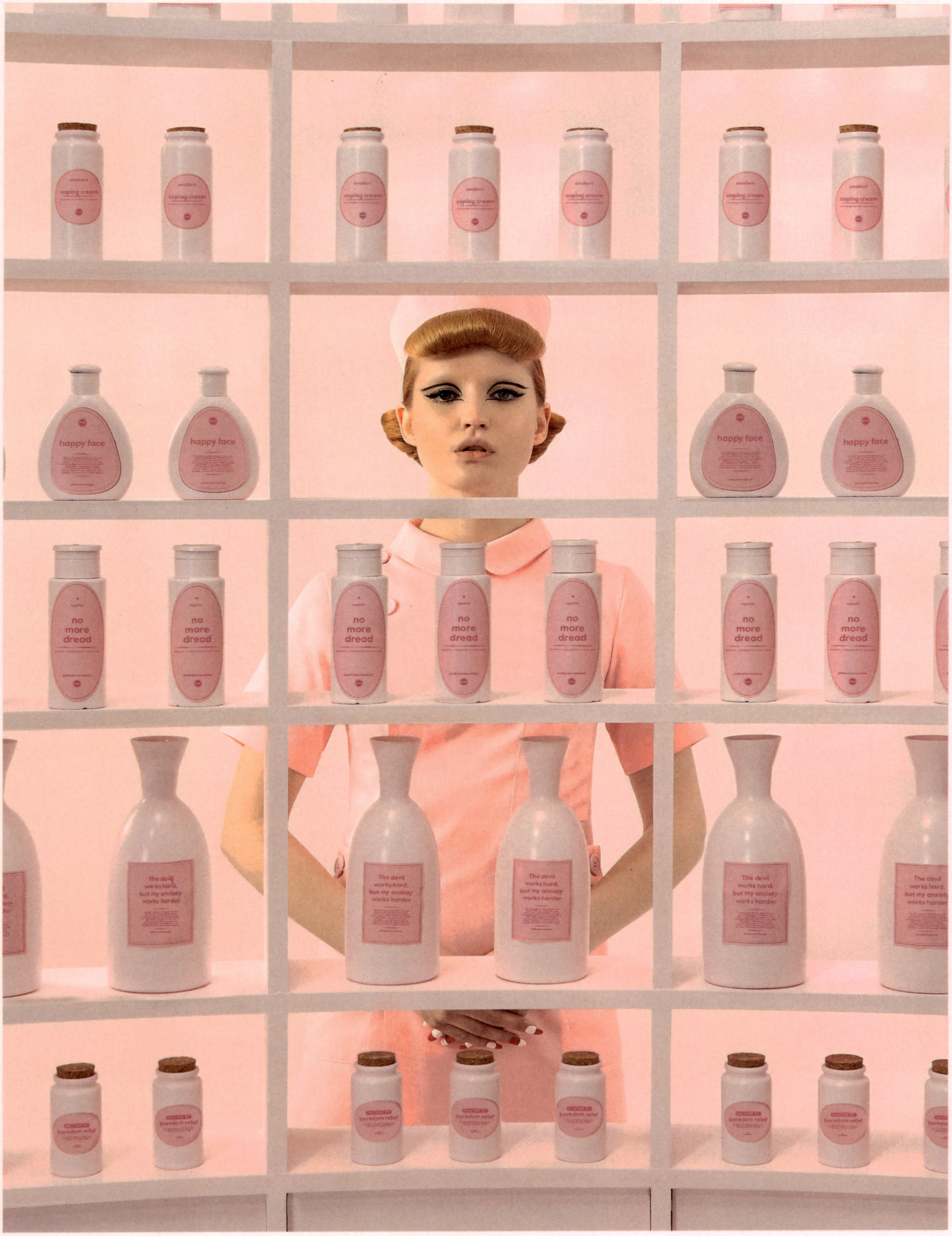
emollient
coping cream
happy face
no more dread
The devil works hard, but my anxiety works harder
boredom relief

ELI REZKALLAH

life in plastik

Lannoo

intro

One could argue that photographer Eli Rezkallah was born in an imaginary world, also known as Lebanon, circa 1986. While there's nothing imaginary about the sectarian conflict and civil war that plagued his native country for decades, Rezkallah lived his formative years sheltered in a picture-perfect beachfront resort on the Lebanese Mediterranean coast, filled with extravagance, fashion, and color, yet surrounded by conflict, anxiety, and trauma.

There's something to be said about living an immaculate childhood that is constantly under threat of annihilation. No matter the false sense of safety, no matter the beauty of one's immediate surroundings, if the foundation is consistently shaken, how can a child find a proper footing during their most crucial formative years?

As every origin story goes, there comes a moment when curiosity for the outside world takes over. When Rezkallah stepped out into the real world, it didn't take long for him to come to the conclusion that it does not live up to the hype. One look outside his carefully curated bubble was enough to make him ask himself: "Is that all there is?"

This book will examine how dark deep-rooted inner conflict can translate into marvelous, vibrant, and whimsical art, through Rezkallah's arduous journey of self-realization, self-acceptance, and healing.

foreword
by jessica walsh

I first met Eli and his partner in New York in 2016, after connecting on Instagram through a mutual admiration of one another's work. Eli's photography stood out through its classical quality: Behind the manicured visuals lie deeper stories of a sullen and imperfect world.

Eli's photographs are layered with sociopolitical innuendos, depicting an underlying tension: Some photos are a commentary on specific issues such as sexism and gender inequality – one of my favorites being "In a Parallel Universe," a series in which he flips gender roles to give the patriarchy a taste of its own poison. It's a great example of how Eli uses this tactic of presenting something pretty while advocating for equality, LGBTQ+ liberation, and mental health awareness.

Another instance is the fundraiser he started with artist Saint Hoax to help the local creative community rebuild some of their studios and bodies of work following the tragic Beirut blast of August 4, 2020.

Over the years, our personal conversations have grown in length and depth, and we have touched on many important subjects. He has never let the atrocities of war and political unrest he has lived through desensitize his sense of empathy and justice. I have always felt drawn to the sensitive artist, the welcoming soul, and the meticulous creative director: the fabric of a true artist and friend, whose cause of fighting oppression with beauty is one I am happy to believe in.

foreword
by saint hoax

Eli's a real aesthete. His eye for detail and love for the arts allow him to create exceptionally composed images that I personally relate to. Looking at his body of work you will find so many Easter eggs; references to quintessential painters, moments from popular culture, and an obsession with celebrity culture that we share. I really like how he relates all of this to his roots, his upbringing, and makes it his own. I remember being introduced to plastik 12 years ago in my undergraduate program, and the impact it made on me and the people around me: Everyone had stars in their eyes.

In a region where people's dreams are often side-tracked by hardship, Eli's photography inspires the artist within – which gives it a universal quality.

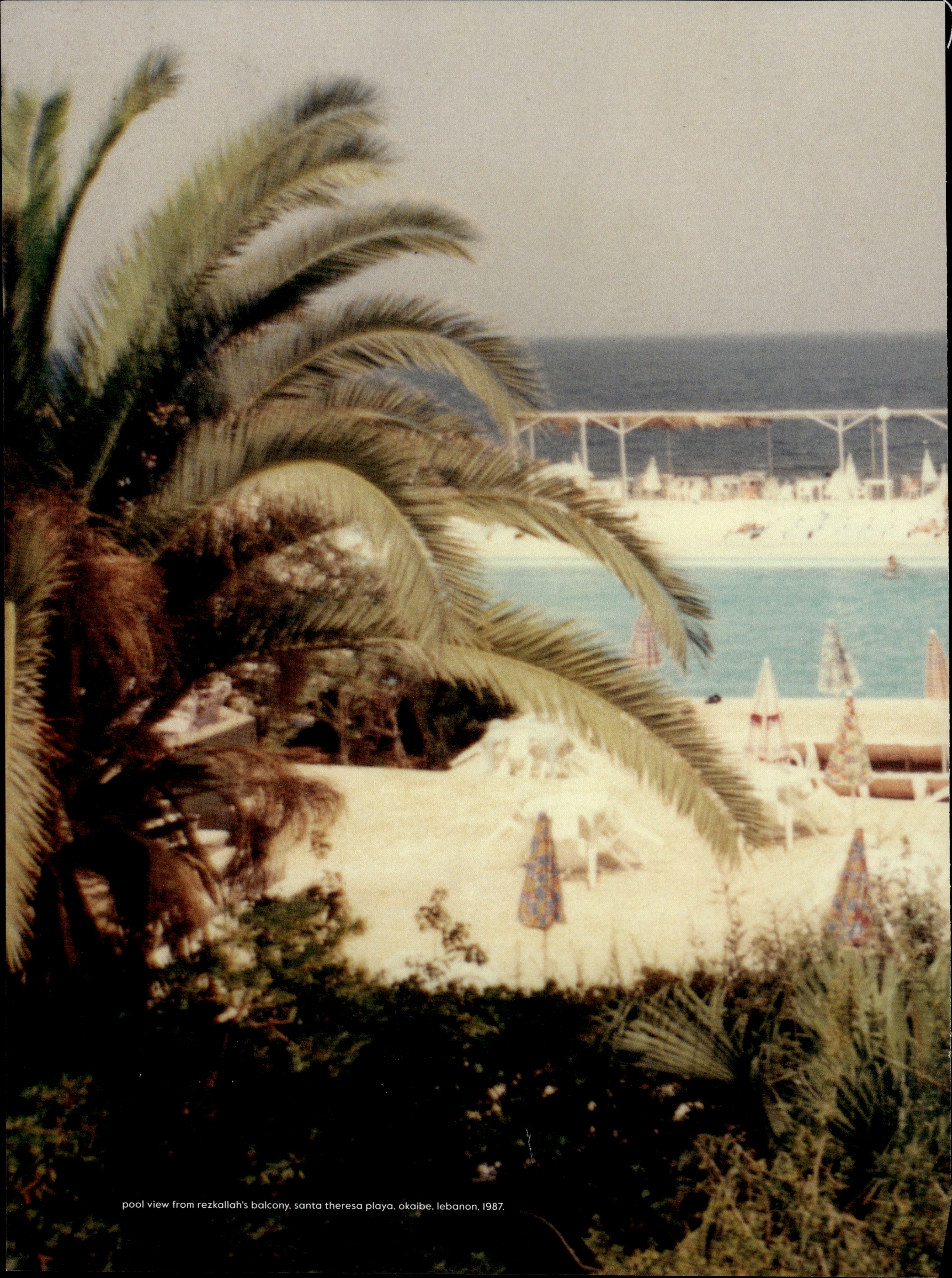

pool view from rezkallah's balcony, santa theresa playa, okaibe, lebanon, 1987.

ACT ONE

summer

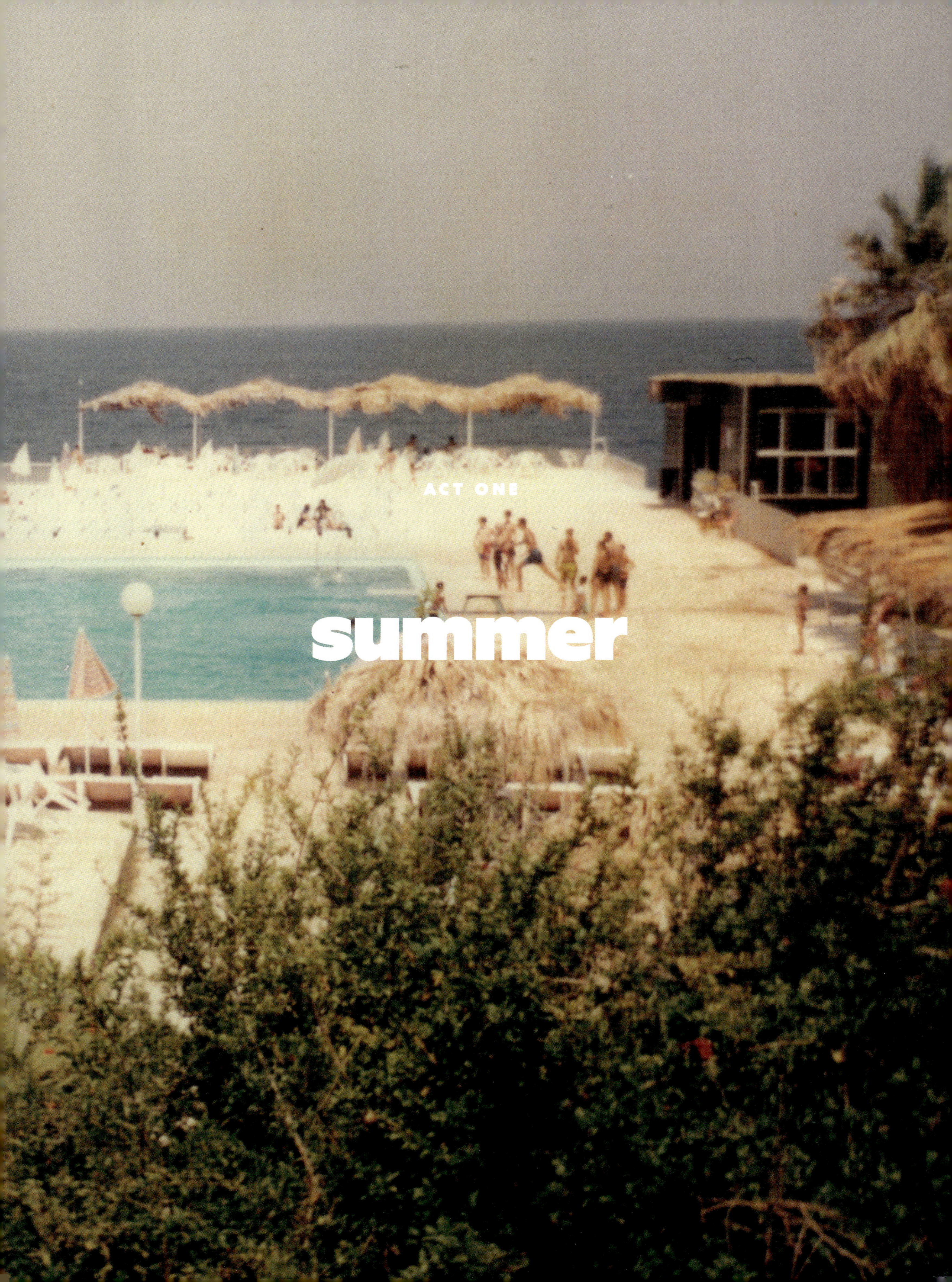

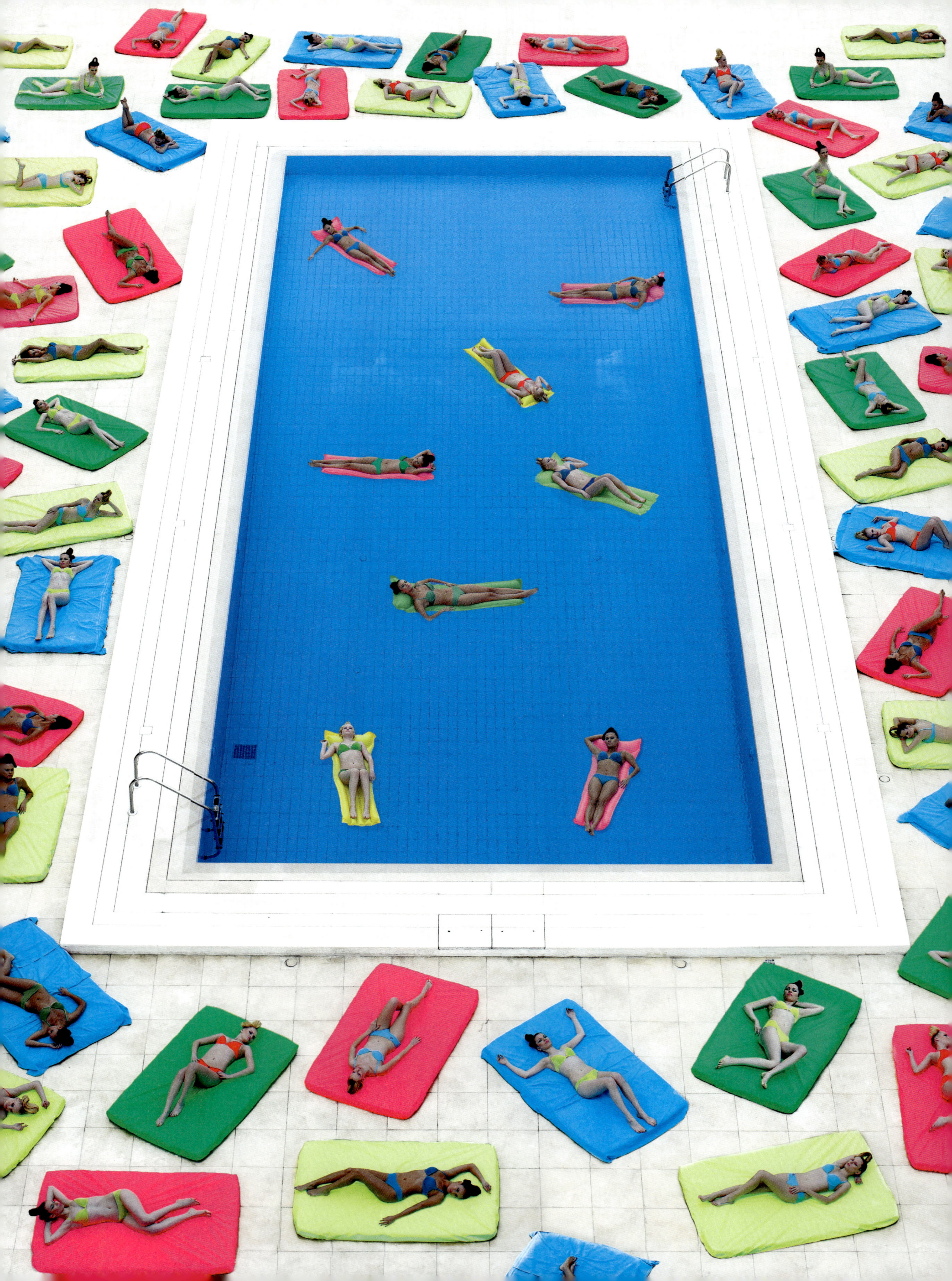

To Rezkallah, summer is not just a season; it's a state of mind - his ultimate emblem of freedom. Inhibitions fade under the heated sun, as colors shine brighter, palm trees cast their shade onto the poolside, clothing becomes optional, and hedonism takes over... until it's gone.

Summer is also a staple of Rezkallah's body of work. Overhead shots of beach bodies basking in the sun's sizzling heat with the unapologetic pursuit of pleasure is an image the photographer often revisits, albeit with a twist. His subjects, whether confronting us with their exposed bodies through bold eye contact or flippantly dismissing the photographer's lens, are carefully manicured to the point of oblivion. Rezkallah's summer is not of the spring break variety, but rather, a more meditative, carefully curated depiction of indulgence and clout – numb, blissful, unaware, and thankless bodies, basking in their privilege till summer's end.

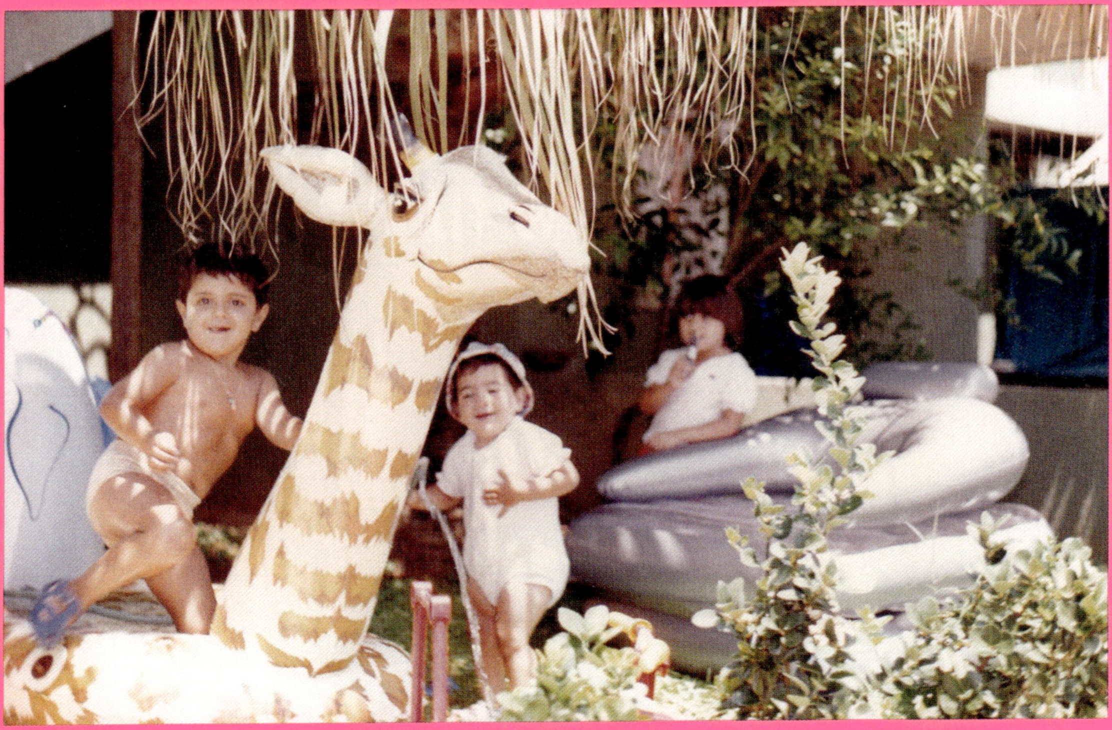

eli and rami rezkallah , santa theresa playa, okaibe, lebanon, 1989.

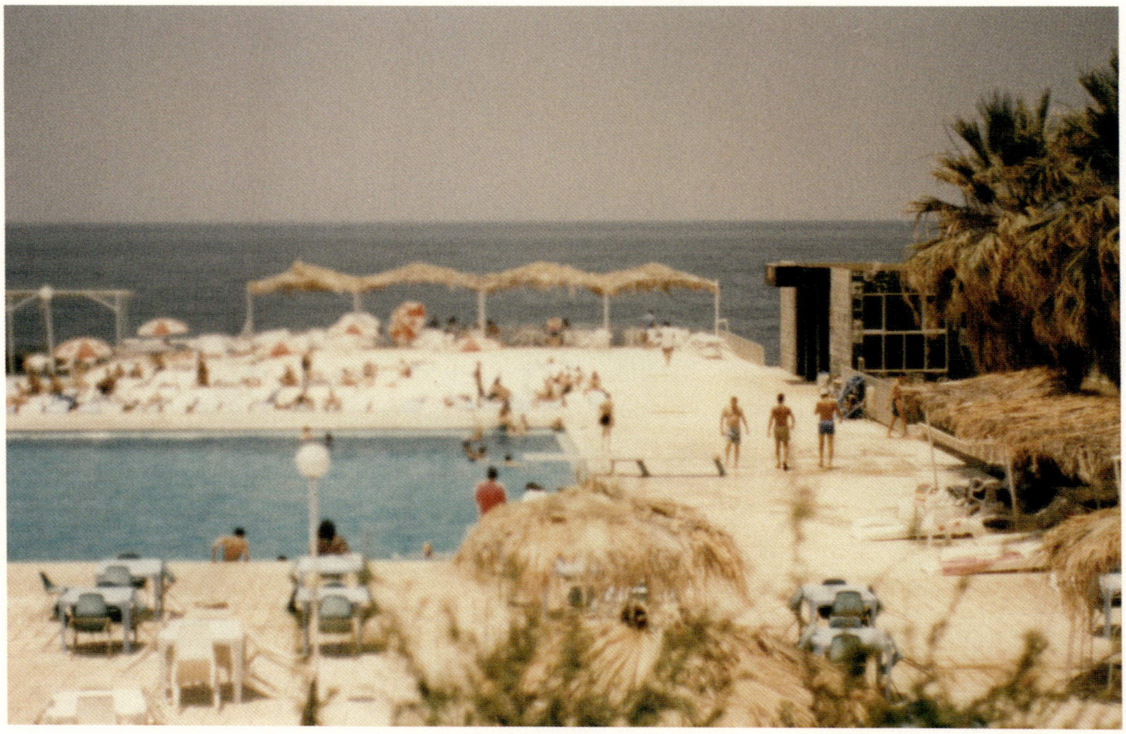

pool view from rezkallah's balcony, santa theresa playa, okaibe, lebanon, 1987.

Rezkallah was born and lived his first years sheltered in Santa Theresa Playa, a coastal summer retreat for Christian families escaping the war. For years, every day was summer paradise, a long-winded whisper, and a blend of vibrant colors and scents: the salt of the Mediterranean Sea, the smell of the effortlessly bronzed local fishermen's sweat, the baby oil and chlorine emanating from poolside melanin enthusiasts, all blended into a haze of stimulating disinhibition. It is there that the young teenager would tentatively let his guard down and explore his inner desires, while, in the back of his mind, a wide-eyed Catholic-raised boy trembled at the thought of being outed and of his haven being permanently shattered.

While everyone around seemed oblivious to his deep-rooted anxieties – privileged bodies begging to escape reality one ray of sunshine at a time - Rezkallah was building his own.

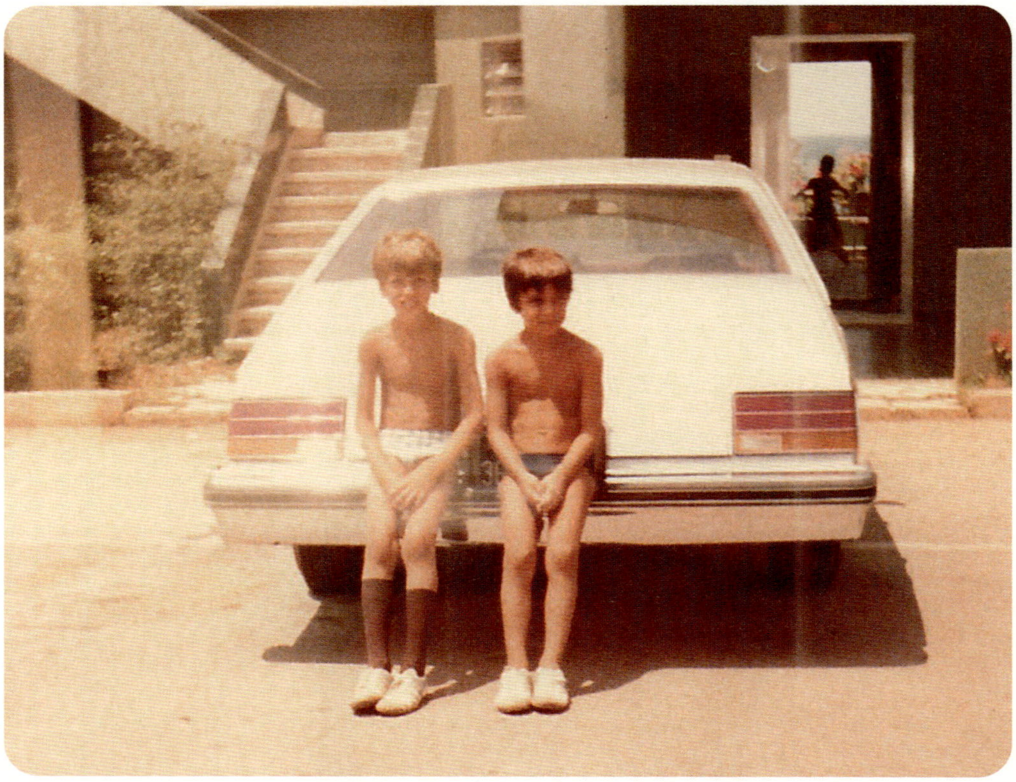

two boys, santa theresa playa, okaibe, lebanon, 1982. photo by alain aad.

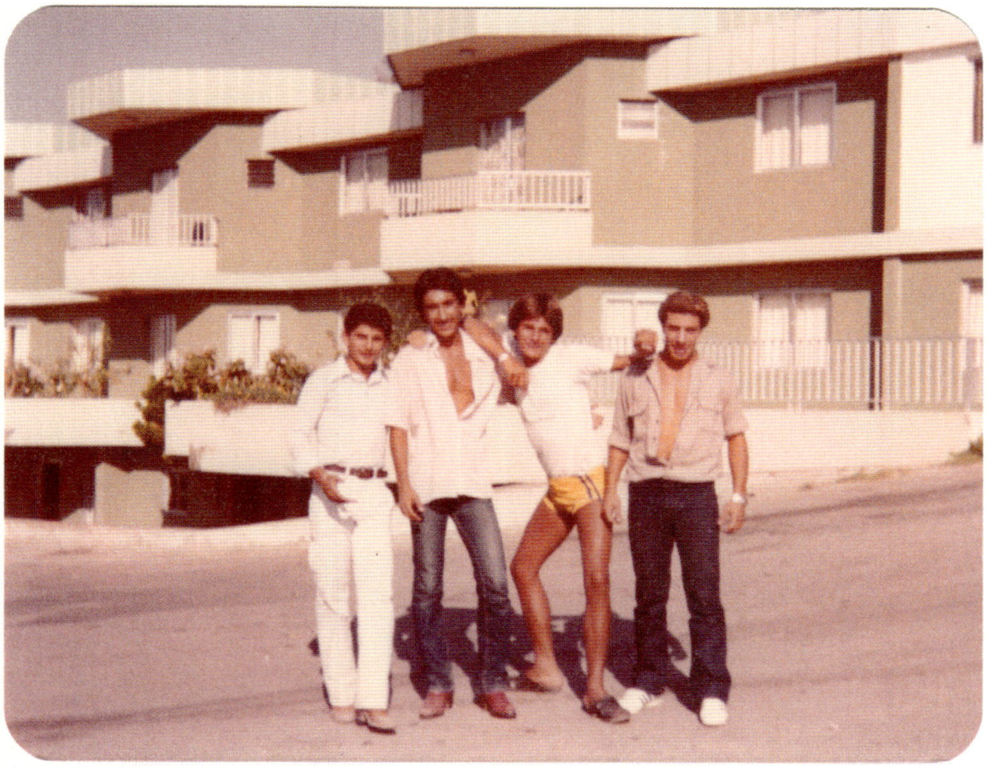

four boys, santa theresa playa, okaibe, lebanon, 1984. photo by elie daye.

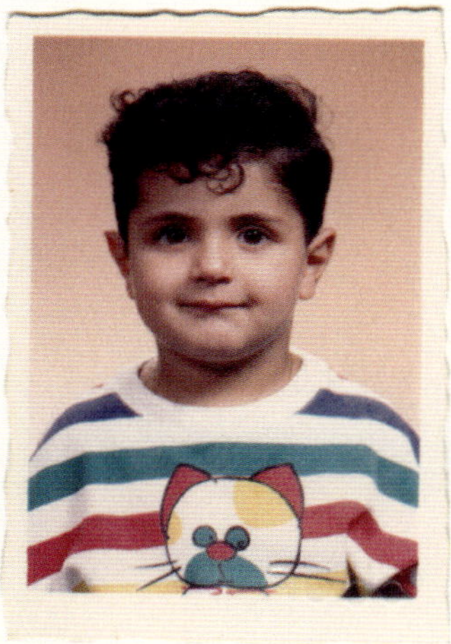

eli rezkallah, passport photo, okaibe, lebanon, 1990.

"Growing up terrified of being outed was my very first encounter with anxiety. And that was all I knew for the longest time."

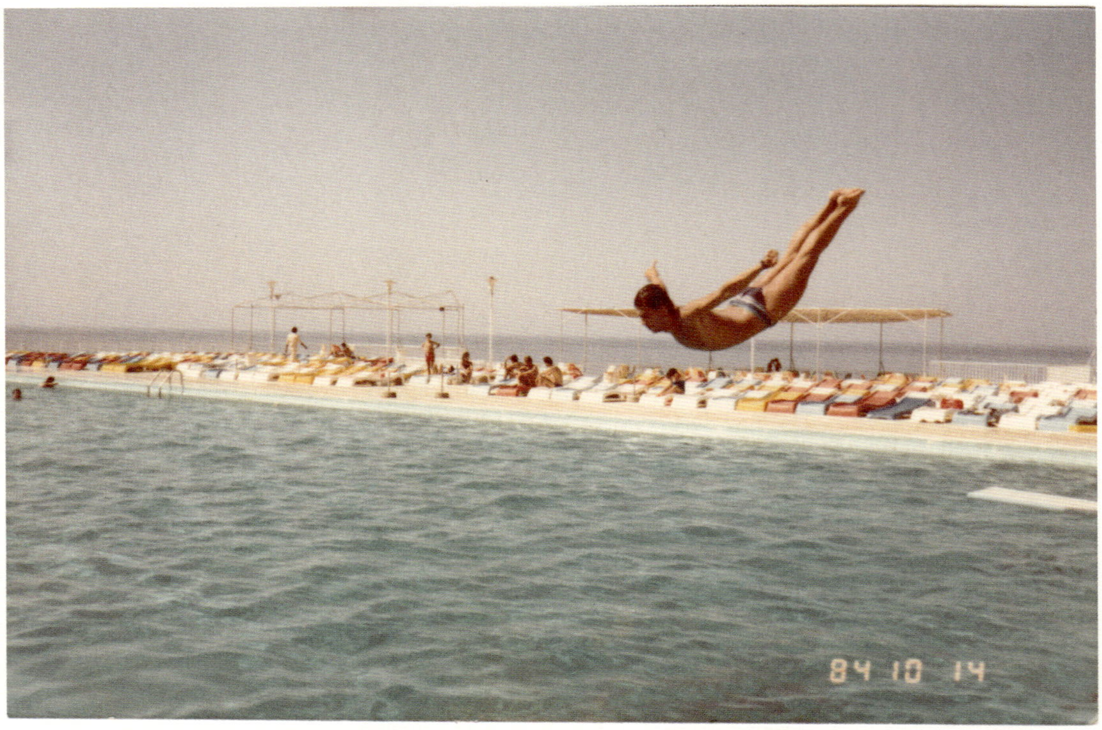

diving man, santa theresa playa, okaibe, lebanon, 1984. photo by elie daye

Despite his acute love for everything summer, Rezkallah could never let go of the fact that the freedom and hedonism that come with this season were only temporary. While most people lived in the resort for the summer season and migrated back to the city in the fall, the Rezkallahs would reside in their beachfront haven all year long. In the blink of an eye, what was once a coastal oasis would turn into a desolate and harsh graveyard of summer memories, triggering months of melancholia as the young boy waited for summer, and the euphoric lifestyle it entailed, to return.

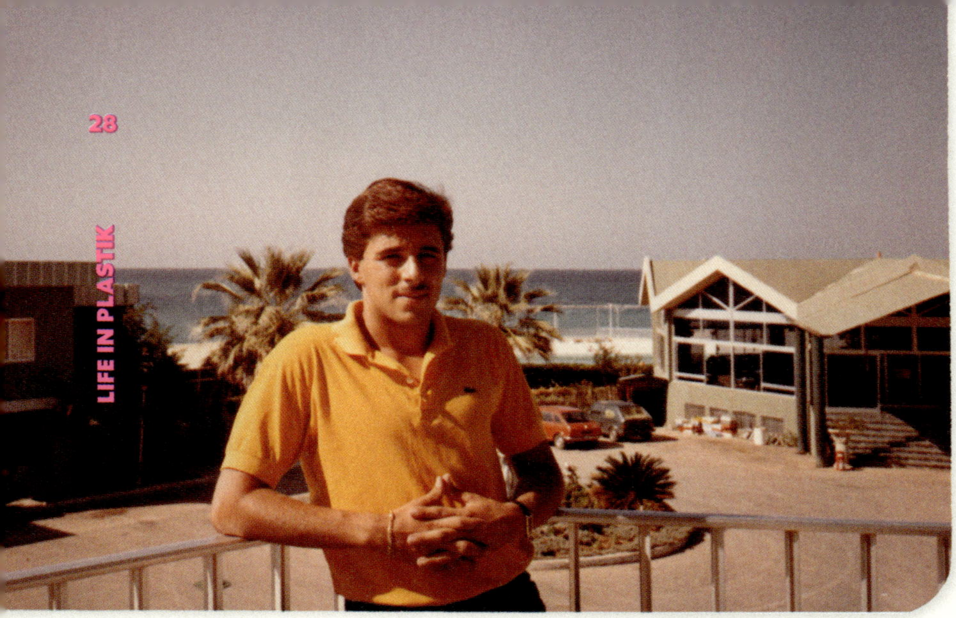

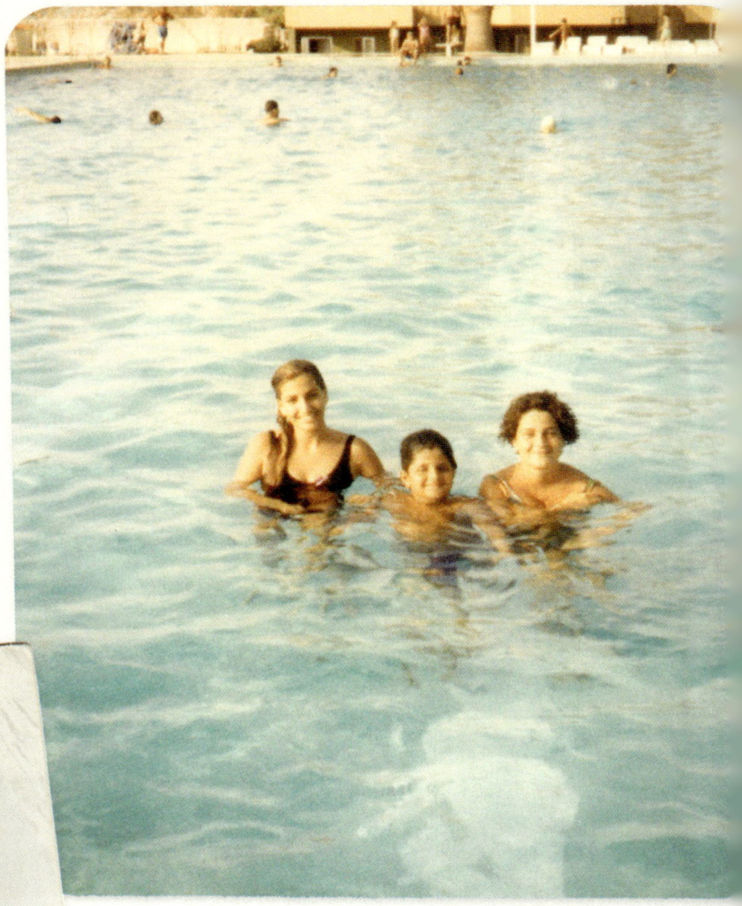

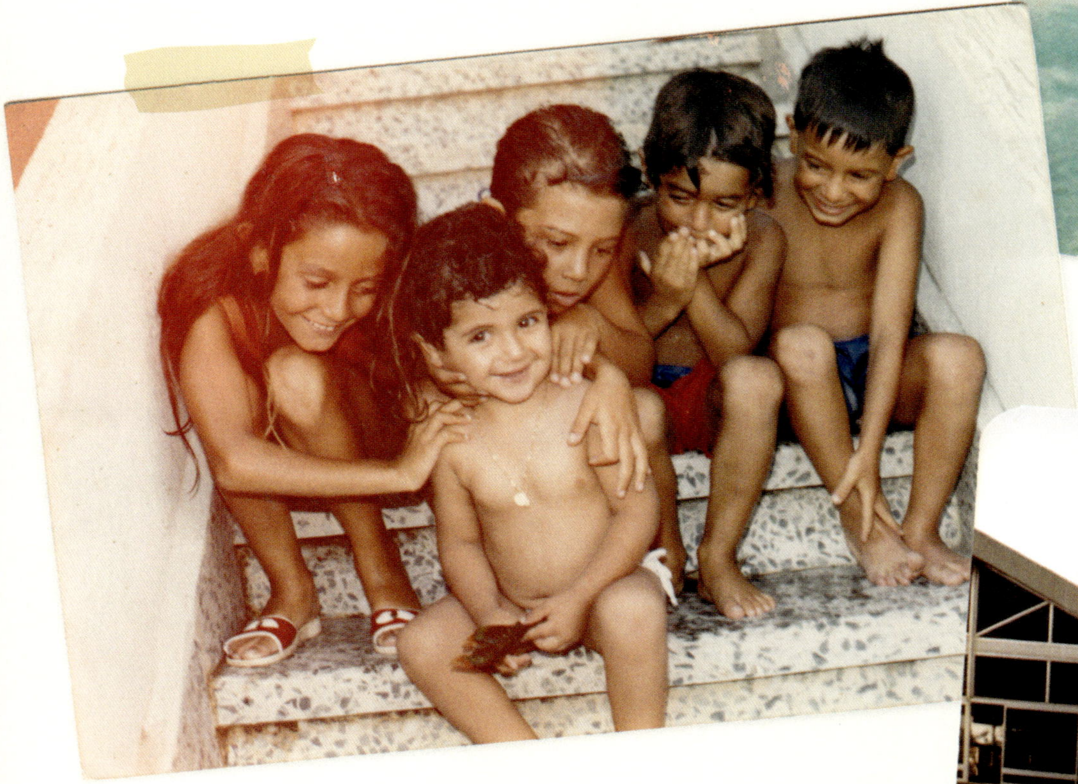

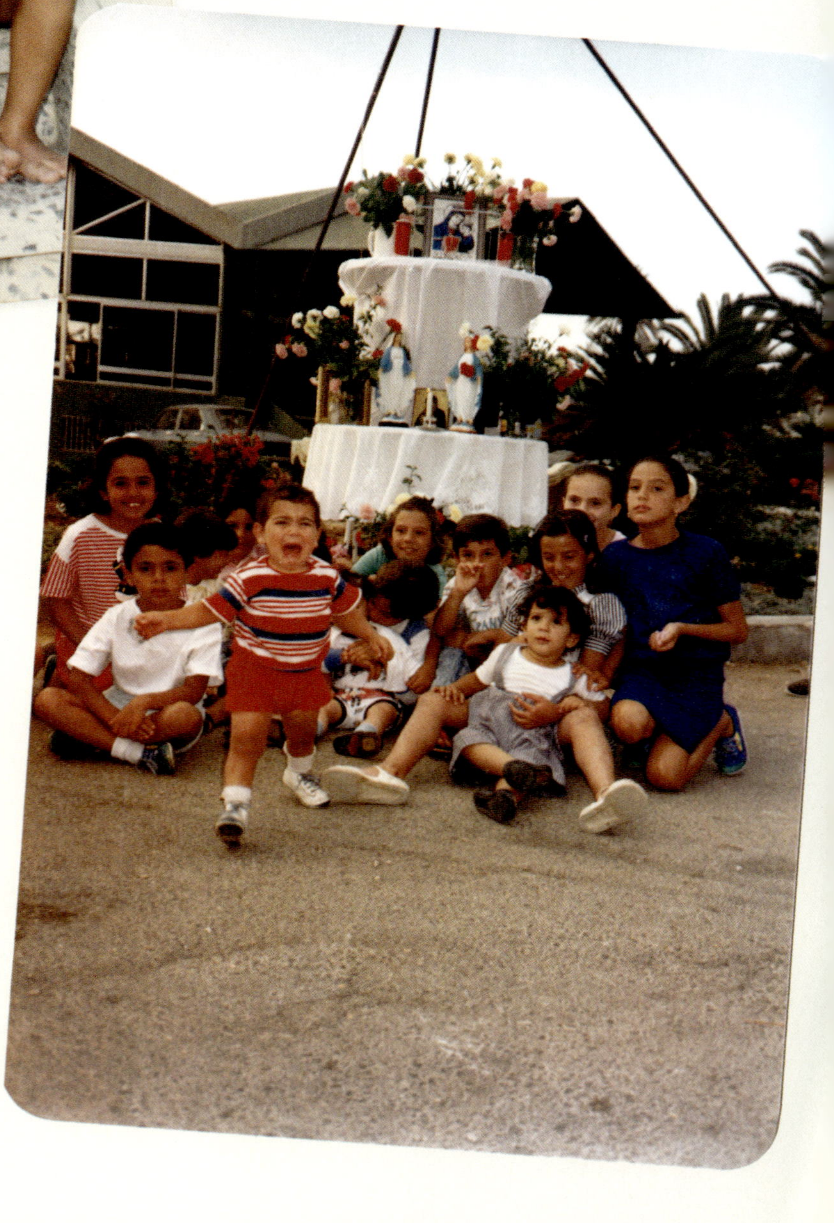

santa theresa lifeguard, 1994.

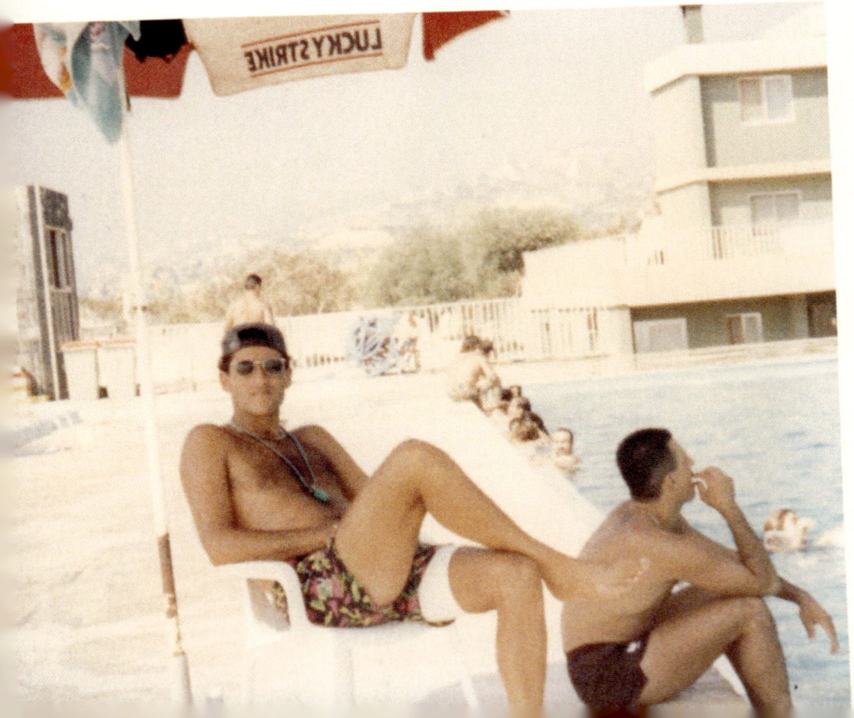

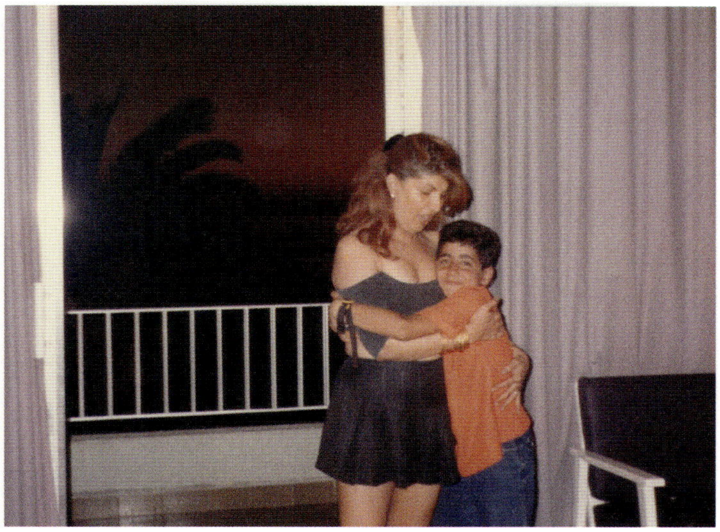

my mom and brother in front of a glorious summer sunset, 1994.

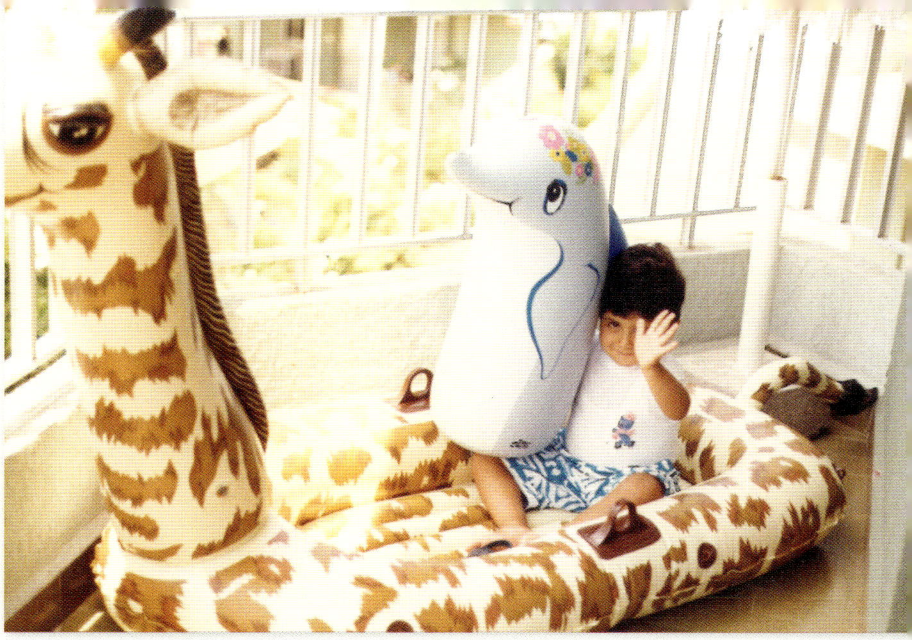

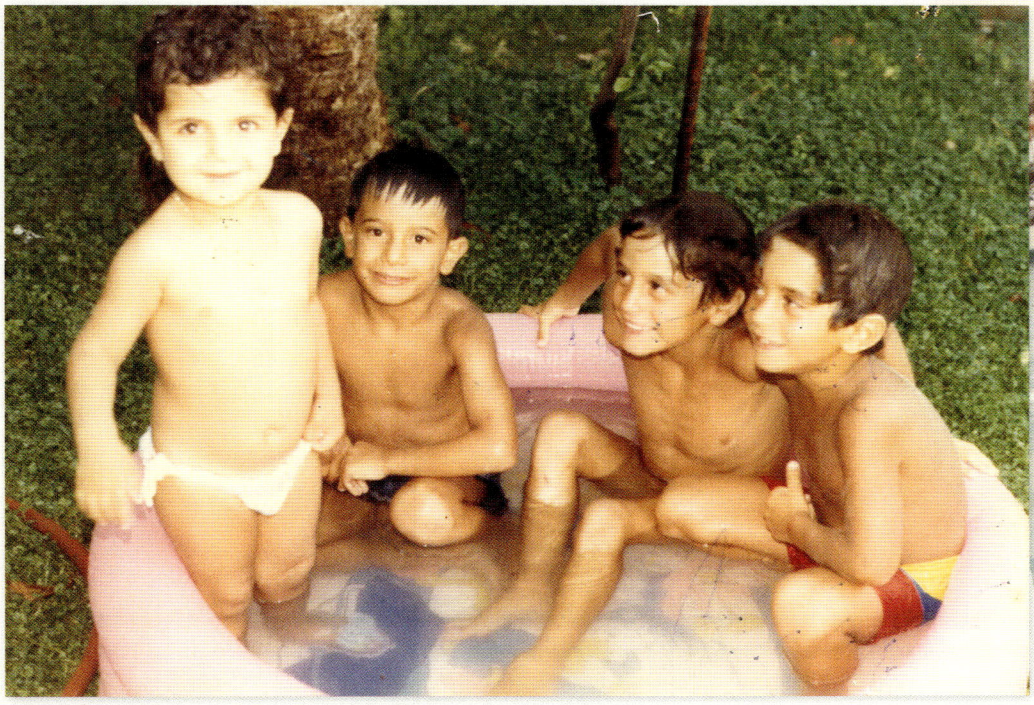

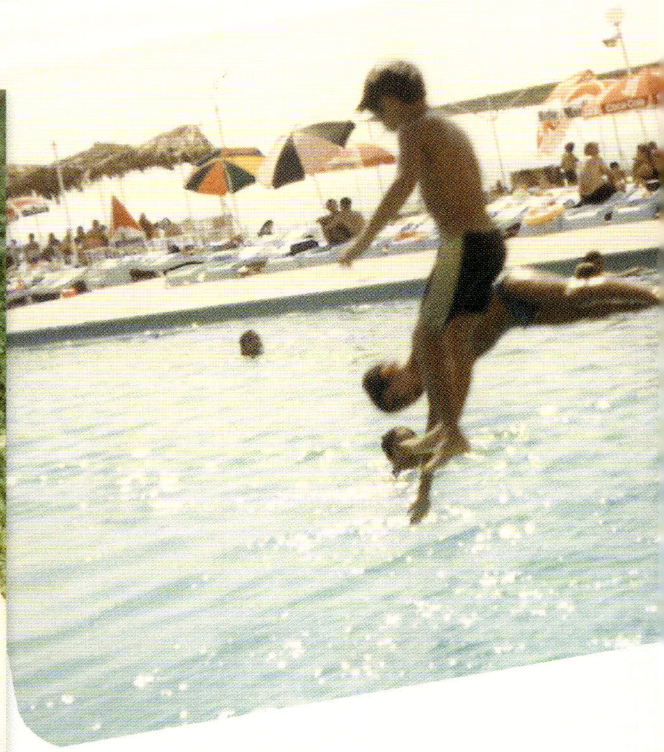

celebrating "saint elie" traditionally: with hand-held fireworks. july 1990.

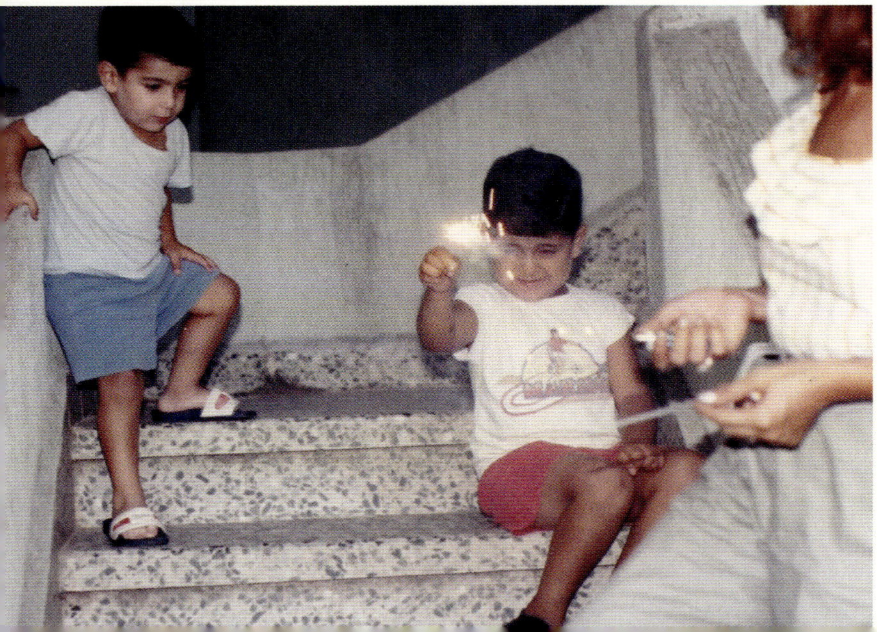

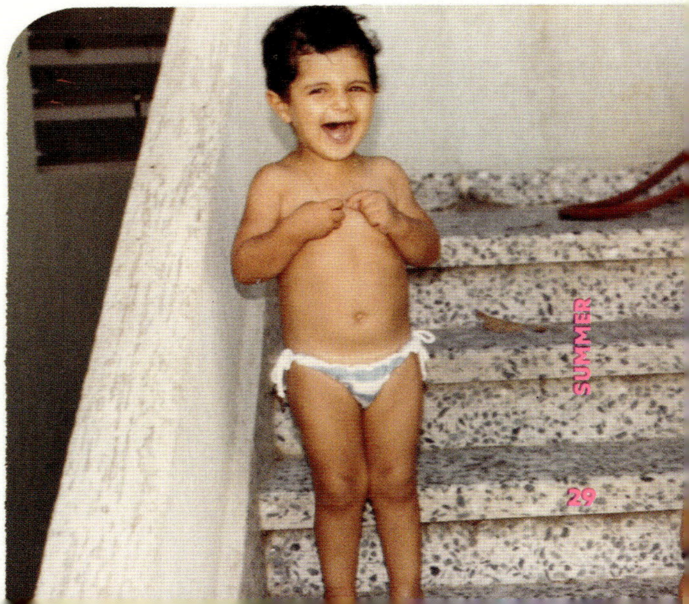

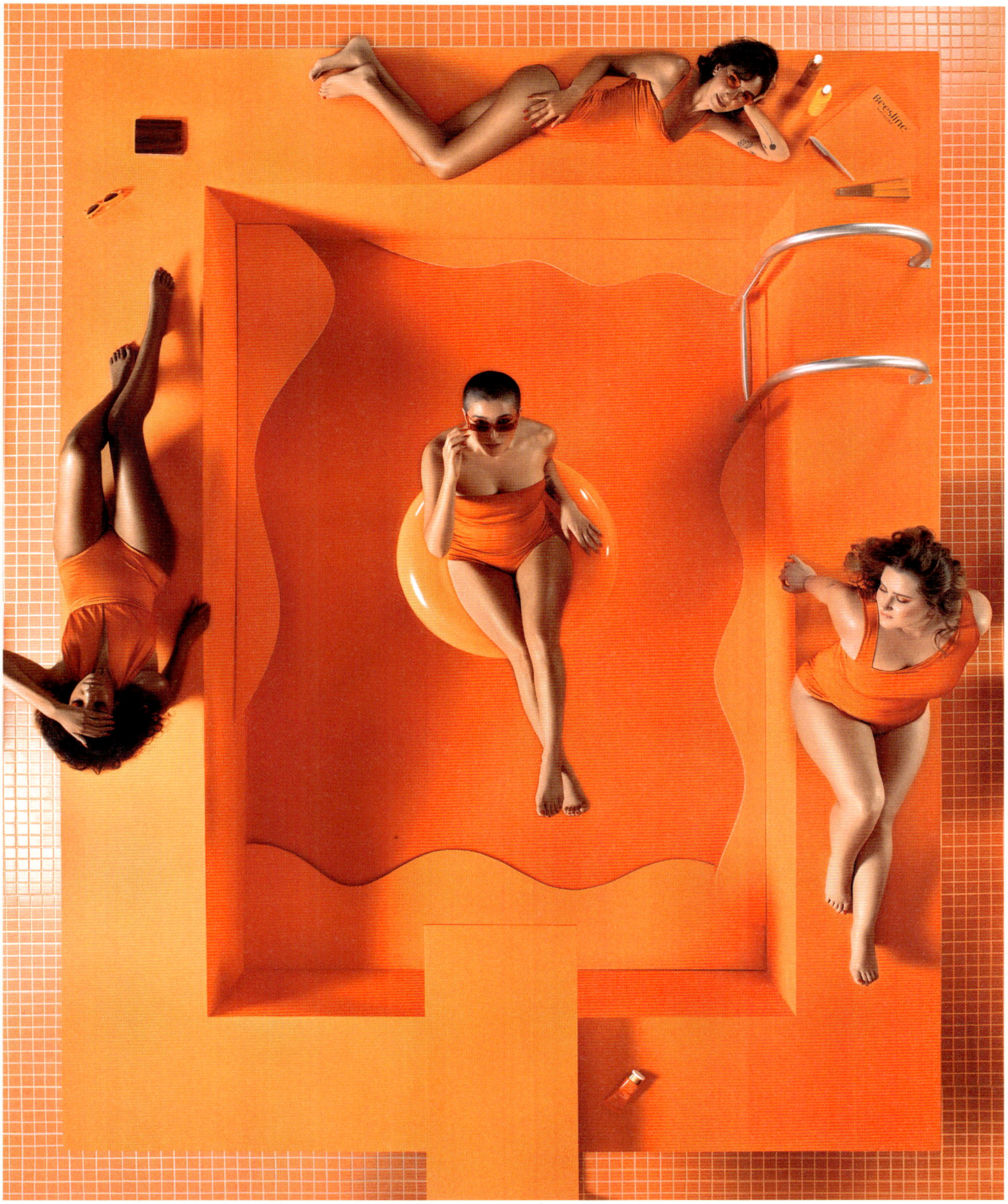
Beesline

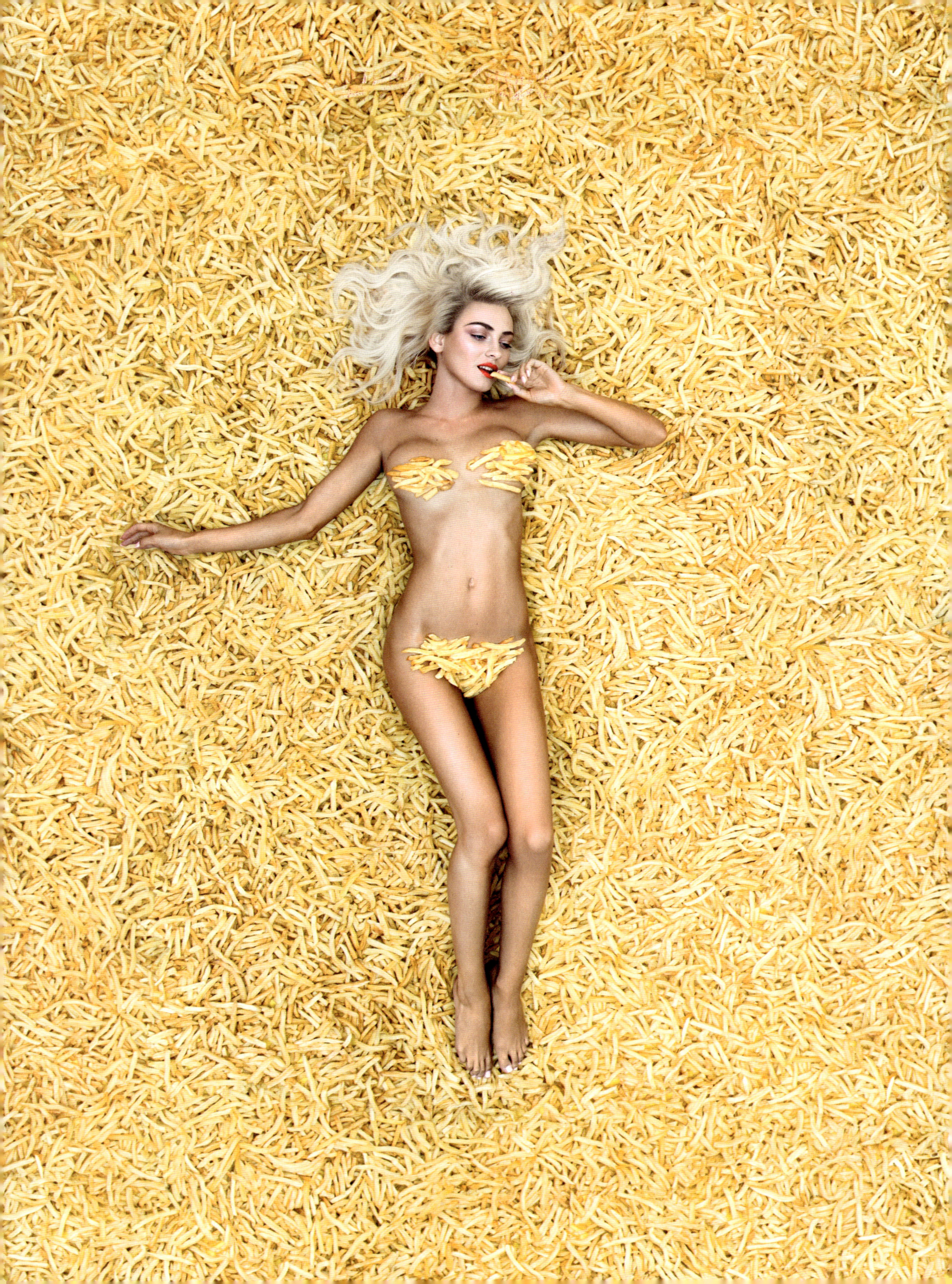

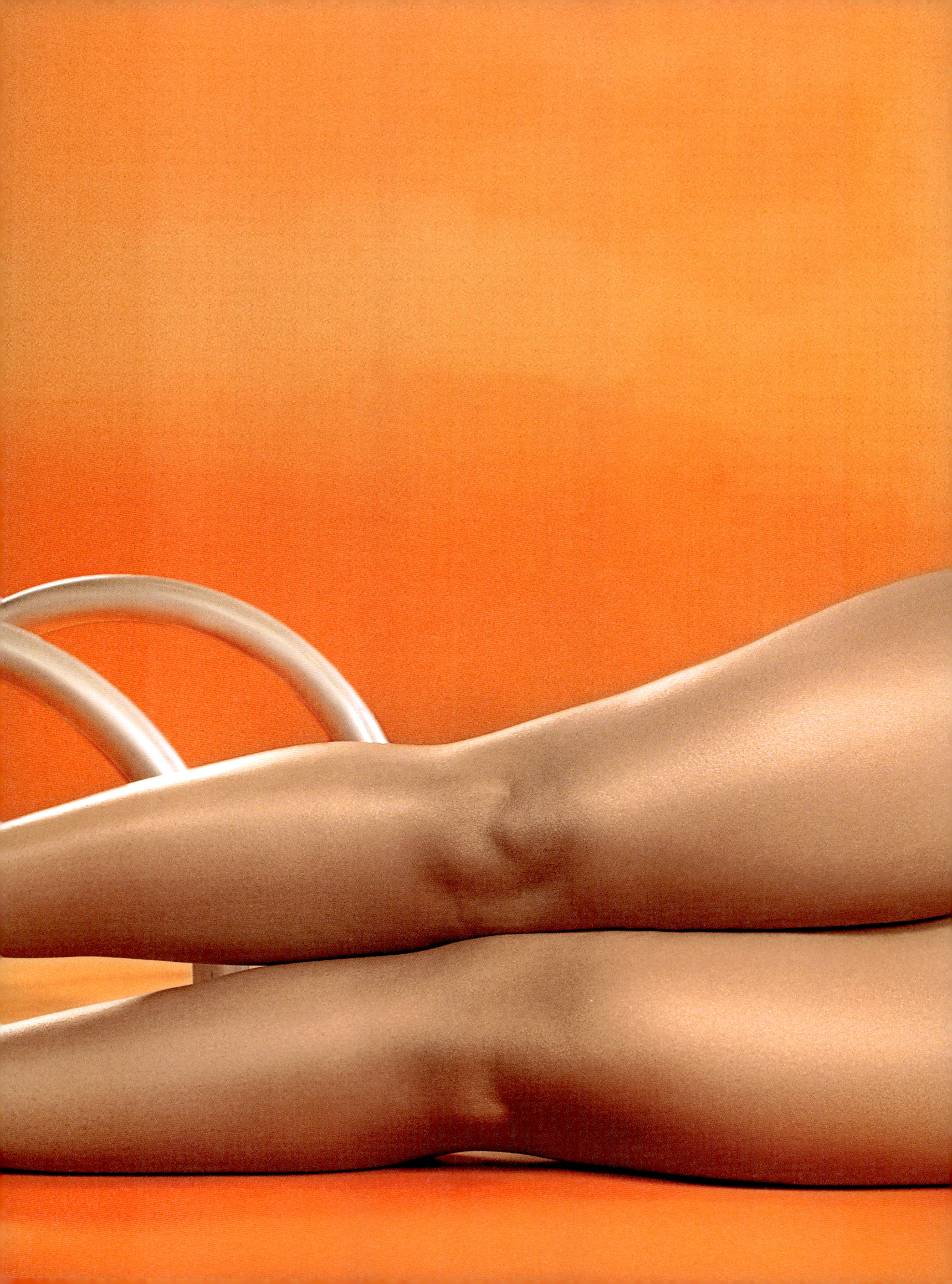

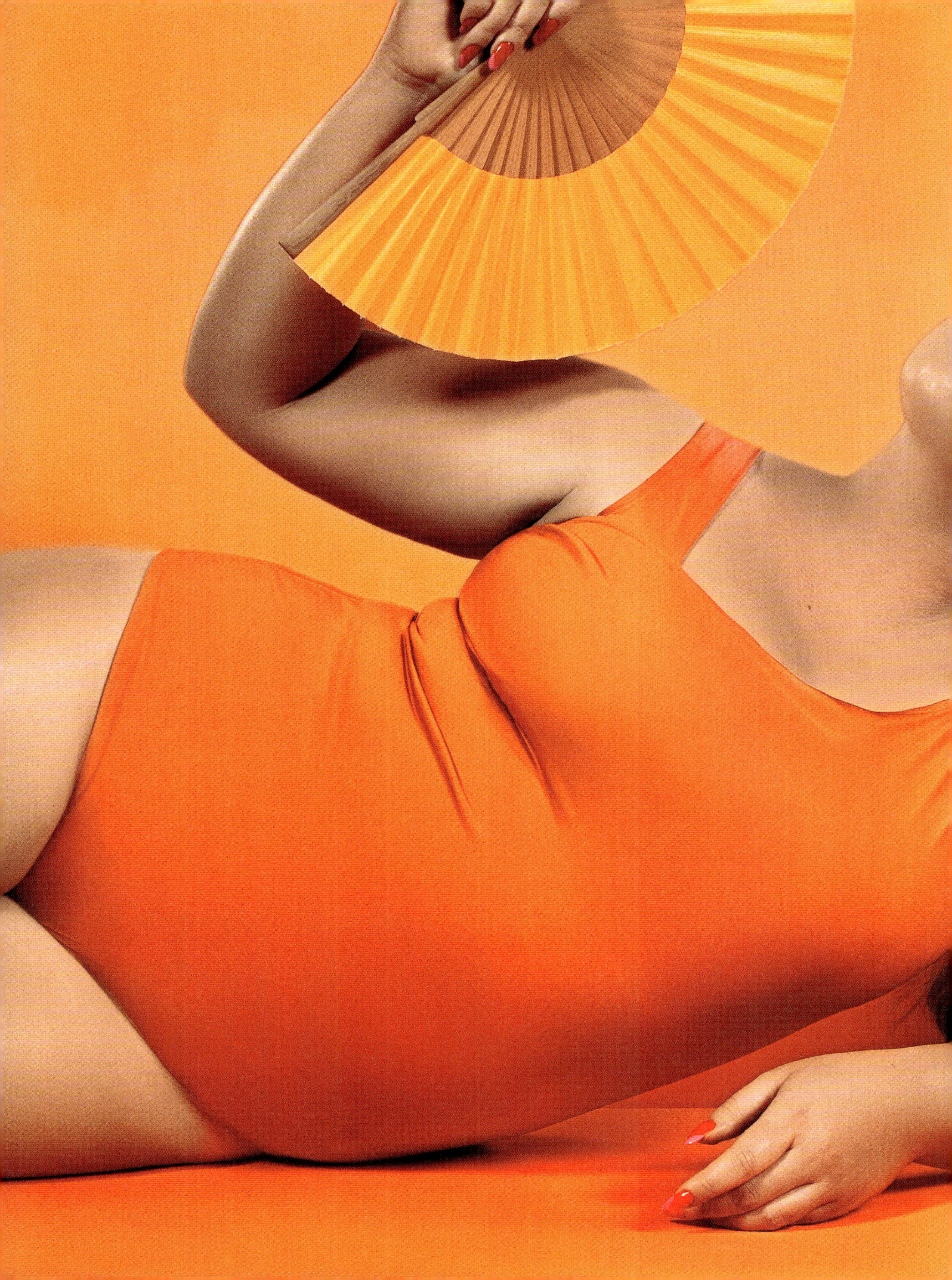

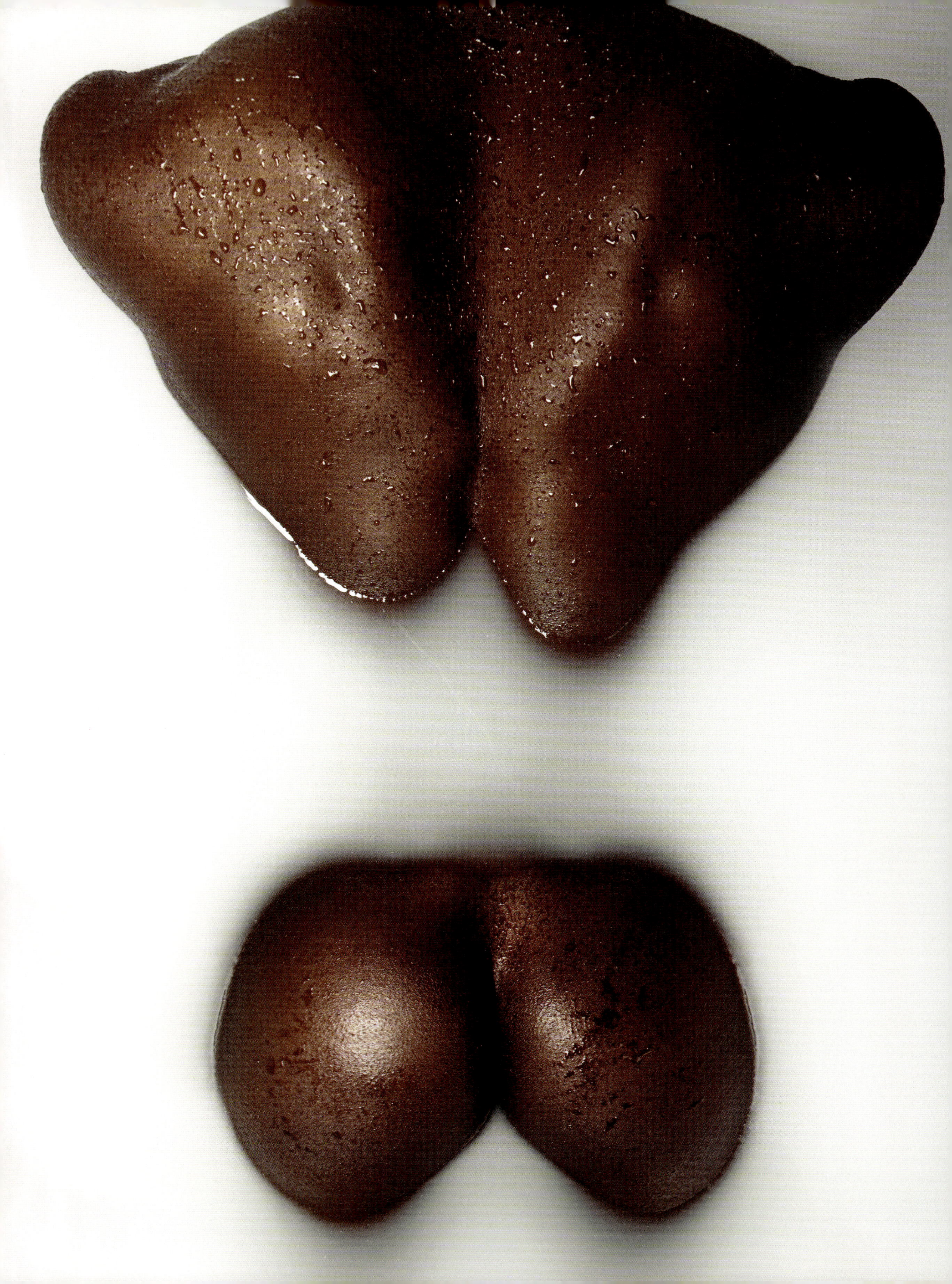

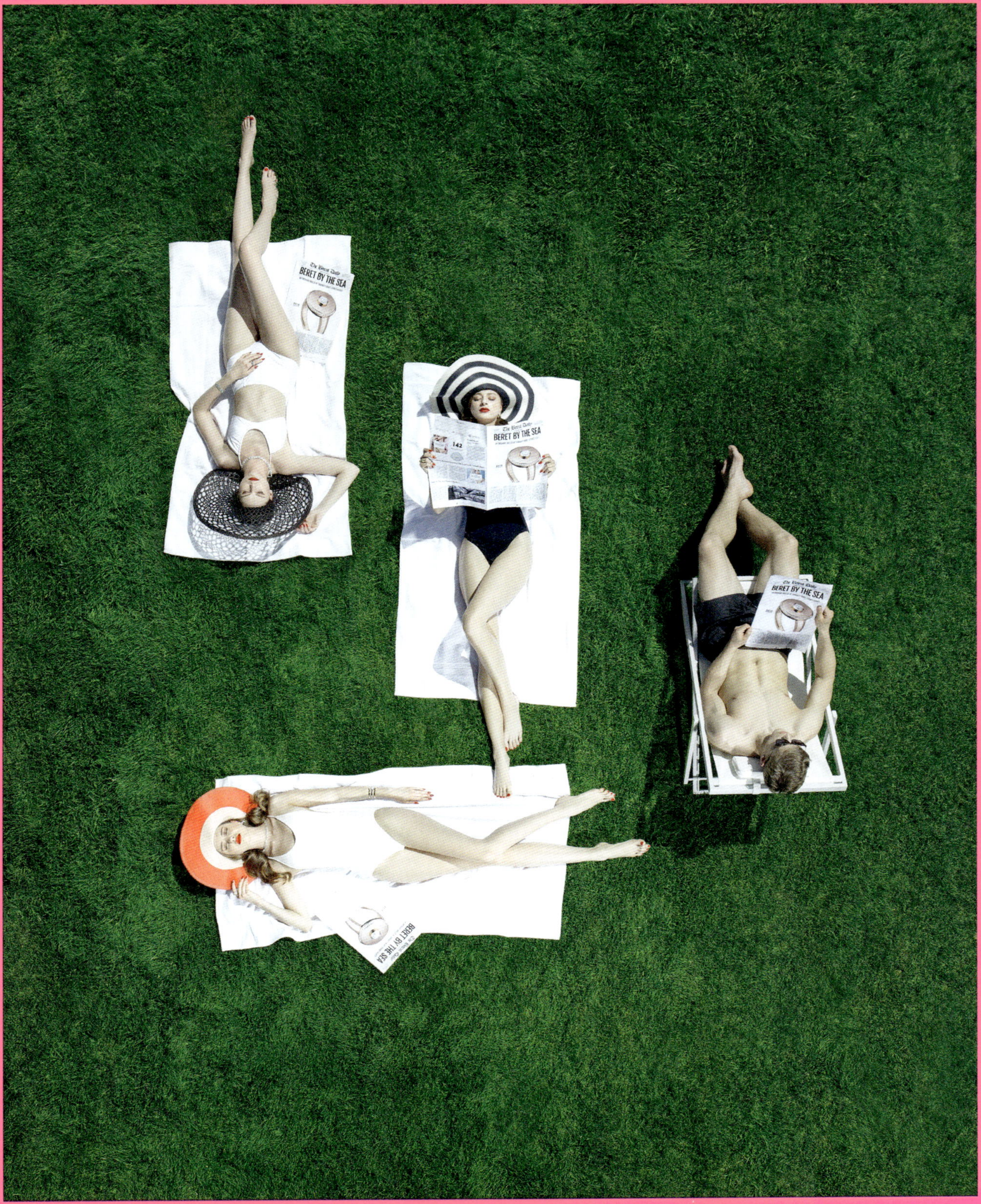
BERET BY THE SEA
BERET BY THE SEA
BERET BY THE SEA
BERET BY THE SEA

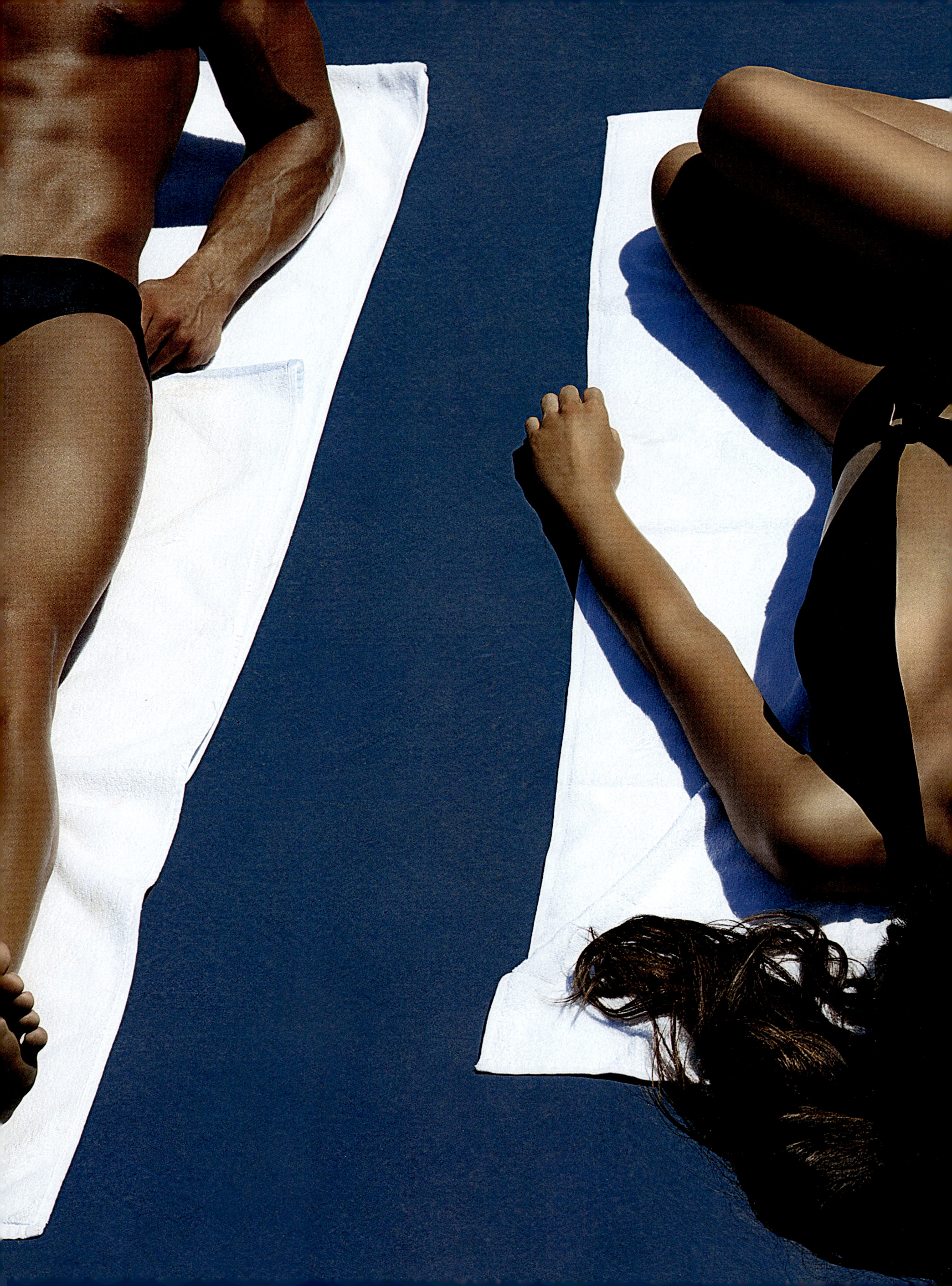

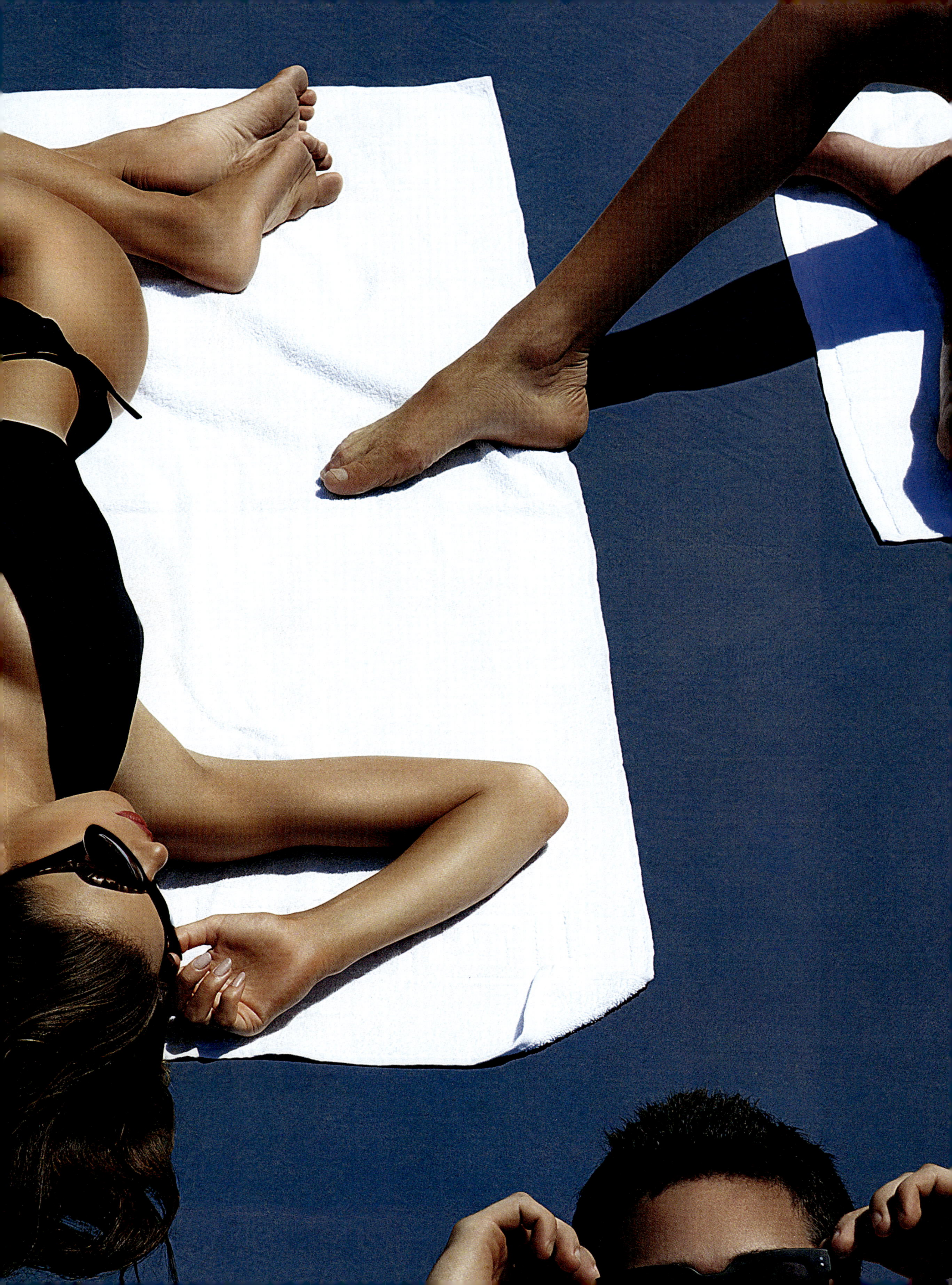

"There's nothing more depressing than an empty pool at the end of a summer."

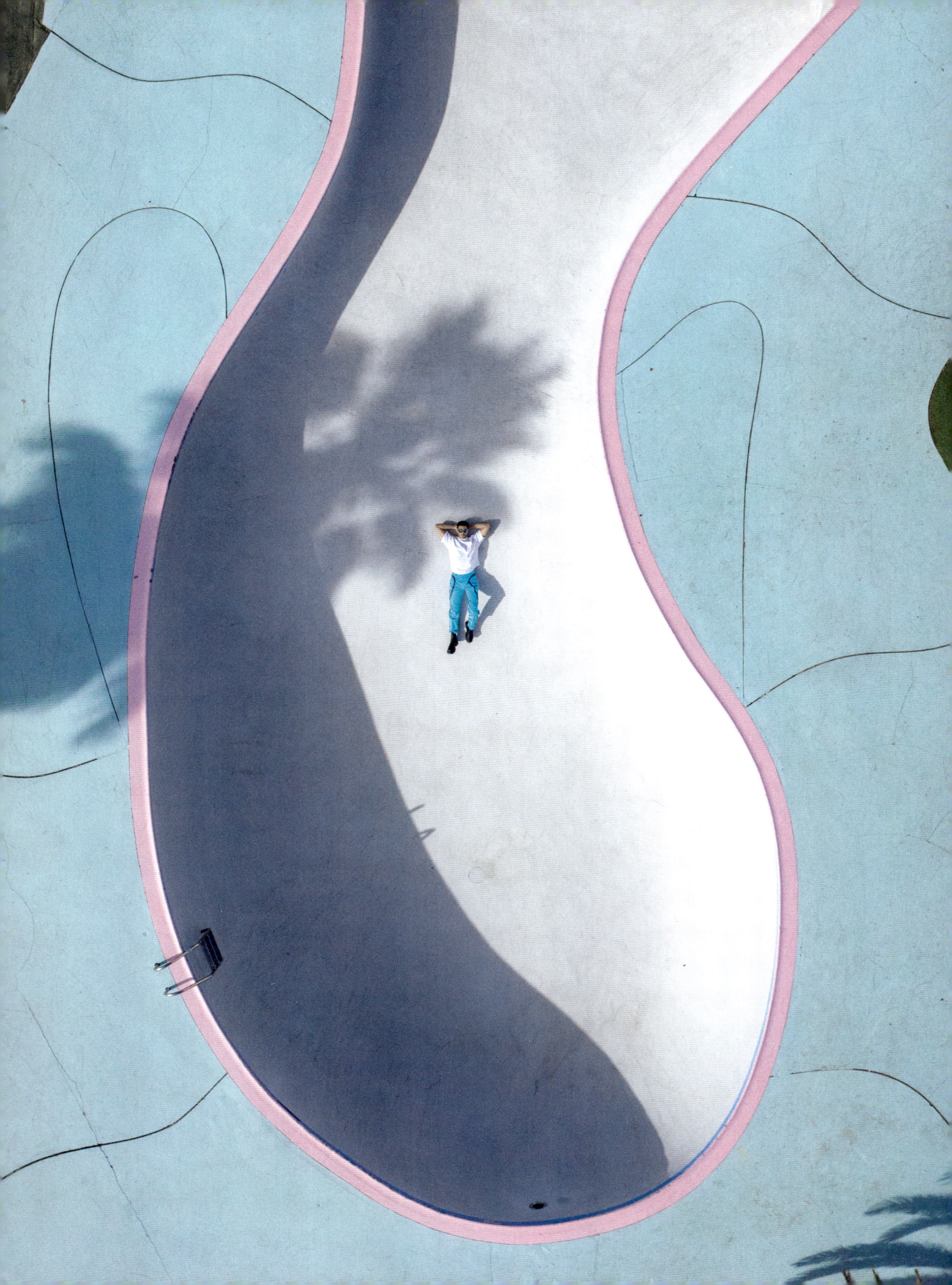

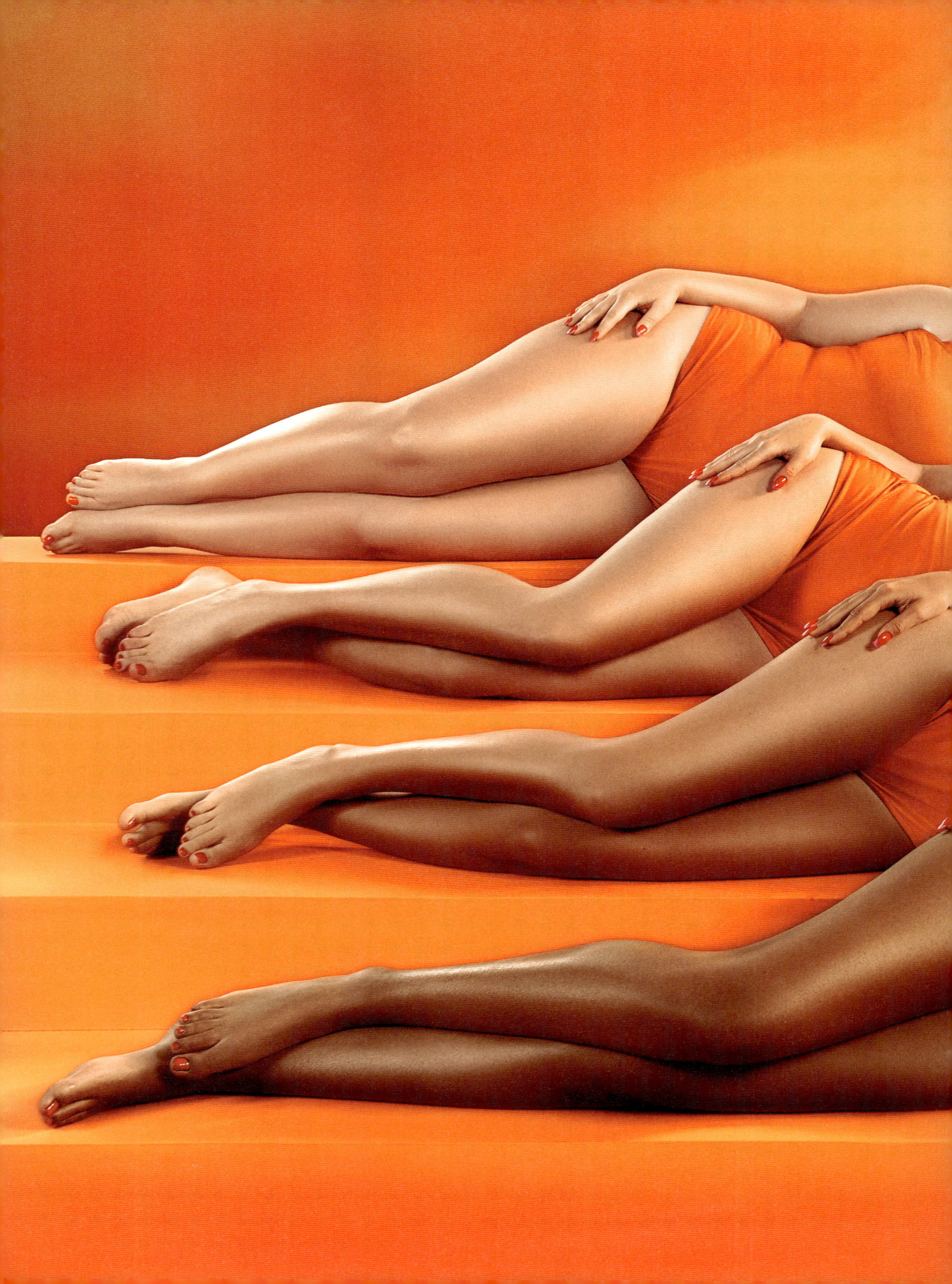

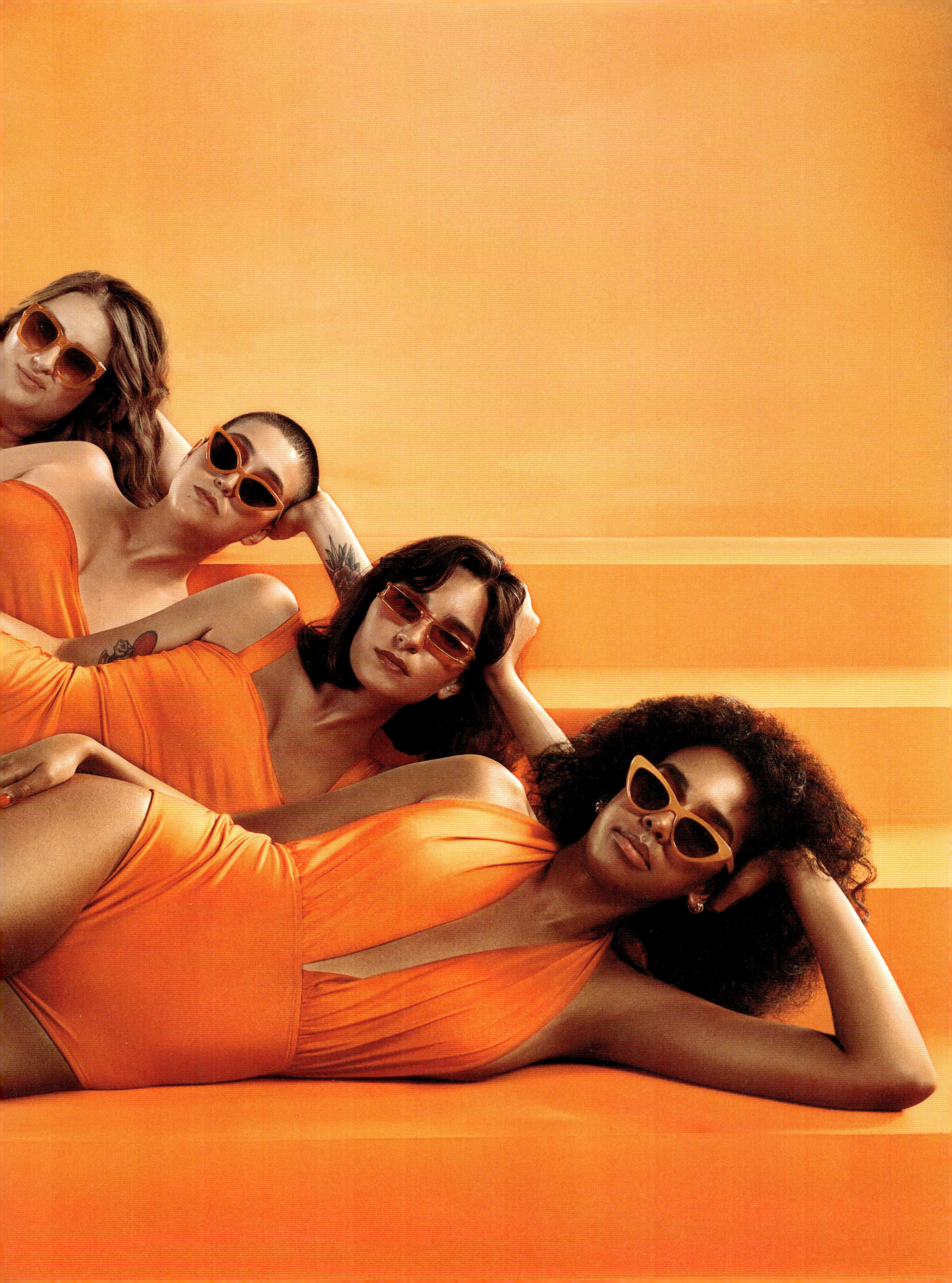

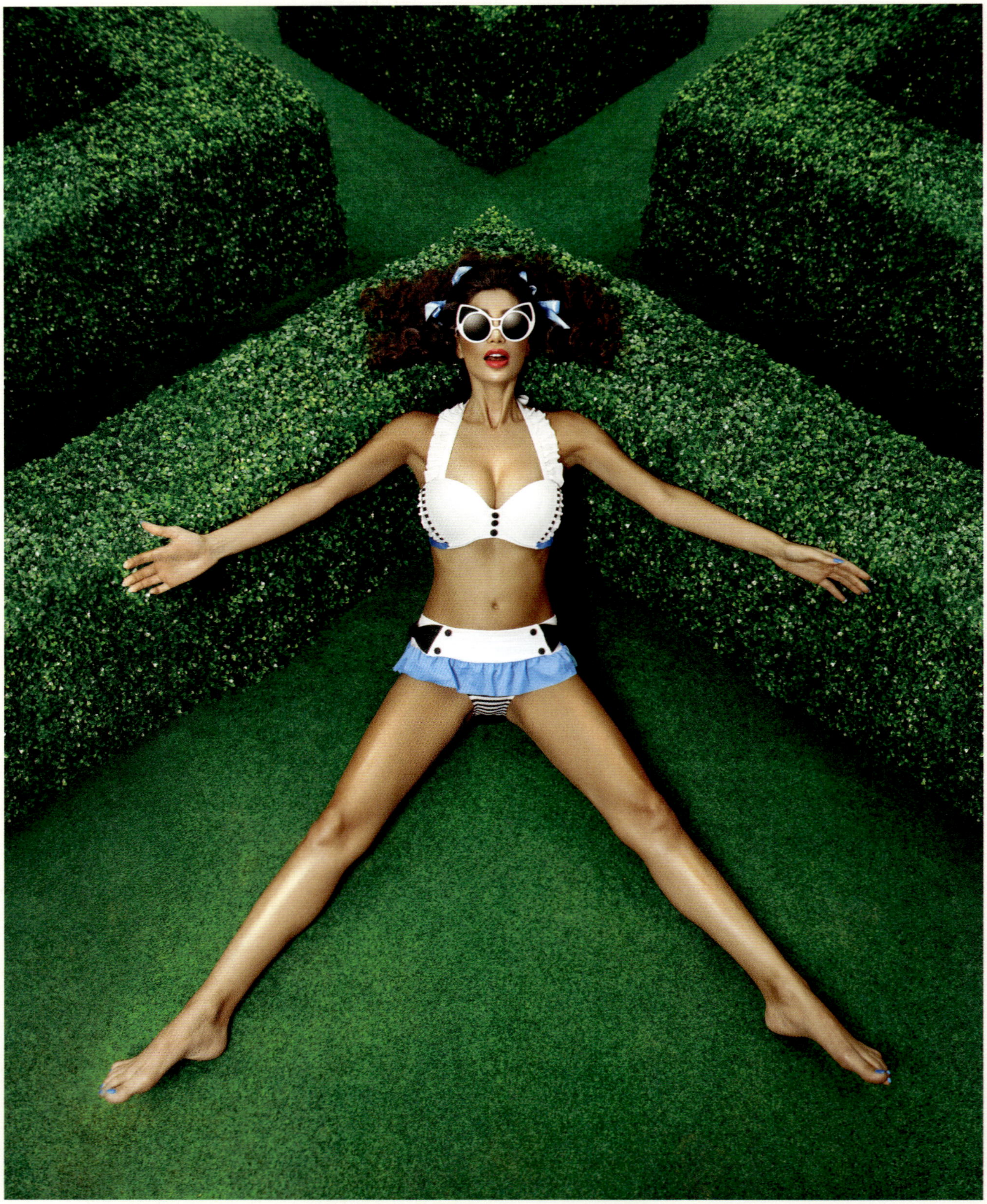

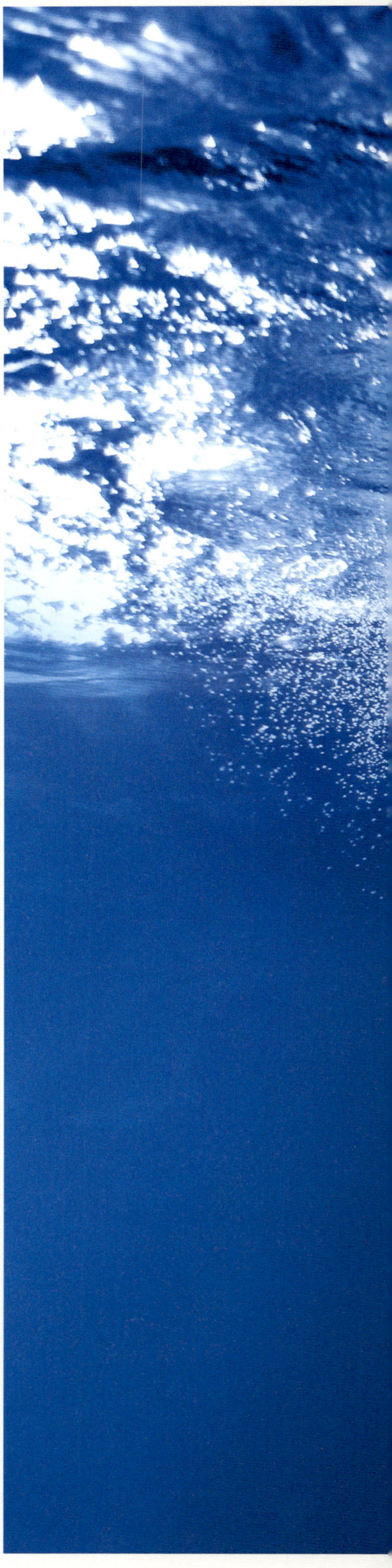

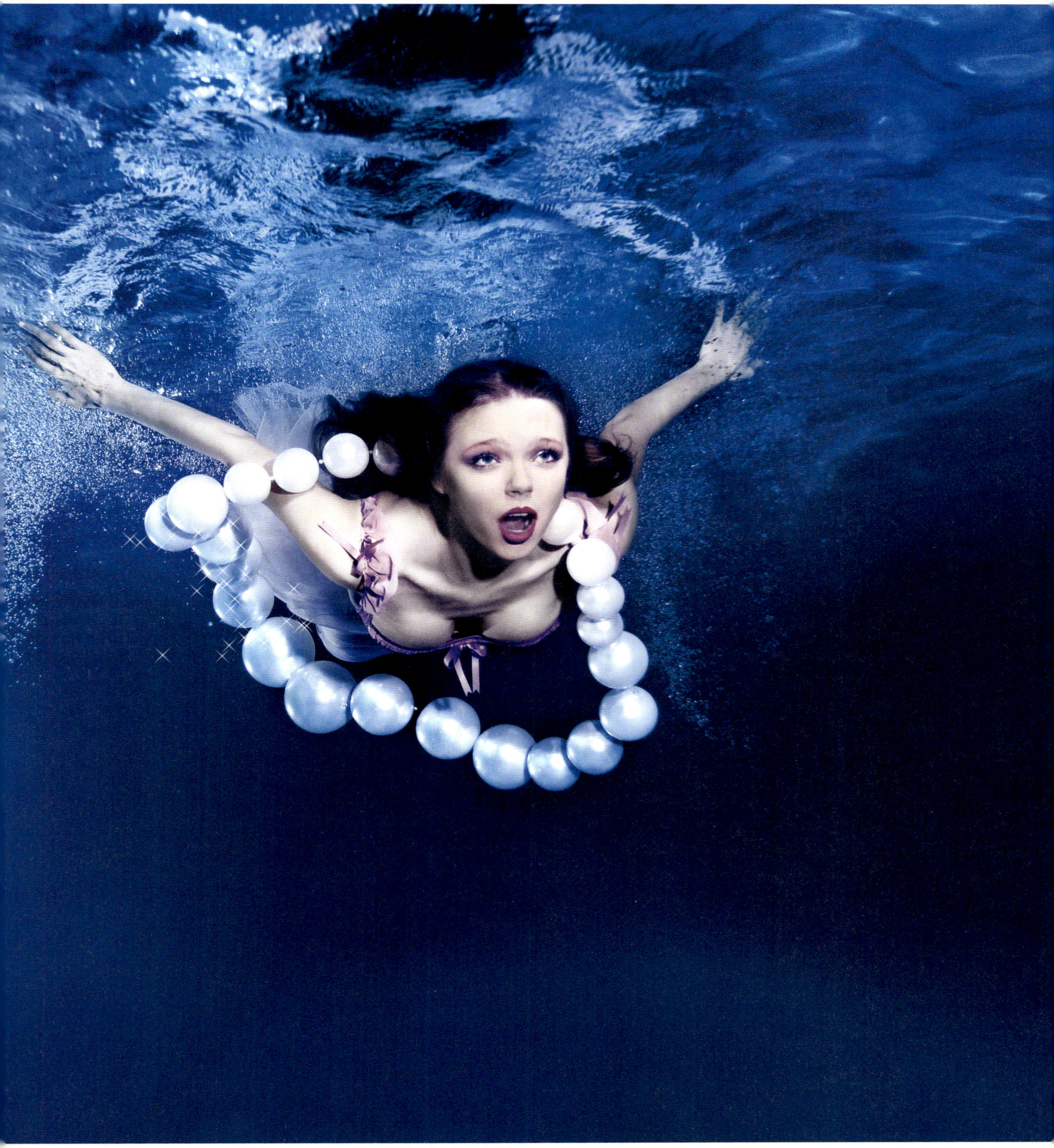

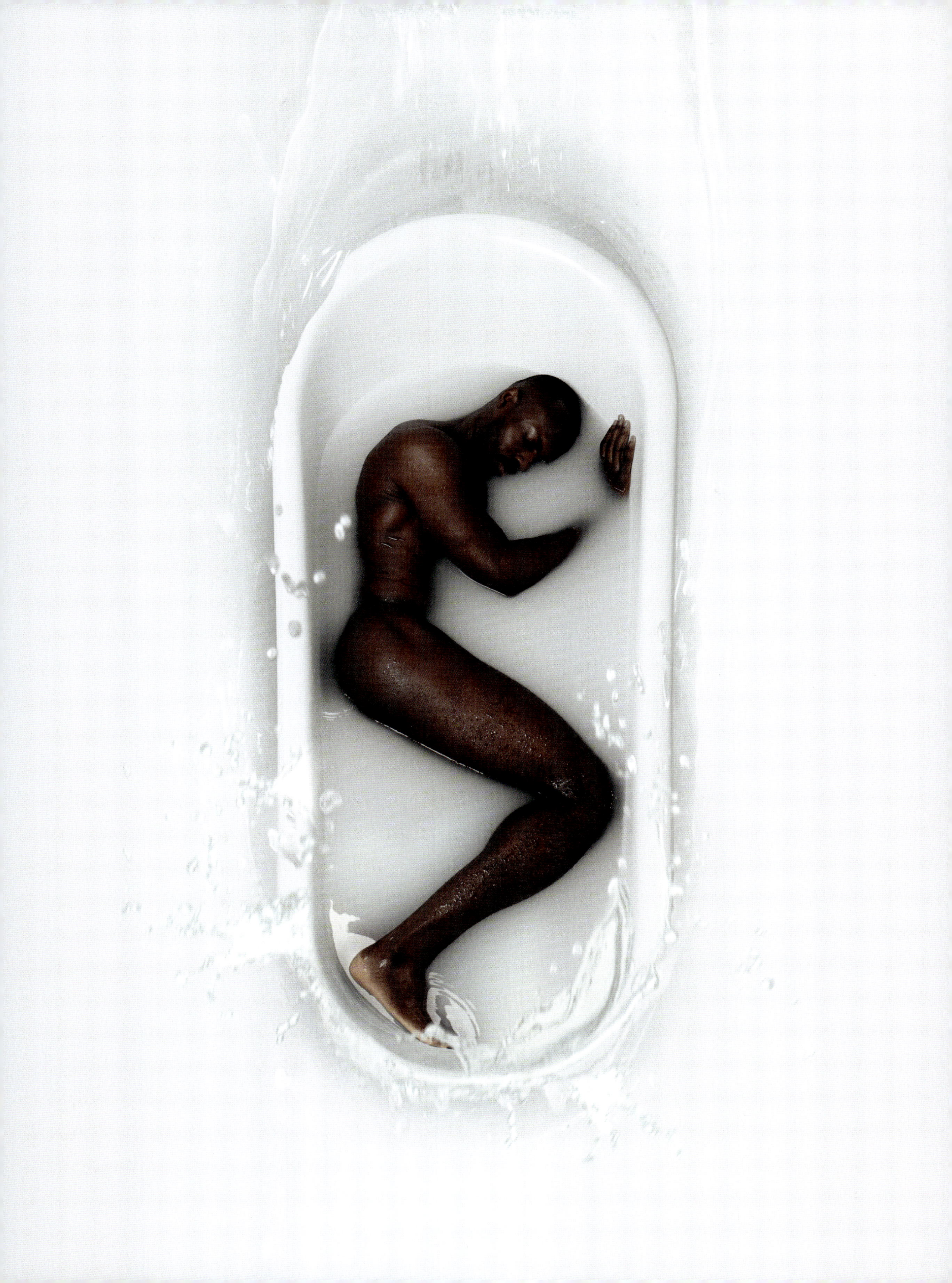

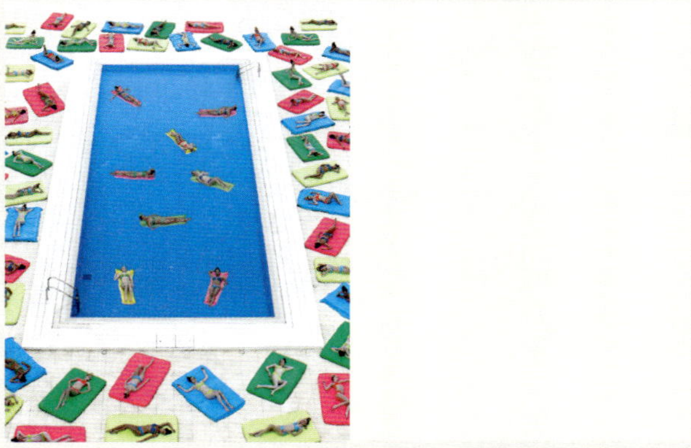

summer of love, ashrafieh, lebanon, *plastik* magazine, 2011.

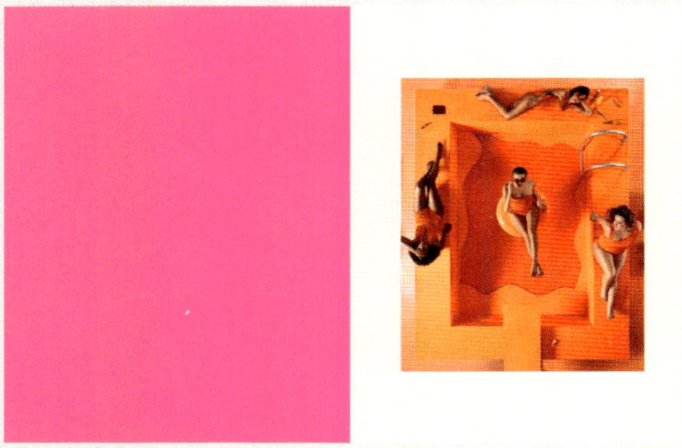

paper pool, beirut, lebanon, beesline campaign, 2020.

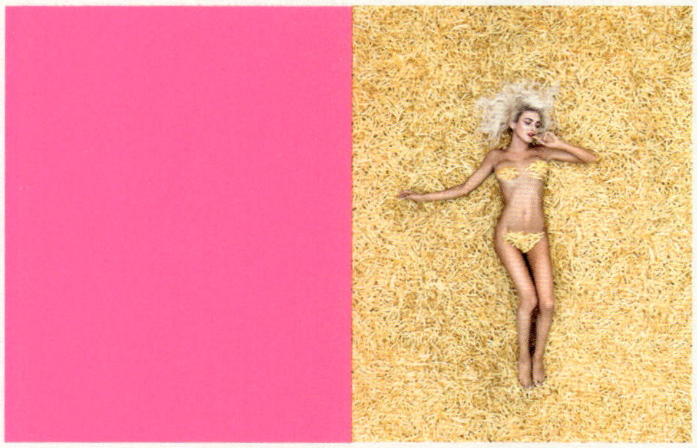

american beauty, beirut, lebanon, *plastik* magazine, 2017.

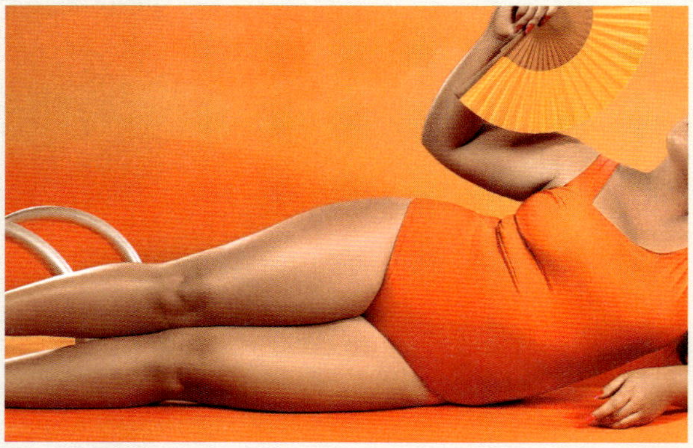

beach body, beirut, lebanon, beesline campaign, 2020.

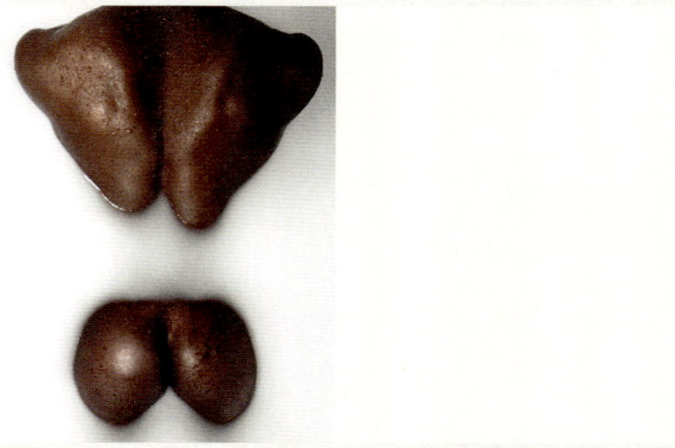

milk II, beirut, lebanon, *plastik* magazine, 2018.

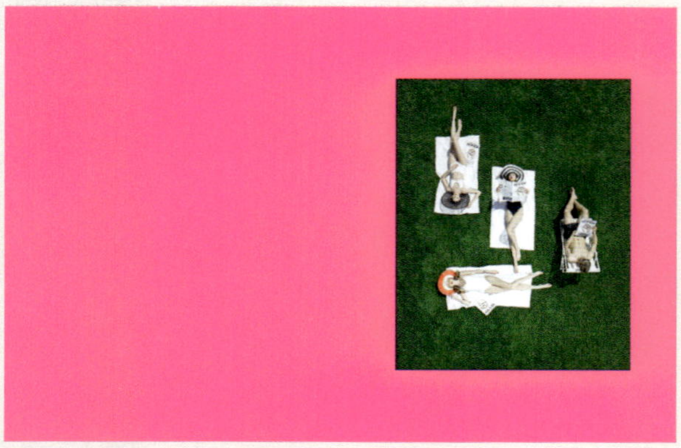

news, beirut, lebanon, tabbah campaign, 2016.

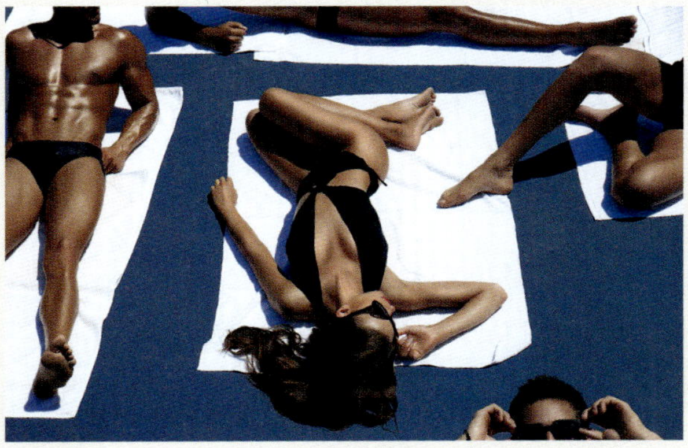

tan club, beirut, lebanon, jk campaign, 2015.

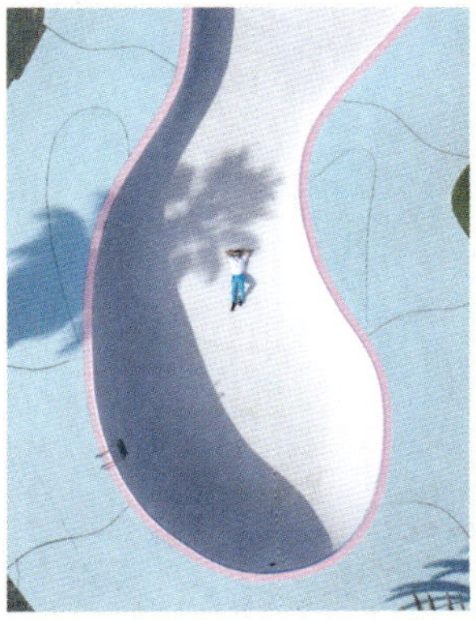

summer interlude, los angeles, usa, eye'm campaign, 2022.

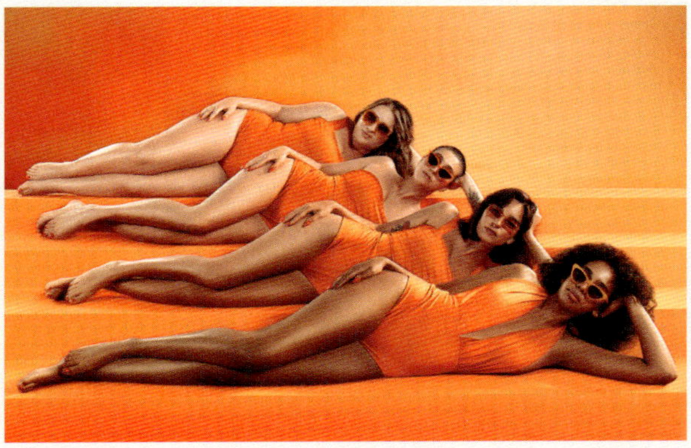

golden beach, beirut, lebanon, beesline campaign, 2020.

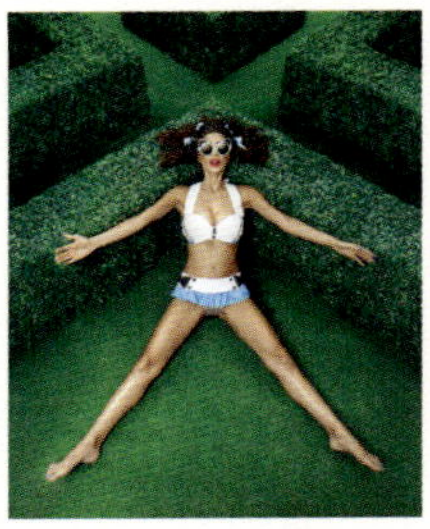

wondertan, beirut, lebanon, wondertan campaign, 2017.

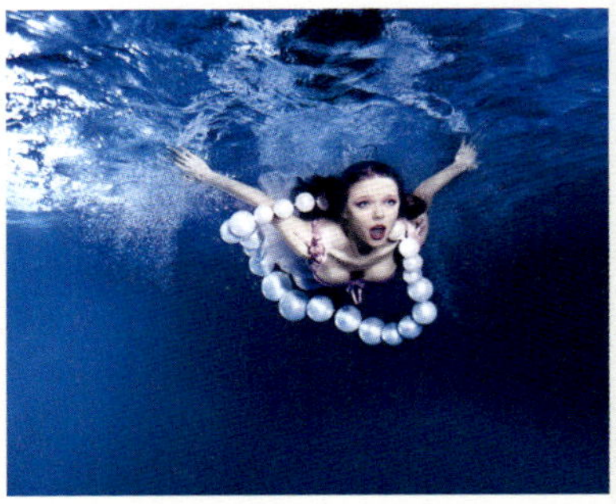

eau de merveilles, kaslik, lebanon, *plastik* magazine, 2010.

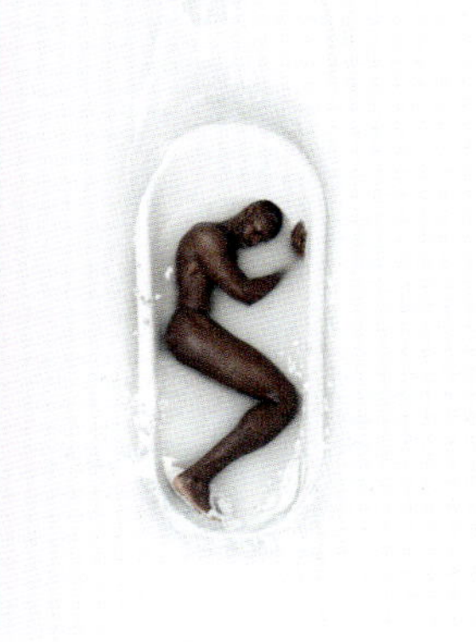

milk I, beirut, lebanon, *plastik* magazine, 2018.

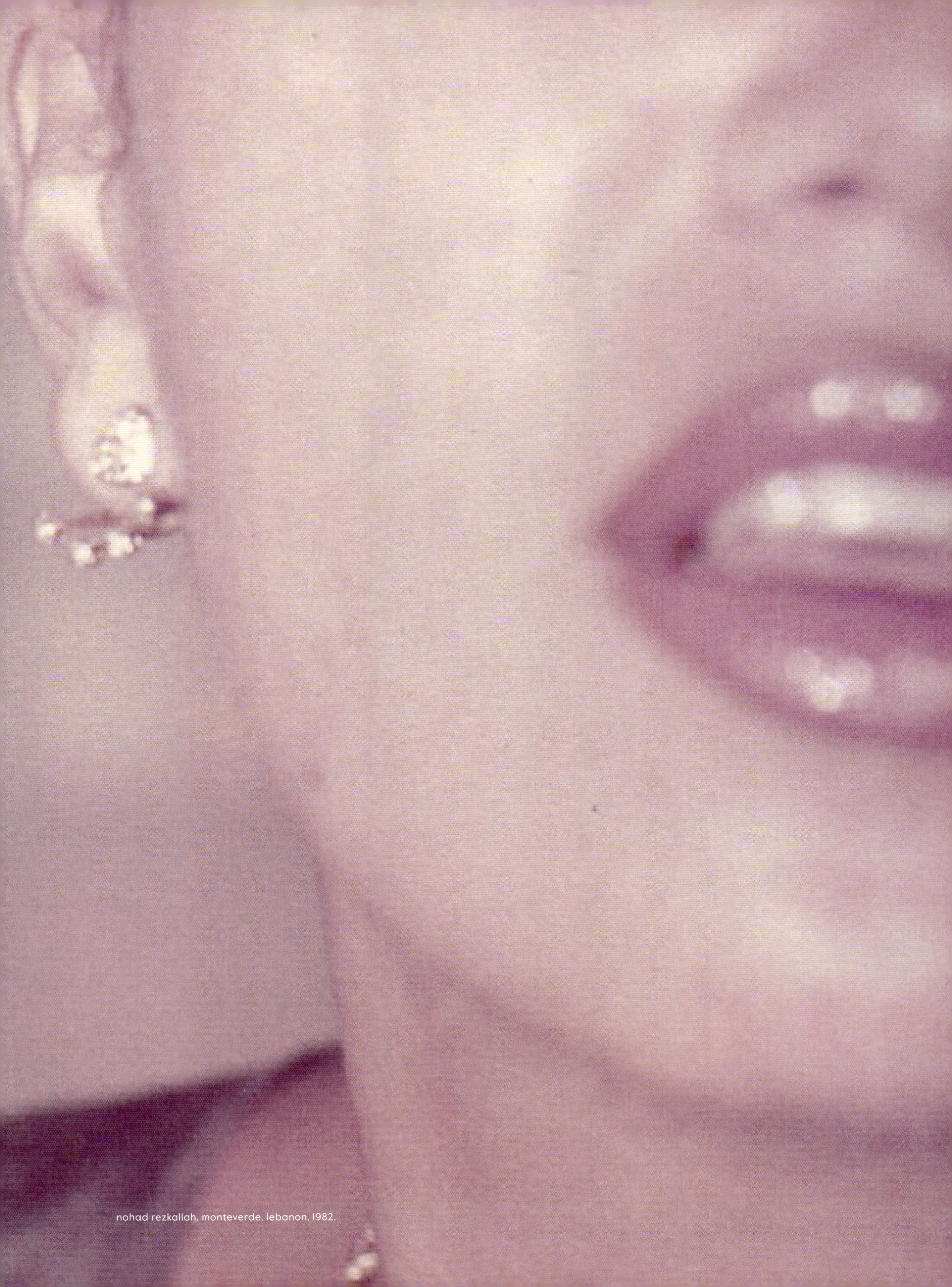

nohad rezkallah, monteverde, lebanon, 1982.

ACT TWO

mother

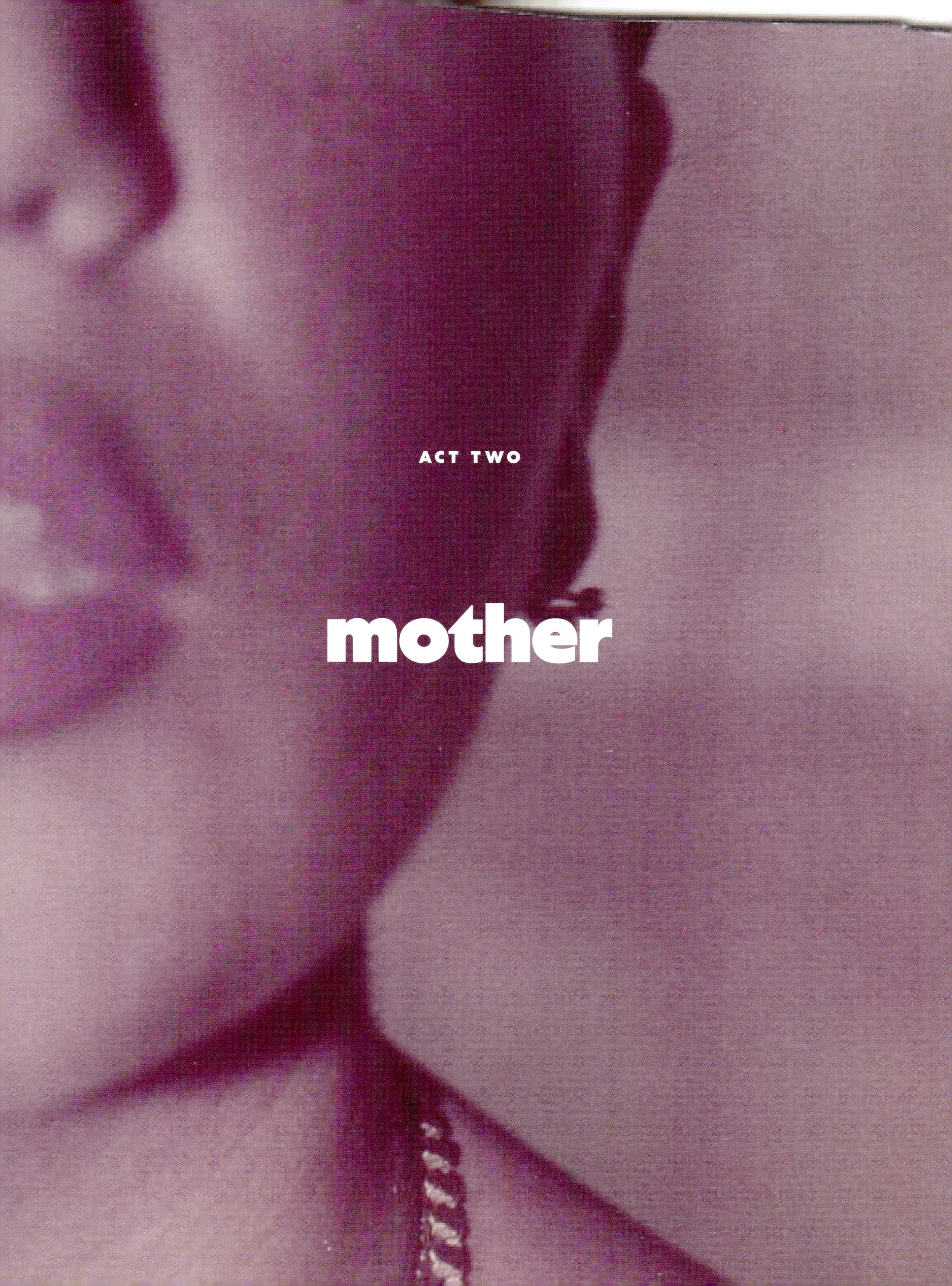

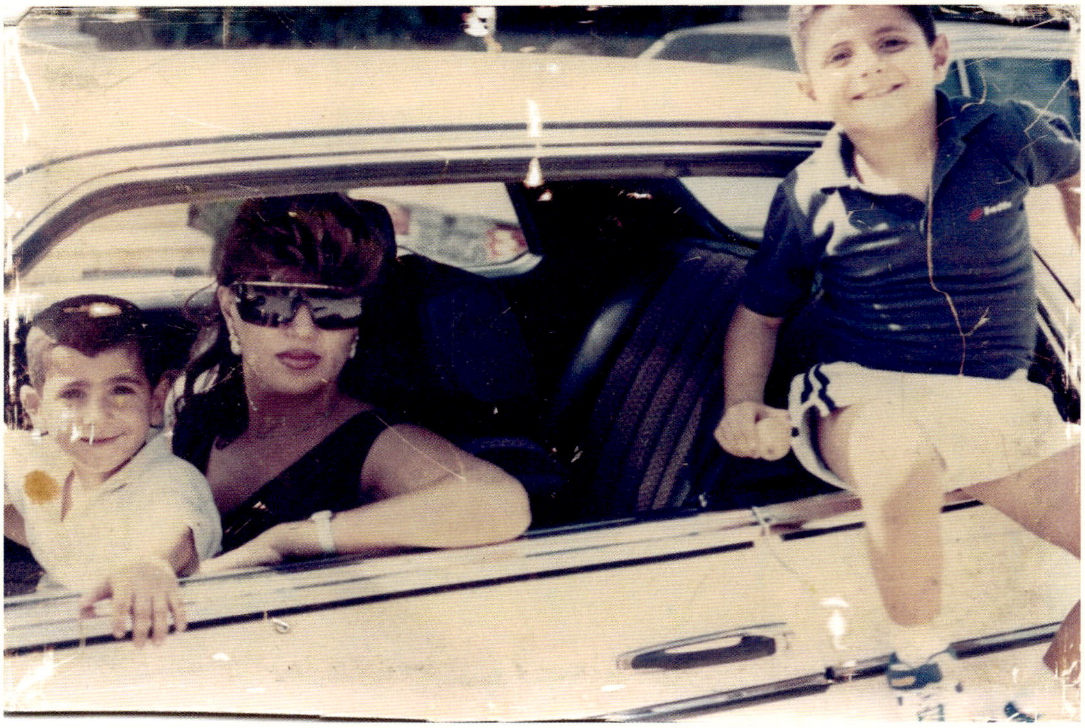

rami, nohad, and eli rezkallah. santa theresa playa, okaibe, lebanon, september 1989.

In 2016, Rezkallah shared his fascination for his mother to the world with a project aptly titled "Mother" in which the photographer reimagined vintage photographs of her through the lens of his carefully tailored imagination. The result was a touching and evocative tribute to the person he calls his very first muse.

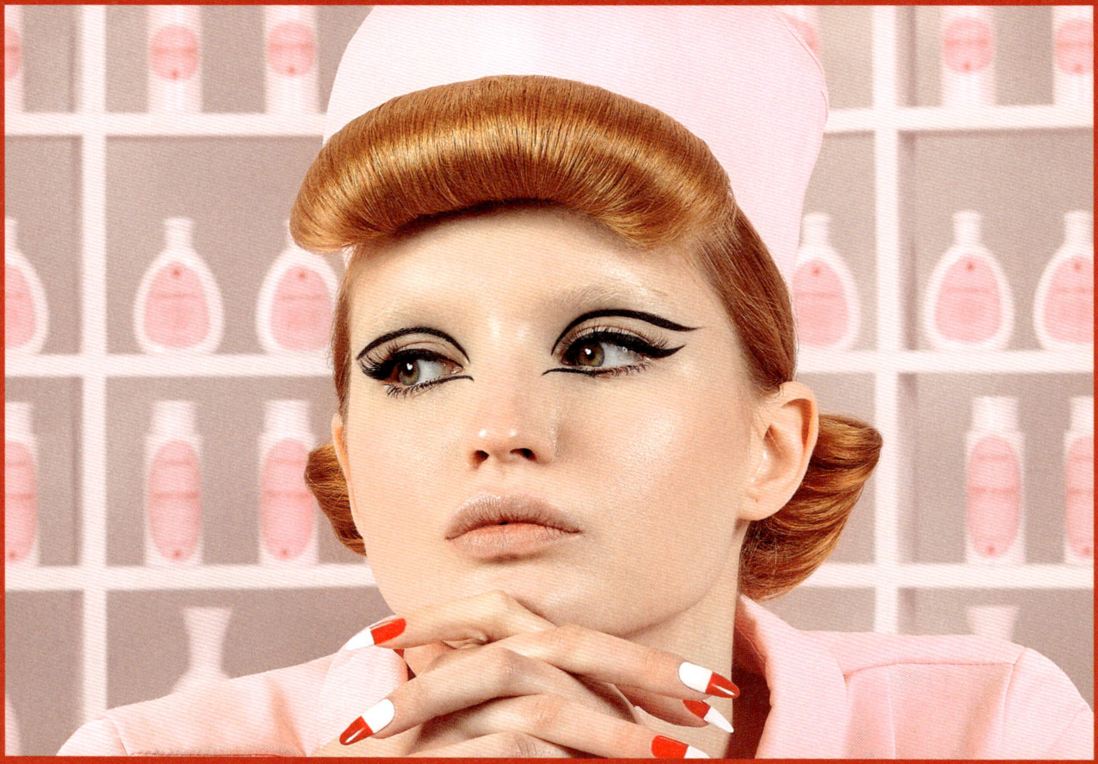

the pharmacist, beirut, lebanon, marzook campaign, 2019.

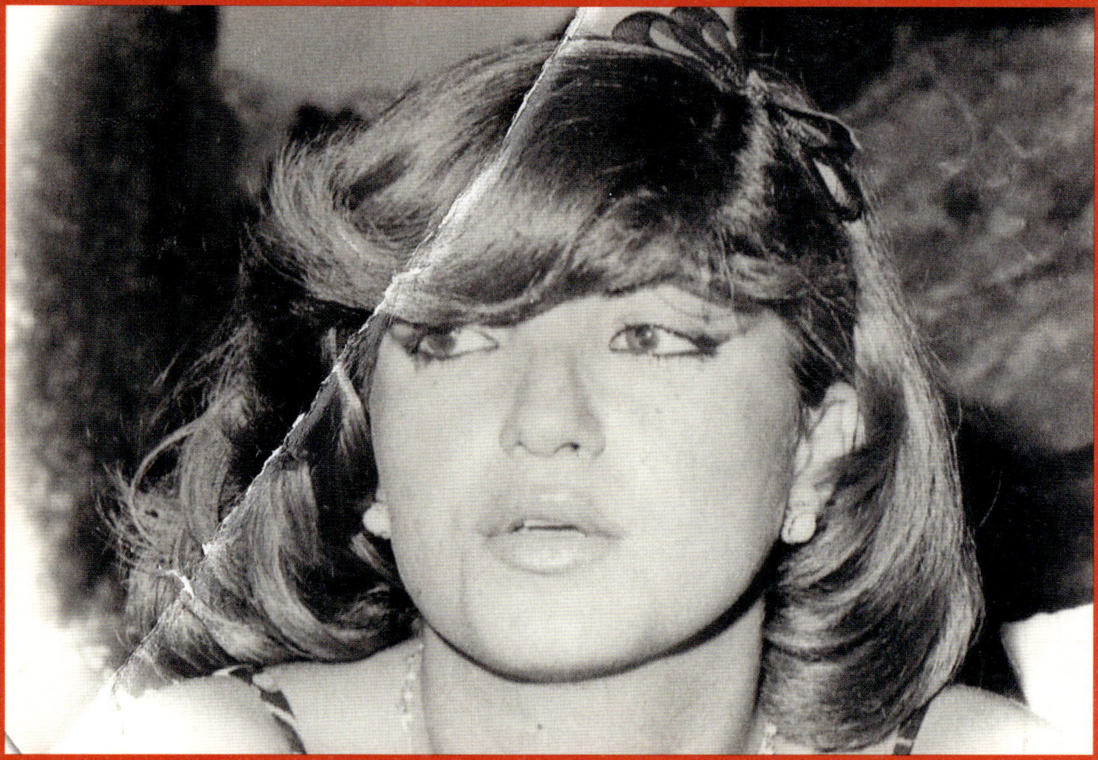

nohad kammoun, egypt, year unknown.

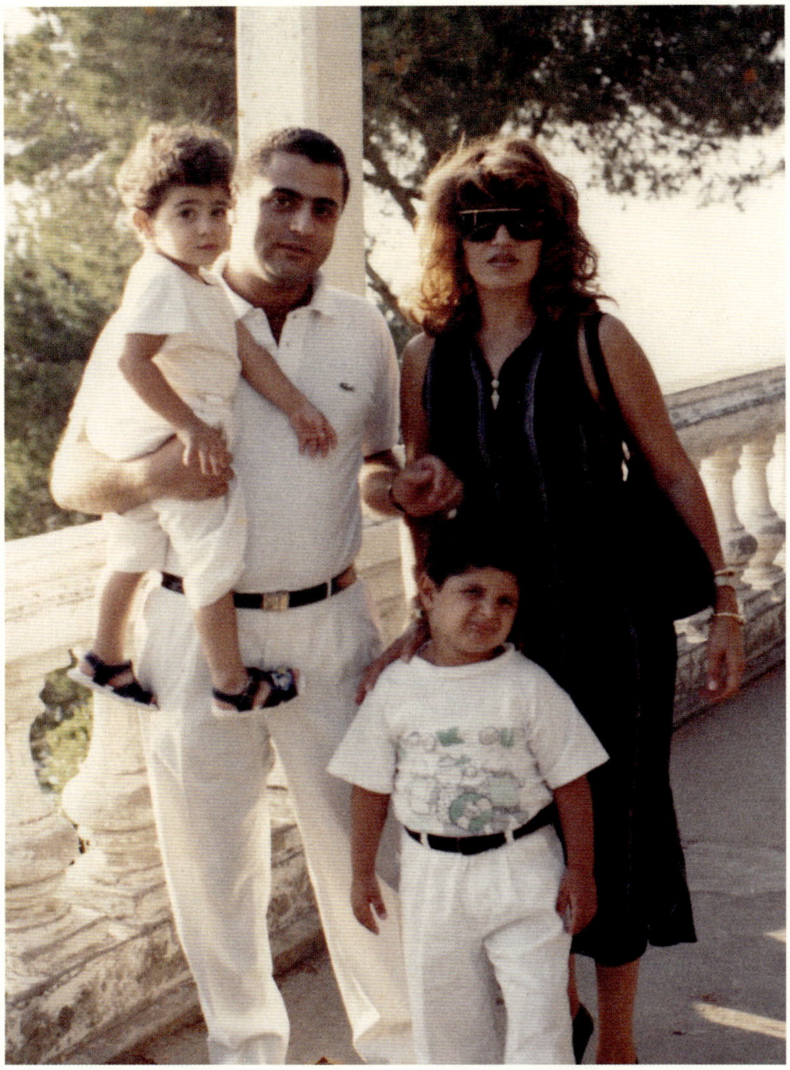

rami, thomas, nohad, and eli rezkallah, harissa, lebanon, september 1989.

Rezkallah's parents got married in Lebanon on March 21, 1982, and gave birth to the photographer, their first child of three, four years later. It must have been a confusing time for them as they celebrated their love and built a family in the midst of war, not knowing things would ever get better. How does one build on a relationship and create a loving family environment in times of destruction and political conflict? Rezkallah's mother resorted to turning all the surrounding negativity into an abstraction, and creating a fantasy world in which she could live the life she had always yearned for...

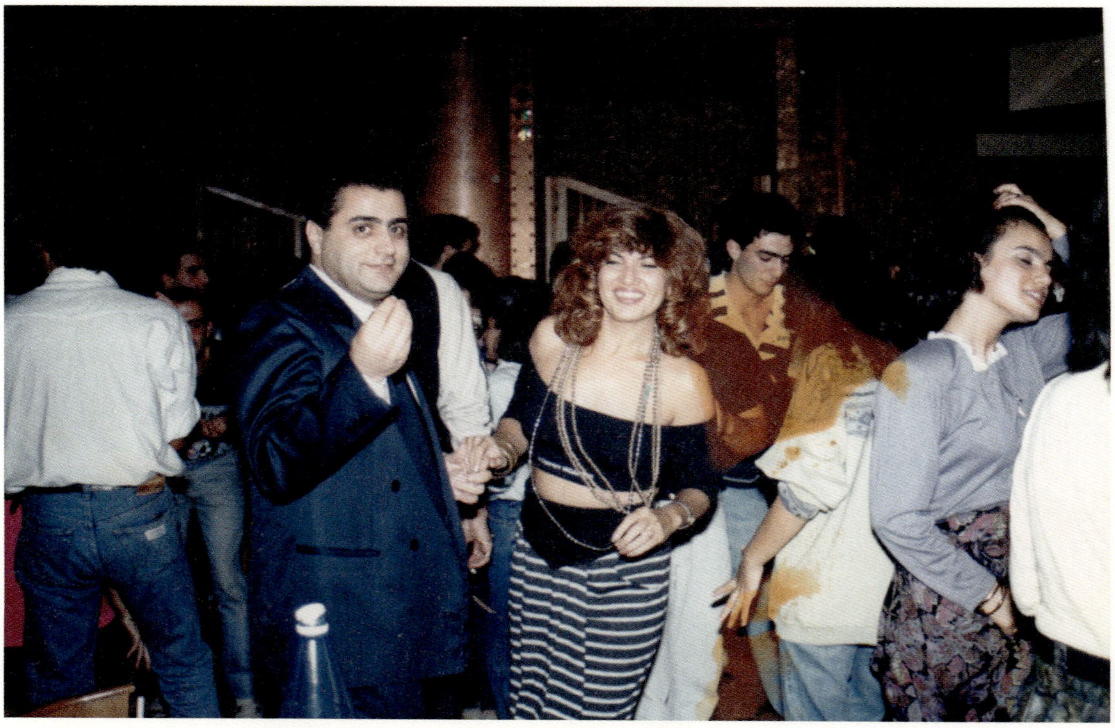

thomas and nohad rezkallah, santa theresa playa, okaibe, lebanon, 1987.

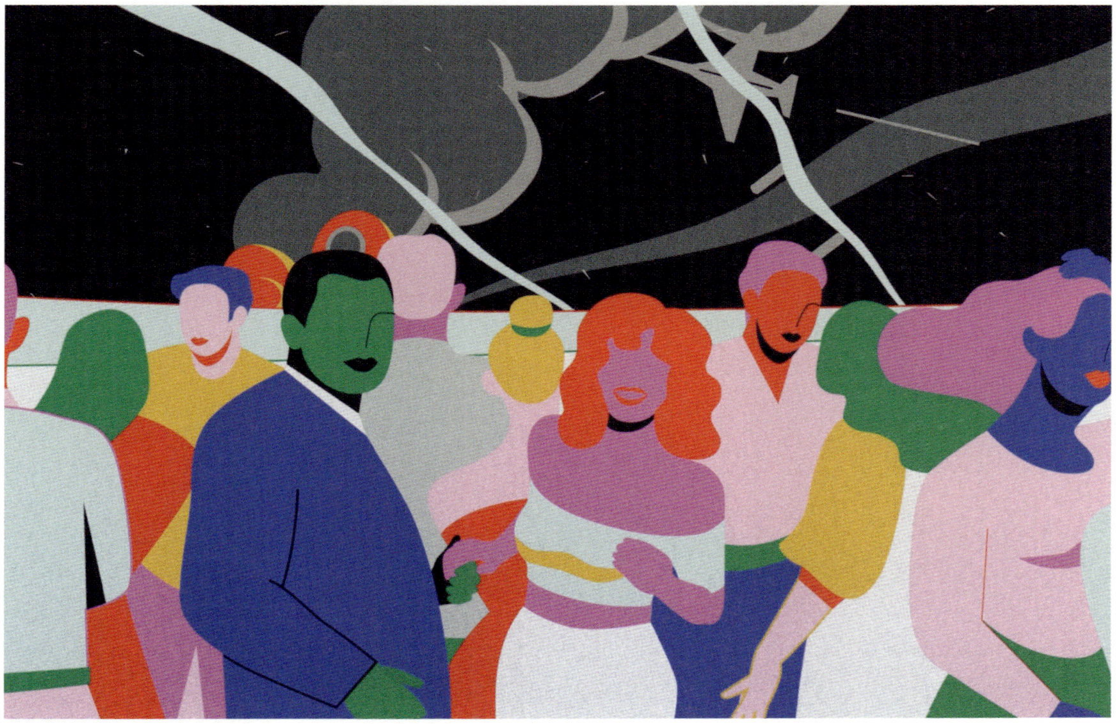

party under the bombs, illustration by minji moon, commissioned by *plastik* studios, 2018.

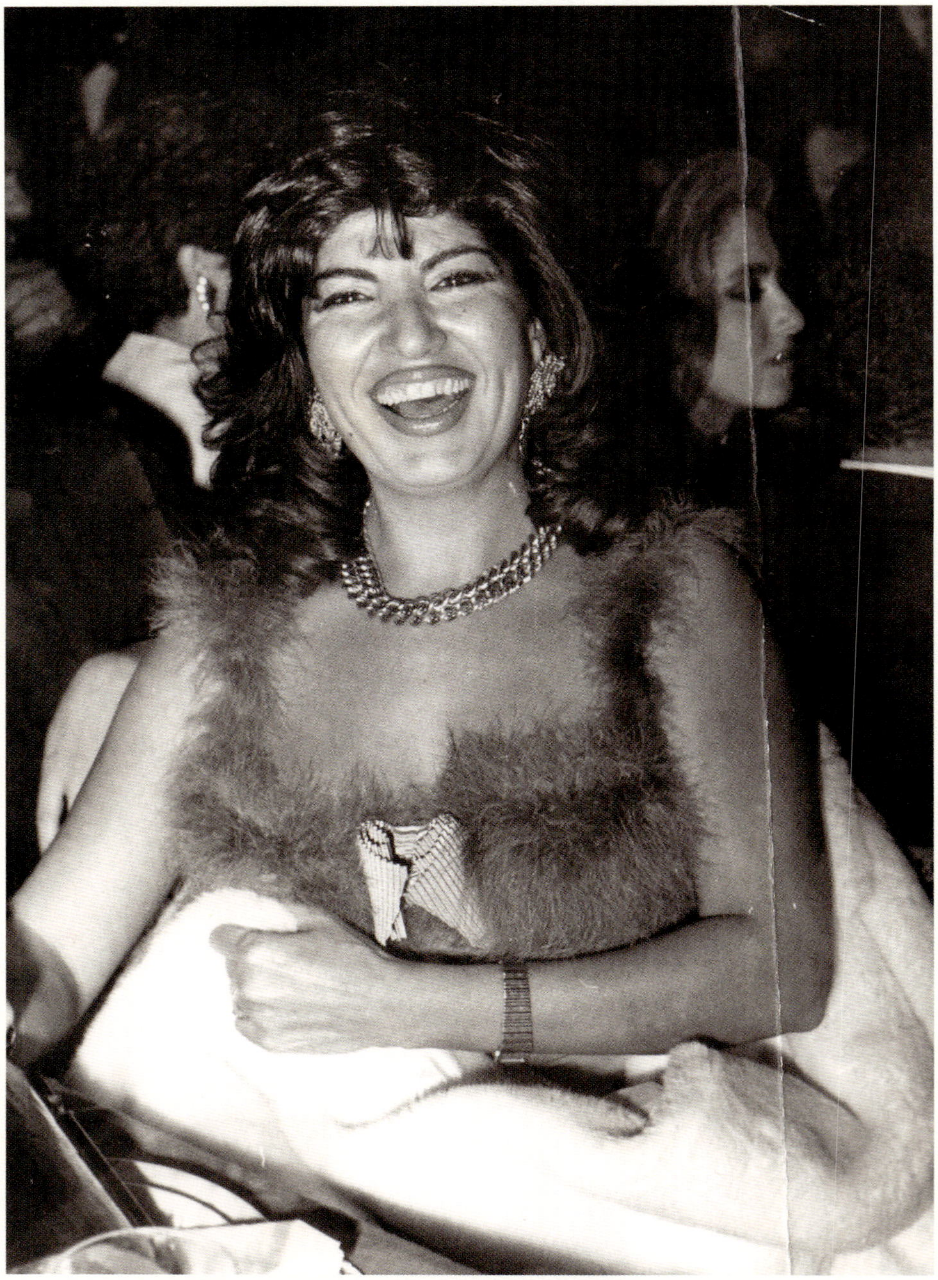

nohad rezkallah, jounieh, lebanon, 1990.

While Rezkallah's father was the provider, his mother became a master illusionist. Every day was a new reason to dress to the nines, revamp one's style, and celebrate life as loudly as the shells exploding next door... She was loud, unfiltered, vain, eccentric, and always the main source of entertainment: Anyone who knew her couldn't help but admire this force of nature who seemed to be in complete control of her own destiny and always living her best life. Little did they know that she was constantly fighting off crippling anxiety that kept trying to surface.

To this day, Rezkallah has a soft spot for his mother, profoundly touched by the fact that she would rather live a fantasy than face reality. Her coping mechanism became a great source of inspiration. With delusion as her weapon, he witnessed how a woman at her most vulnerable, could mask her fears and anxieties using the power of denial and project strength, joy, and light instead.

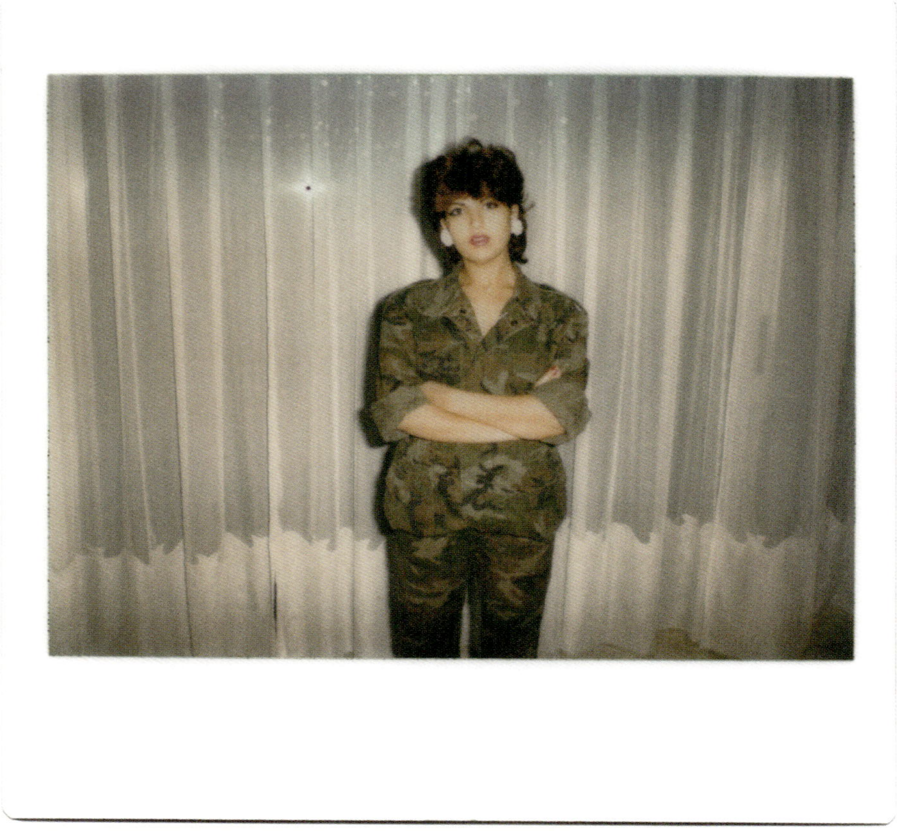

nohad rezkallah playing dress-up in a military costume. monteverde, lebanon, 1983.

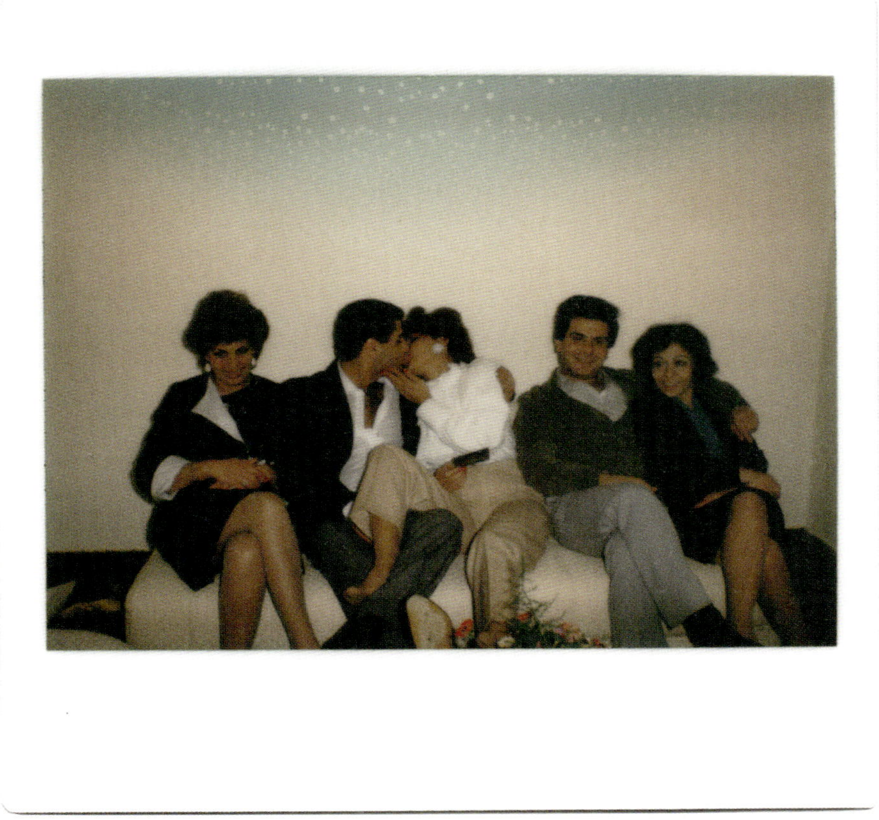

nazik zeidan, thomas and nohad rezkallah, ramez and sabah kammoun. monteverde, lebanon, 1983.

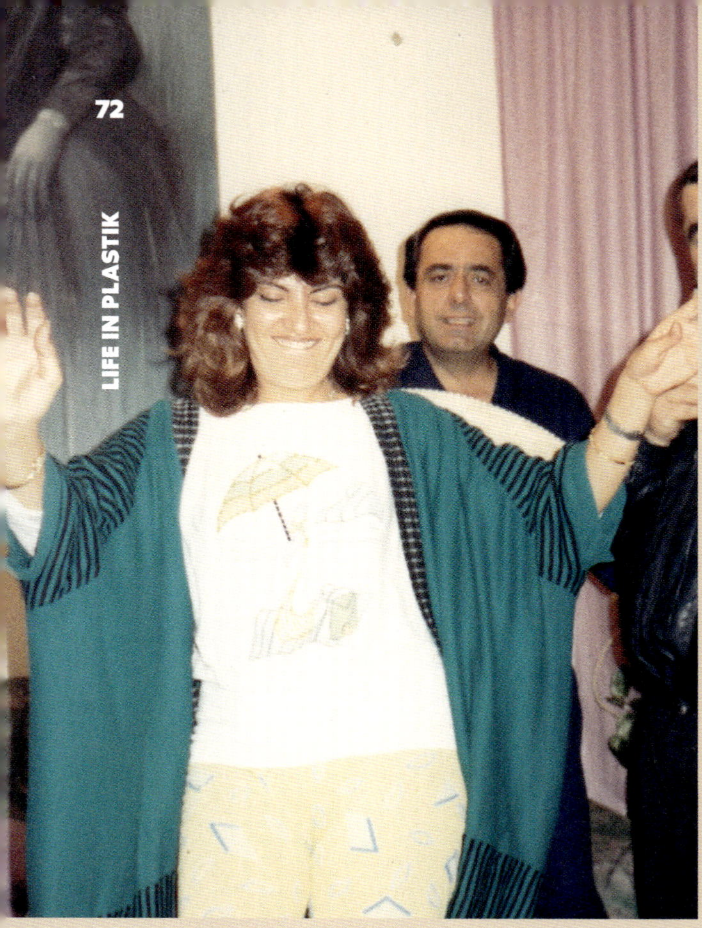

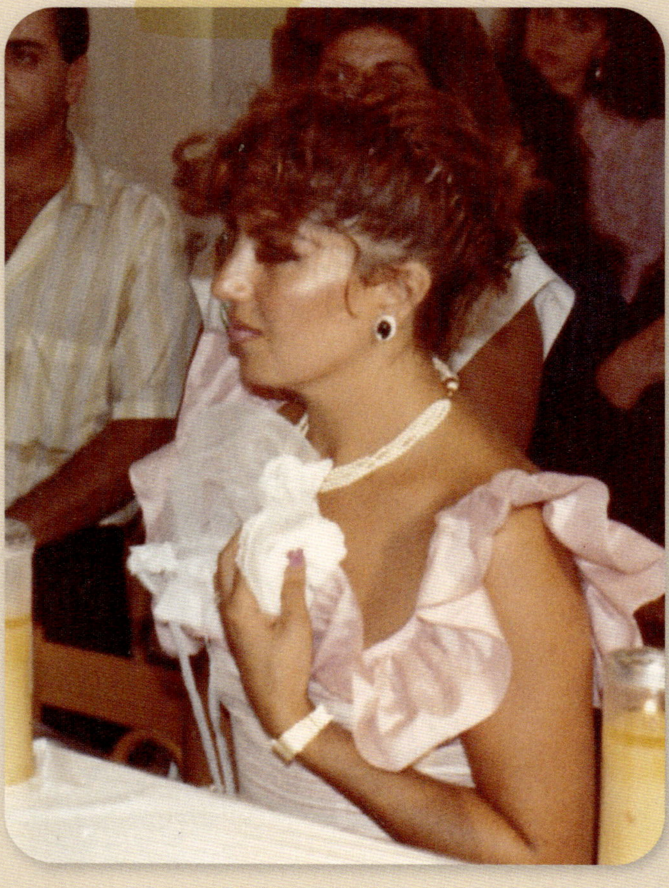

mom at my baptism 1986.

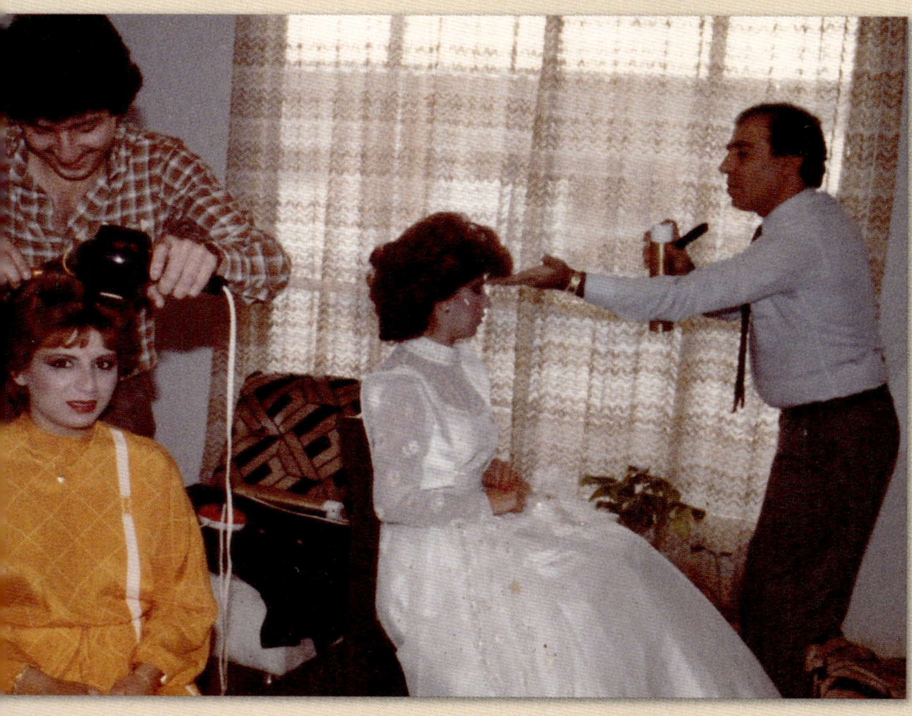

nohad getting ready for her wedding.
she tells me later that she hated her hair that day.

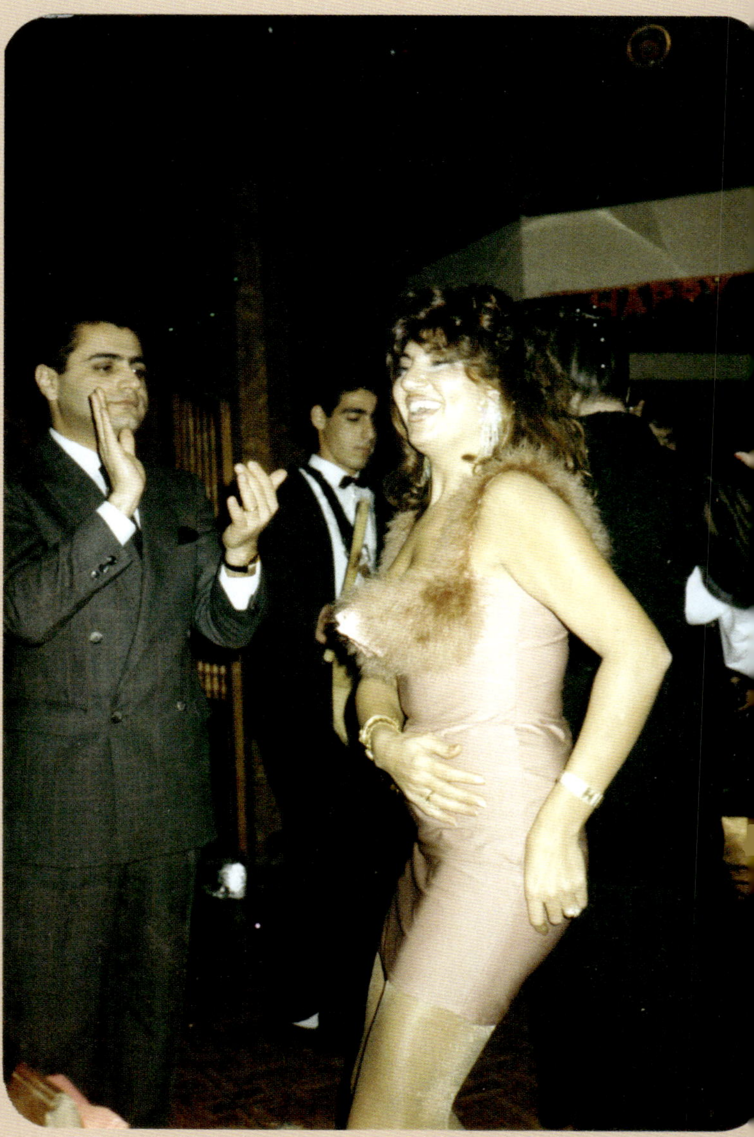

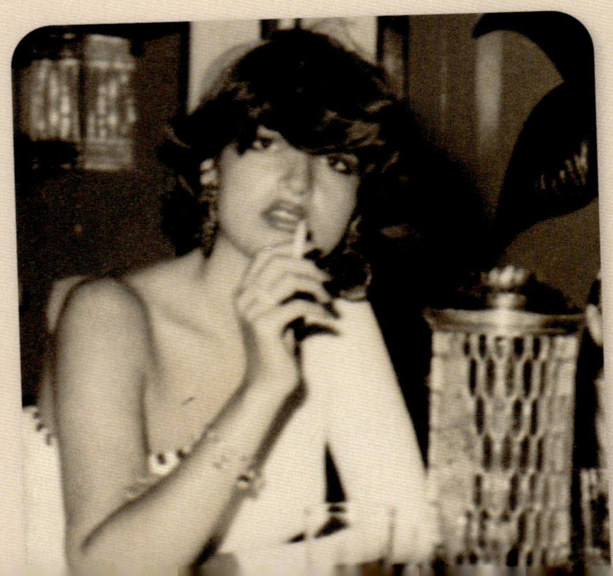

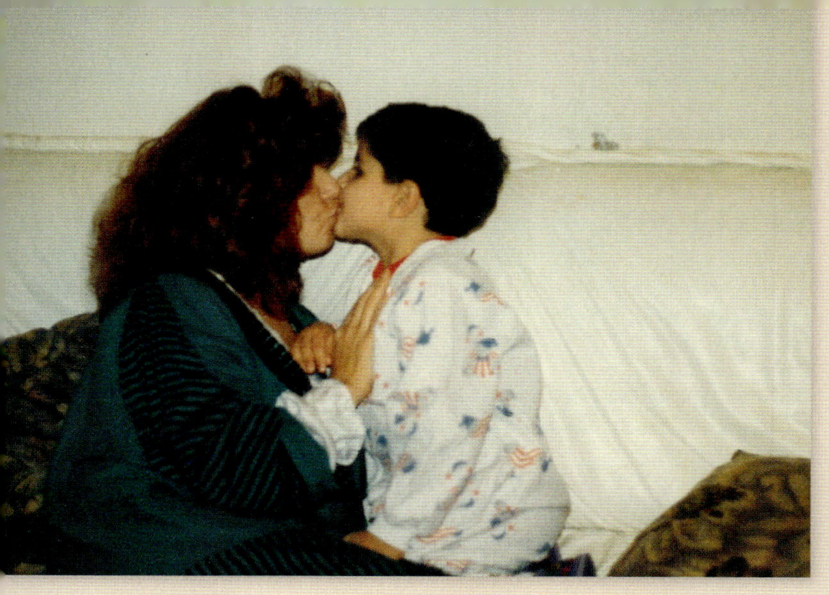

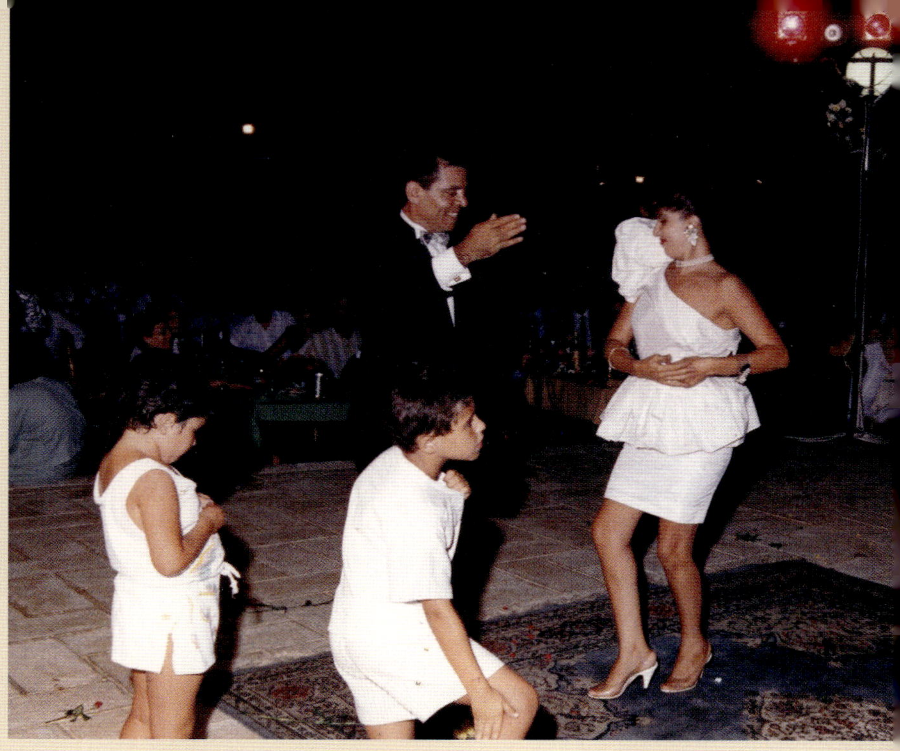

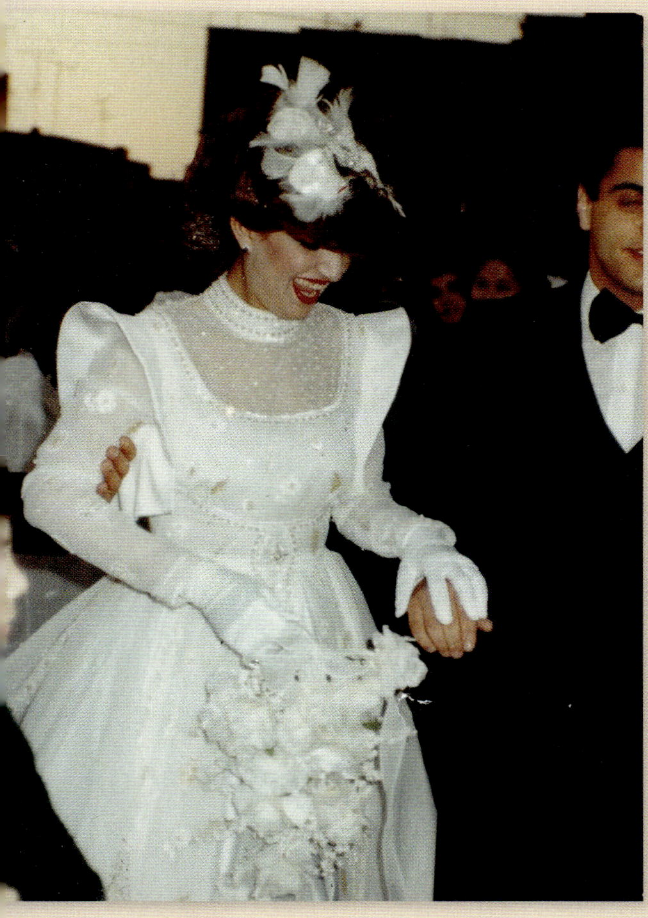

mom and dad on their wedding day.
first day of spring 1982.

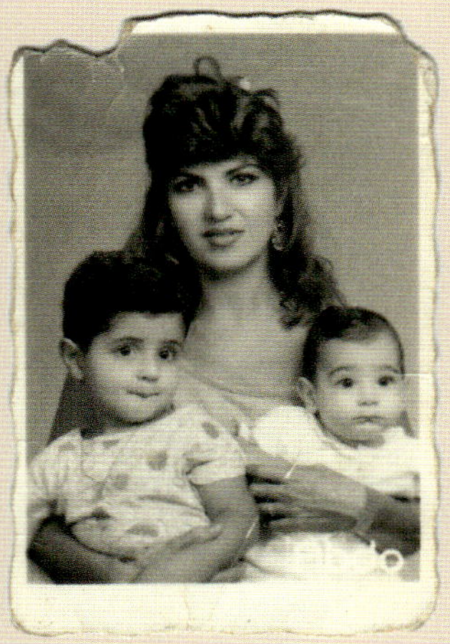

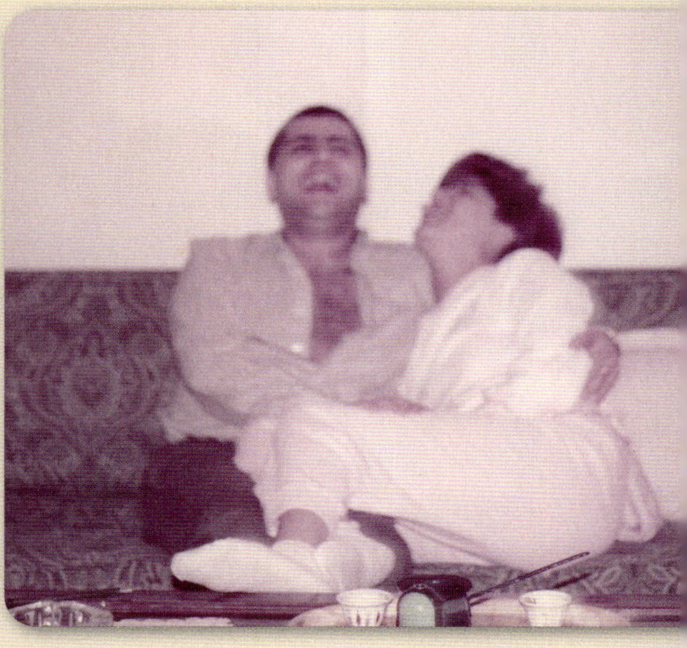

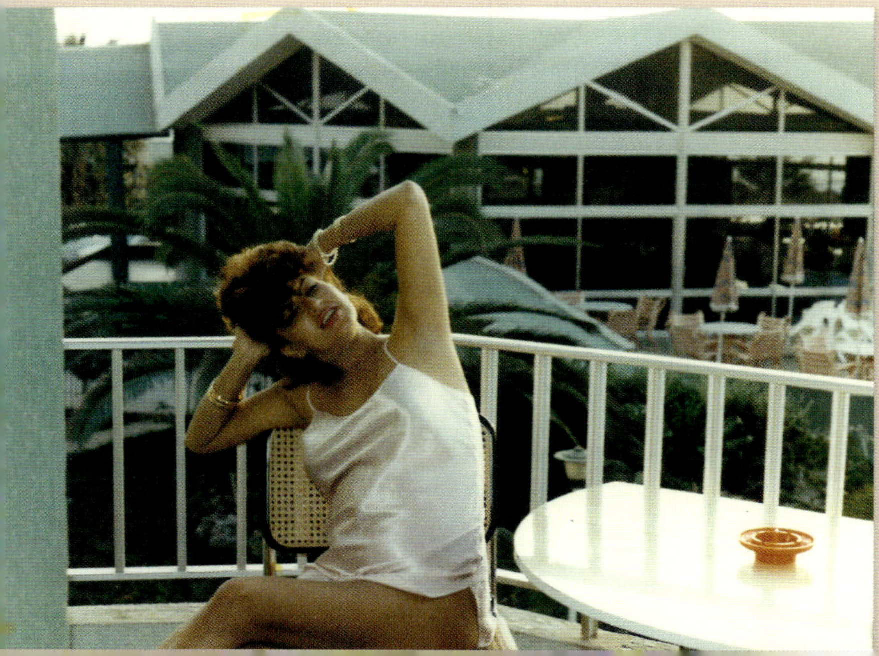

nohad pregnant with me 1985

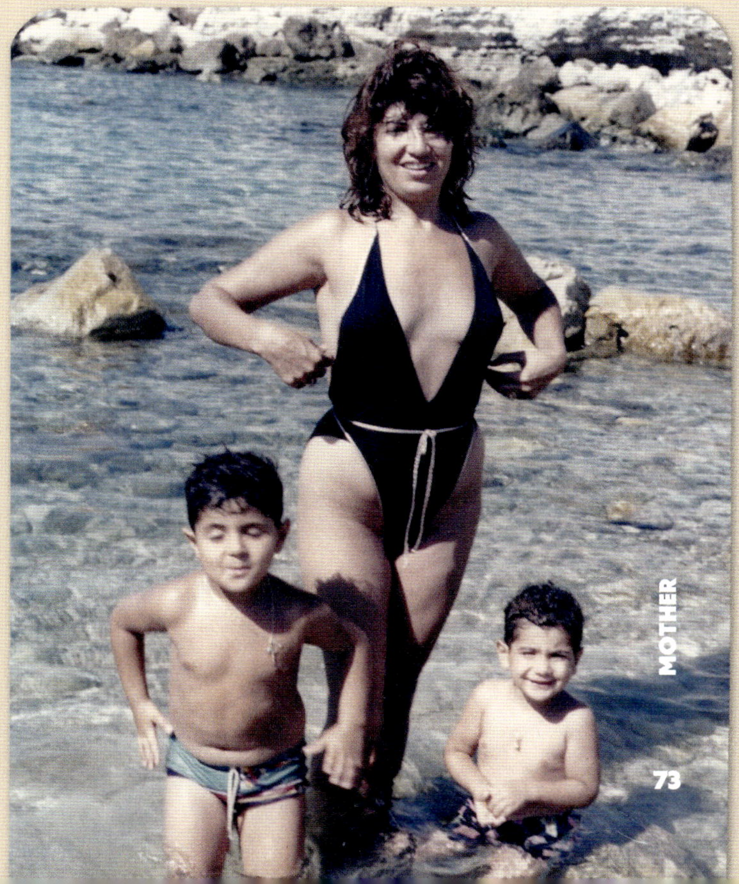

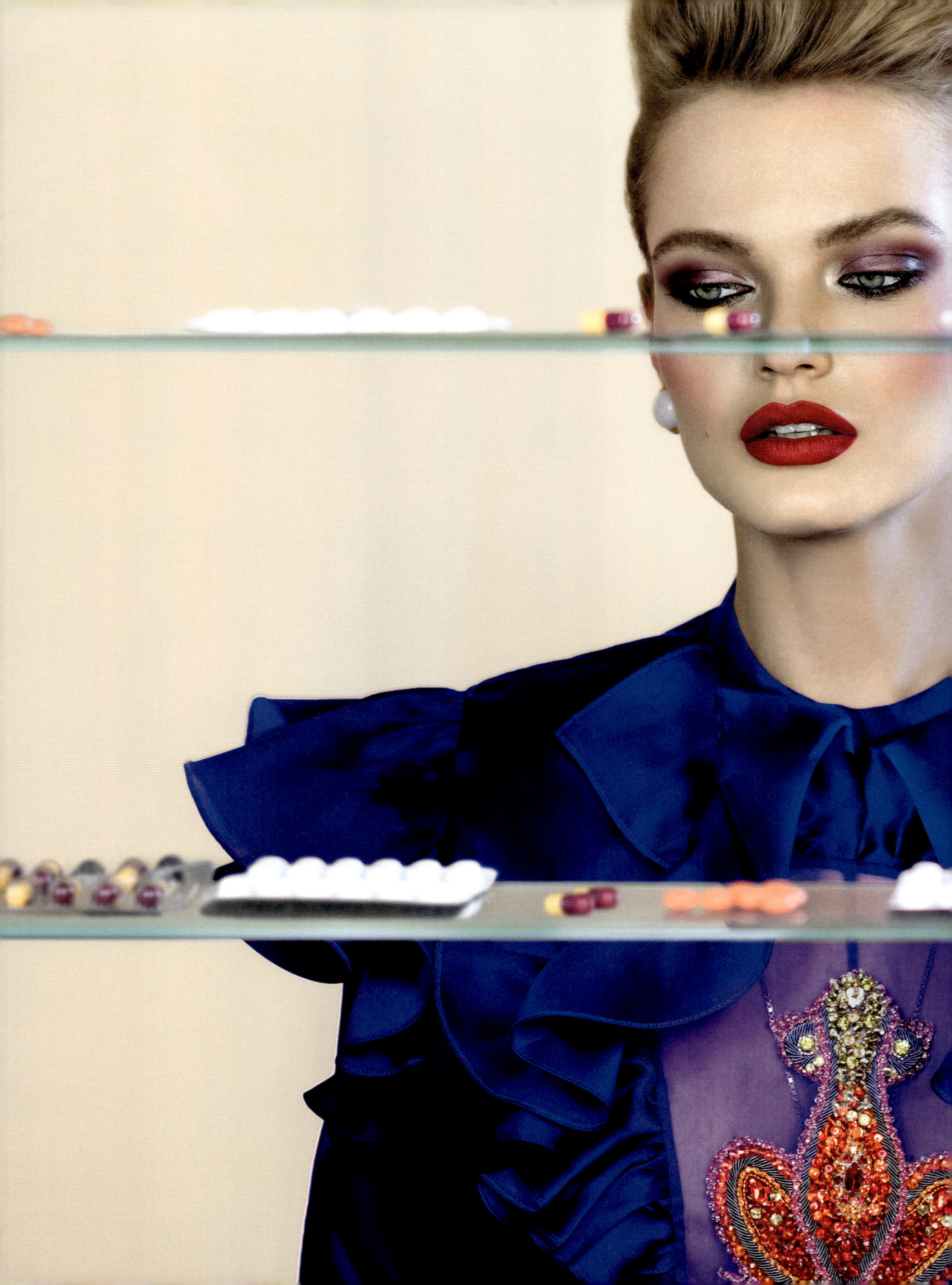

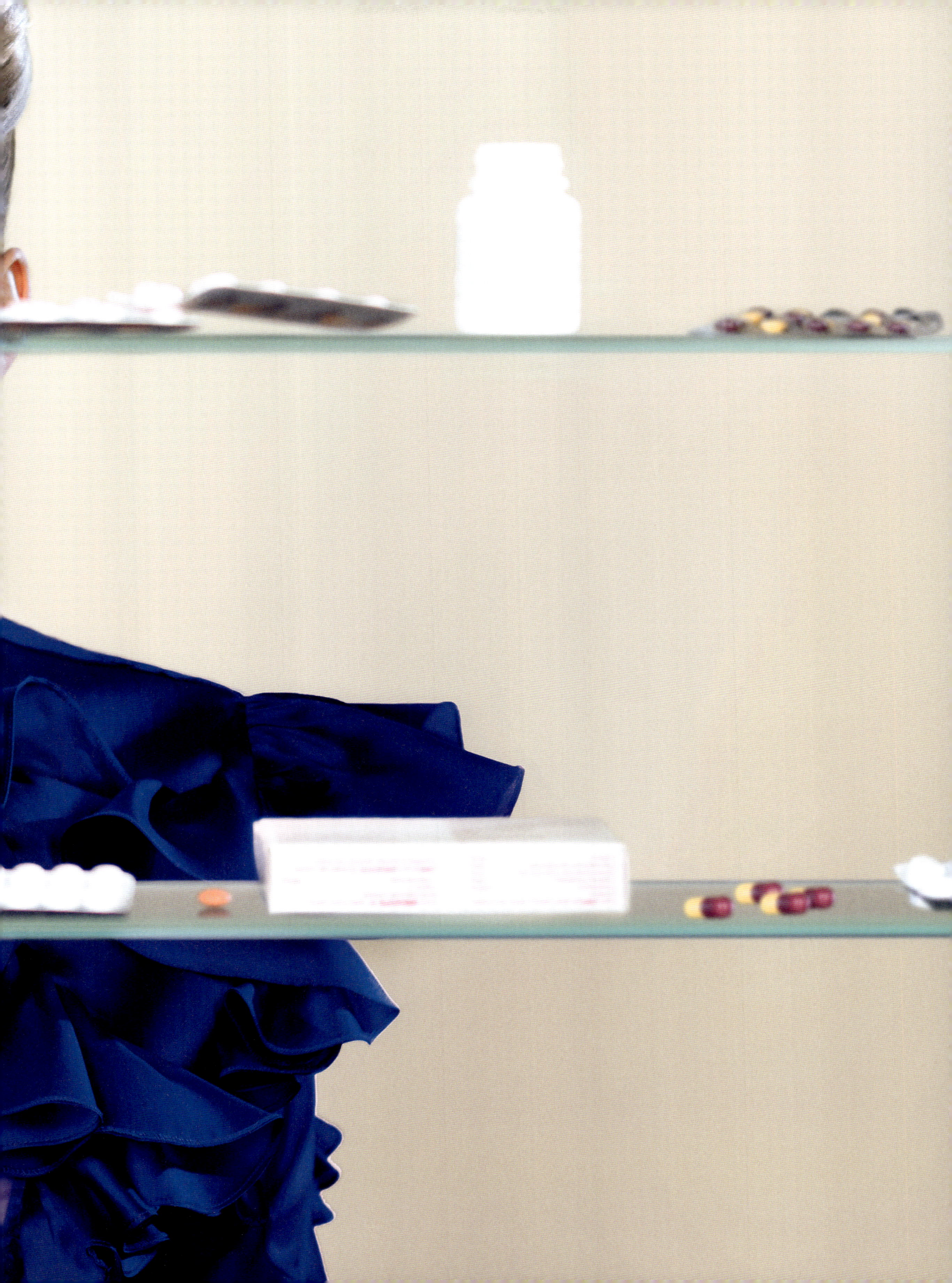

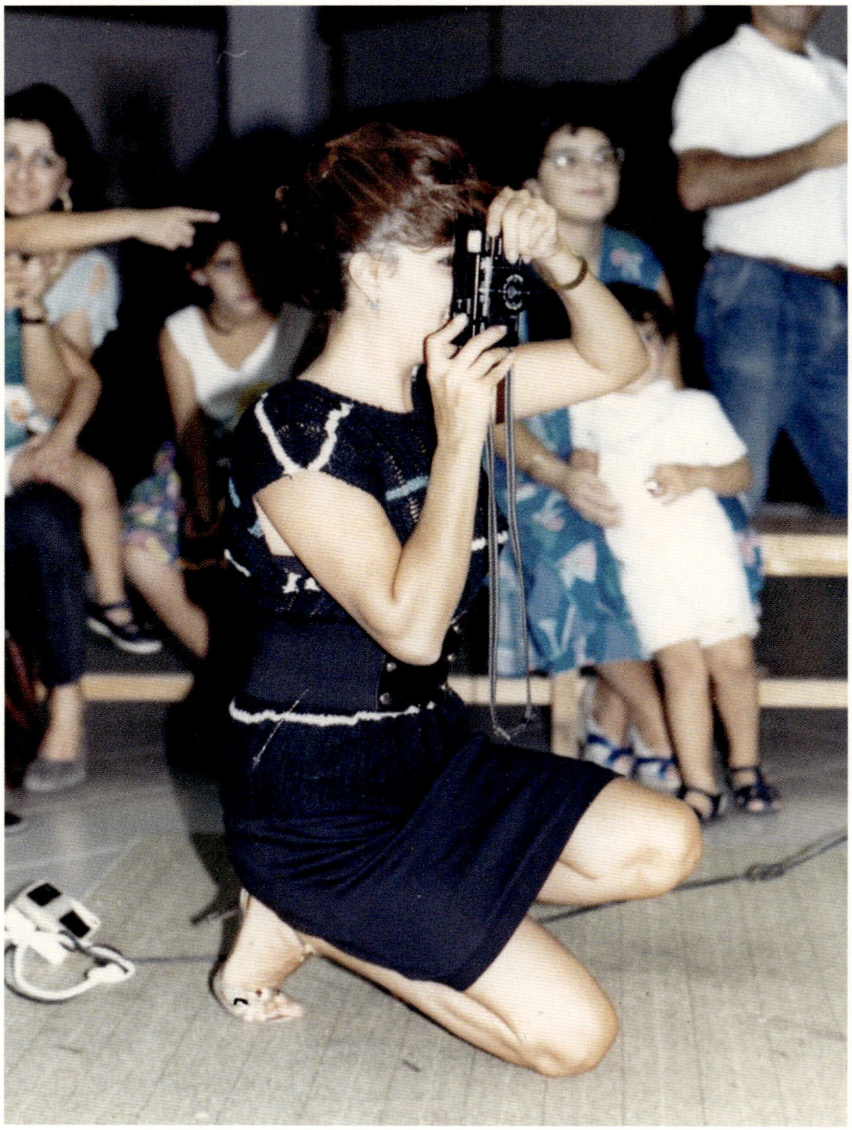

nohad rezkallah, saframarine, safra, lebanon, september 1988.

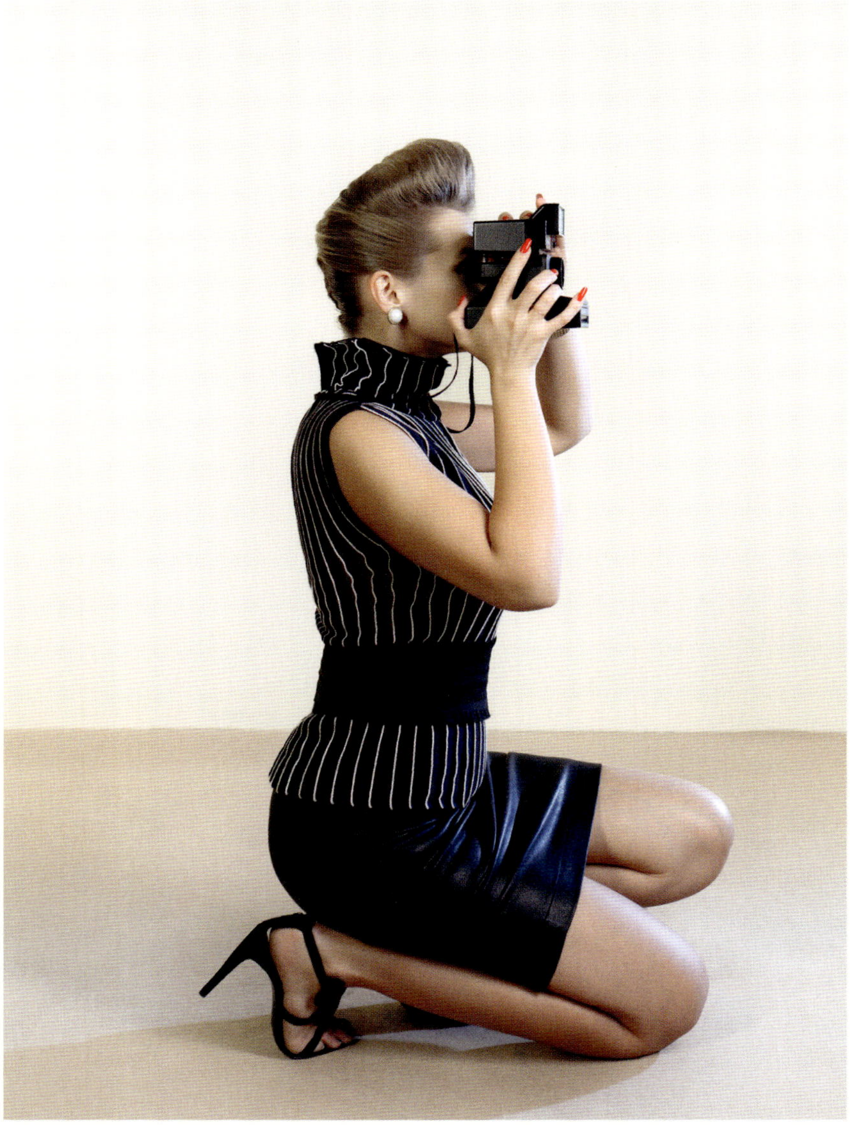

mother with a camera, beirut, lebanon, dare greatly documentary, 2017.

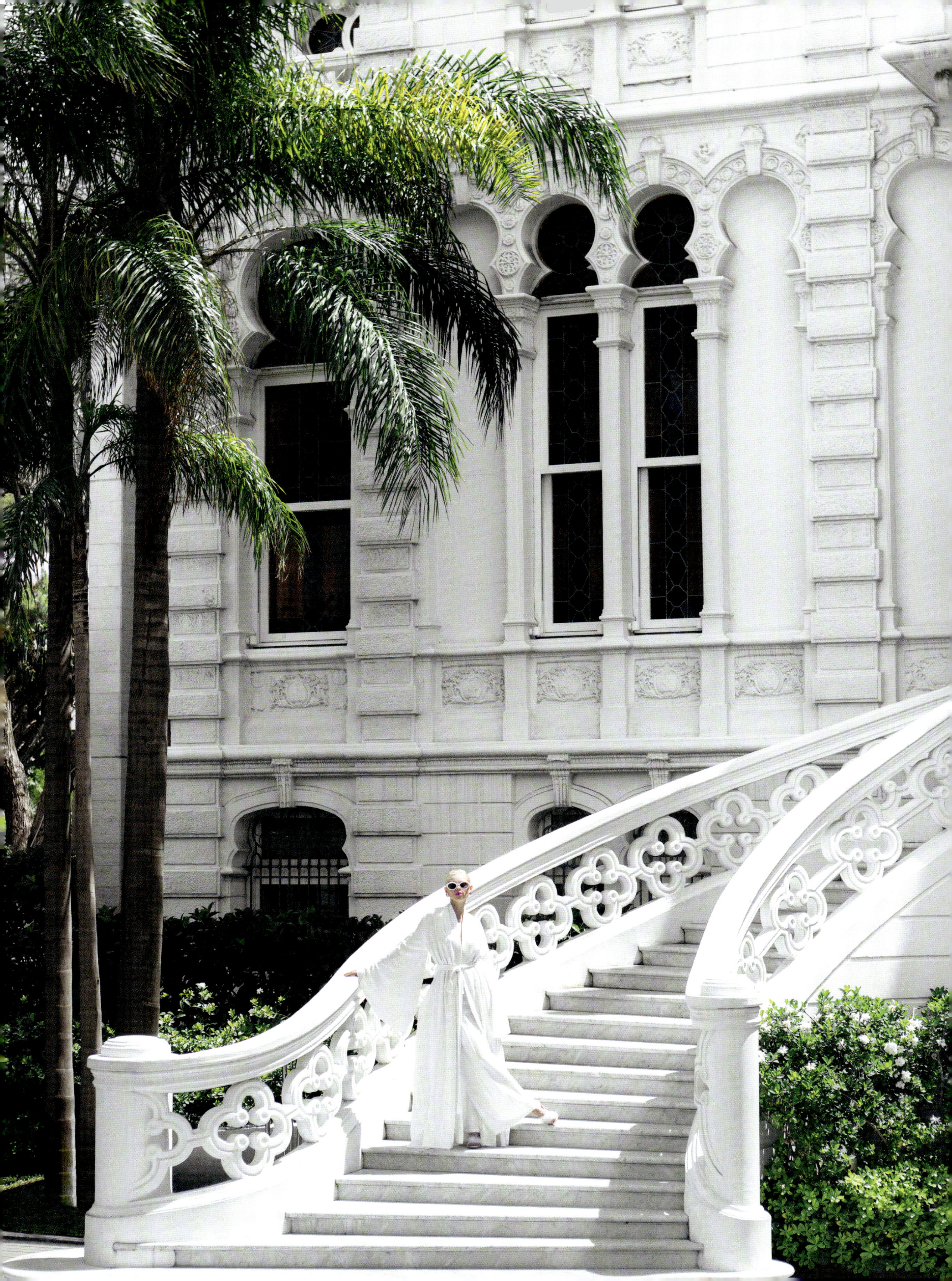

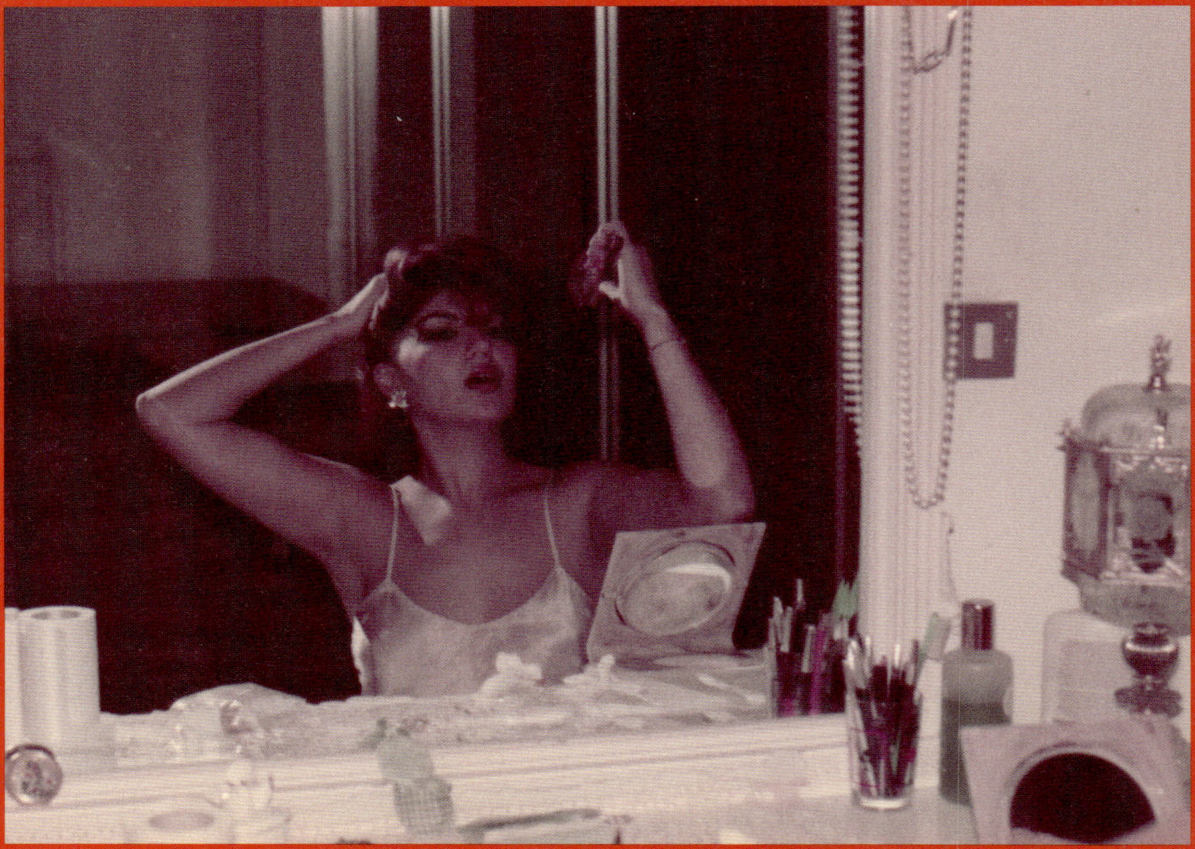

nohad rezkallah, monteverde, lebanon, 1982.

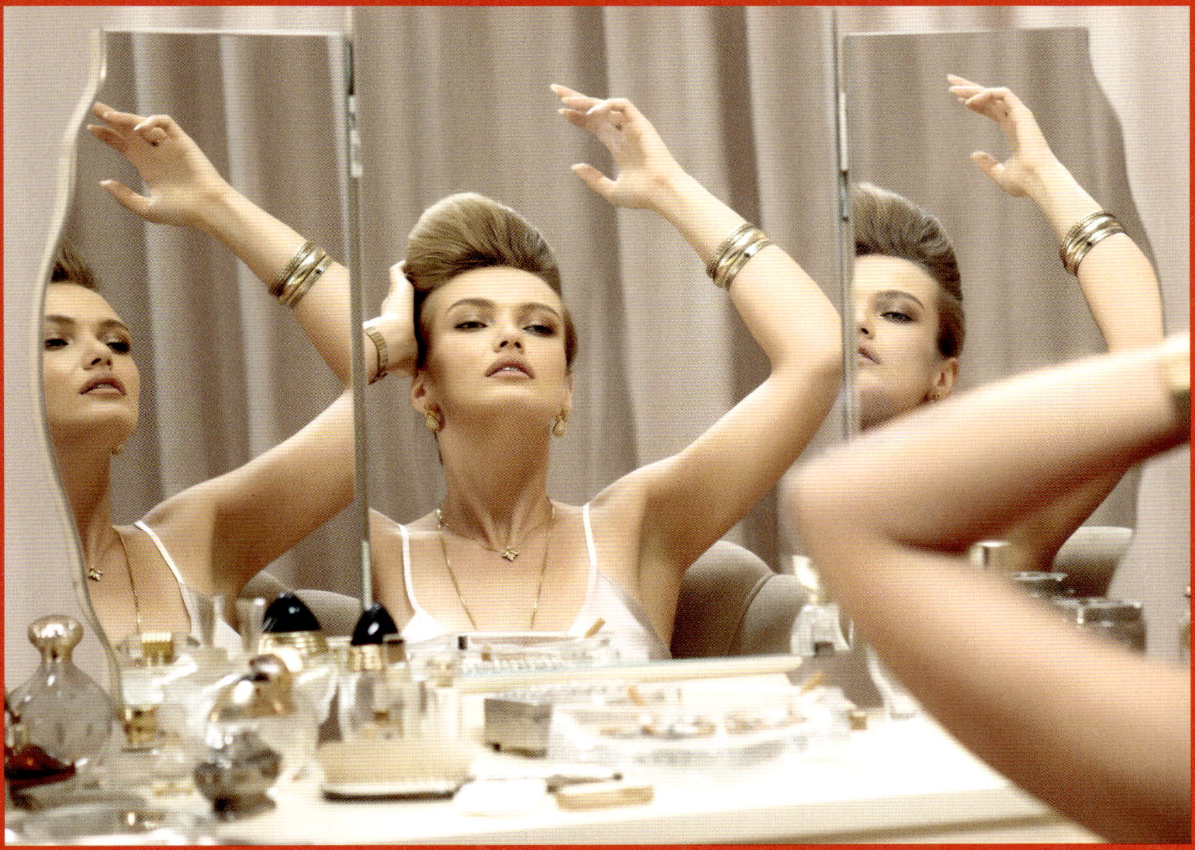

vanity, mother, beirut, lebanon, dare greatly documentary, 2017.

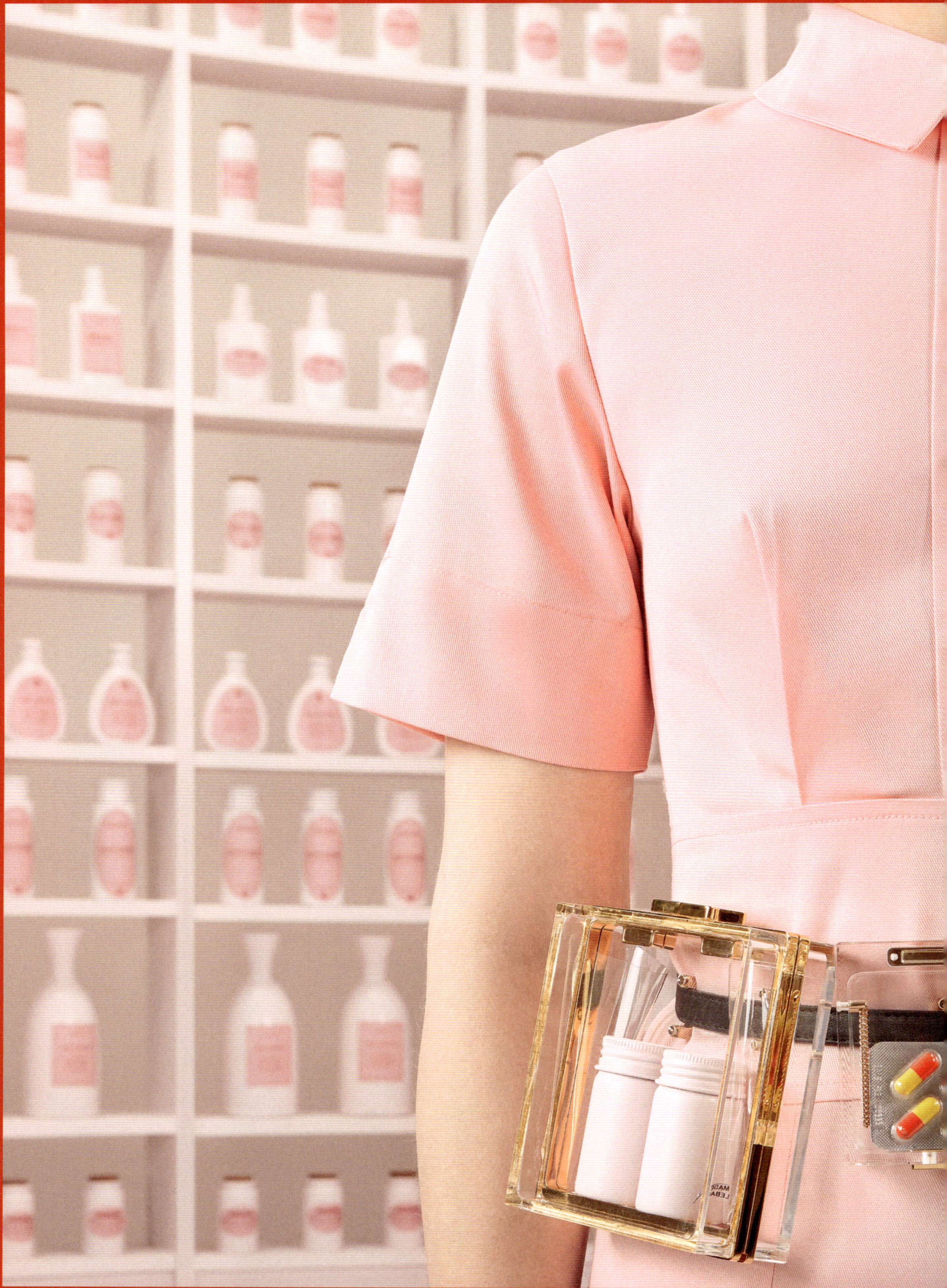

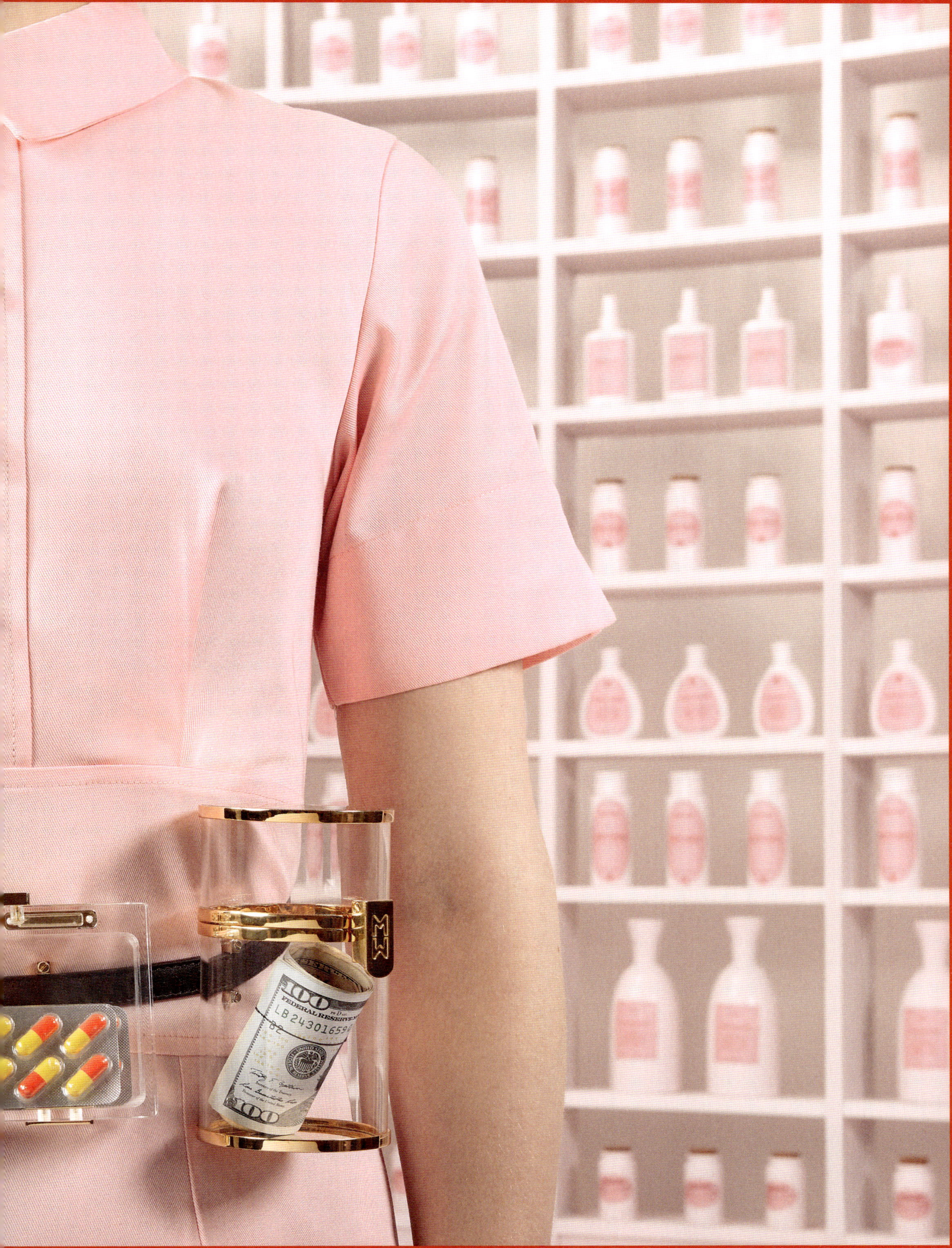
100

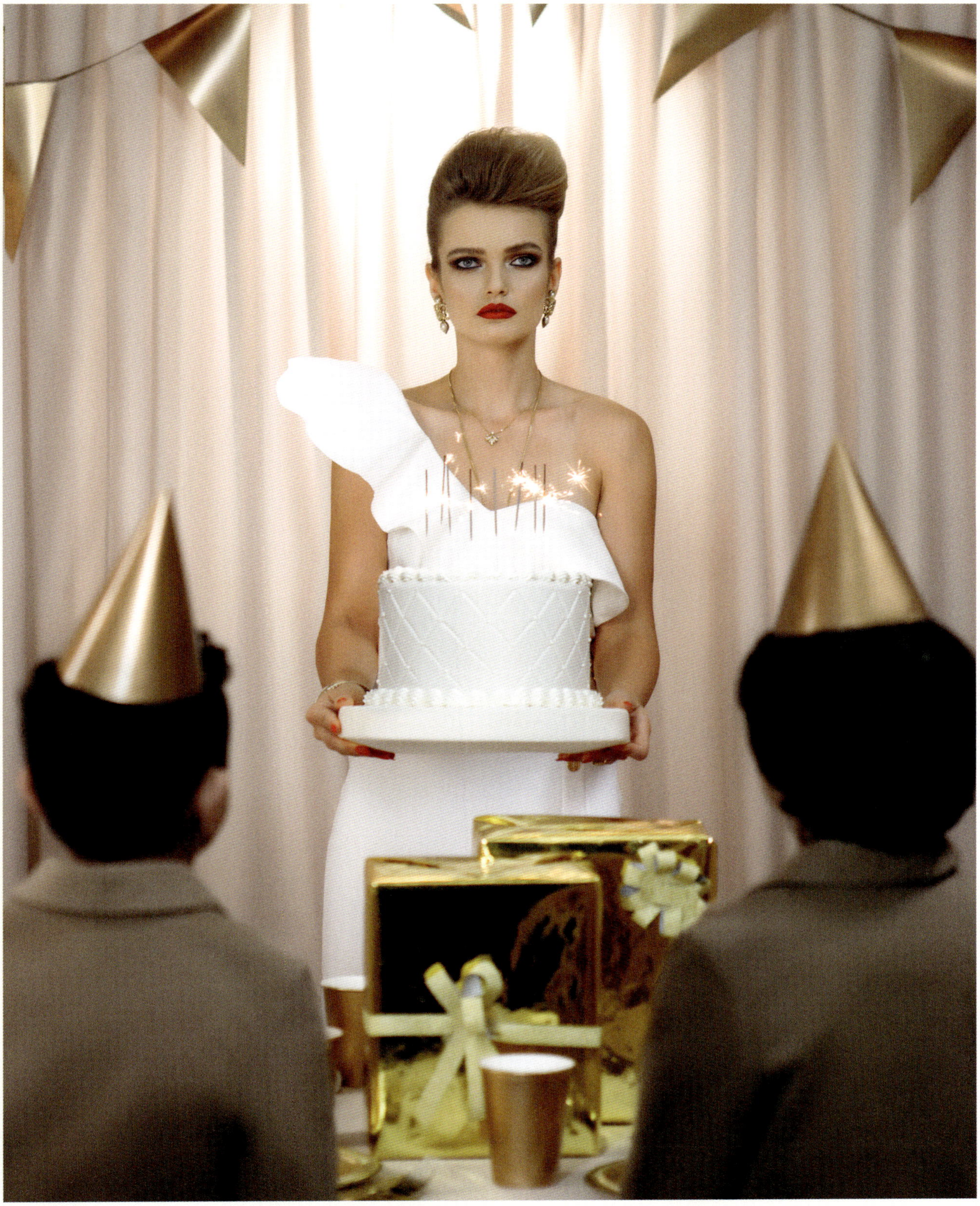

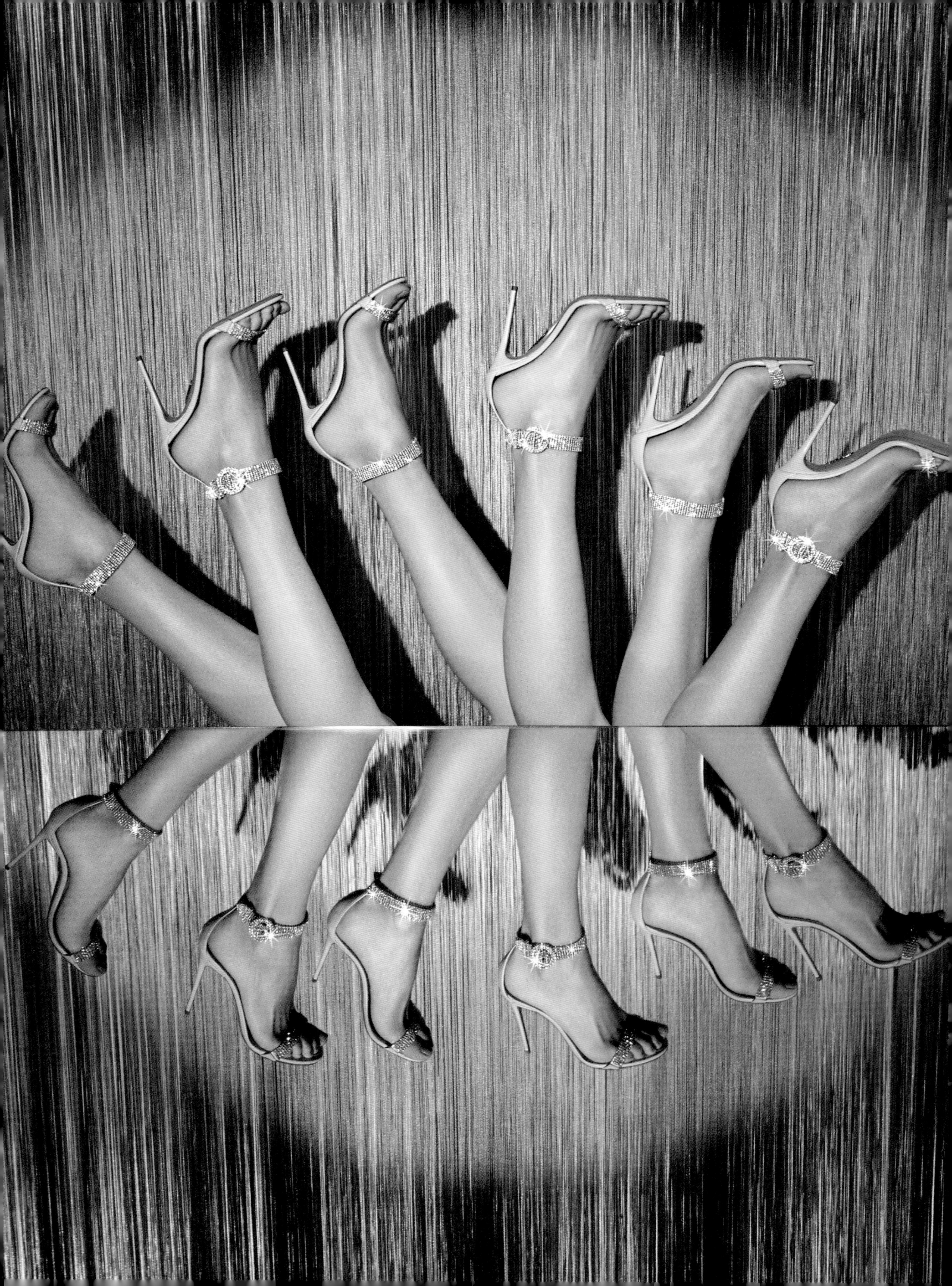

"Everyone knew my mom was arriving from the sound of her jewelry clinking with her every step."

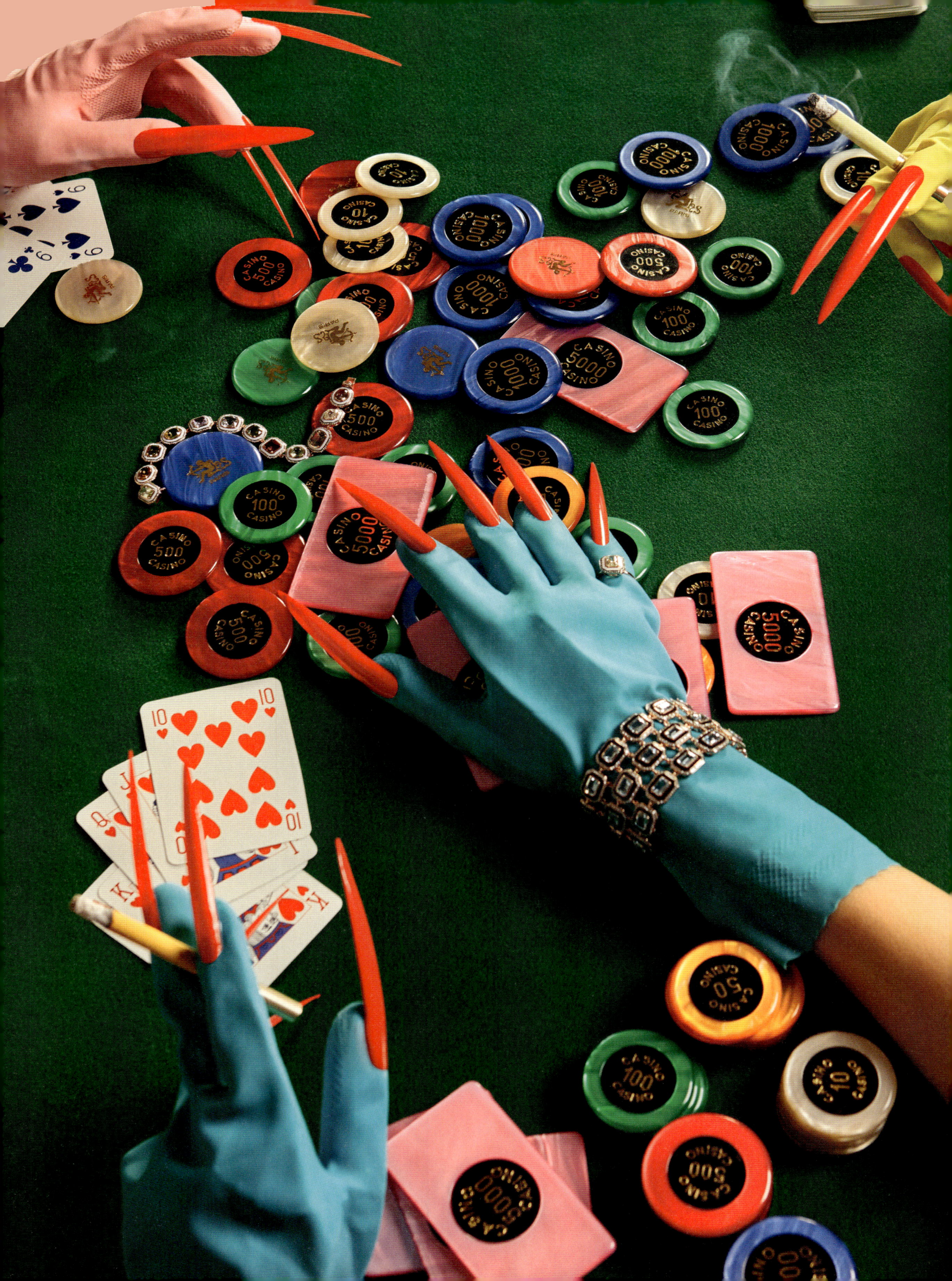
CASINO 5000 CASINO
CASINO 1000 CASINO
CASINO 500 CASINO
CASINO 100 CASINO
CASINO 10 CASINO
CASINO 50 CASINO

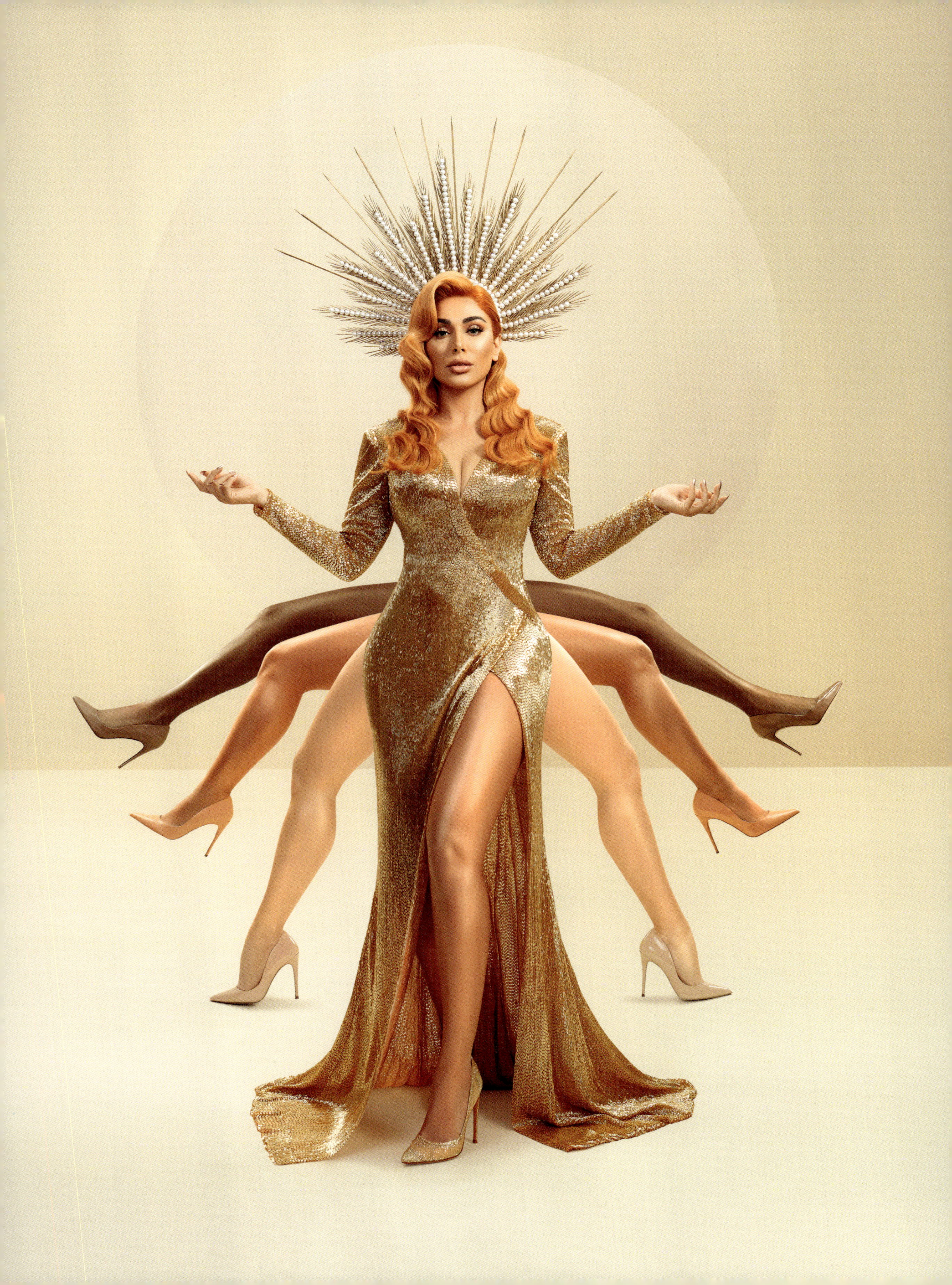

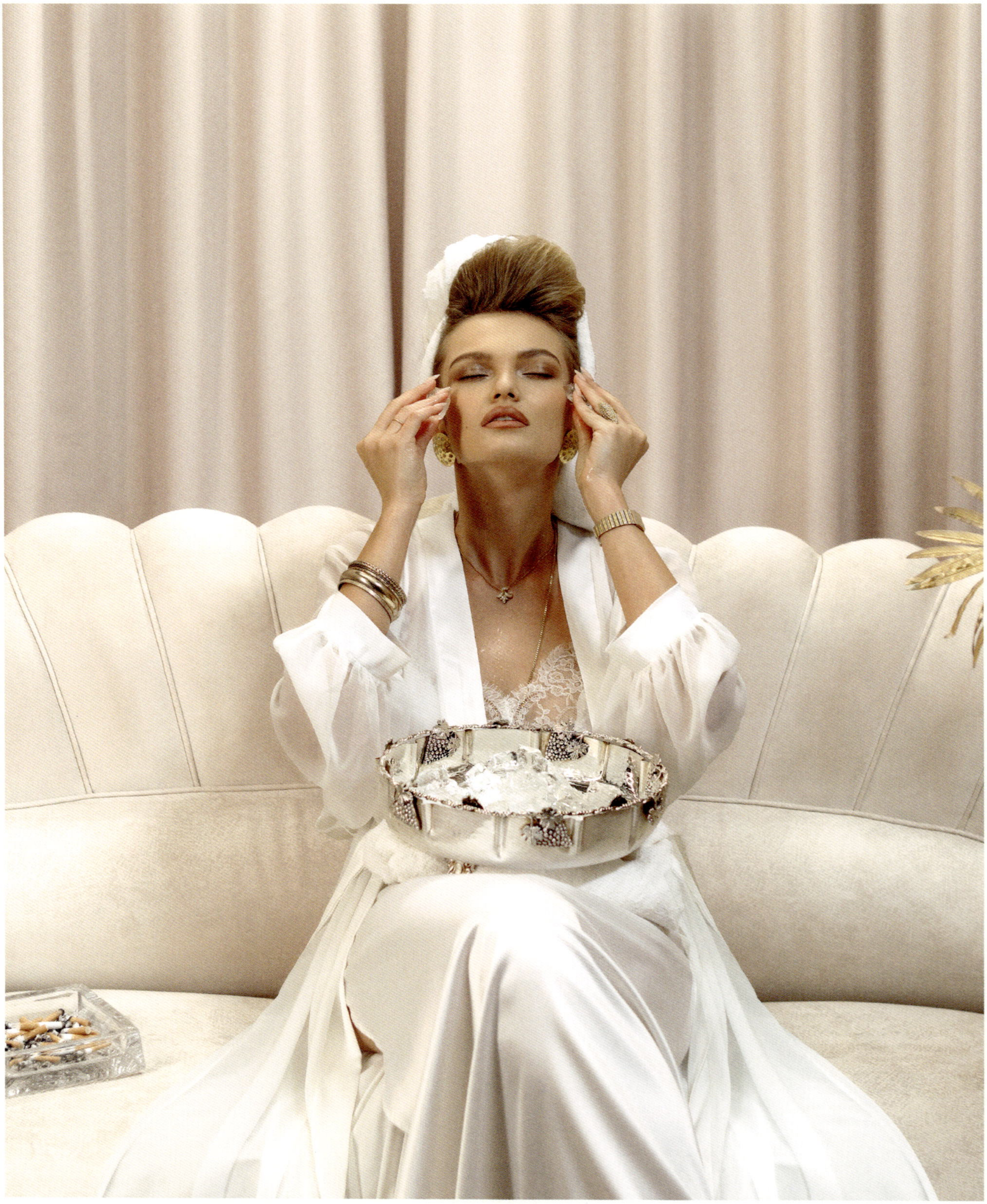

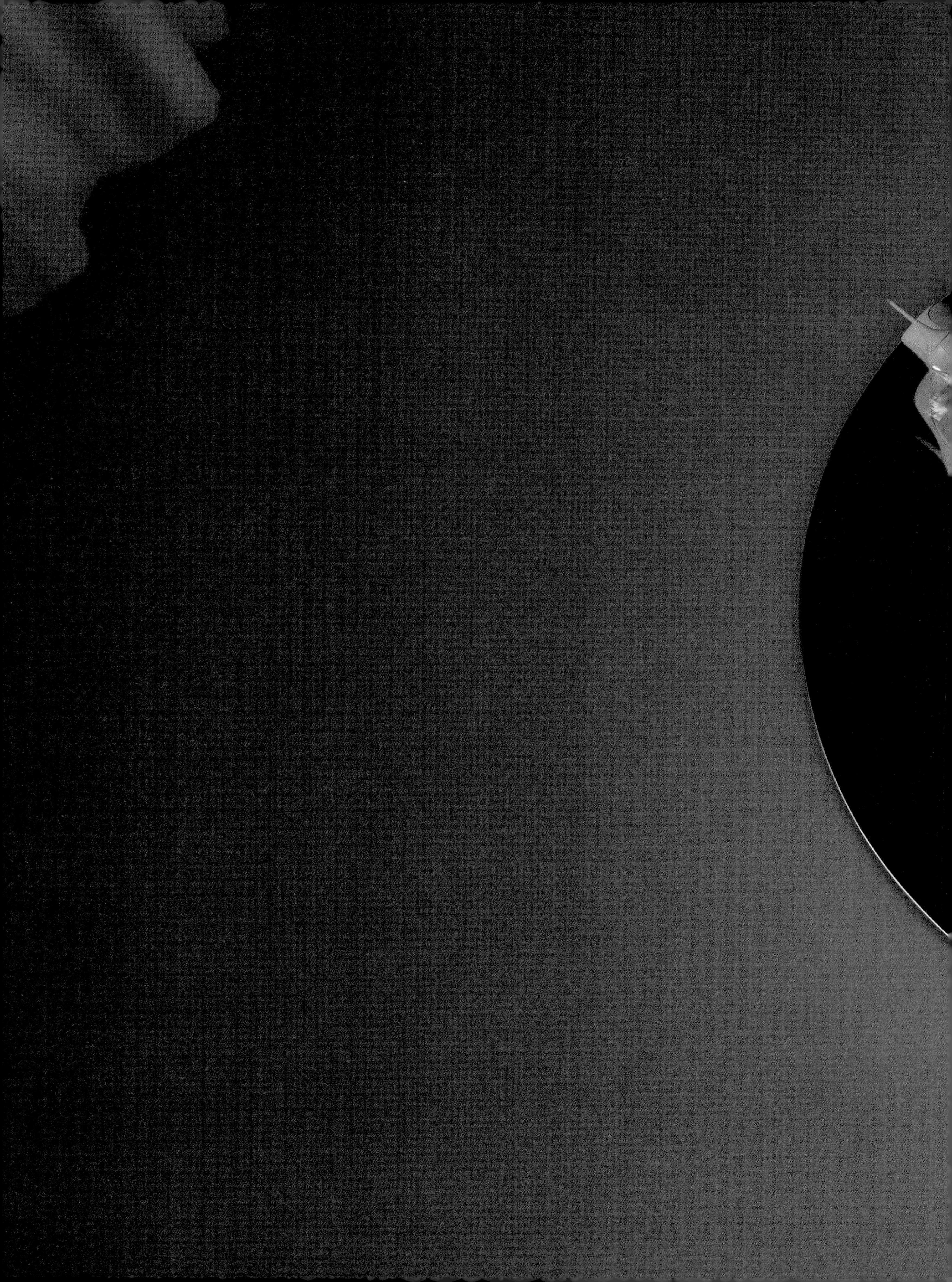

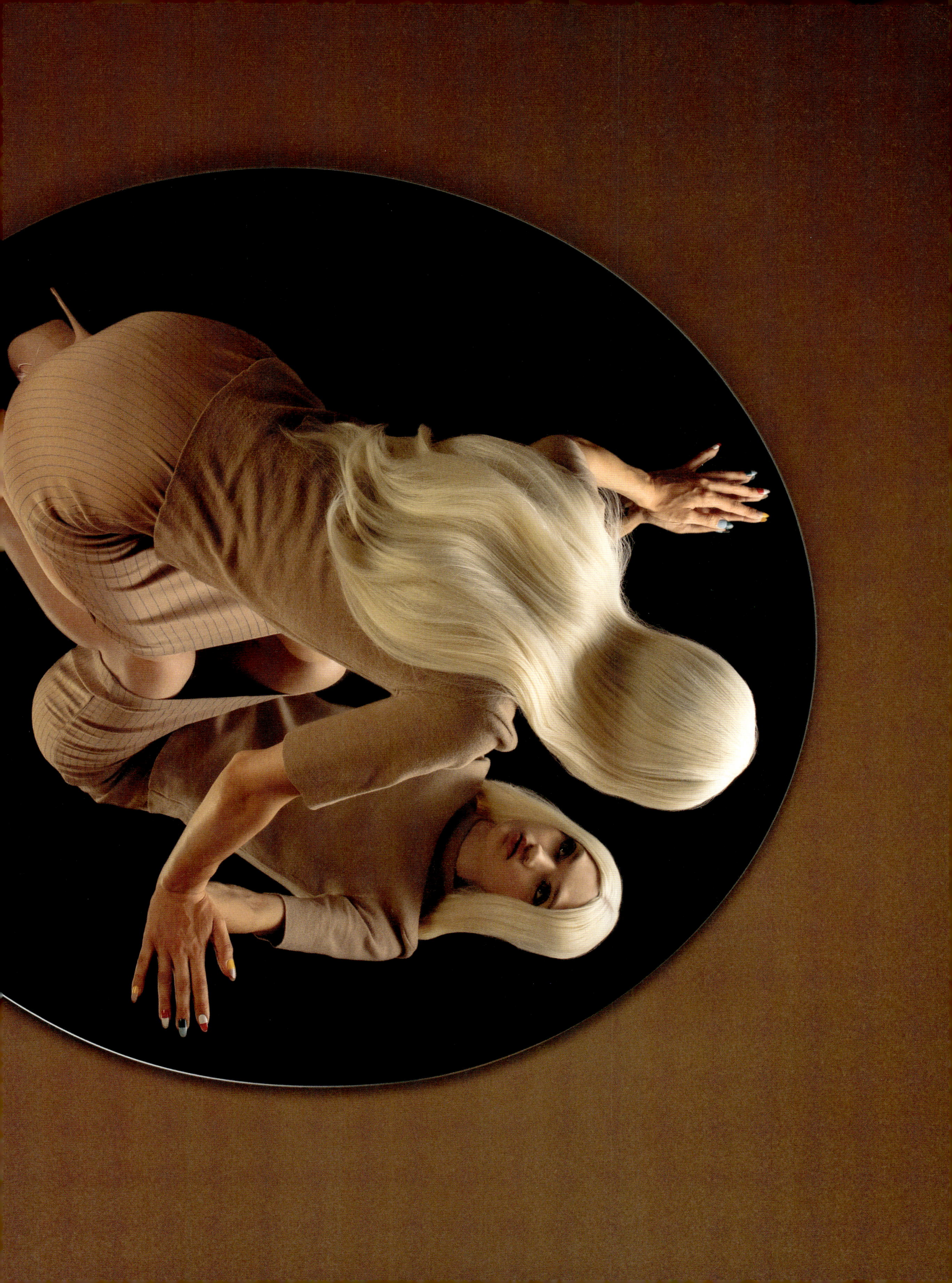

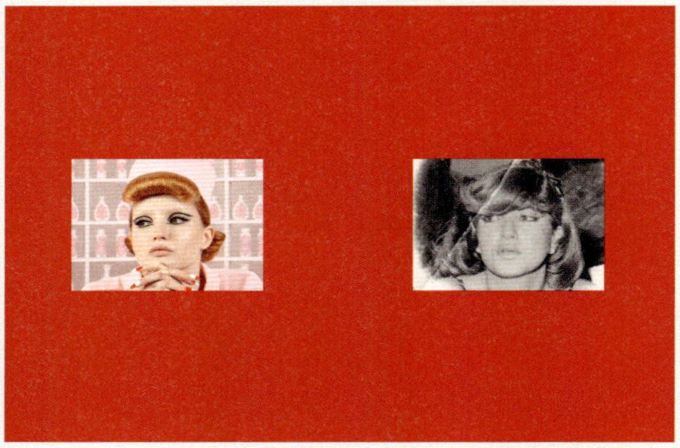

the pharmacist, beirut, lebanon, marzook campaign, 2019.

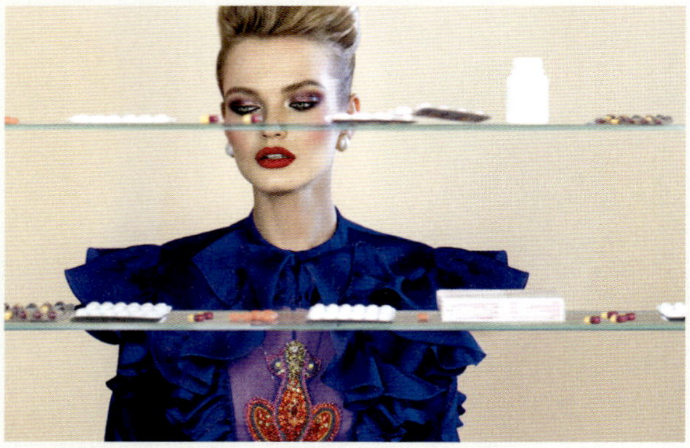

mother I, beirut, lebanon, *dare greatly* documentary, 2017.

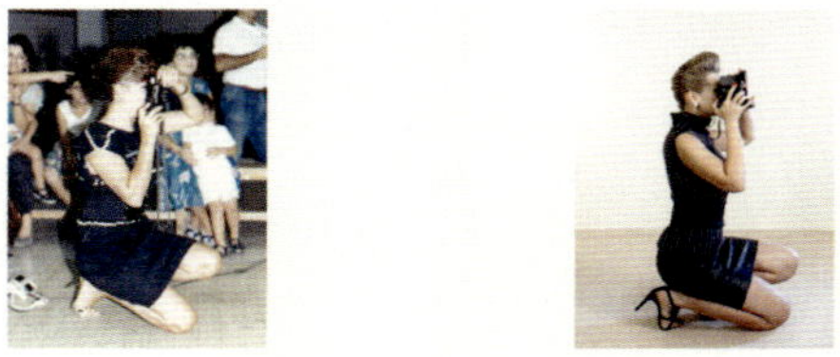

mother with camera, beirut, lebanon,
dare greatly documentary, 2017.

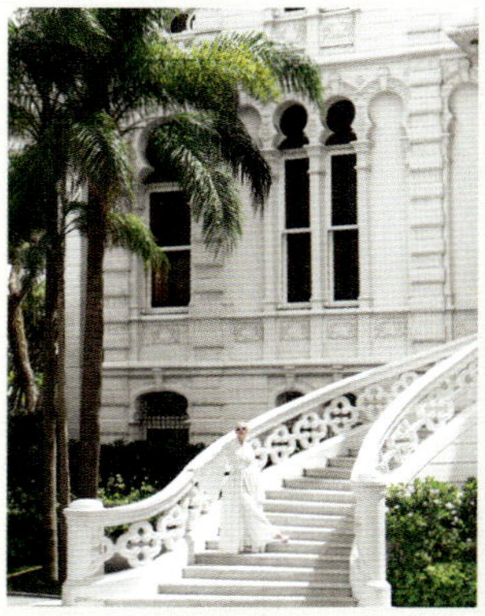

sursock stairs, beirut, lebanon, marzook campaign, 2018.

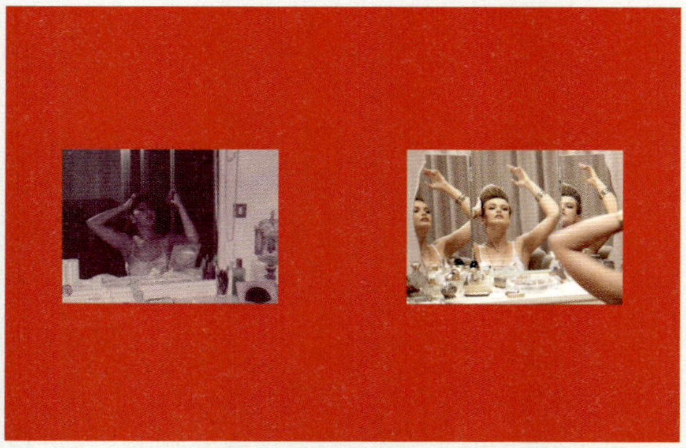

vanity, beirut, lebanon, *dare greatly* documentary, 2017.

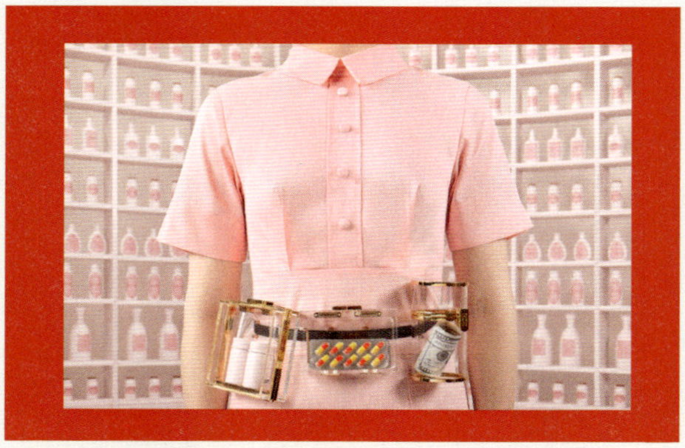

emergency belt, beirut, lebanon, marzook campaign, 2019.

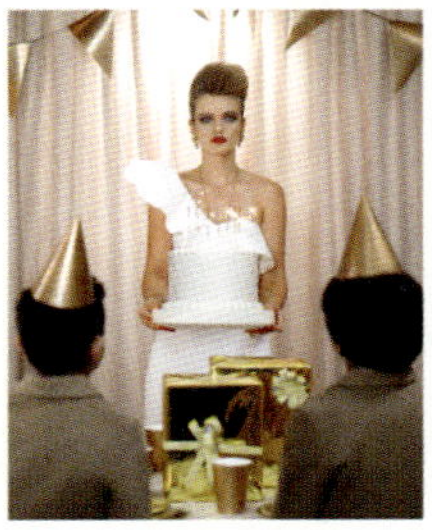

feb 18, beirut, lebanon, *dare greatly* documentary, 2017.

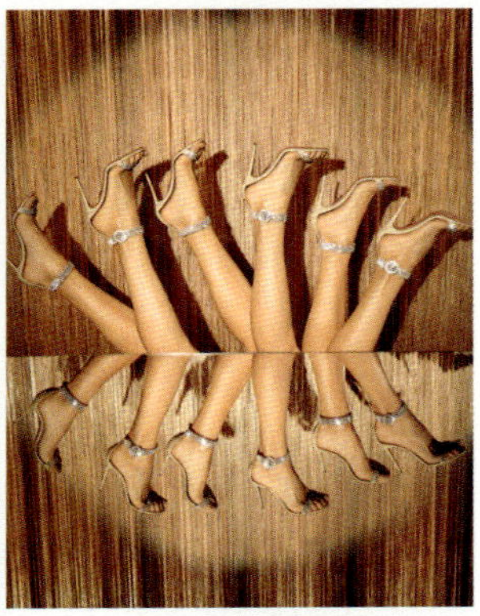

glam wheel, beirut, lebanon, aquazzura campaign, 2020.

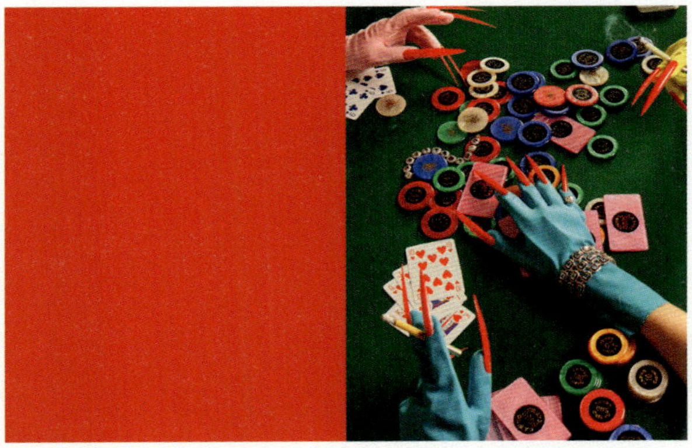

poker? i barely know her, beirut, lebanon, *plastik* magazine, 2020.

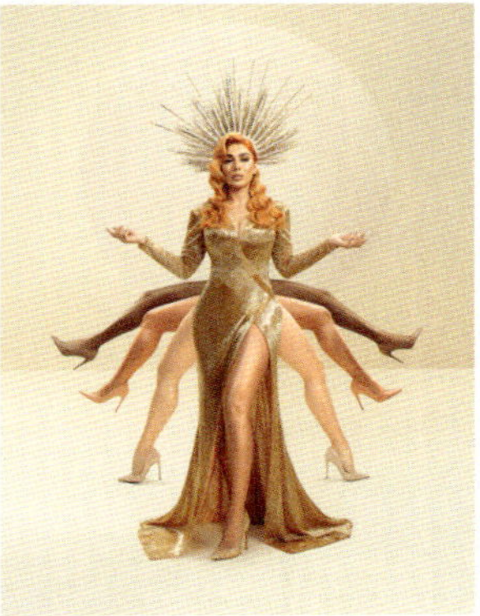

array of light, dubai, uae, huda beauty campaign, 2019.

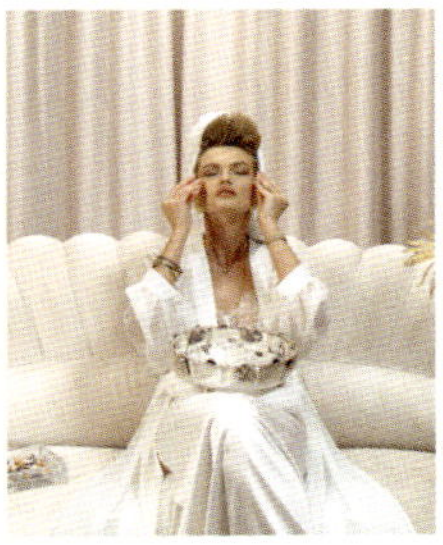

ice queen, beirut, lebanon, *dare greatly* documentary, 2017.

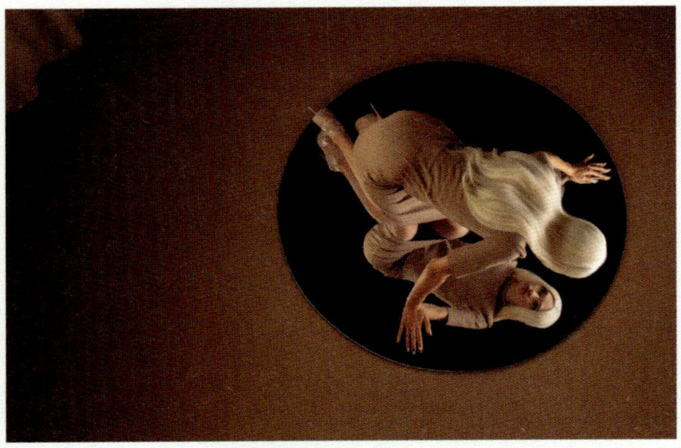

the void, beirut, lebanon, marzook campaign, 2018.

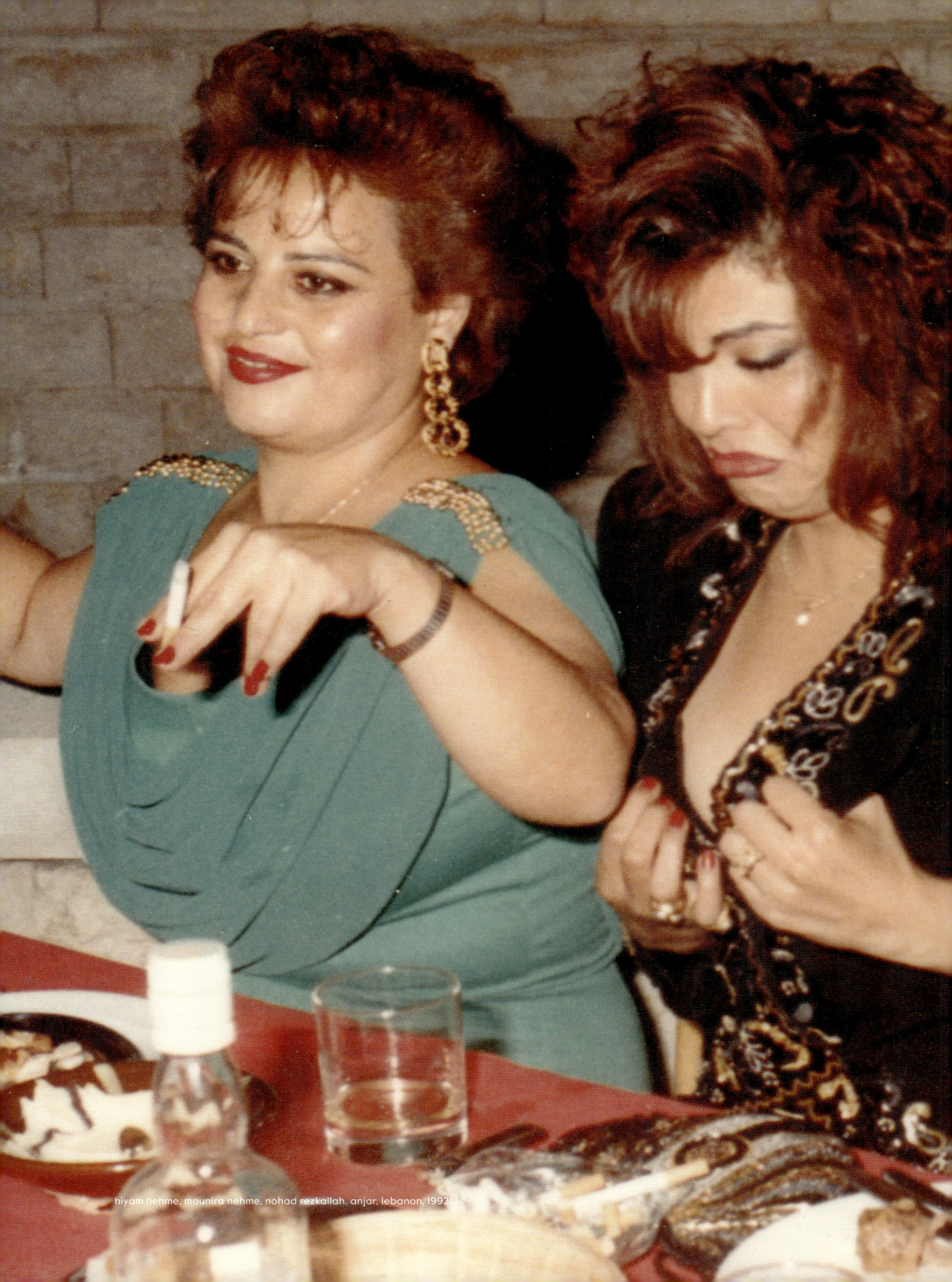

hiyam nehme, mounira nehme, nohad rezkallah. anjar, lebanon, 1992

ACT THREE

women

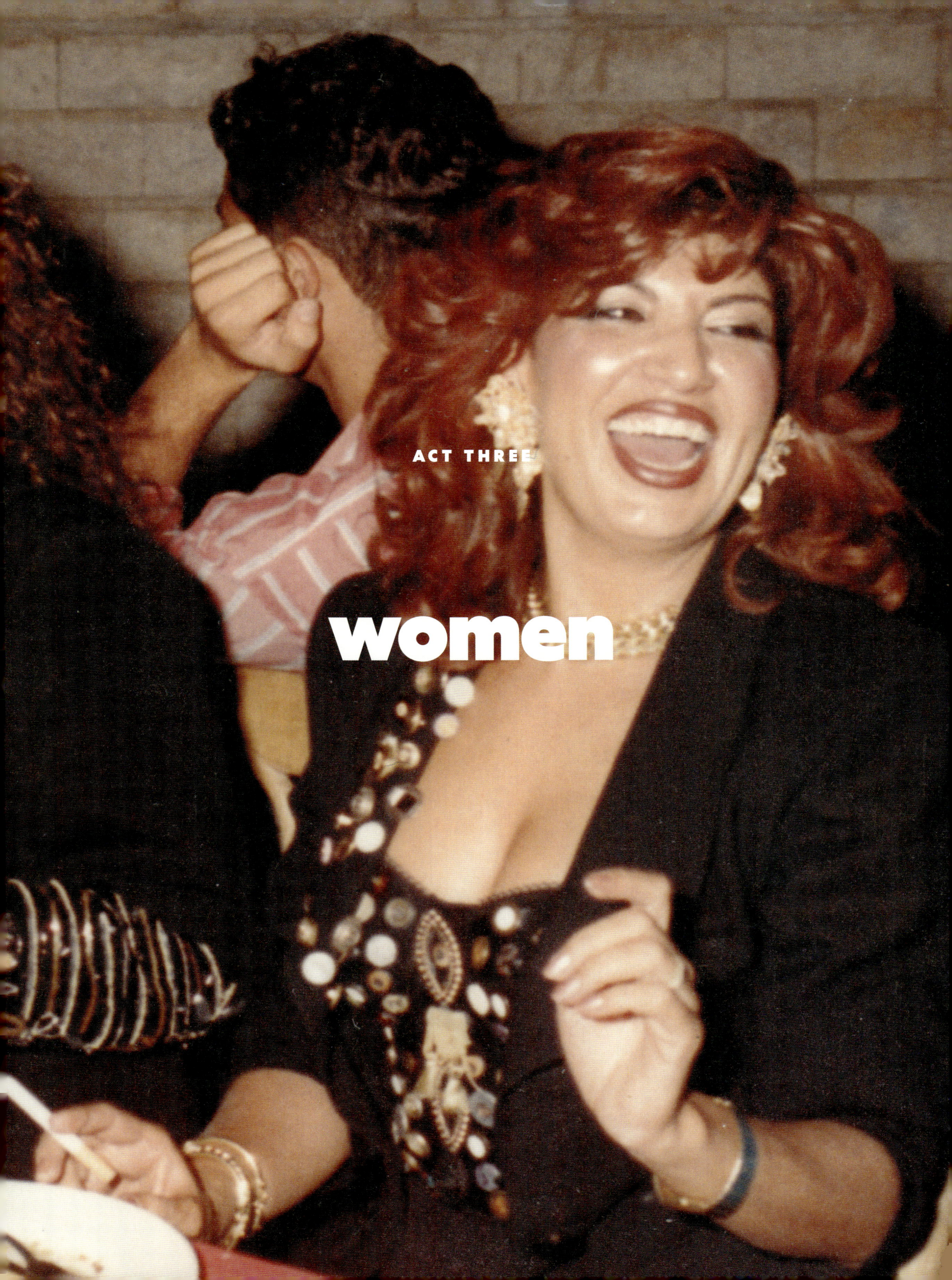

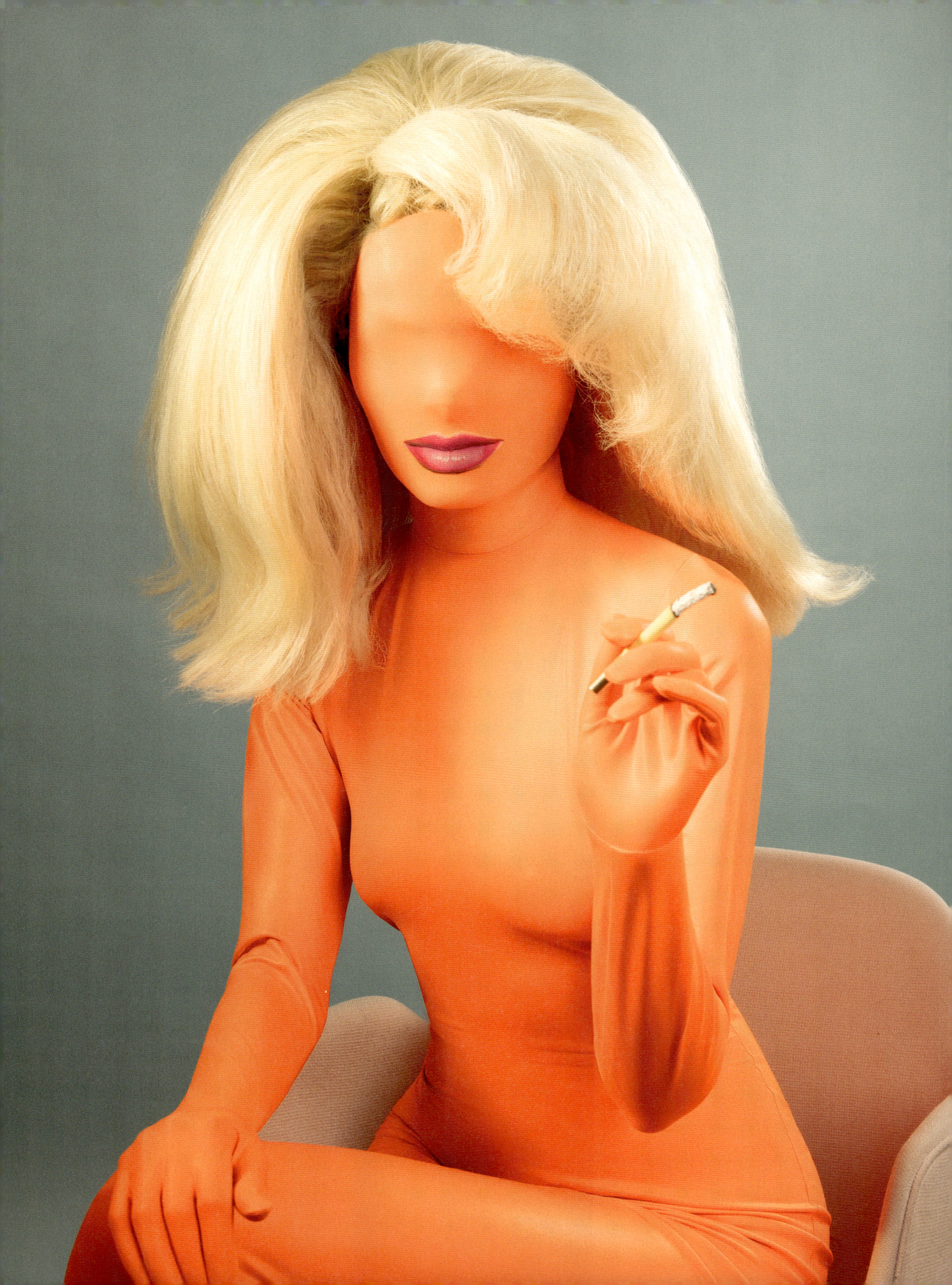

There's something to be said about the fact that Rezkallah's first muse was his mother. However, after careful observation, it becomes apparent that the photographer's mother is a visible influence in many of his portrayals of women throughout his career.

His women, just like his mother – carefully manicured to emanate beauty, wealth, and class – are typically isolated, contemplative, and compelled by their own reflection, as though trying to come to terms with the disparity between the inner and the outer. Rezkallah voyeuristically captures his women as performers of social ideals, artists behind the scenes, during those rare moments of solitude, as they long for an instance of serenity and solace that would finally allow them to shed their layers.

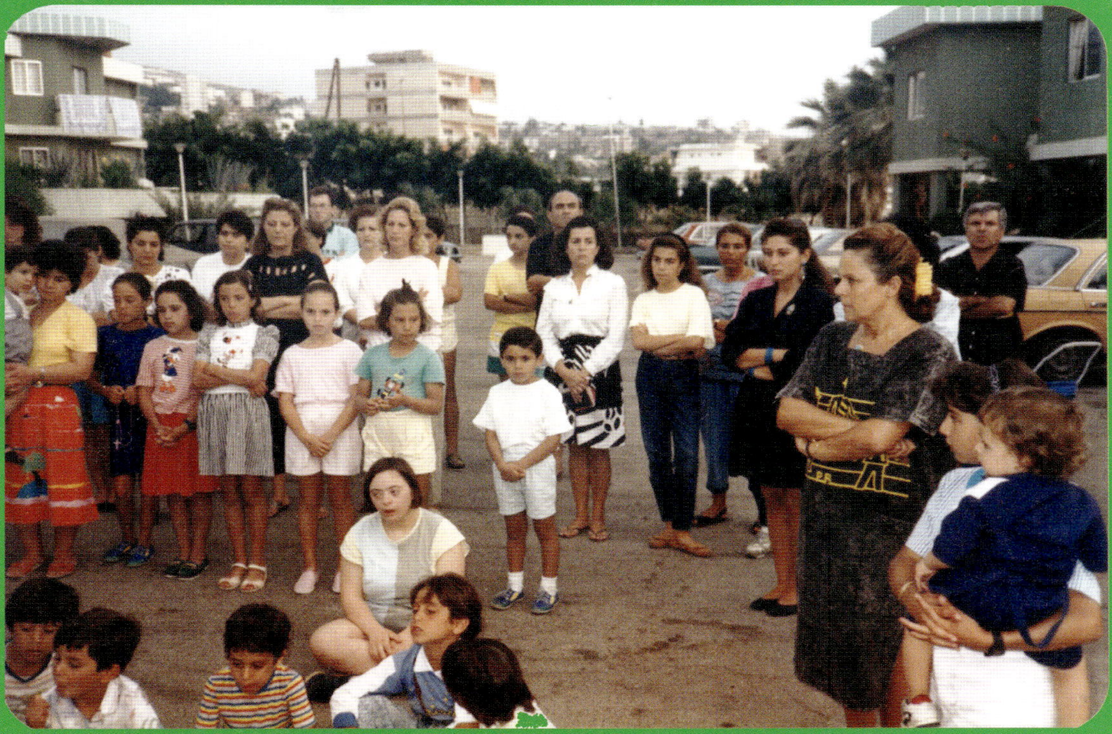

the women and children of santa theresa playa, okaibe, lebanon, june 1989.

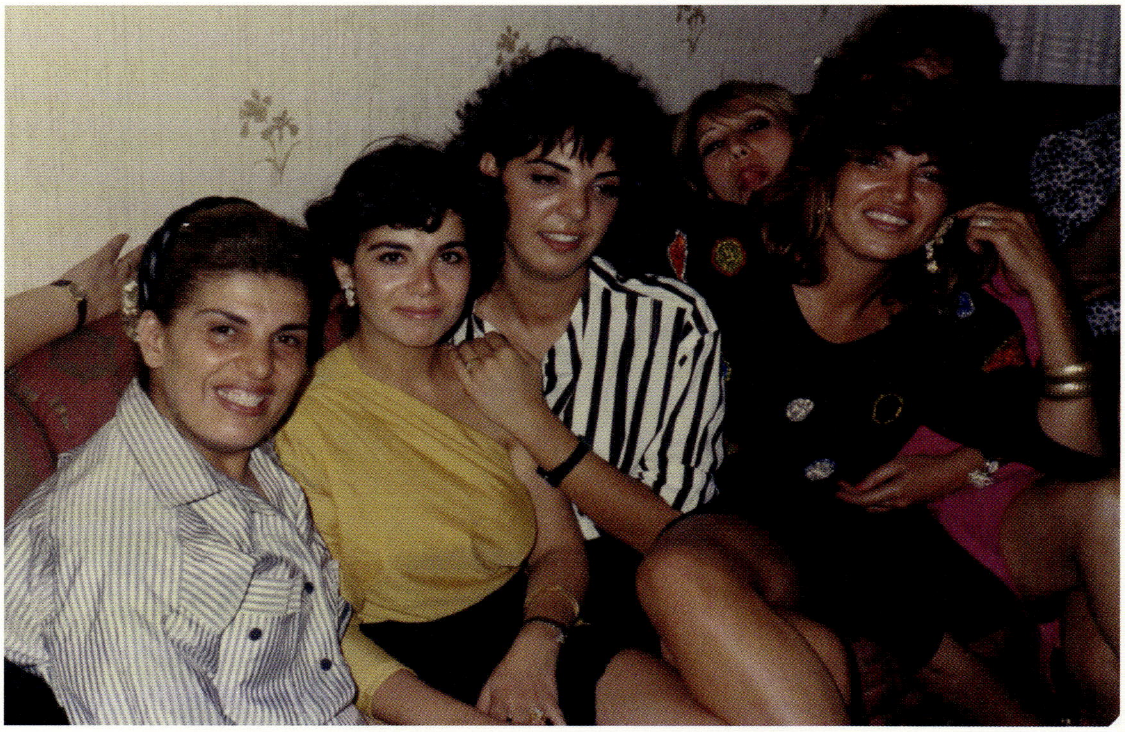

nazik zeidan, caroline zeidan, nada kammoun, nohad rezkallah, lody kammoun, ain el remmaneh, lebanon, 1990.

As a child, Rezkallah was surrounded by women who, at every waking moment, had to choose between facing the harsh reality of war or escaping it within the confines of their minds. While most would choose the latter and indulge in the smaller pleasures of life, external conflicts always managed to disturb their peace. Anything ranging from a husband late from work, to a loud noise resonating from beyond the compound's walls, would instantly trigger acute anxiety and shatter the thin veil of oblivion they worked so hard to maintain. Such was the fabric of the photographer's childhood, a delicate house of cards built on shaky grounds, constantly on the verge of collapse. These women were, and continue to be, unsung heroes to Rezkallah, who, to this day, continues to tell their stories one picture at a time.

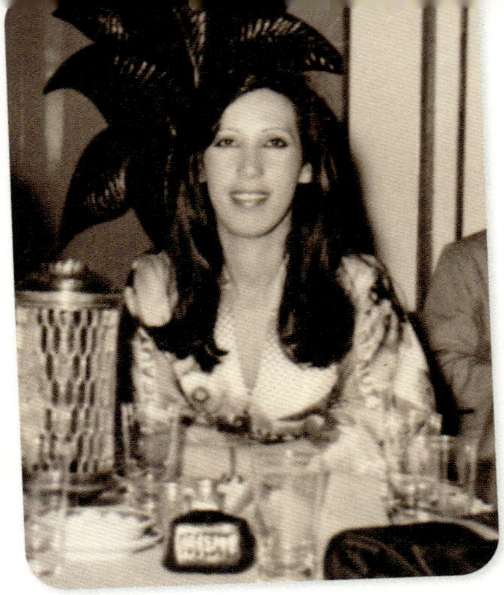

aunty lody:
a little bit of love, a little bit of insanity, loads of fun.

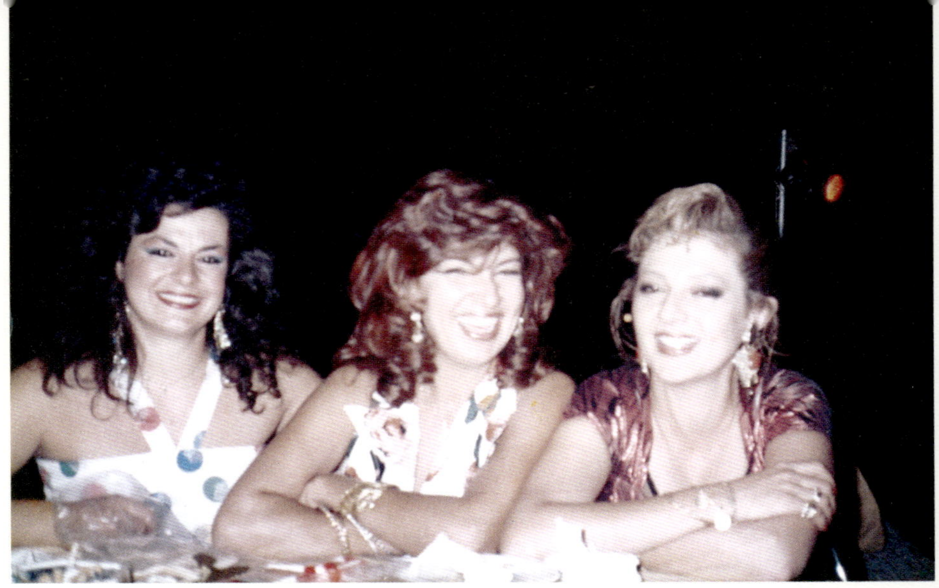

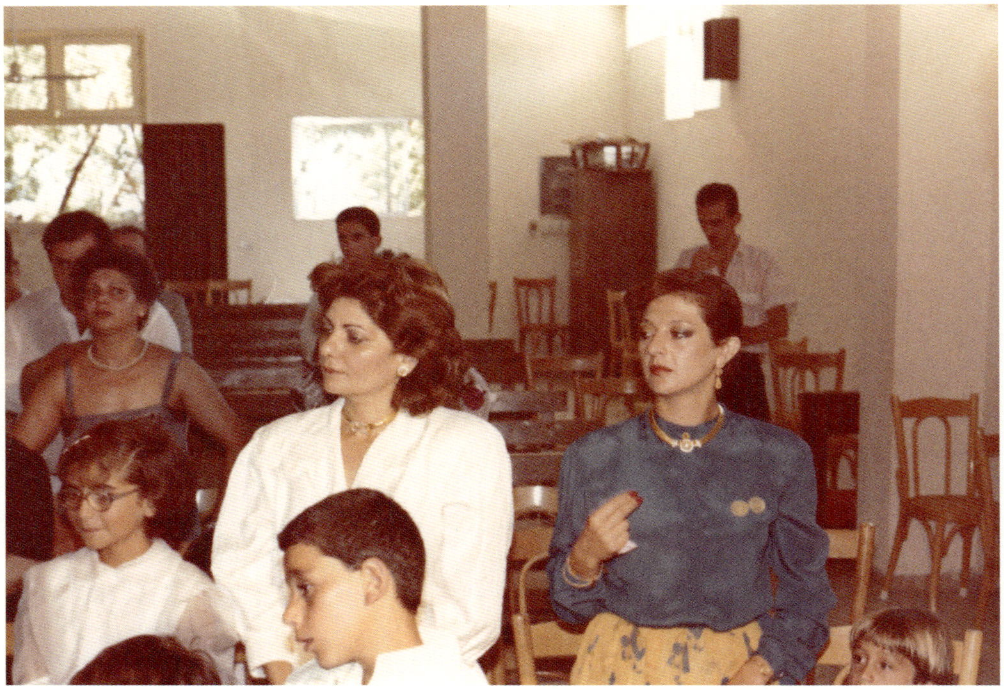

najla, claudette and randa making the cross sign at church during my baptism. 1986.

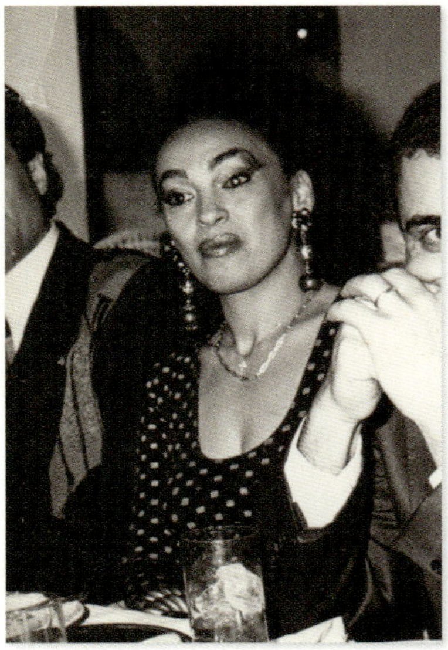

mira wakim, one of the kindest women I knew,
who used to read me bedtime stories.

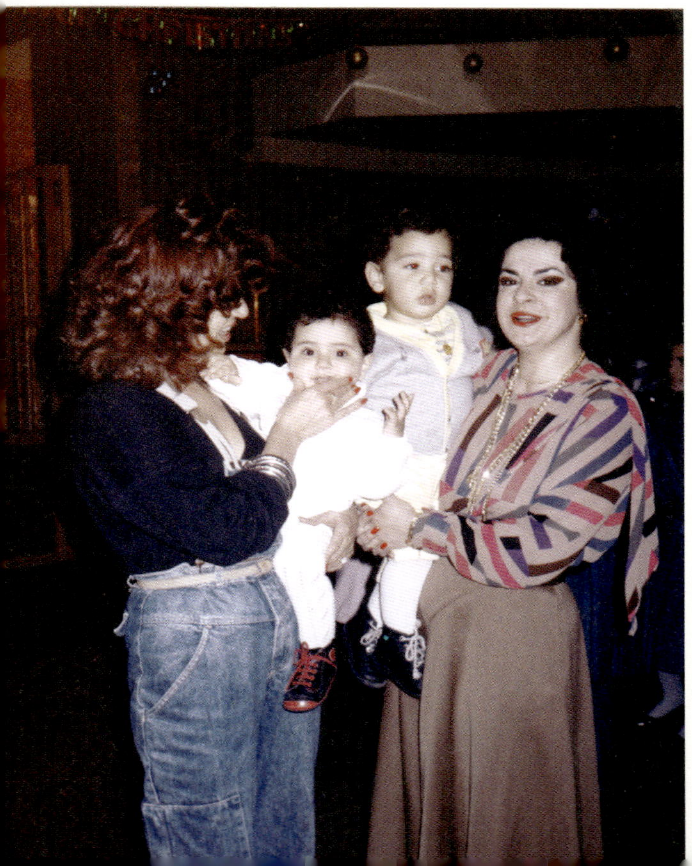

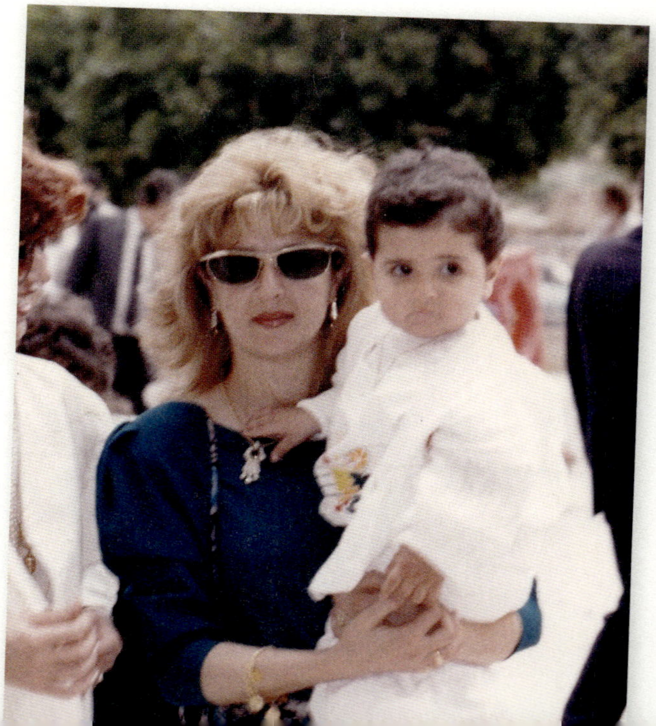

my mom as a baby with her sisters nazik and najala (the bride).

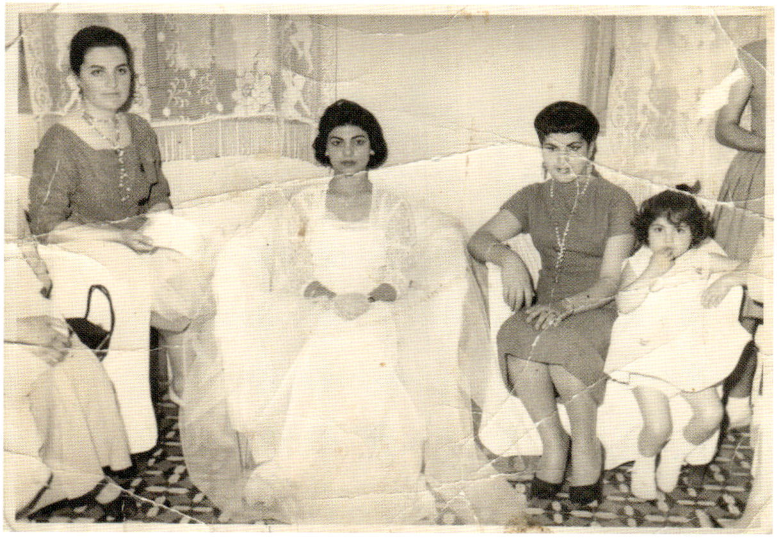

my mom never knew her father, when you see the age difference between her and her sisters you understand why.

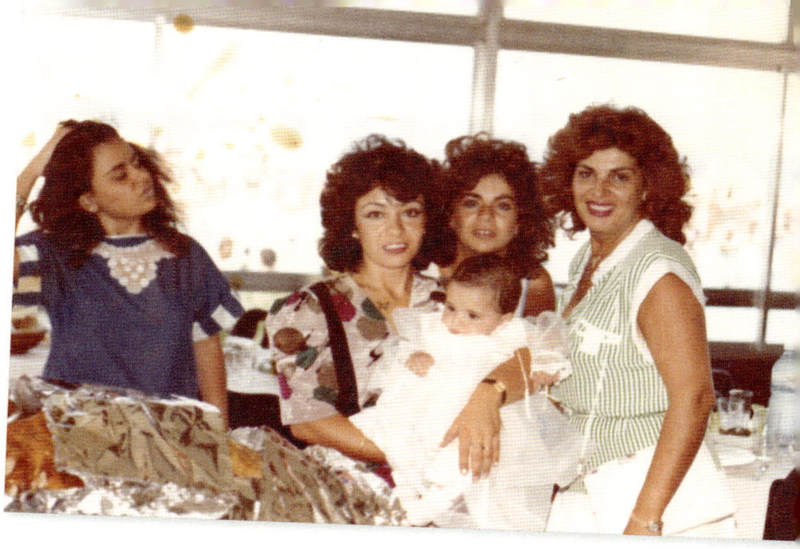

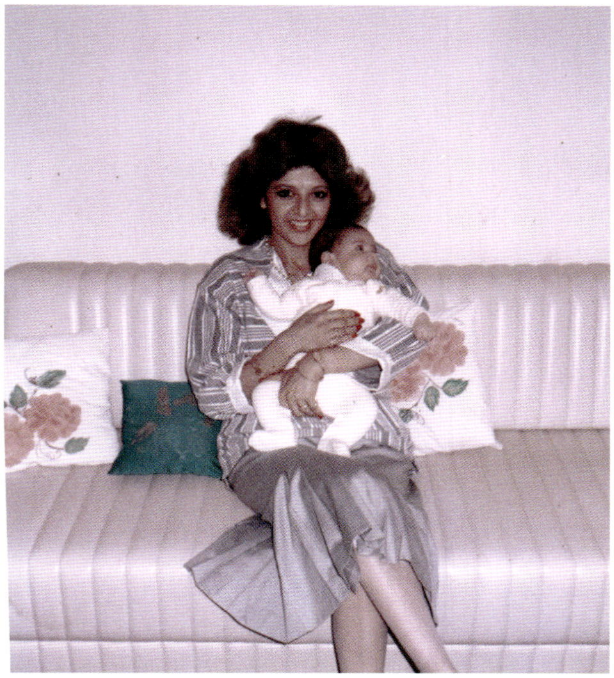

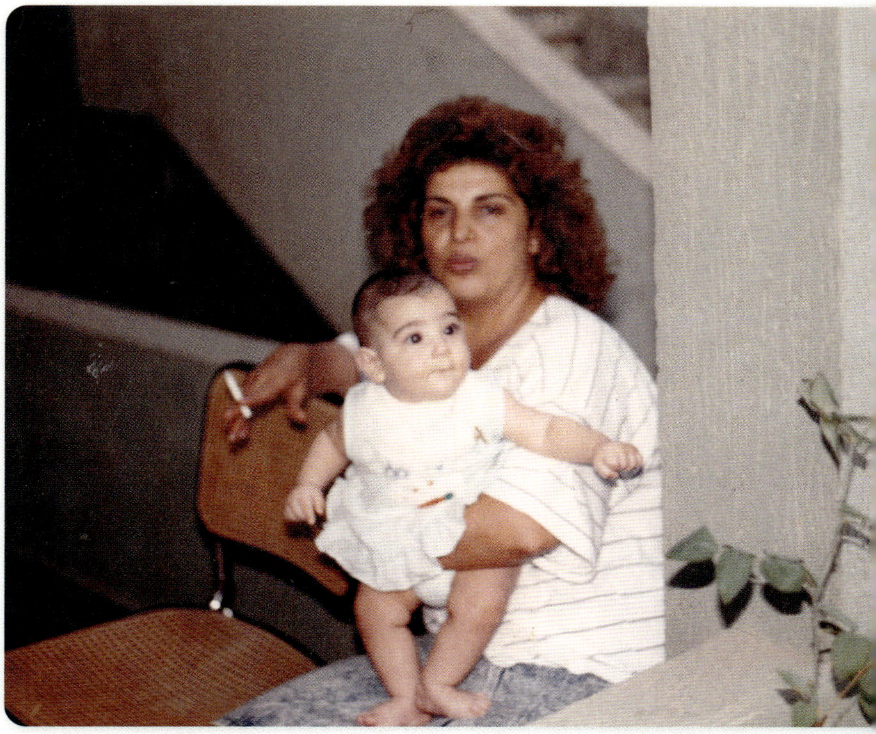

aunty nazik, aka the og supreme:
my brother rami in one hand, a cigarette in the other.
quintessential 90's moment.

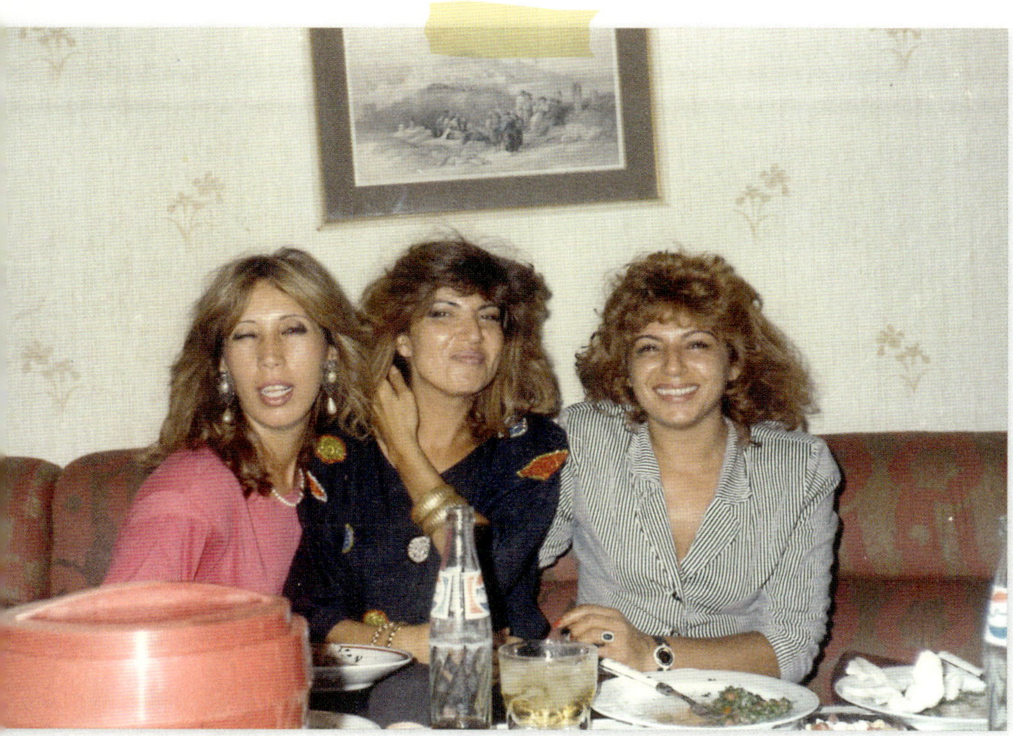

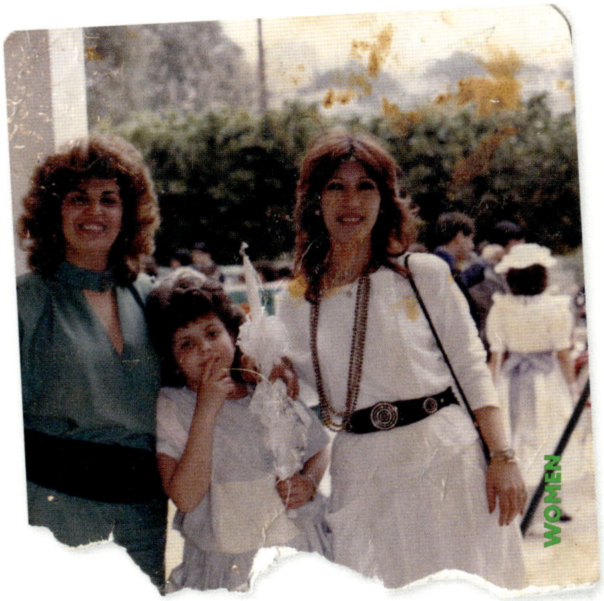

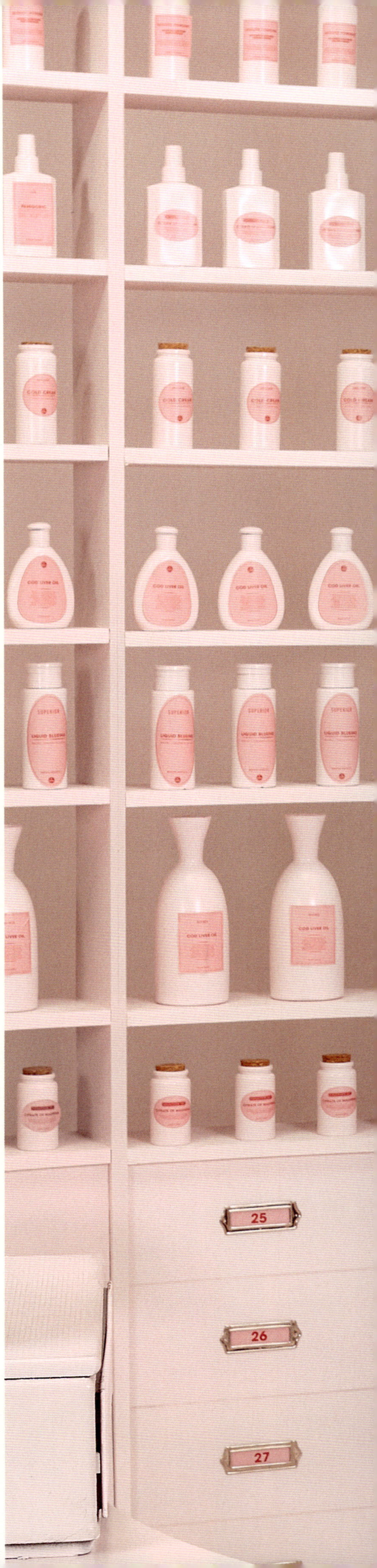
25
26
27

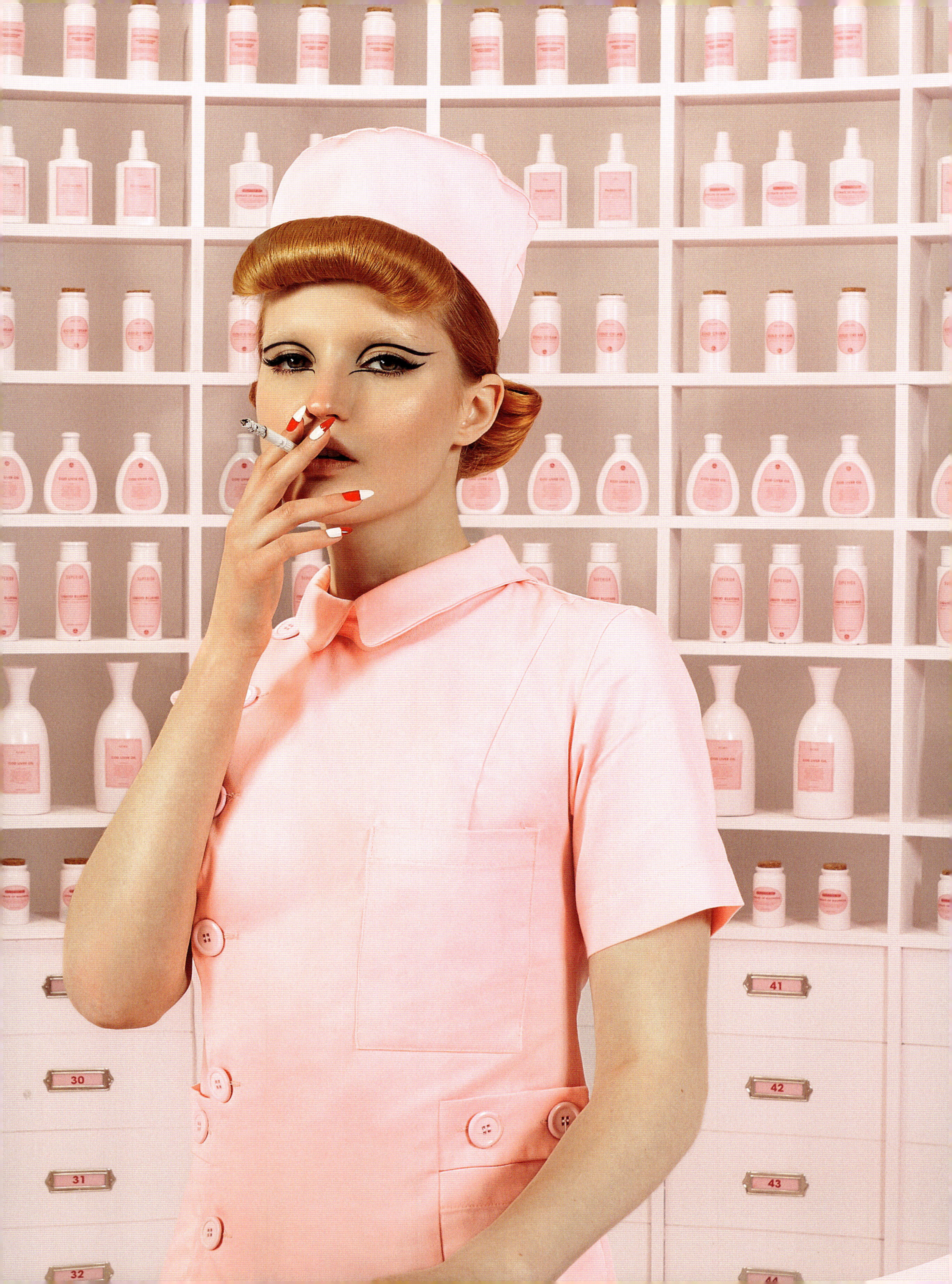
41
30
42
31
43
32

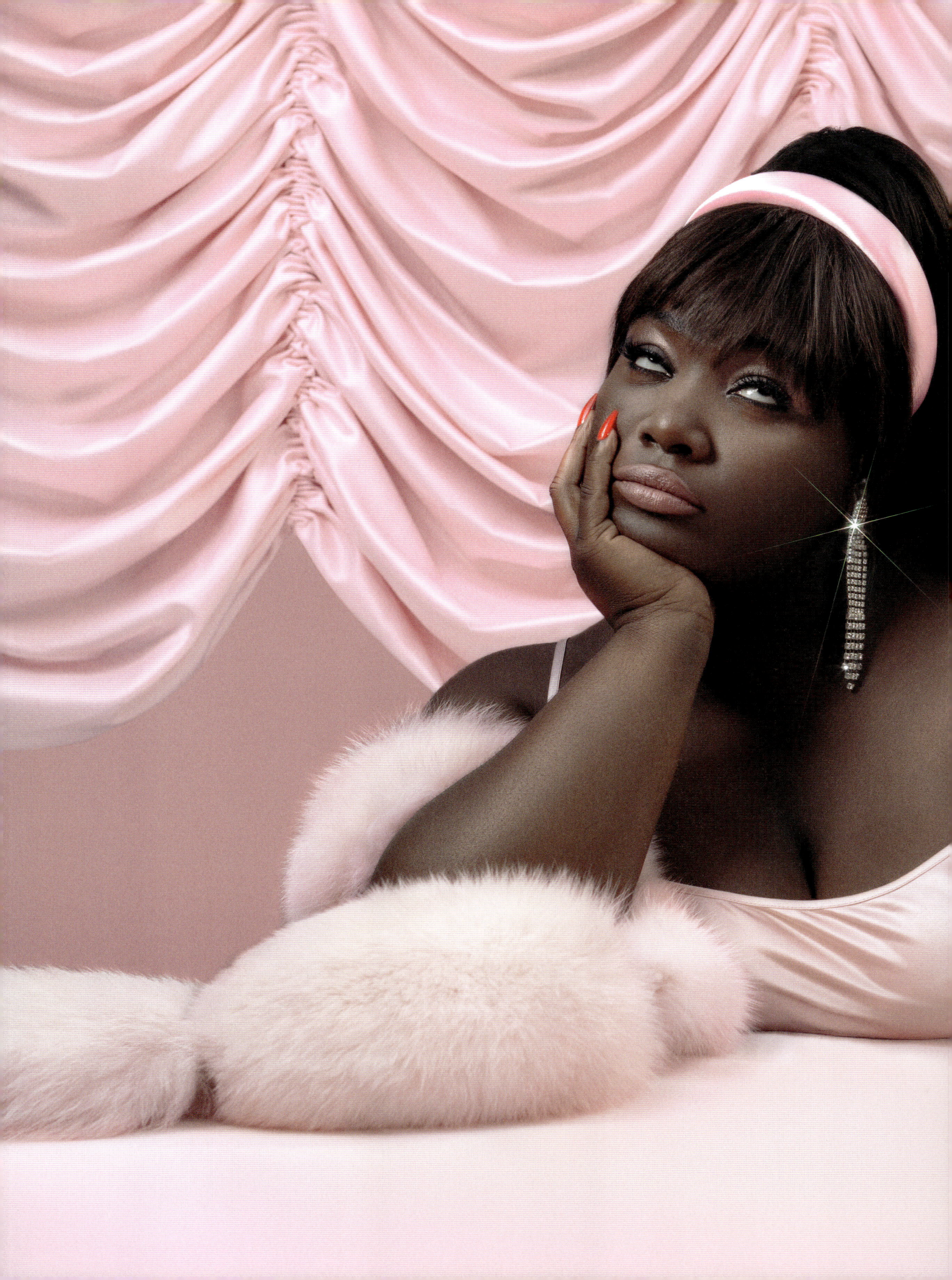

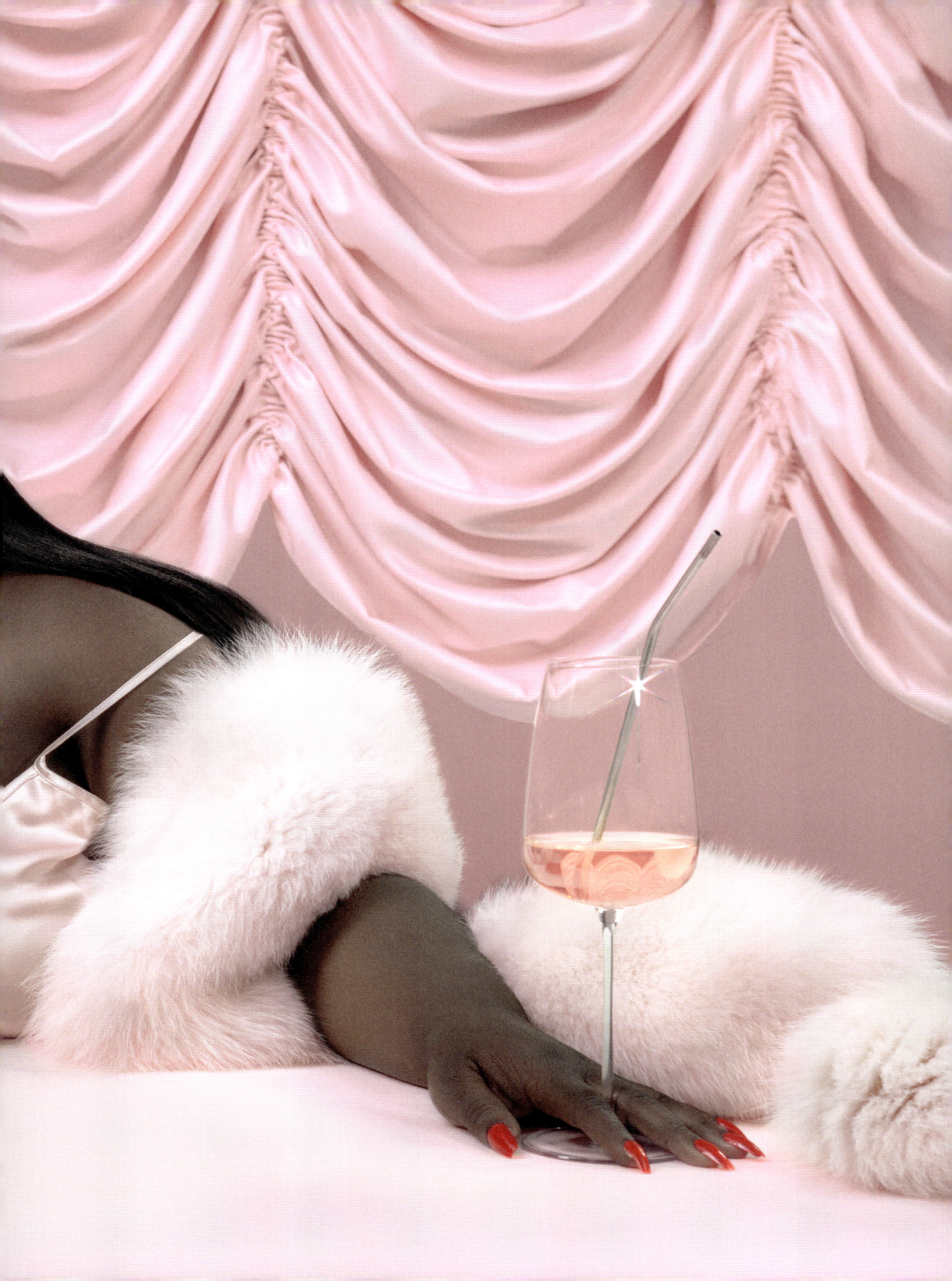

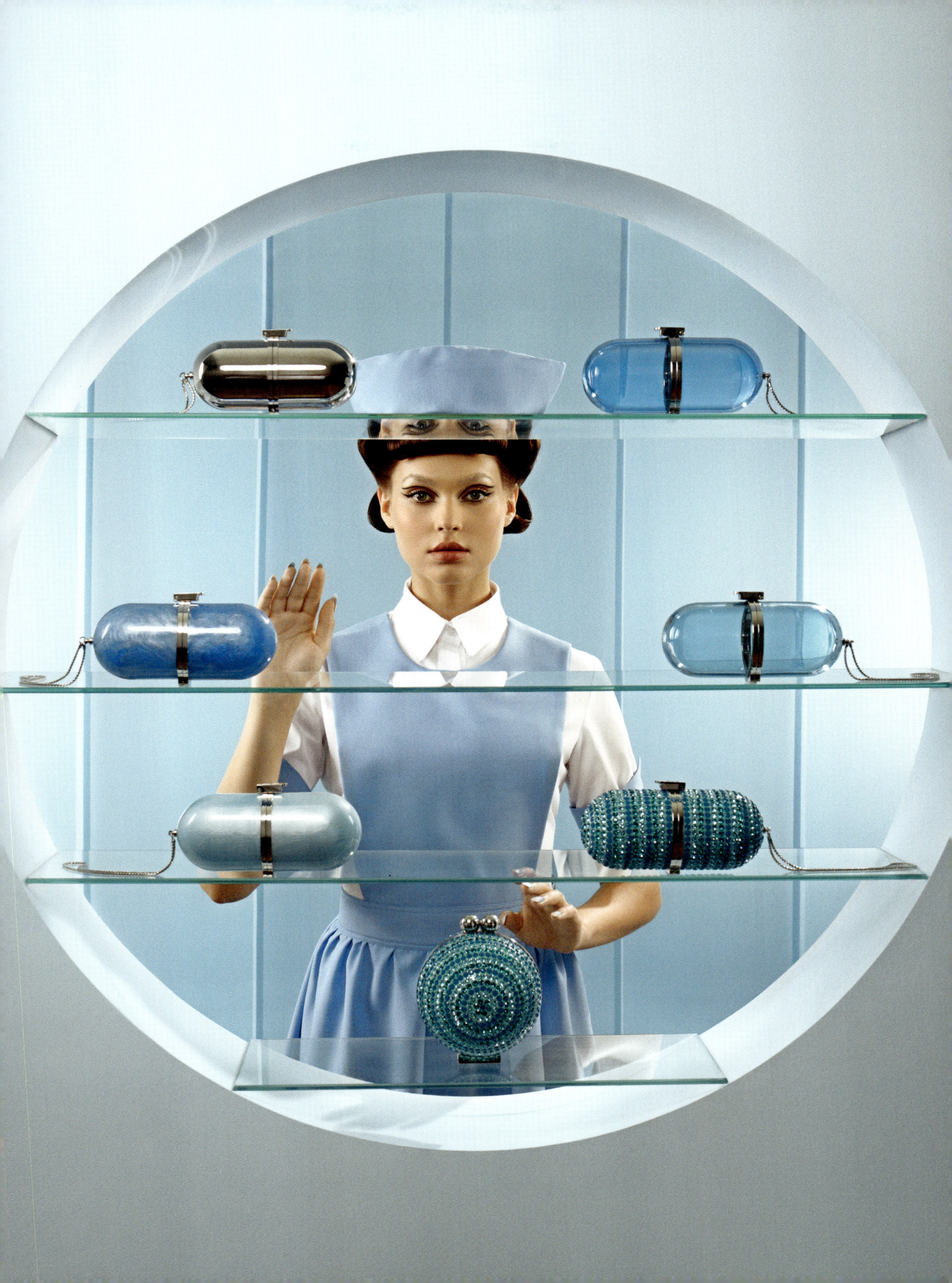

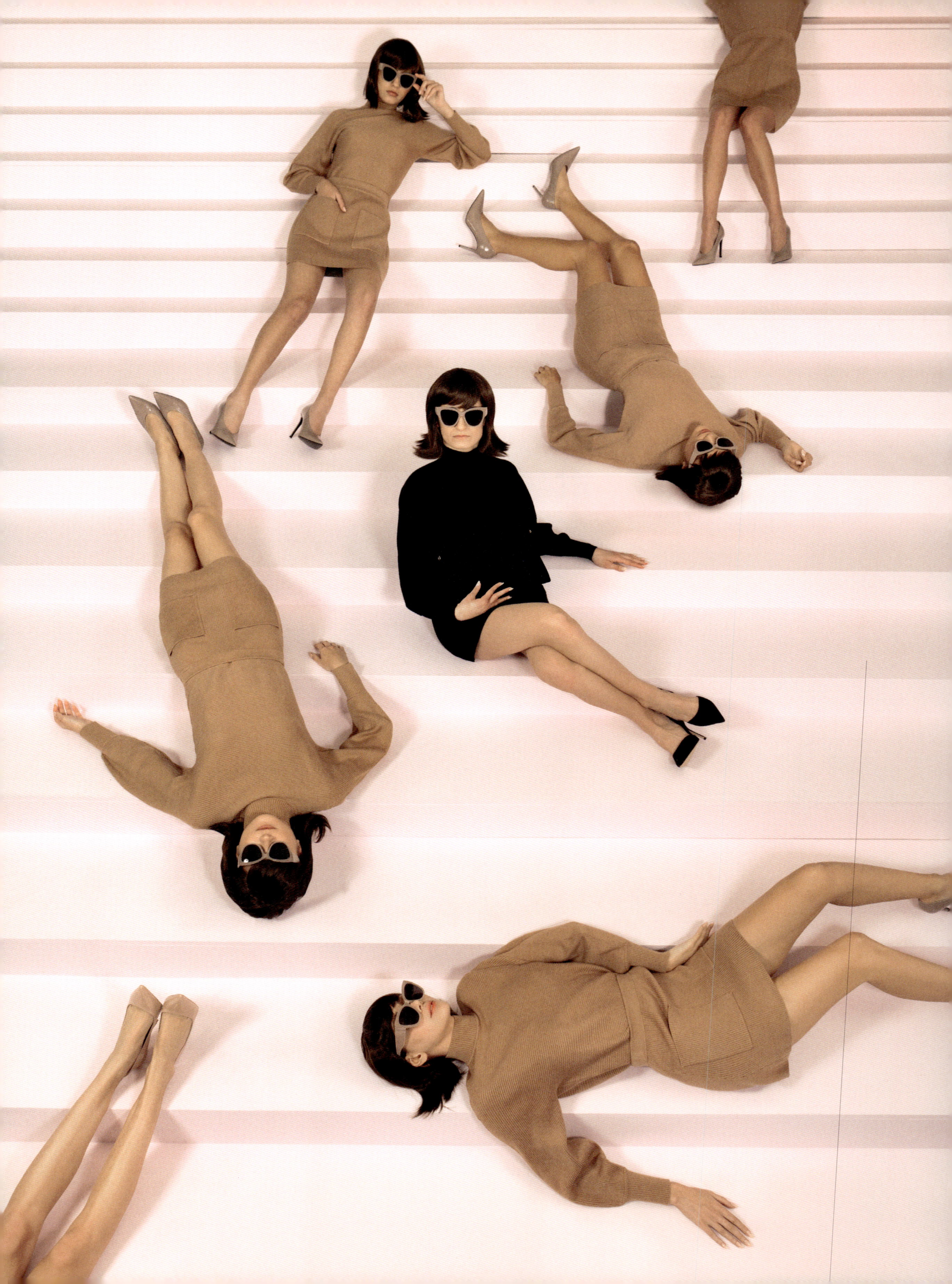

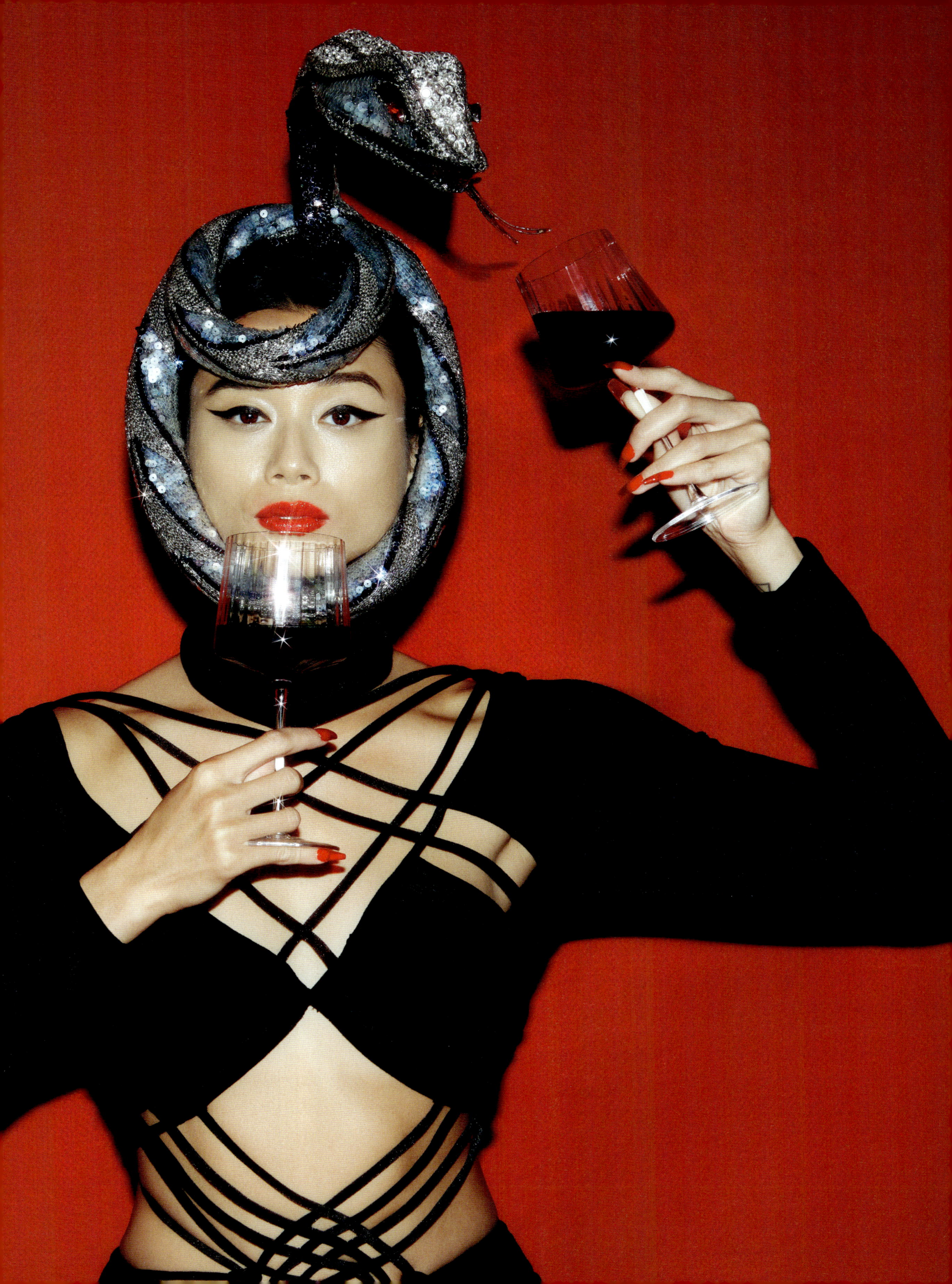

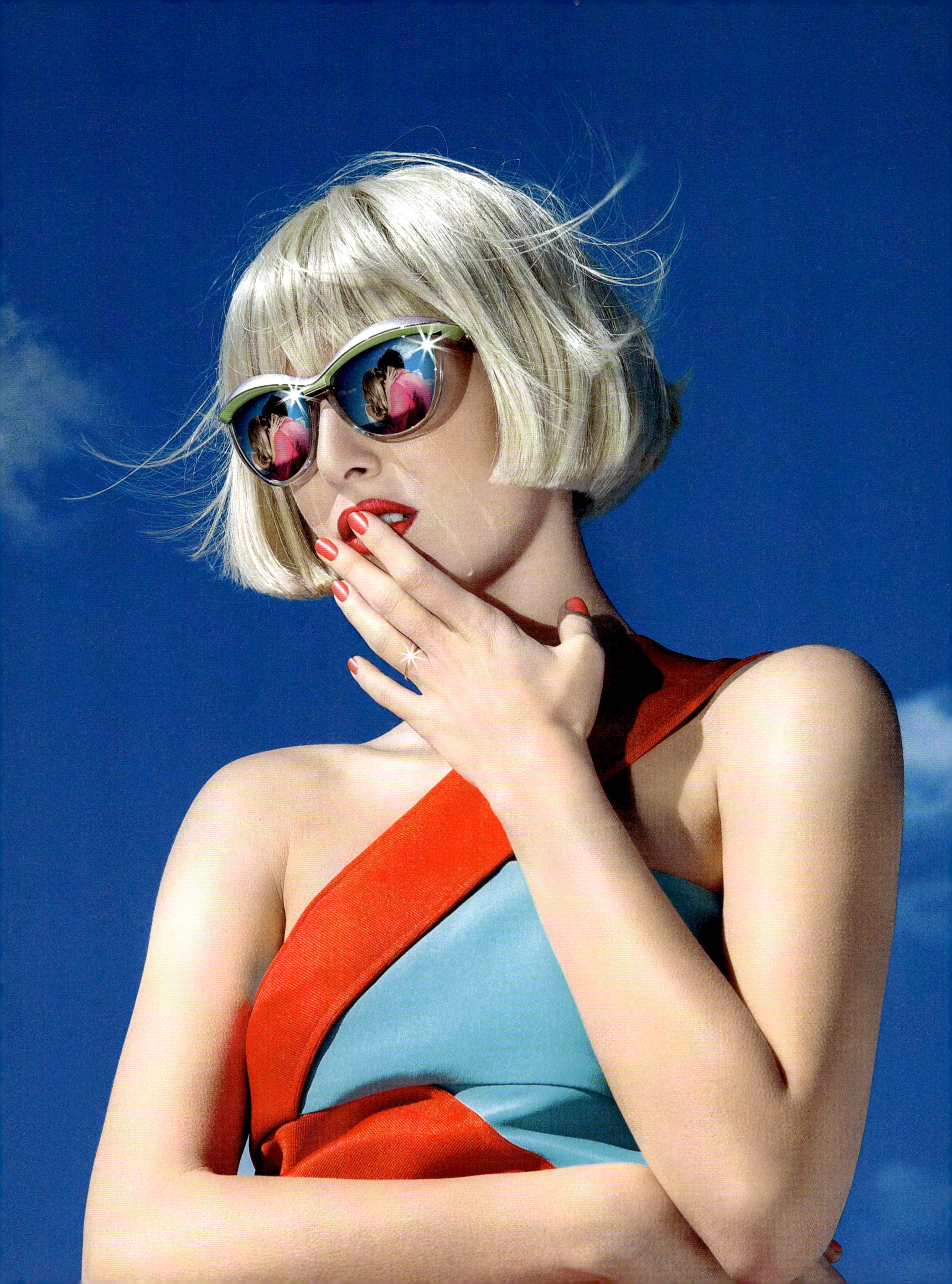

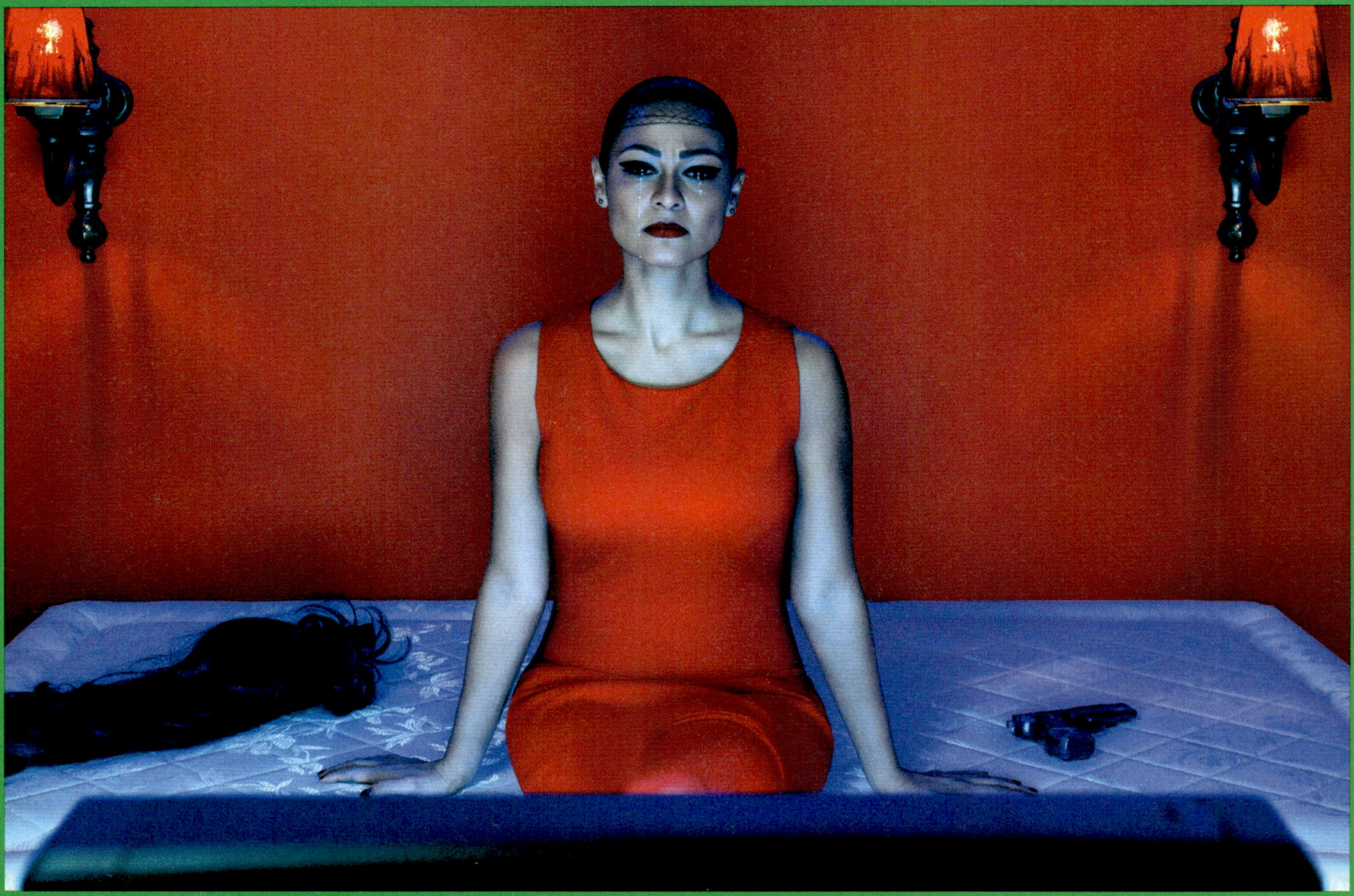

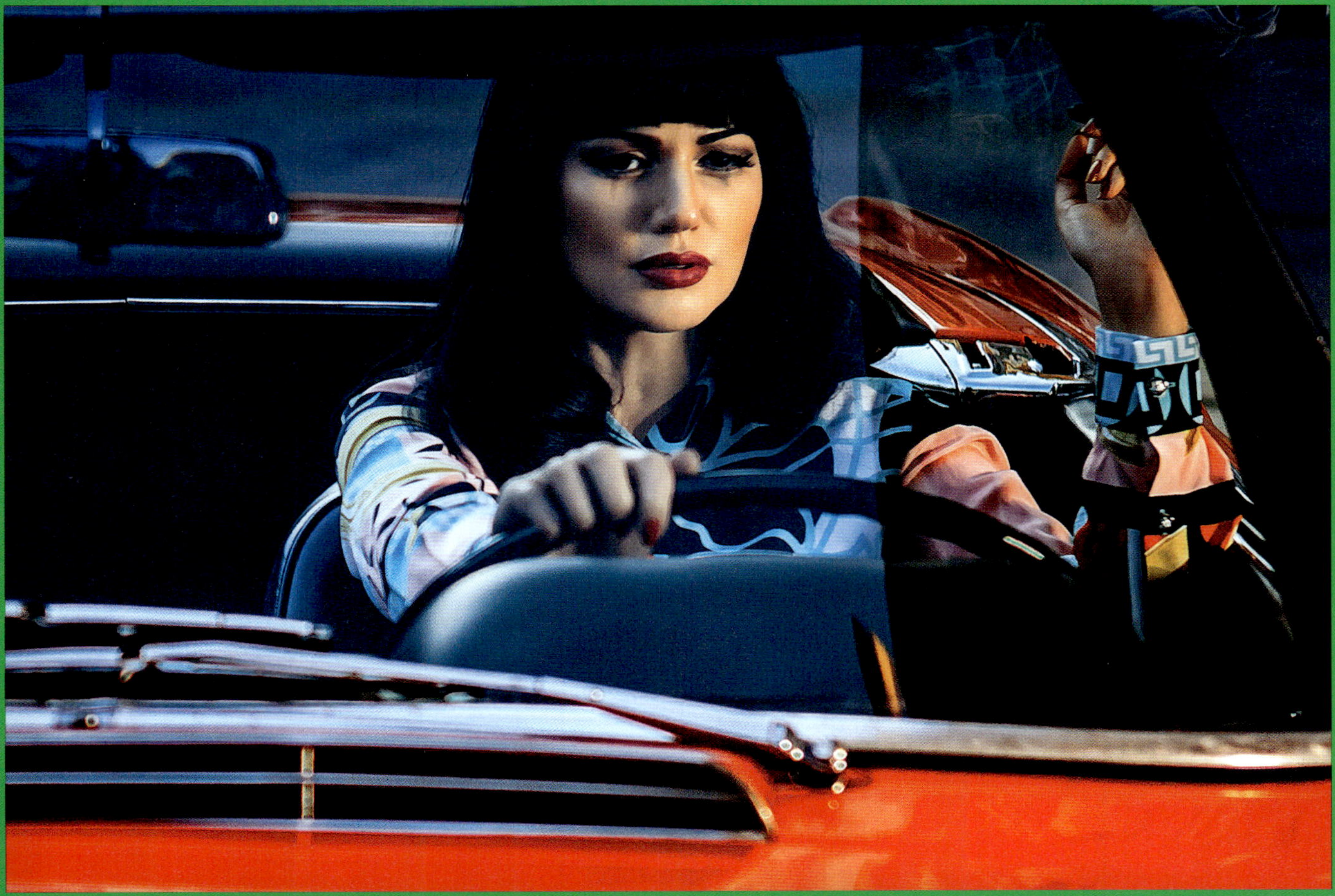

"As a child I had an infatuation with all of my mother's friends. Today, a part of me falls in love with an aspect of every woman I photograph."

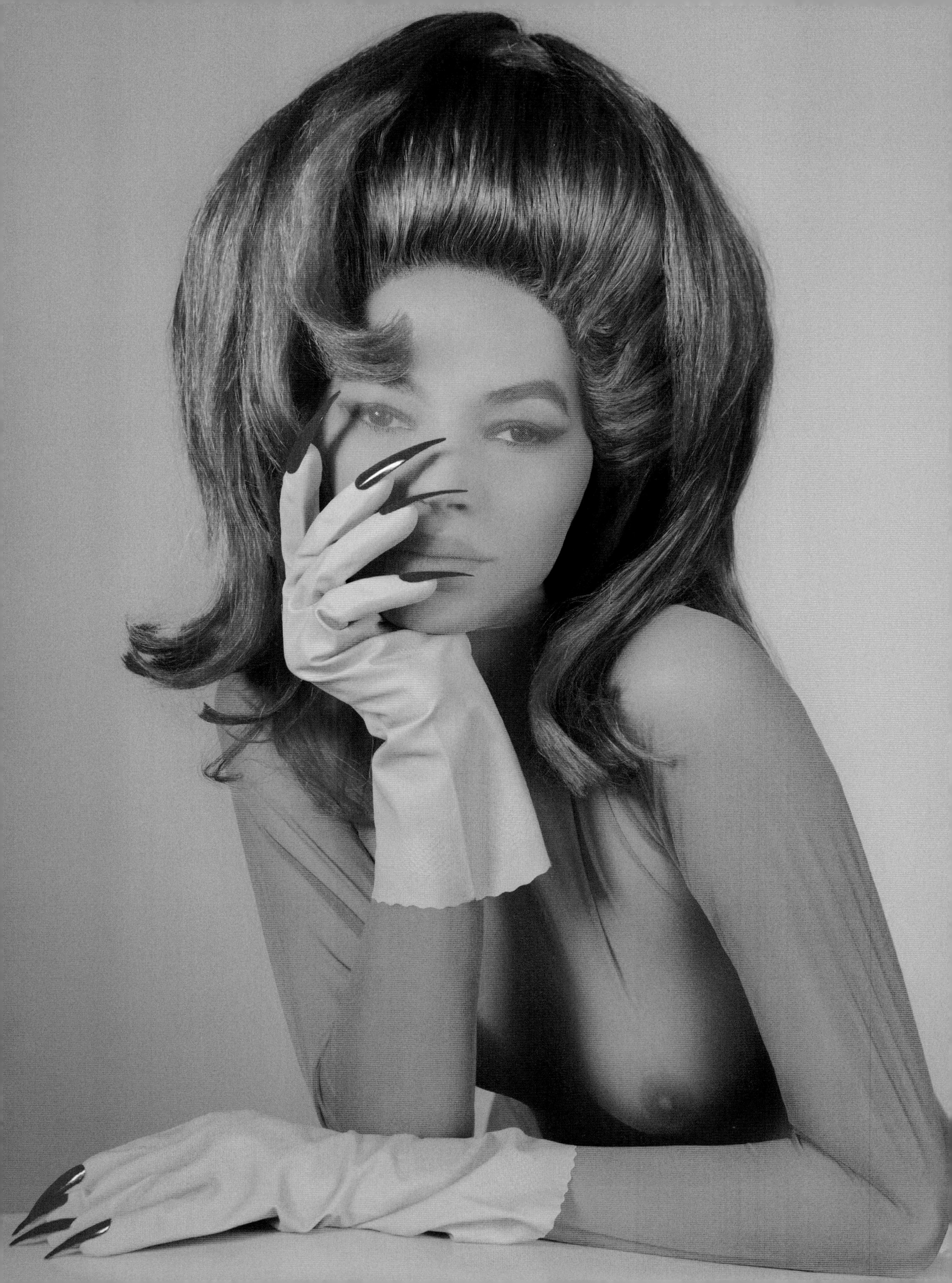

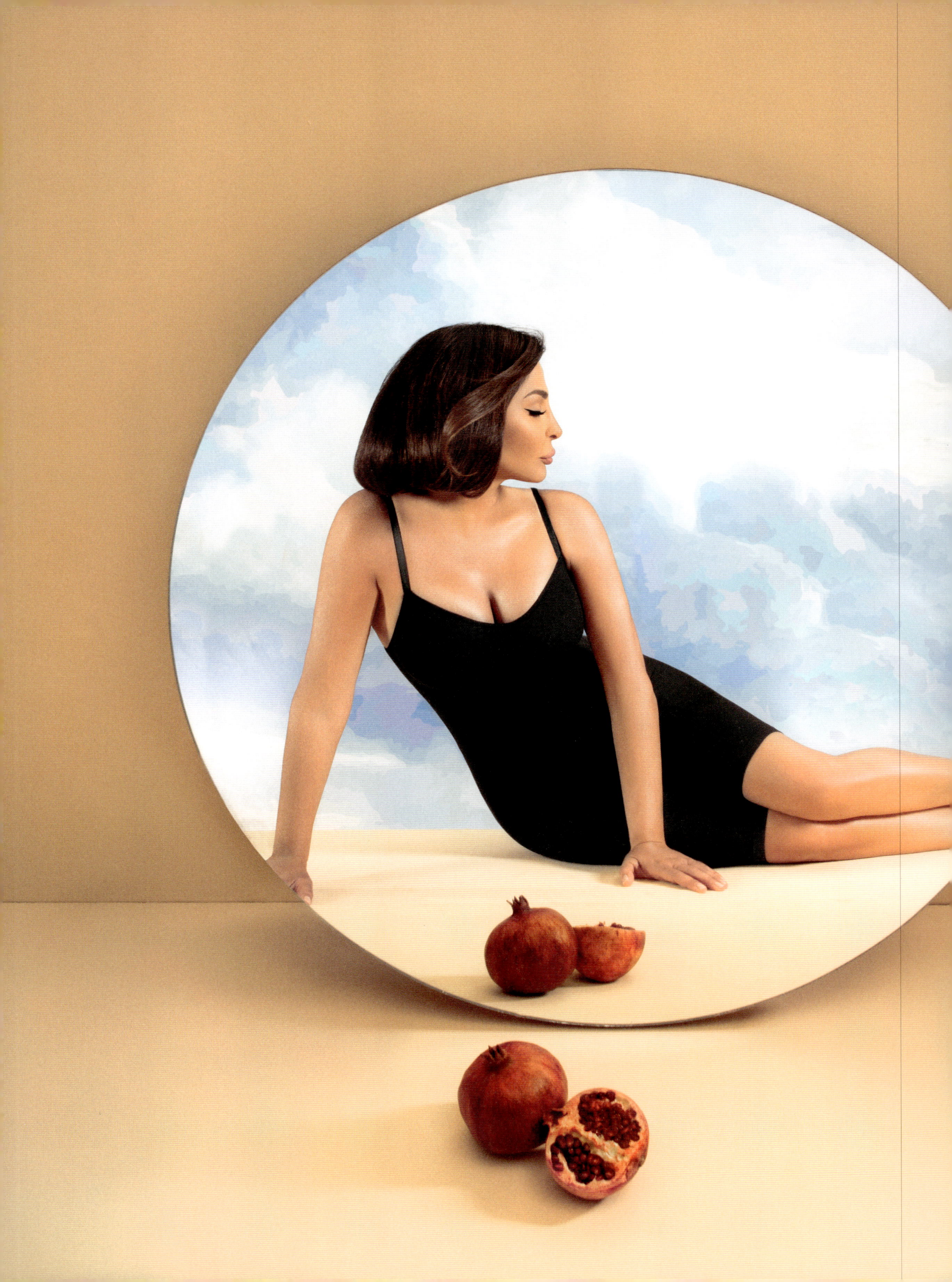

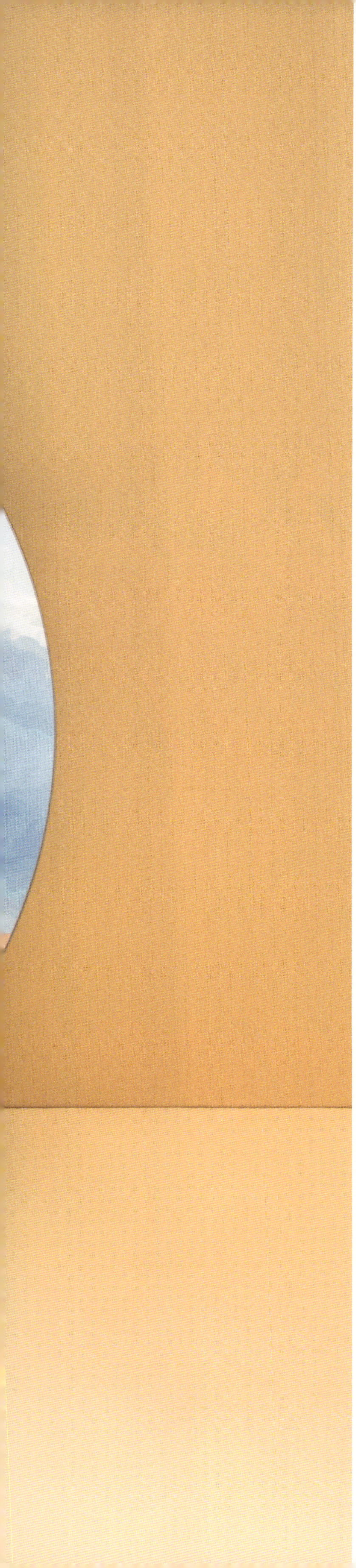

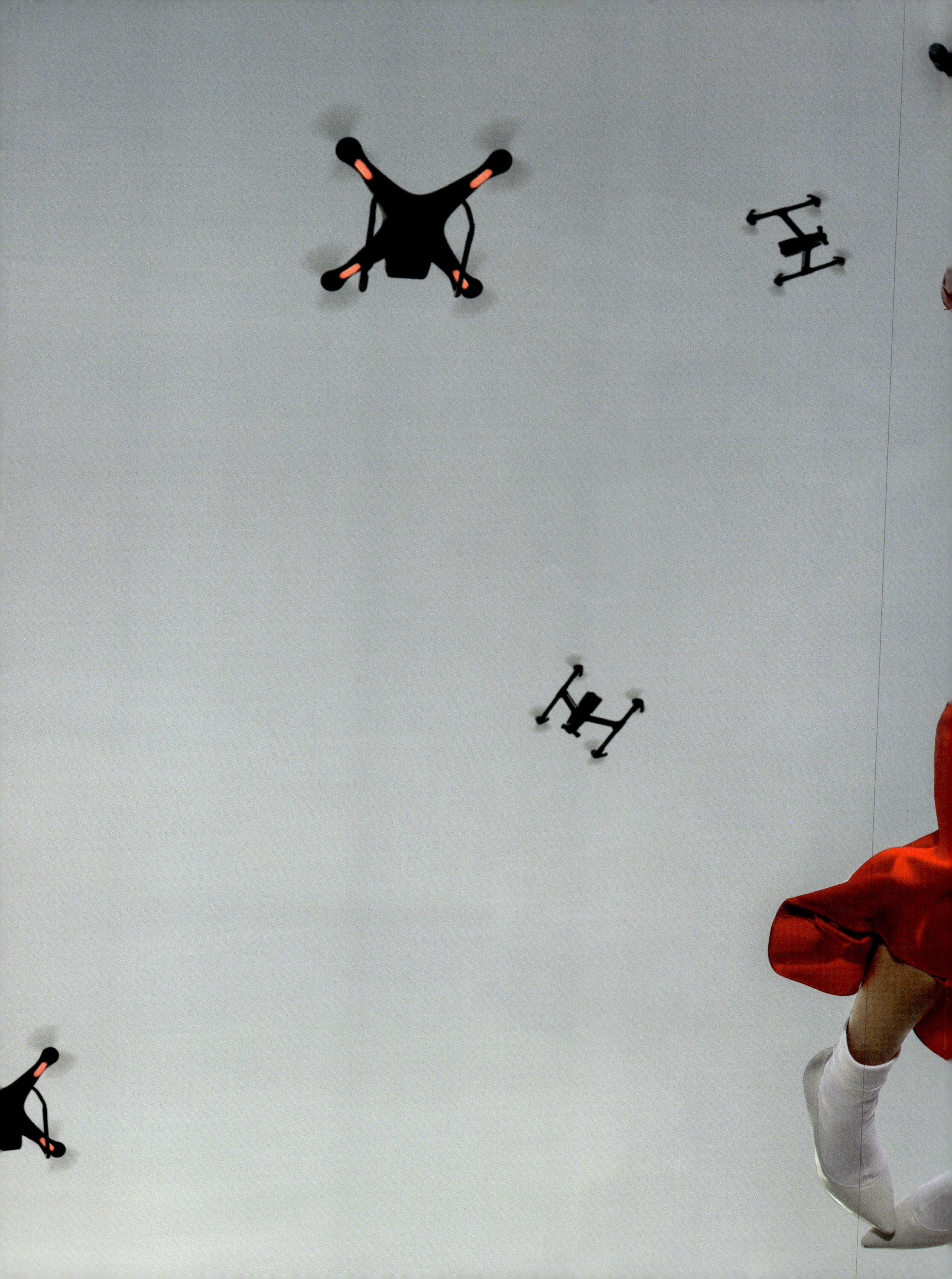

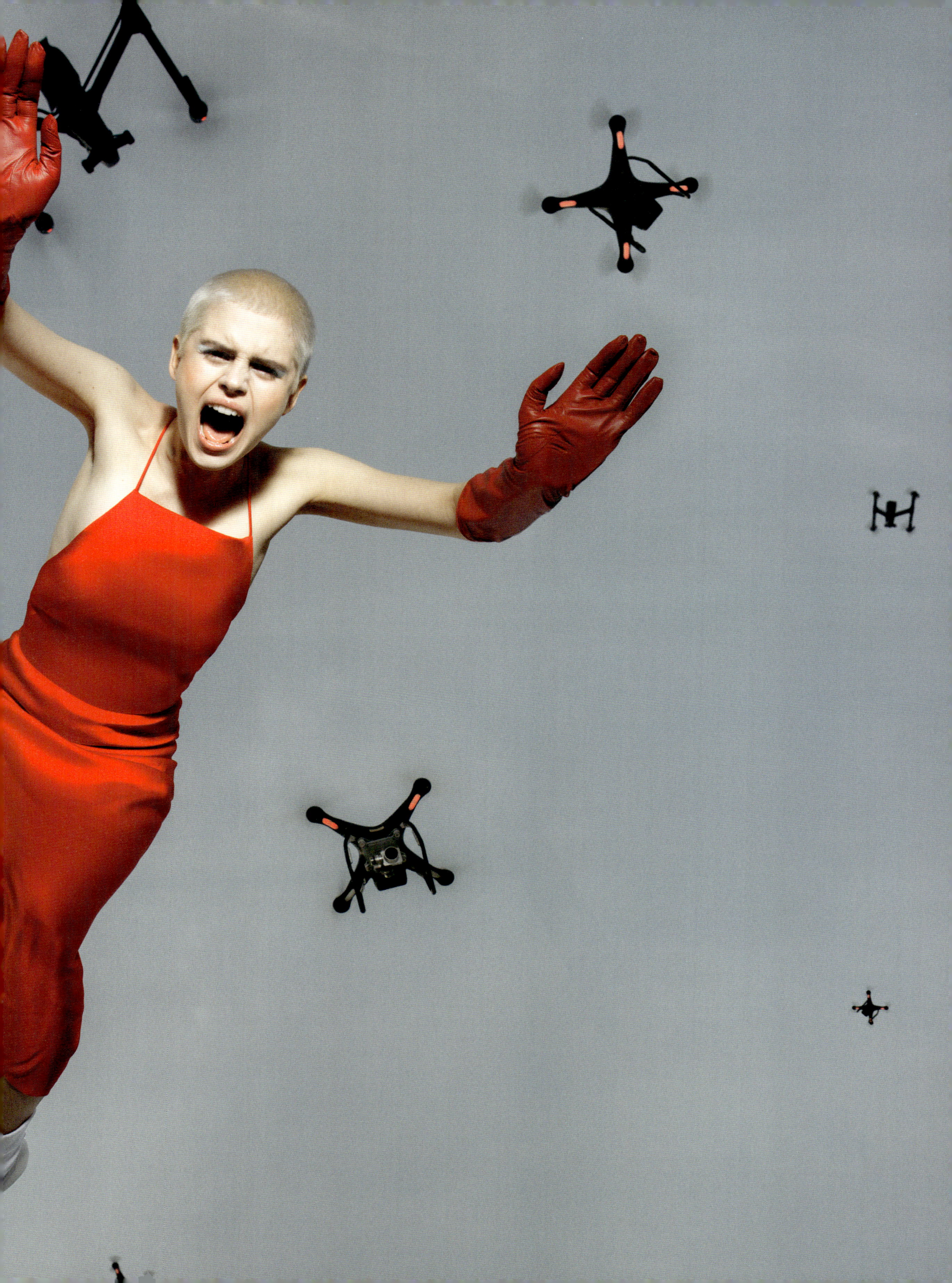

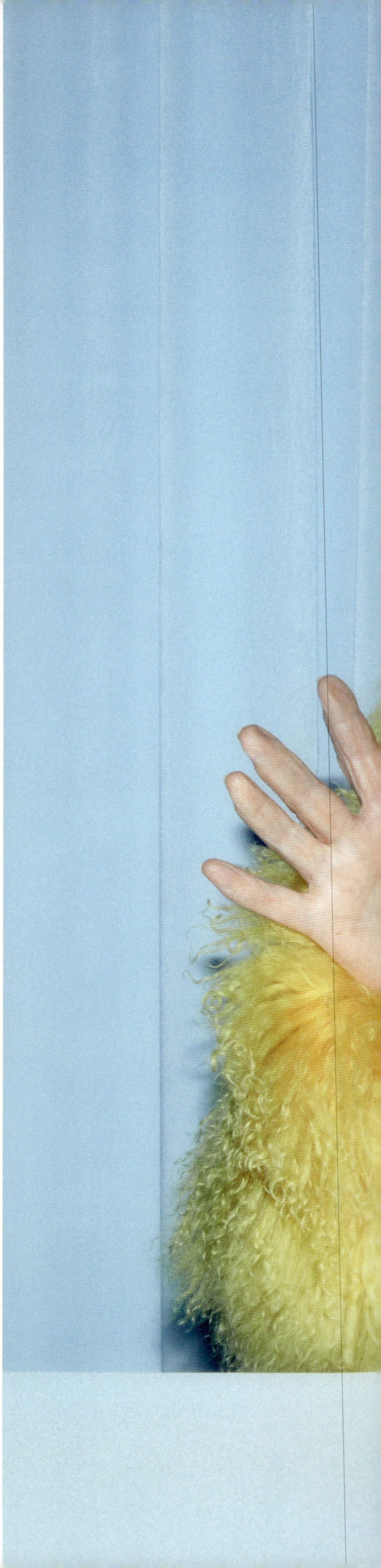

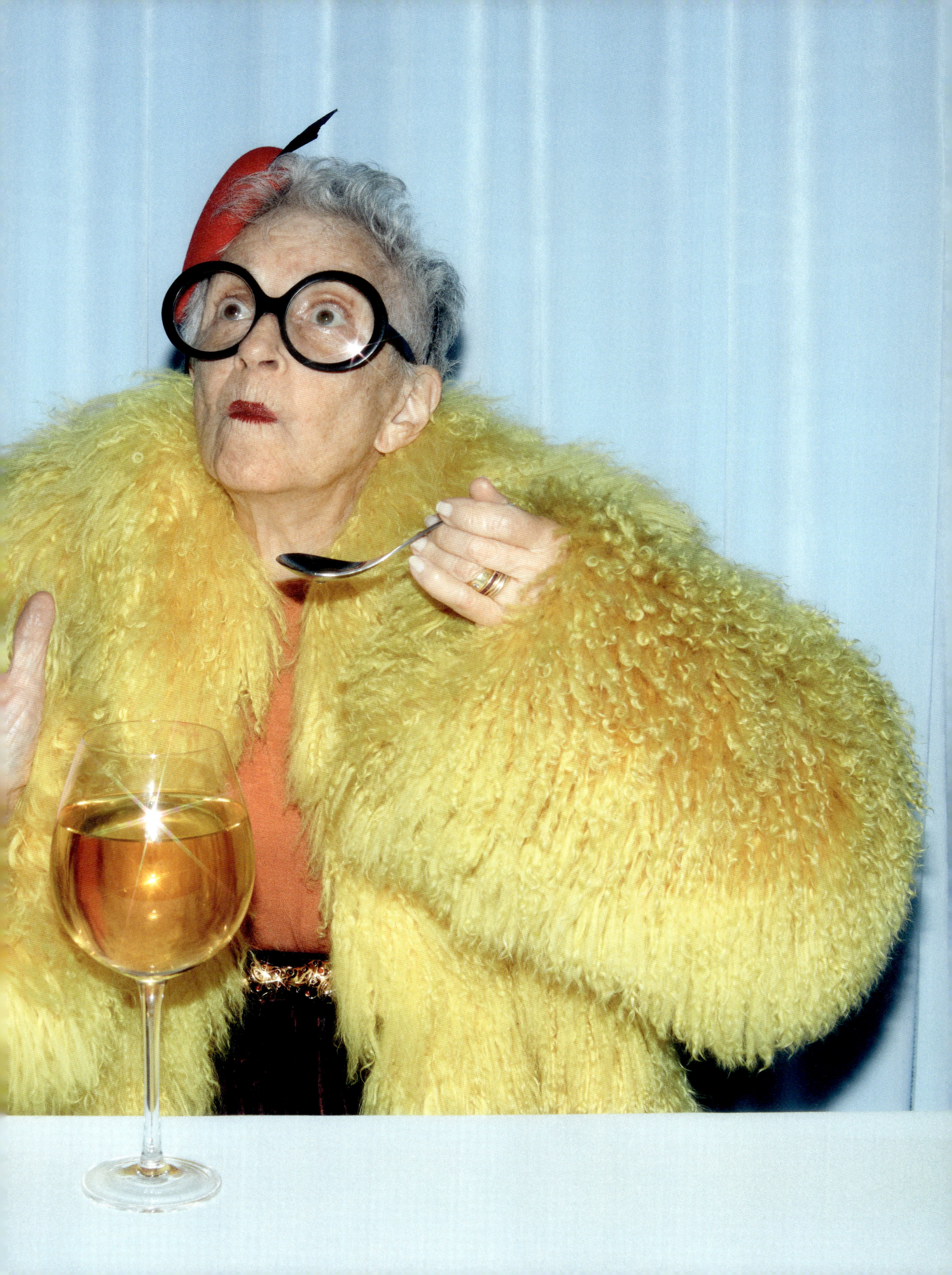

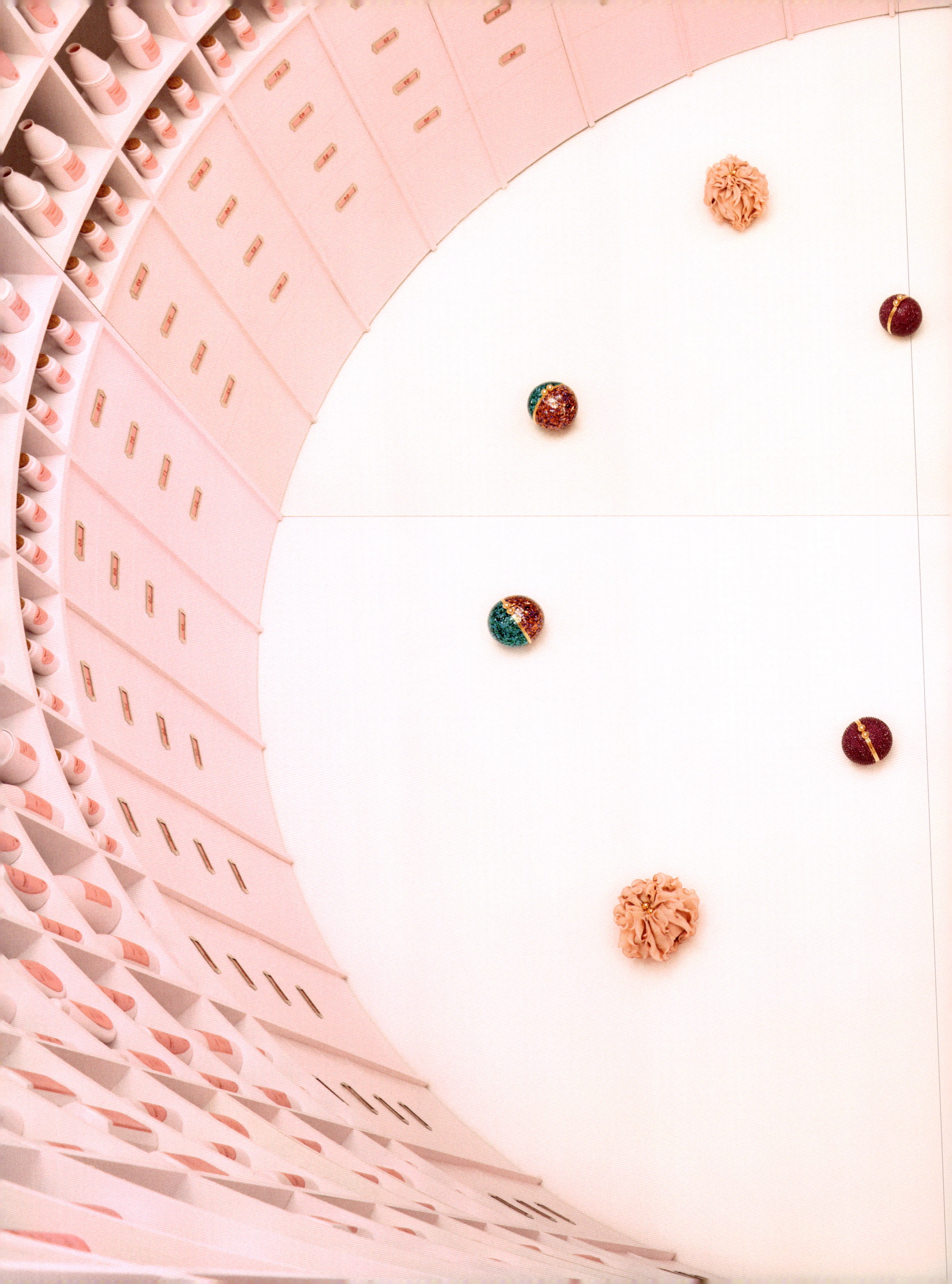

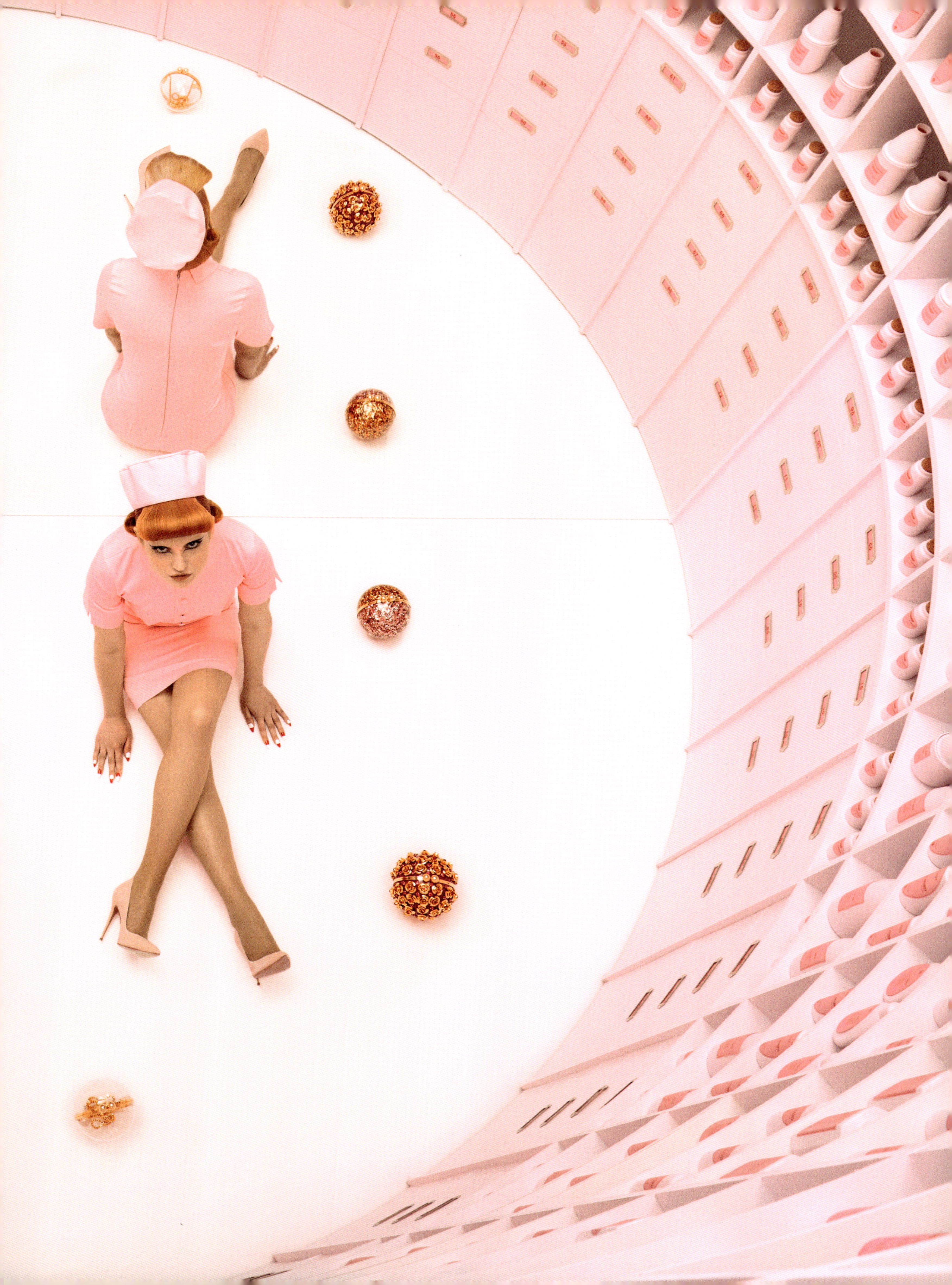

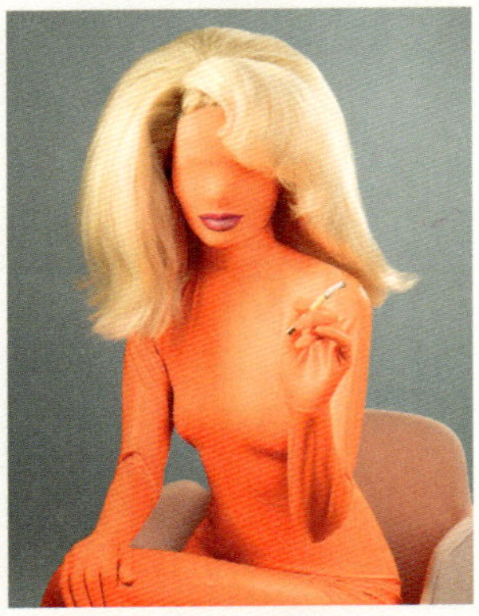

quarantine queen II, beirut, lebanon, *plastik* magazine, 2020.

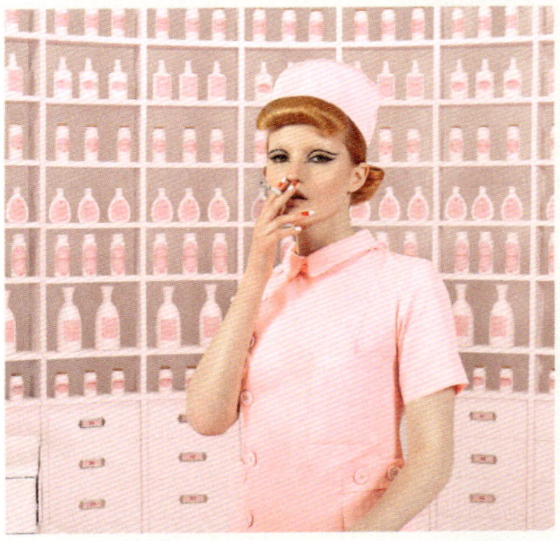

pills and cigarettes, beirut, lebanon, marzook campaign, 2019.

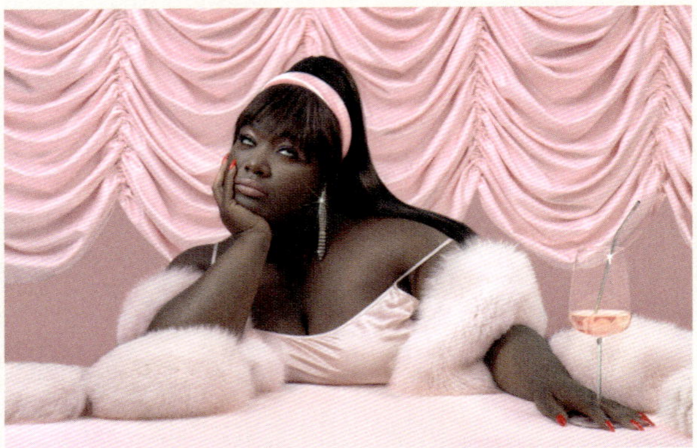

the bored and beautiful, new york, usa, pasqua campaign, 2021.

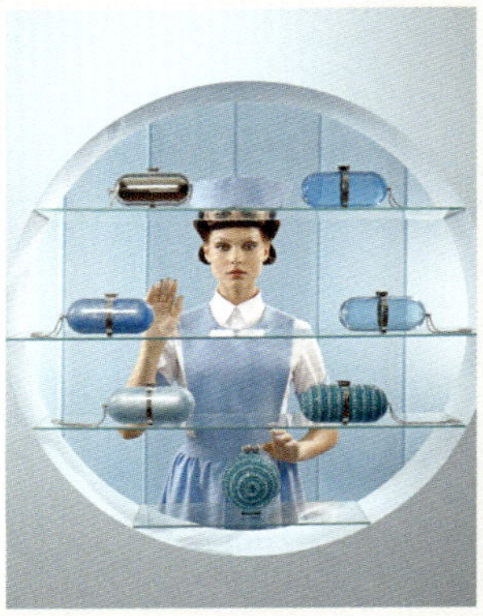

through the pills glass, beirut, lebanon, marzook campaign, 2019.

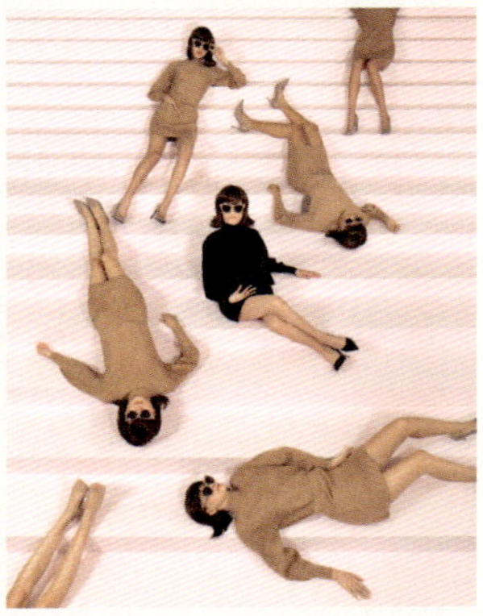

crumbling, beirut, lebanon, le marais campaign, 2019.

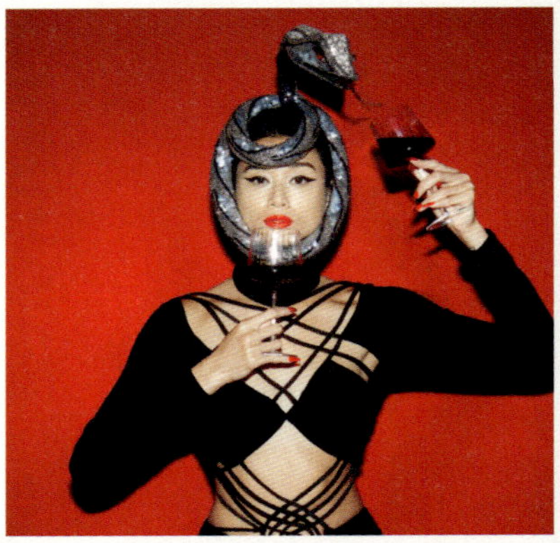

venemous, new york, usa, pasqua campaign, 2021.

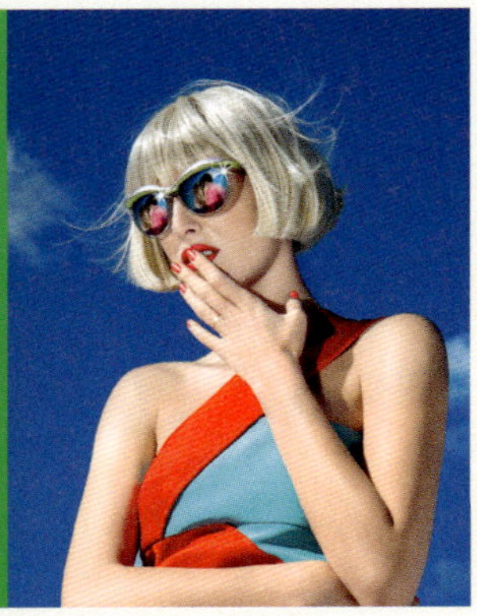

plastik tears I, beirut, lebanon, *plastik* magazine, 2015.

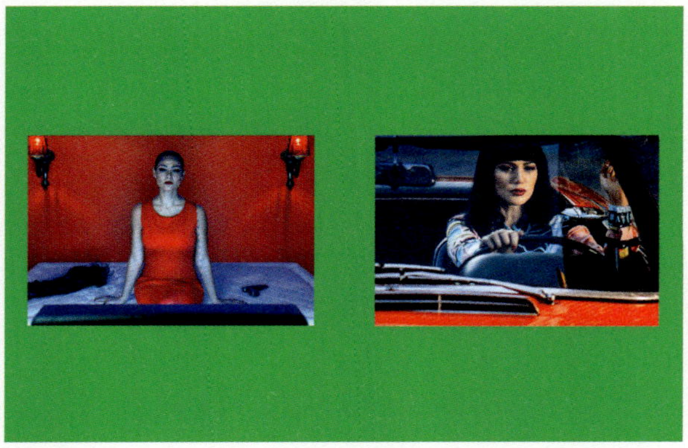

plastik tears III, beirut, lebanon, *plastik* magazine, 2015.

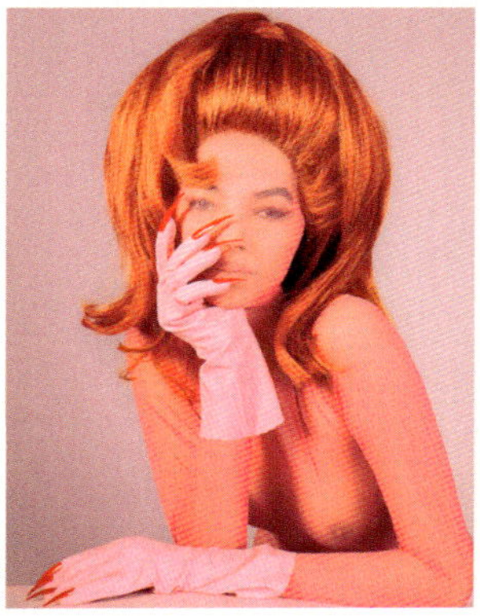

quarantine queen III, beirut, lebanon, *plastik* magazine, 2020.

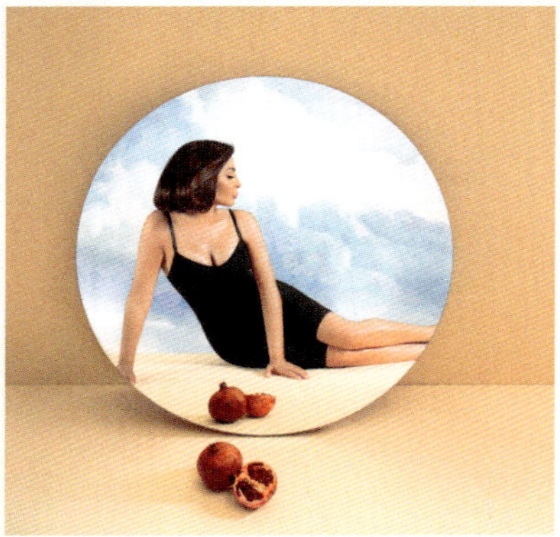

elissa, beirut, lebanon, elissa album cover, 2020.

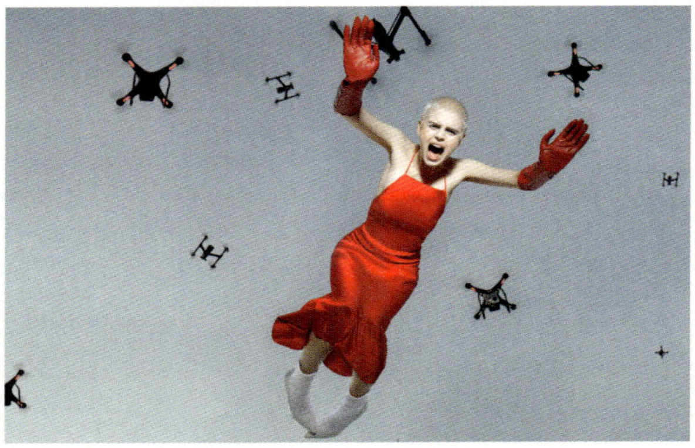

the drones, al shoof, lebanon, *plastik* magazine, 2018.

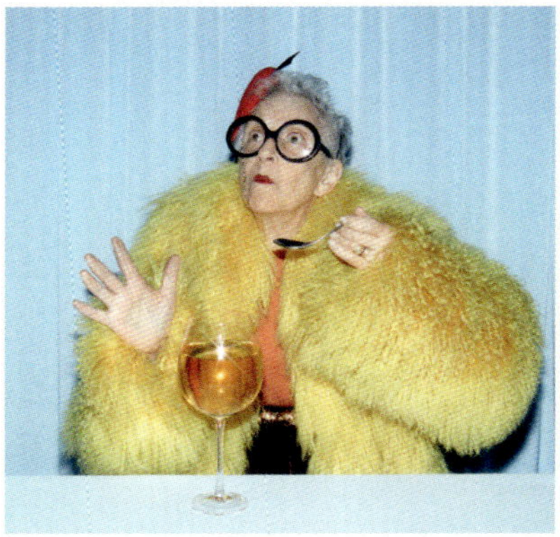

sylvia, new york, usa, pasqua campaign, 2021.

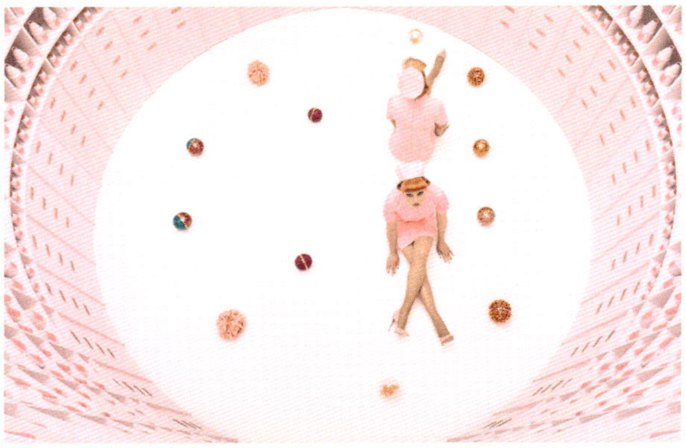

the maze, beirut, lebanon, marzook campaign, 2019.

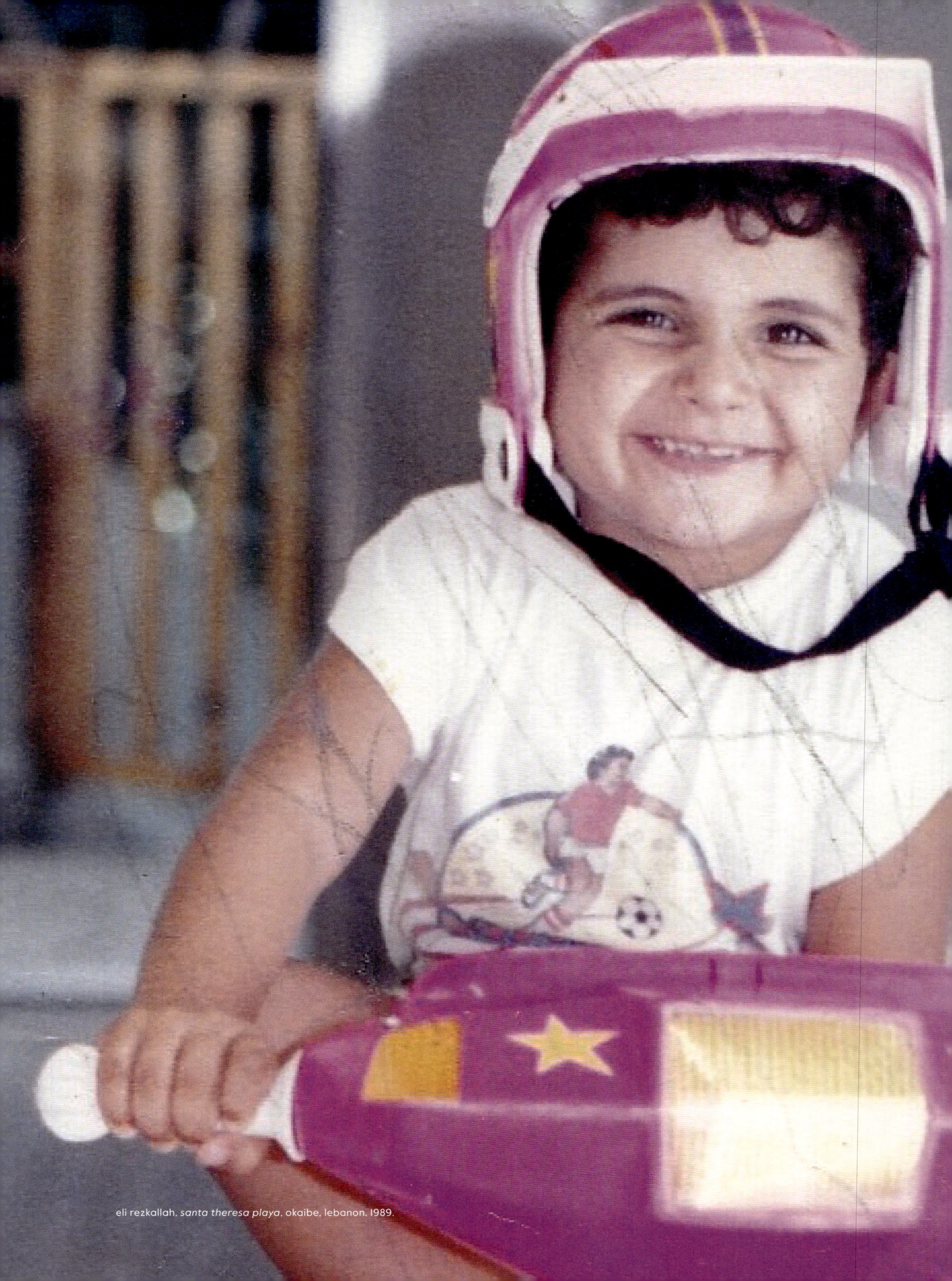

eli rezkallah, *santa theresa playa*, okaibe, lebanon, 1989.

ACT FOUR

play

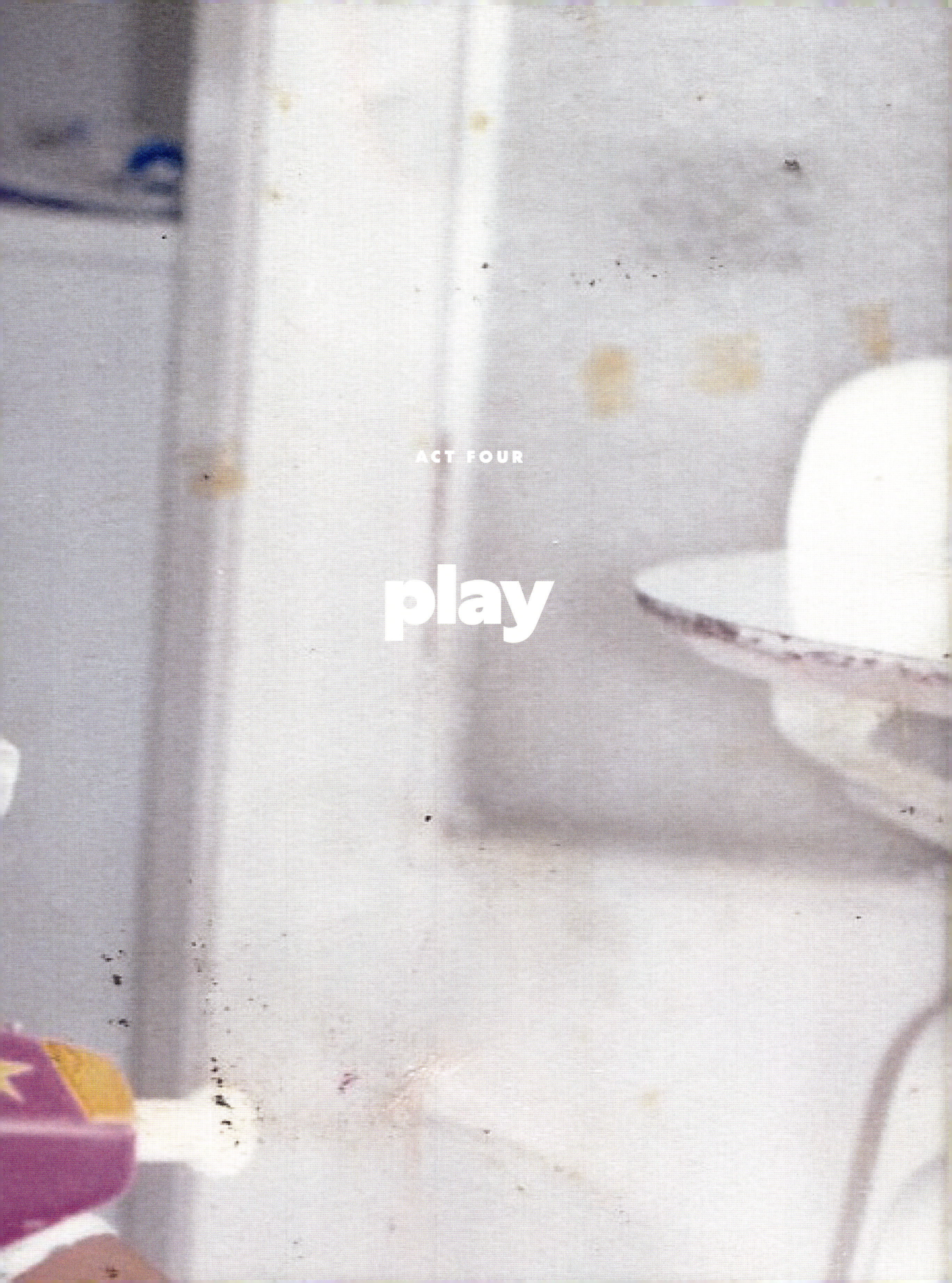

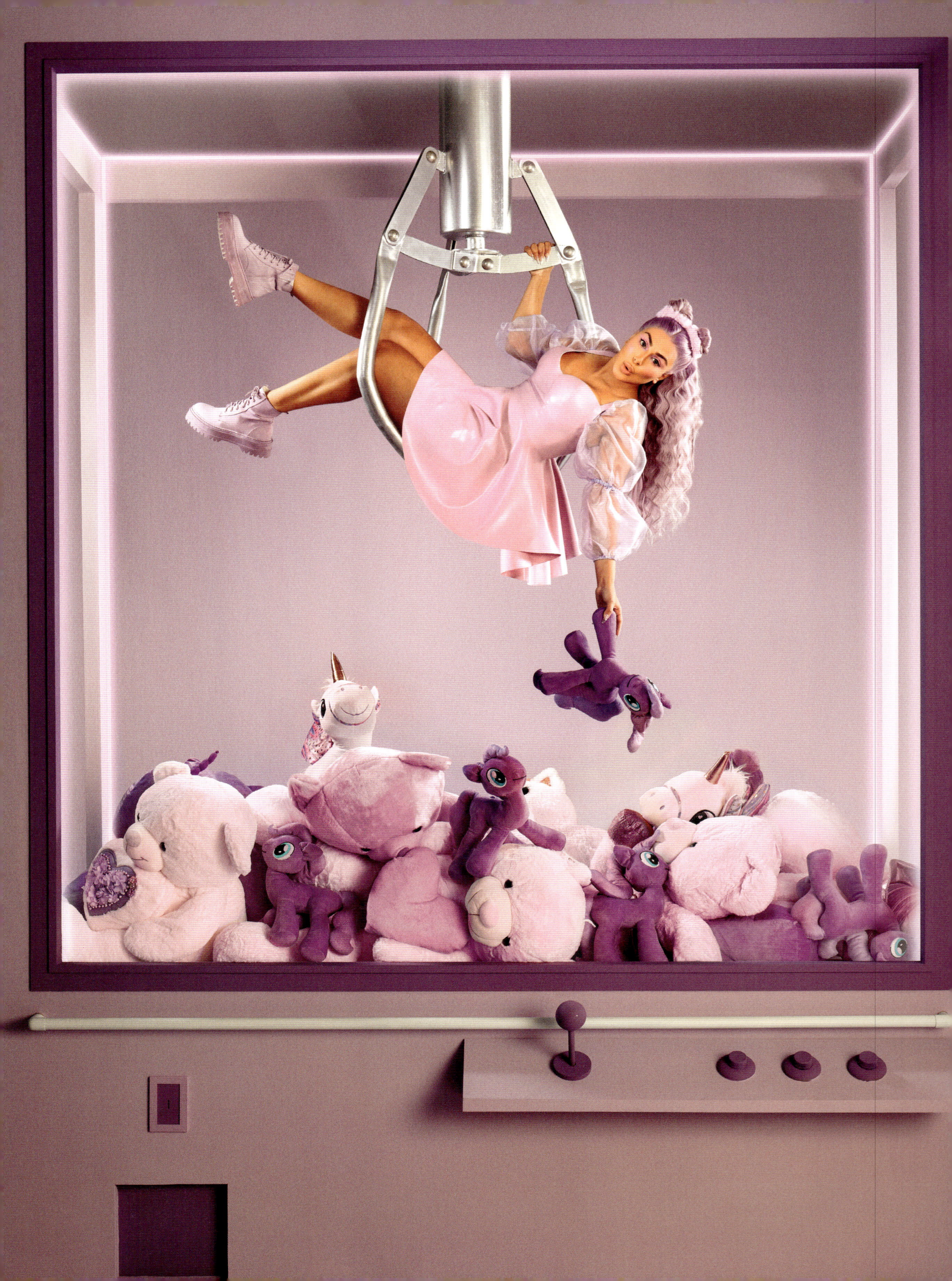

There's an undeniable playfulness in Rezkallah's work that stems from his eternally spirited state of mind. Rezkallah has a knack for deconstructing pop culture codes and traditional photography by refurbishing all too familiar stereotypes with a new sense of meaning: dollhouses for adults, frosted cakes for the visibly depressed, fast food for queens...
The juxtaposition of the grandiose with the mundane depicts society as a massive role-playing stage – a testament to the notion that people are rarely as serious as they seem.

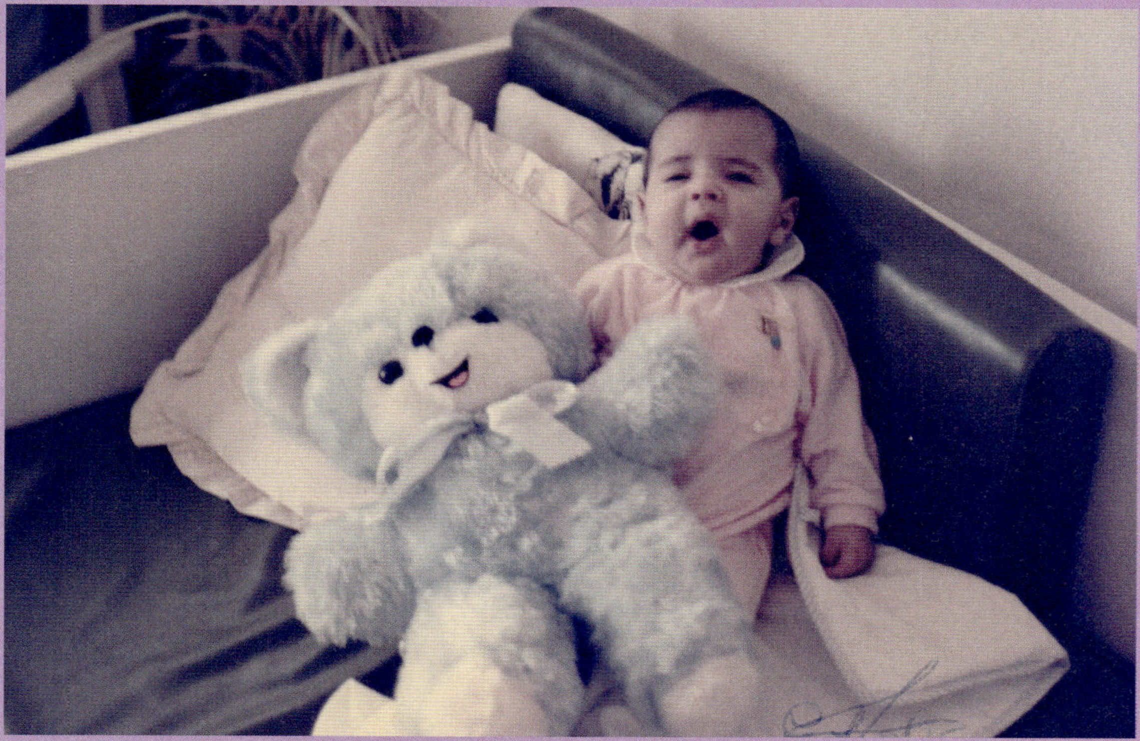

eli rezkallah, santa theresa playa, okaibe, lebanon, may 1986.

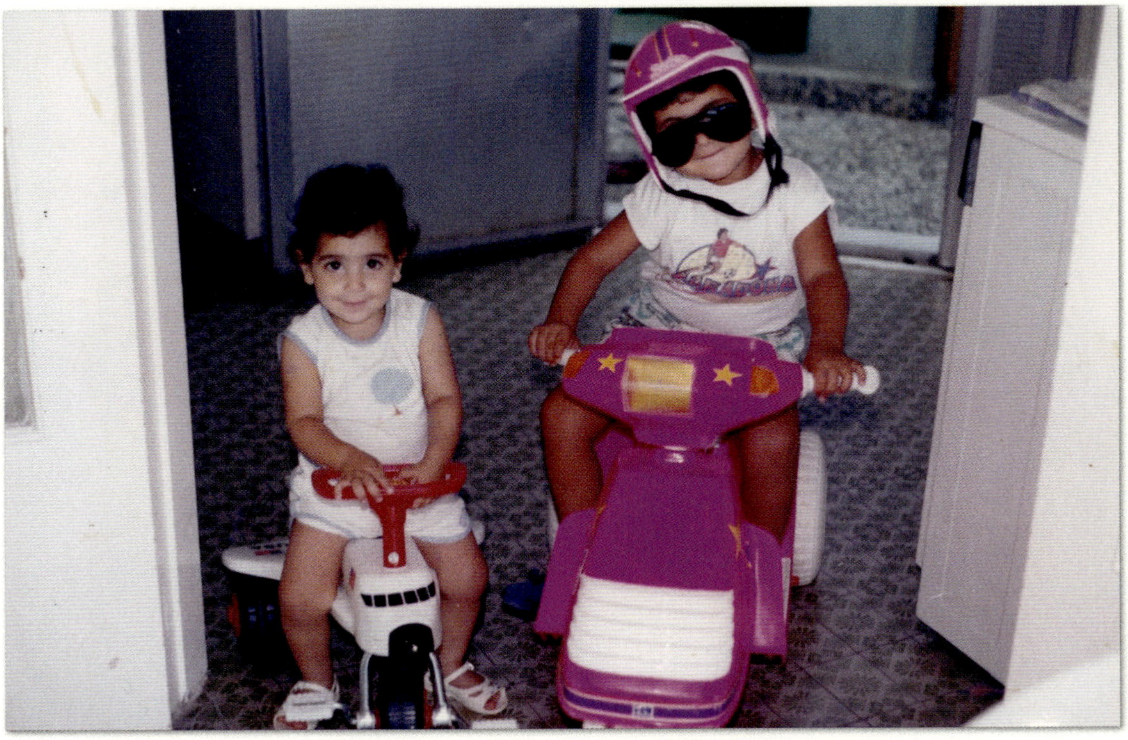

rami and eli rezkallah, santa theresa playa, okaibe, lebanon, 1989.

One of the very first pages of the very first issue of *plastik* reads: "Grow up but never stop playing", an injuction that was a direct reflection of Rezkallah's mindset at the time – young, carefree, and fearless. Since then, ironically, one of the photographer's biggest struggles has been finding a balance between the serious, responsible adult and the whimsical artist within, an inner conflict that, if anything, has become more apparent in his work throughout the years. What he creates are vibrant fantasy realms for the apathetic, where both time and joy stand still and where relics of the past long to be part of the present.

thomas, rami, and eli rezkallah, laklouk, lebanon, 1991.

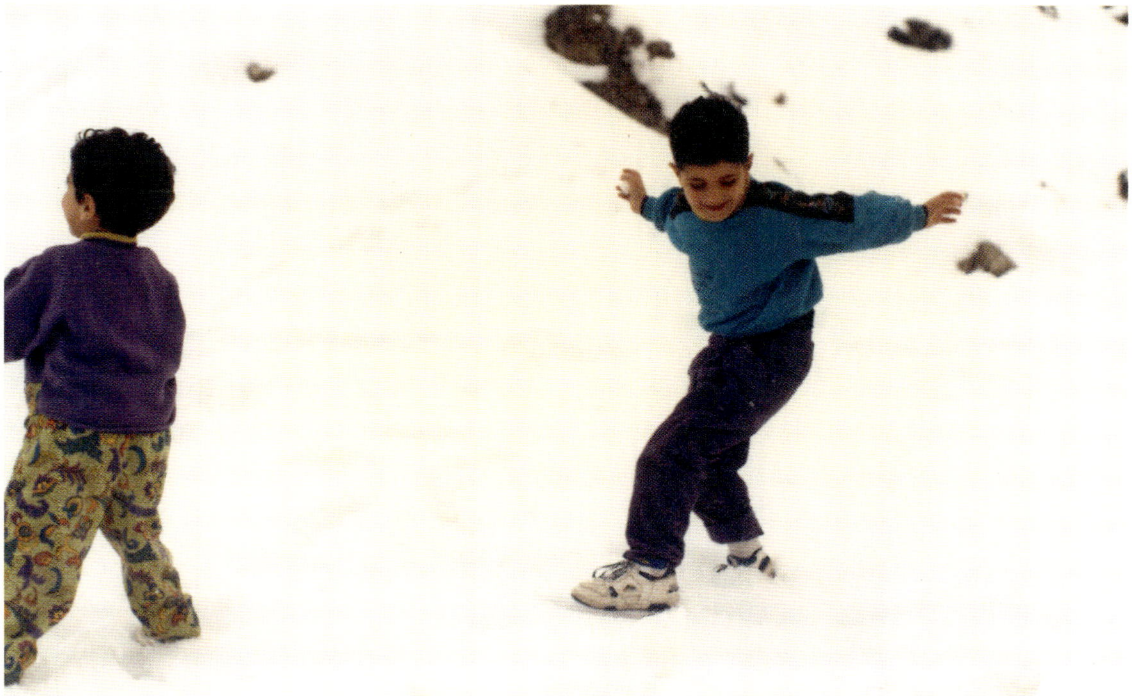

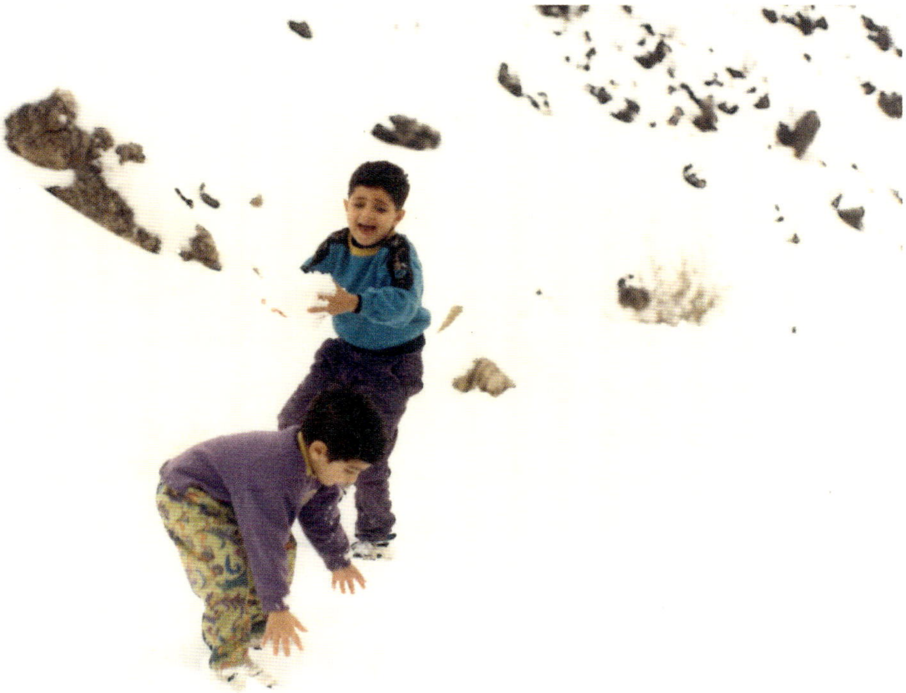

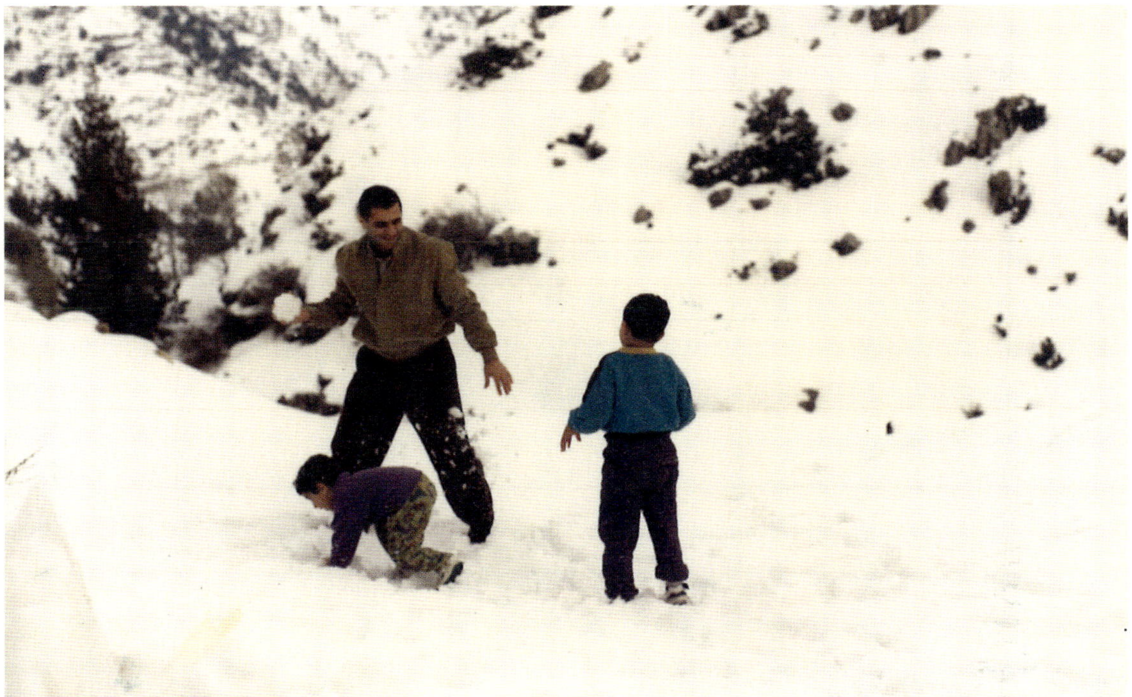

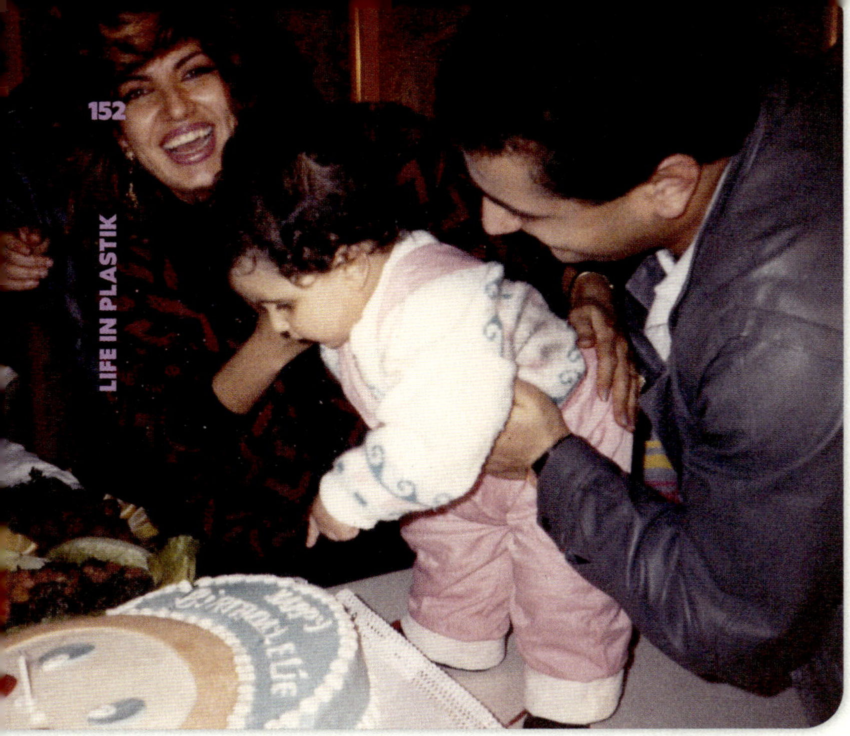

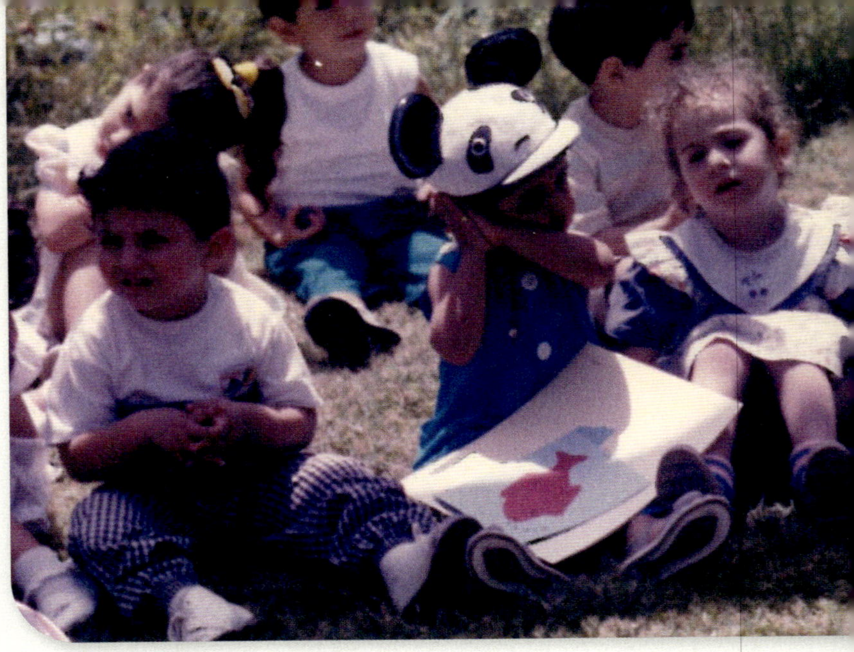

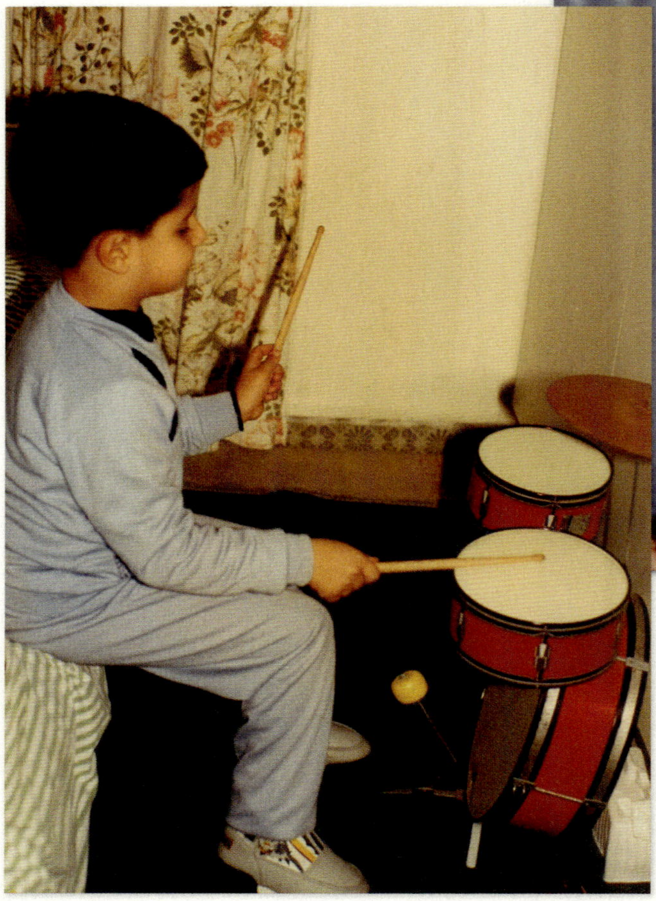

i will remember this christmas gift forever
it was brutally destroyed the next morning by one of the santa theresa bullies.

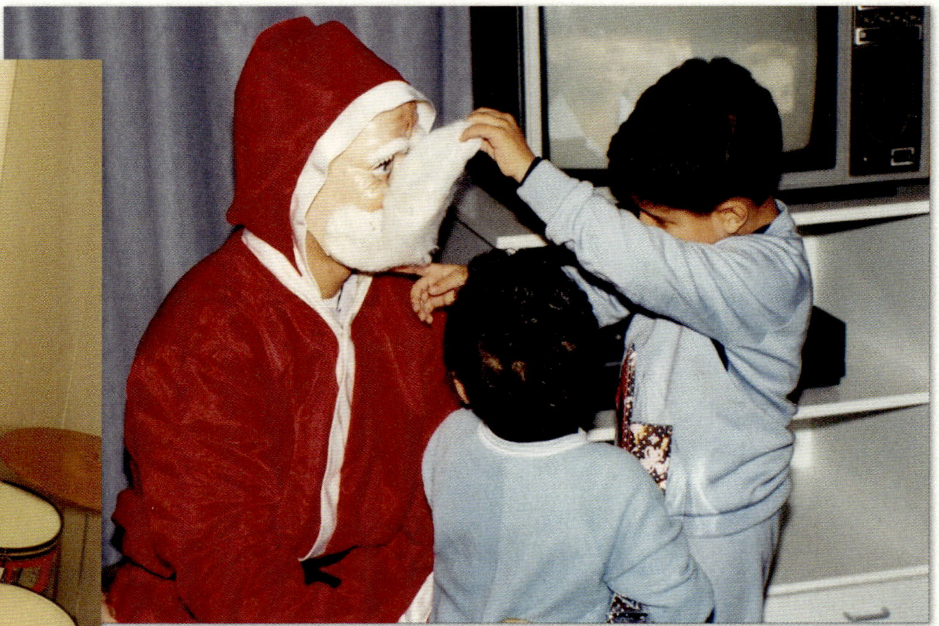

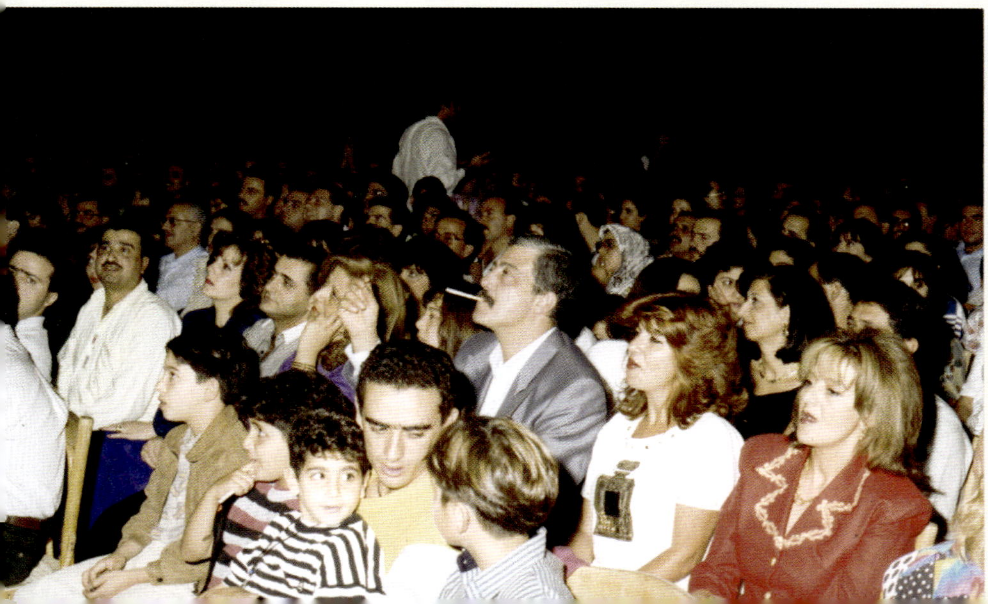

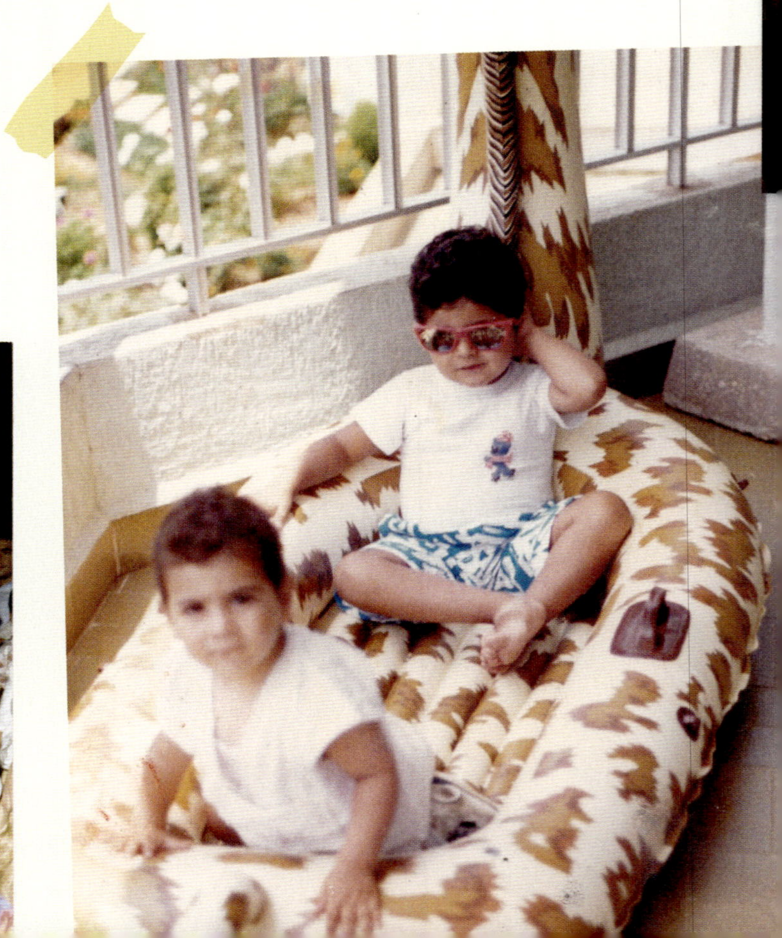

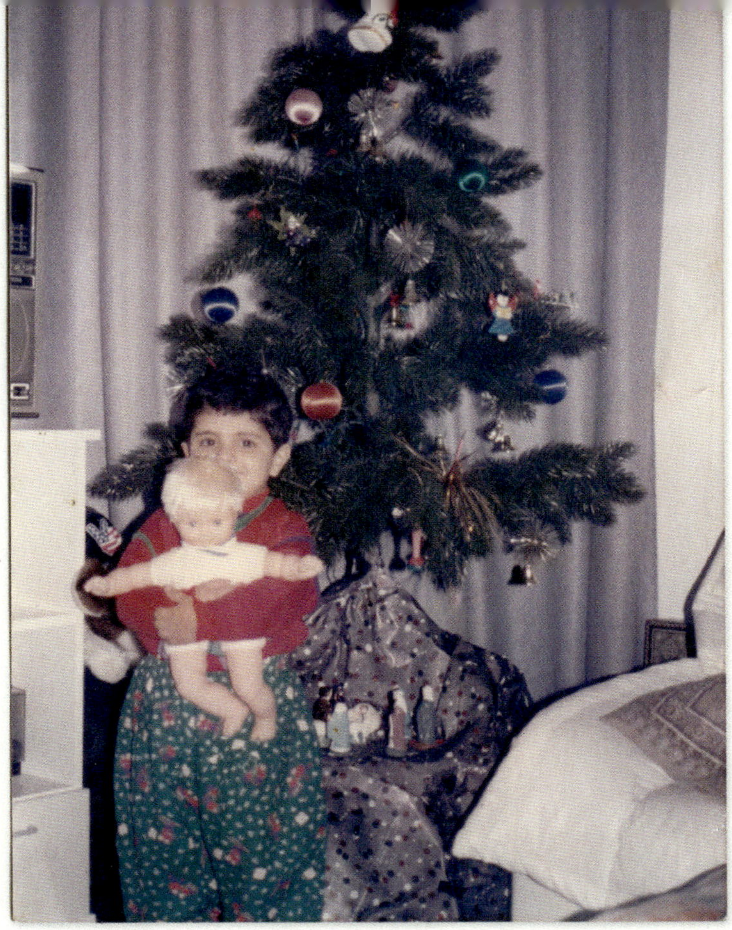

my first doll.

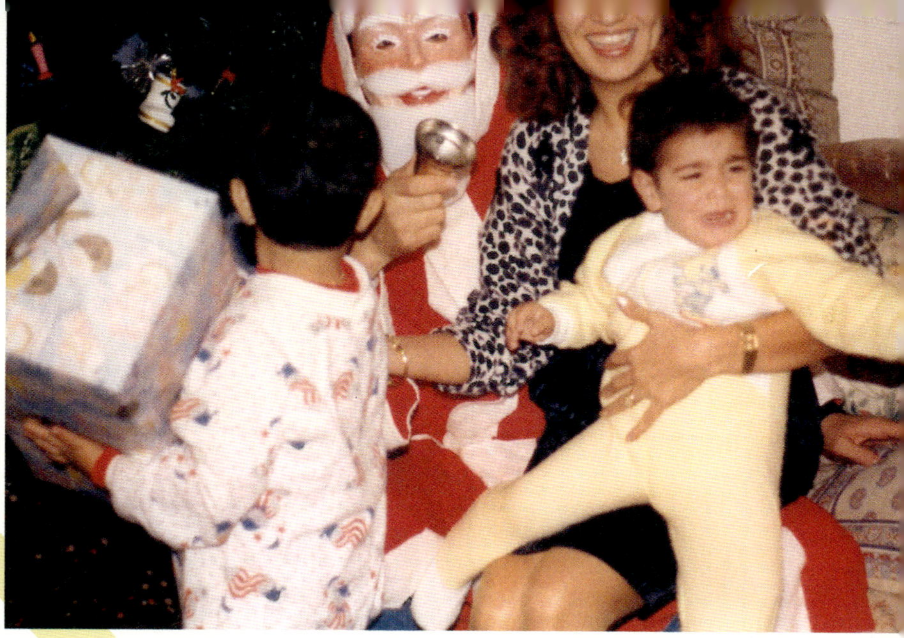

christmas horror.

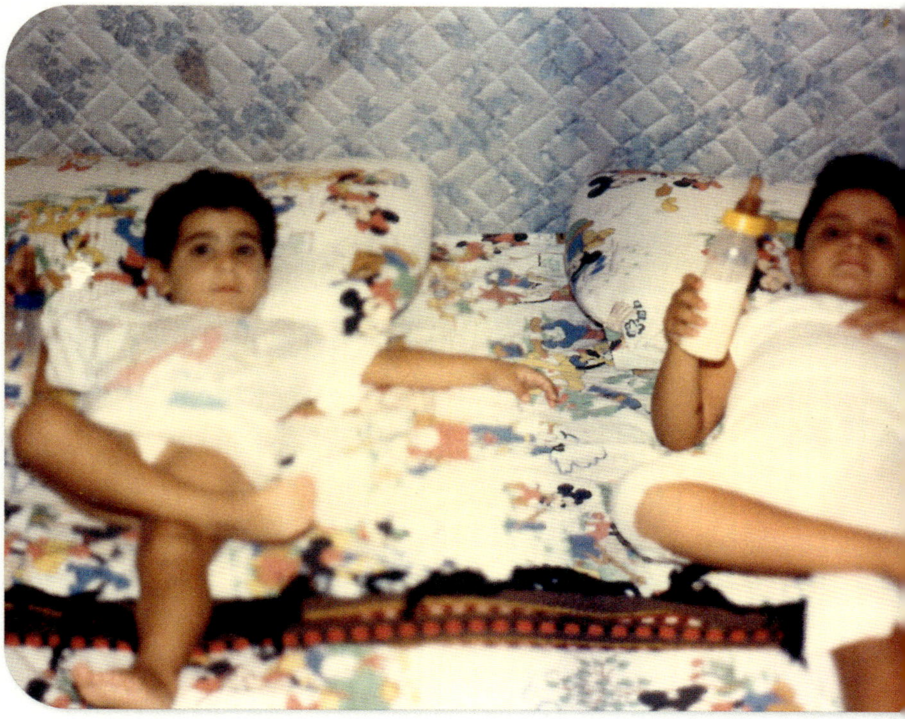

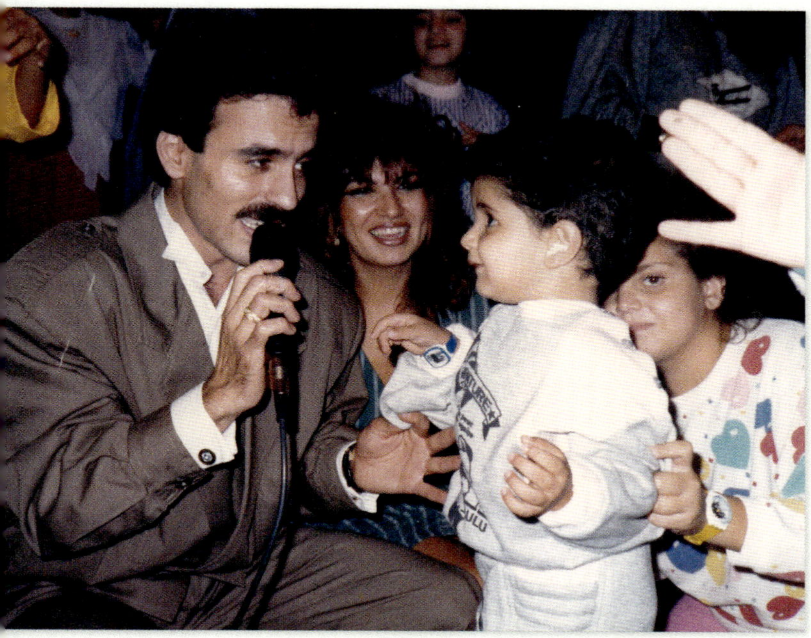

as a child, I'd celebrate my birthday twice:
the day I was born, and on the day of "st. elie" which was a national holiday, no less.

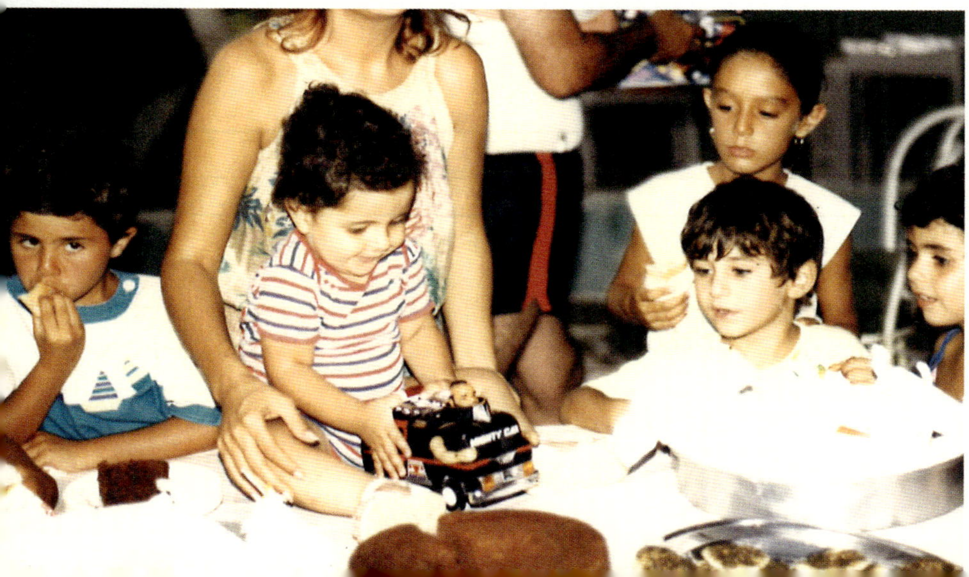

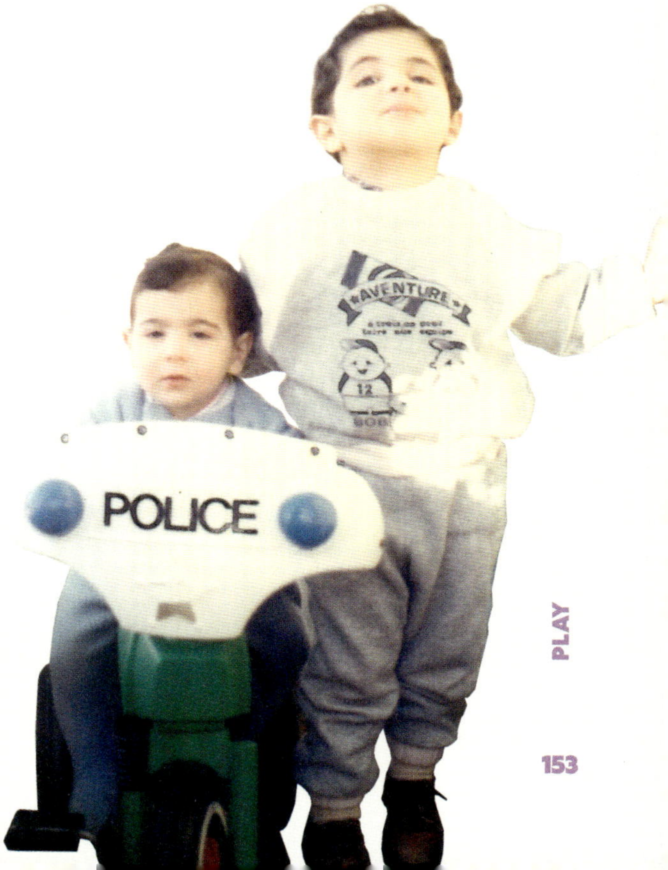

PLAY

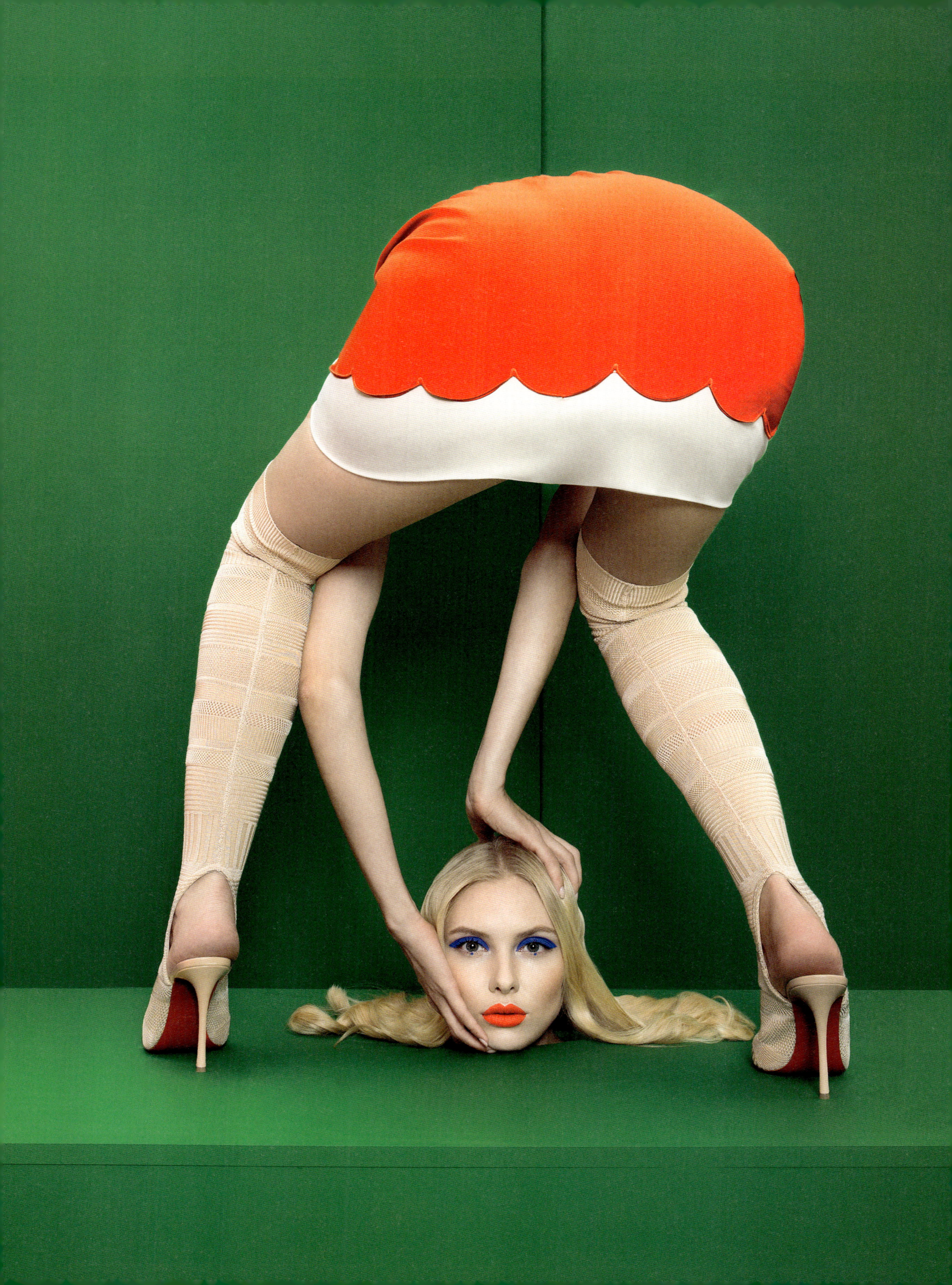

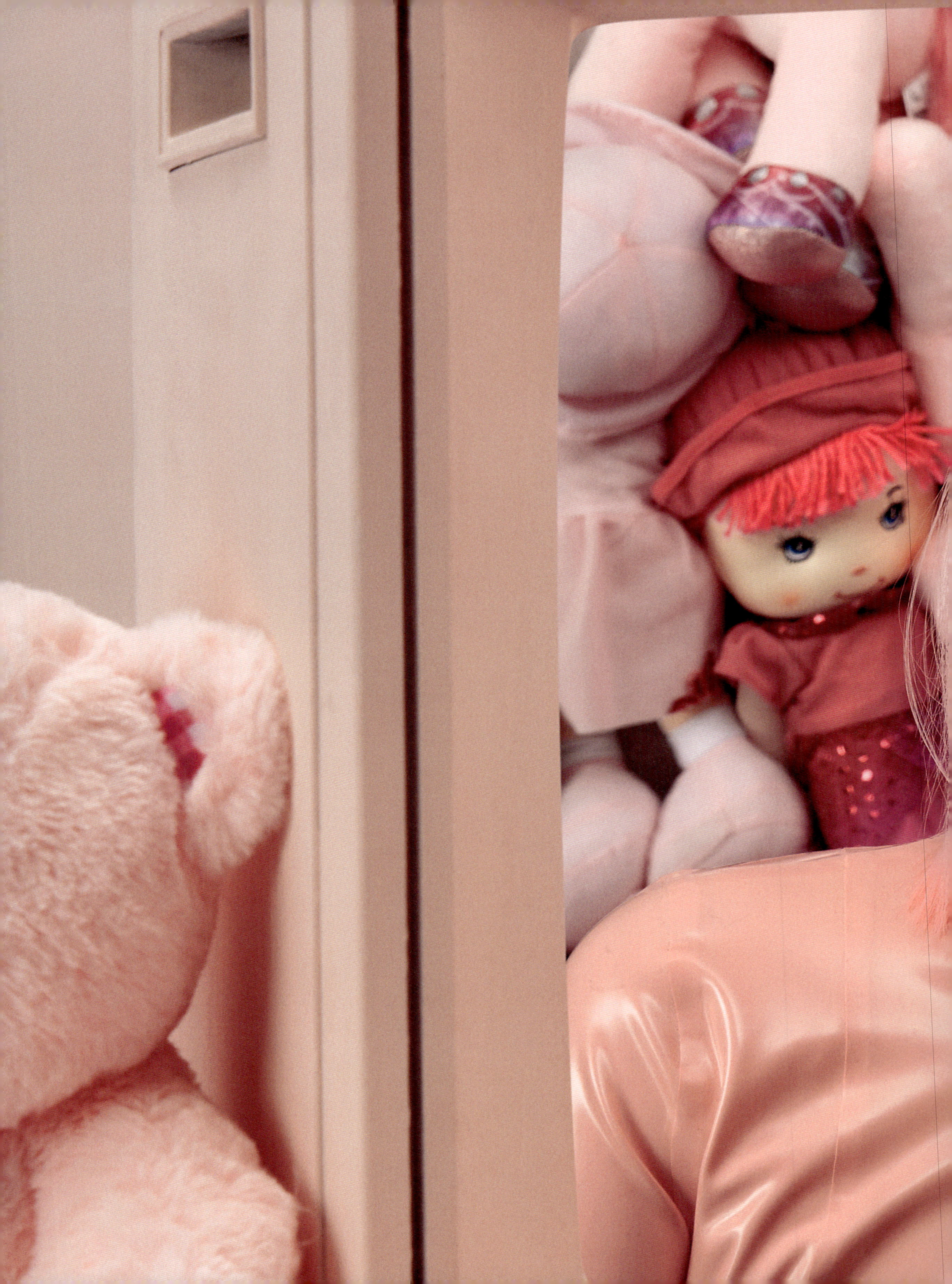

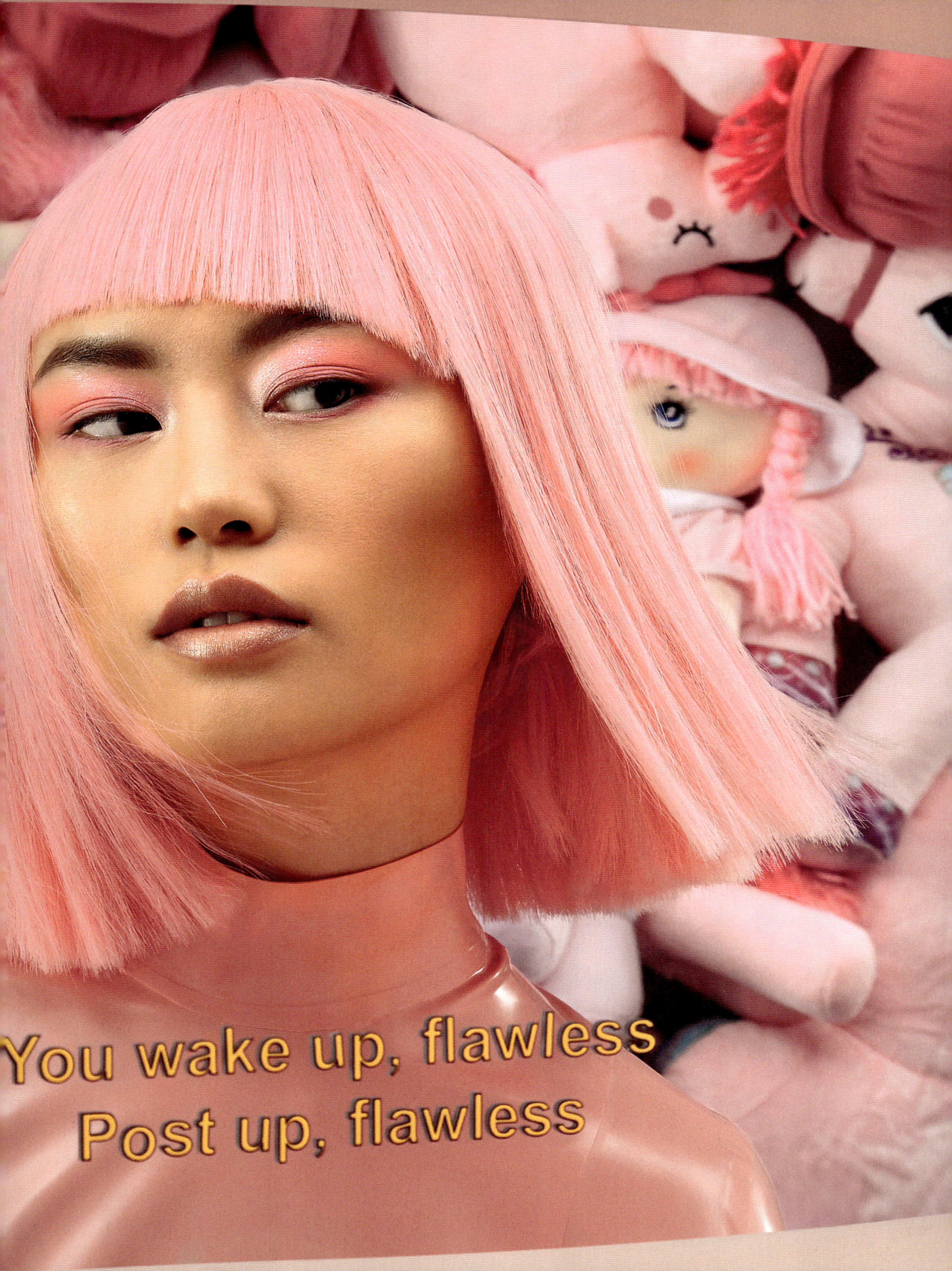
You wake up, flawless
Post up, flawless

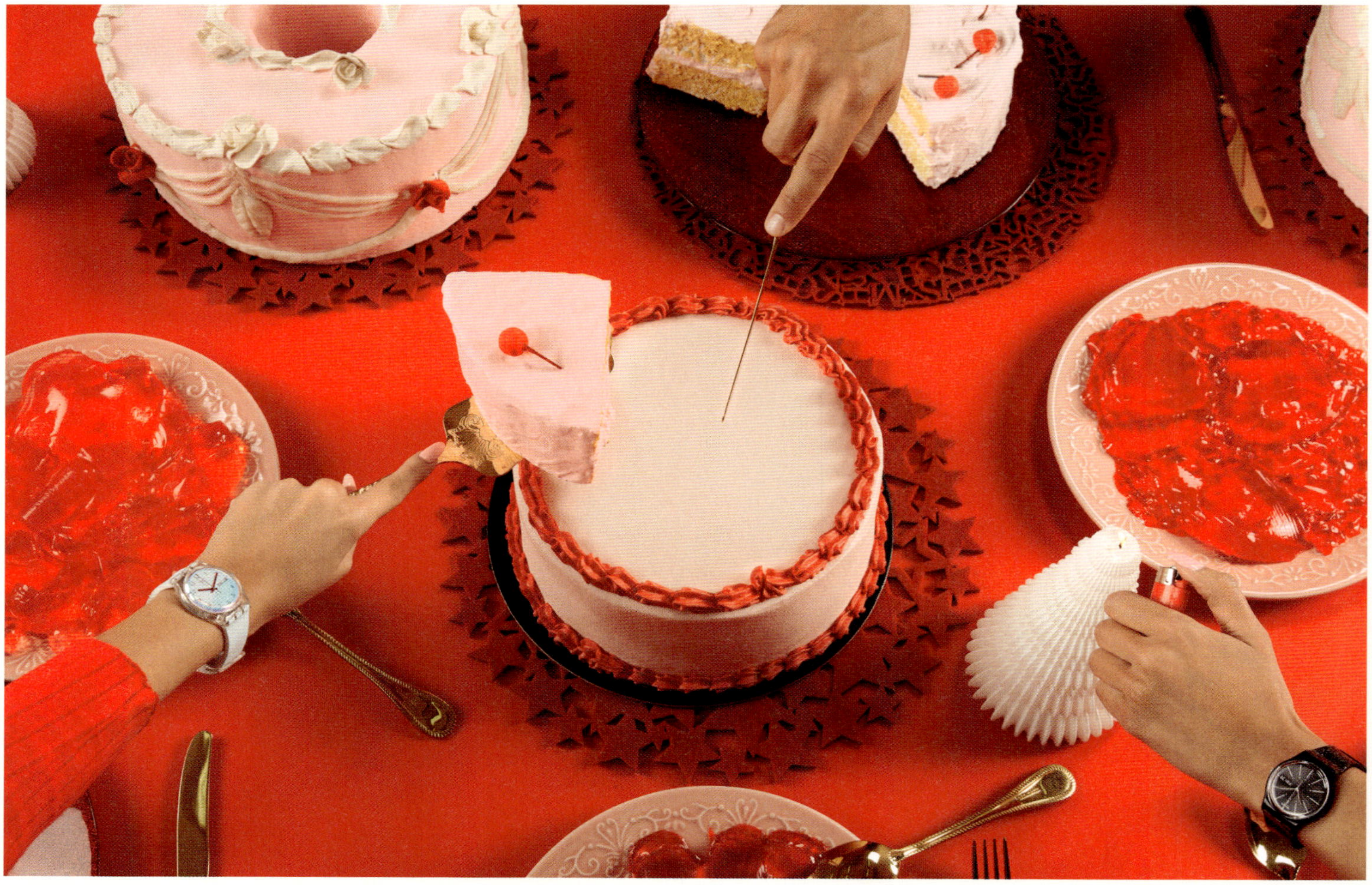

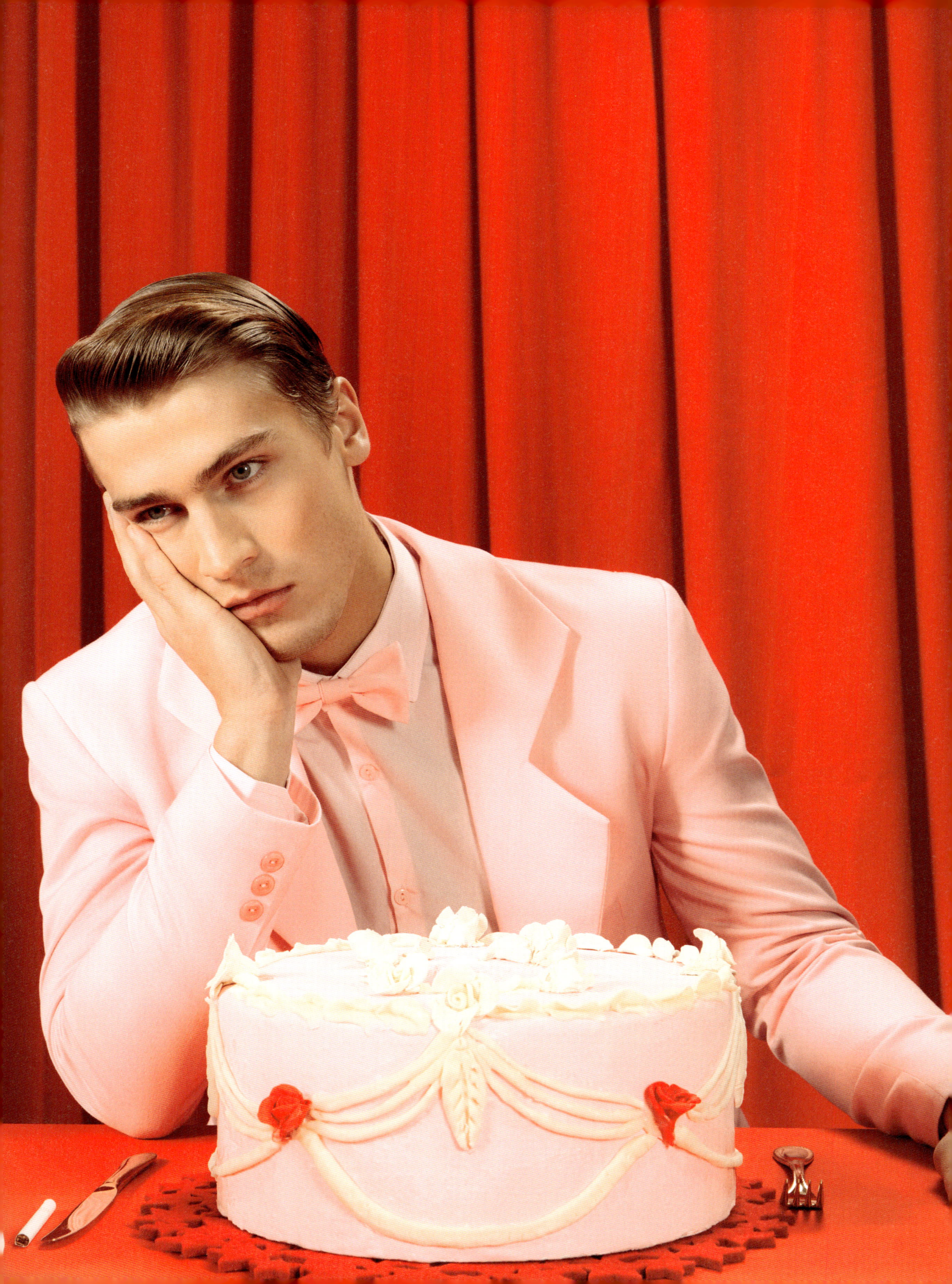

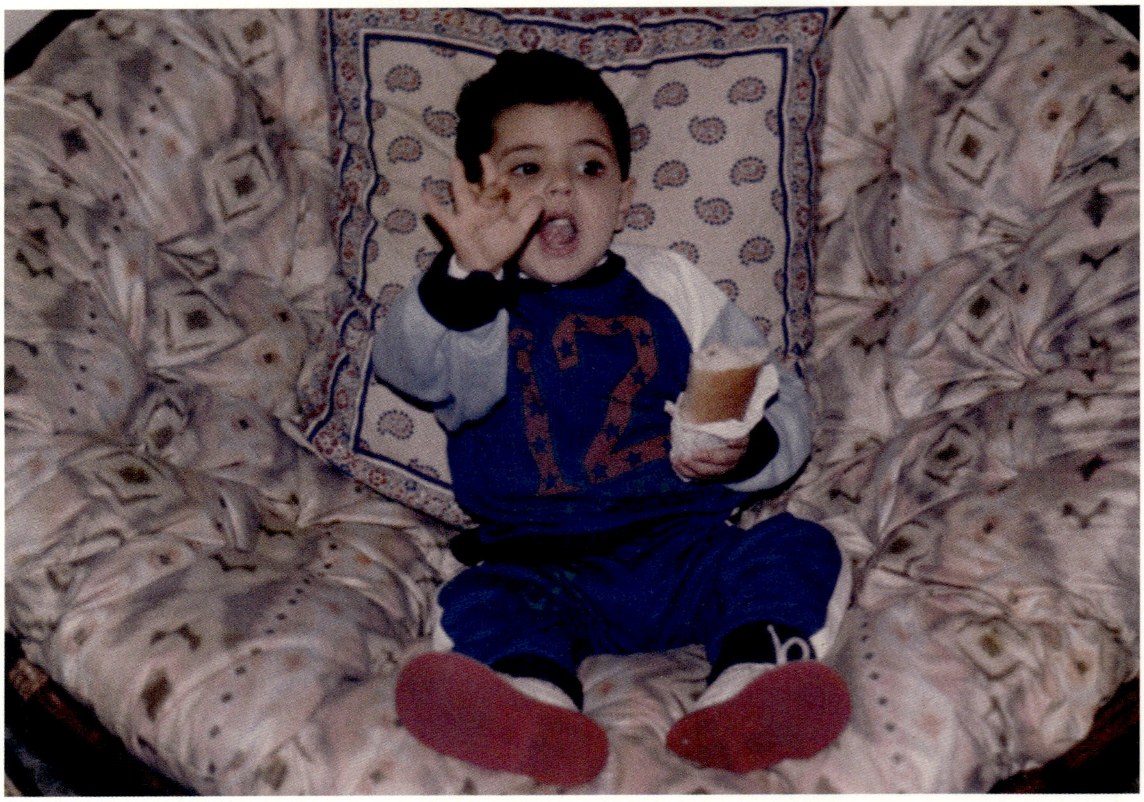

eli rezkallah, santa theresa playa, okaibe, lebanon, 1988.

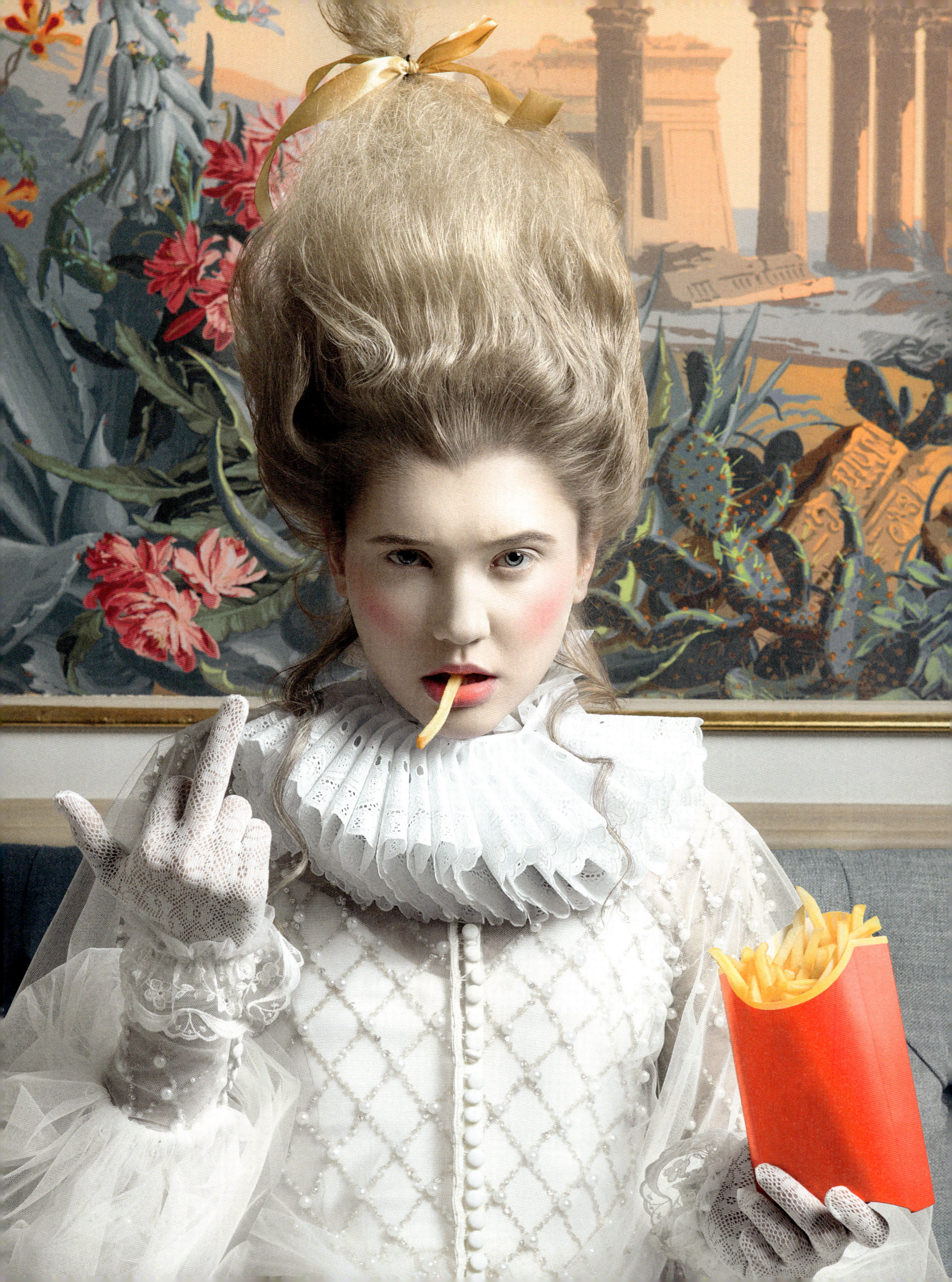

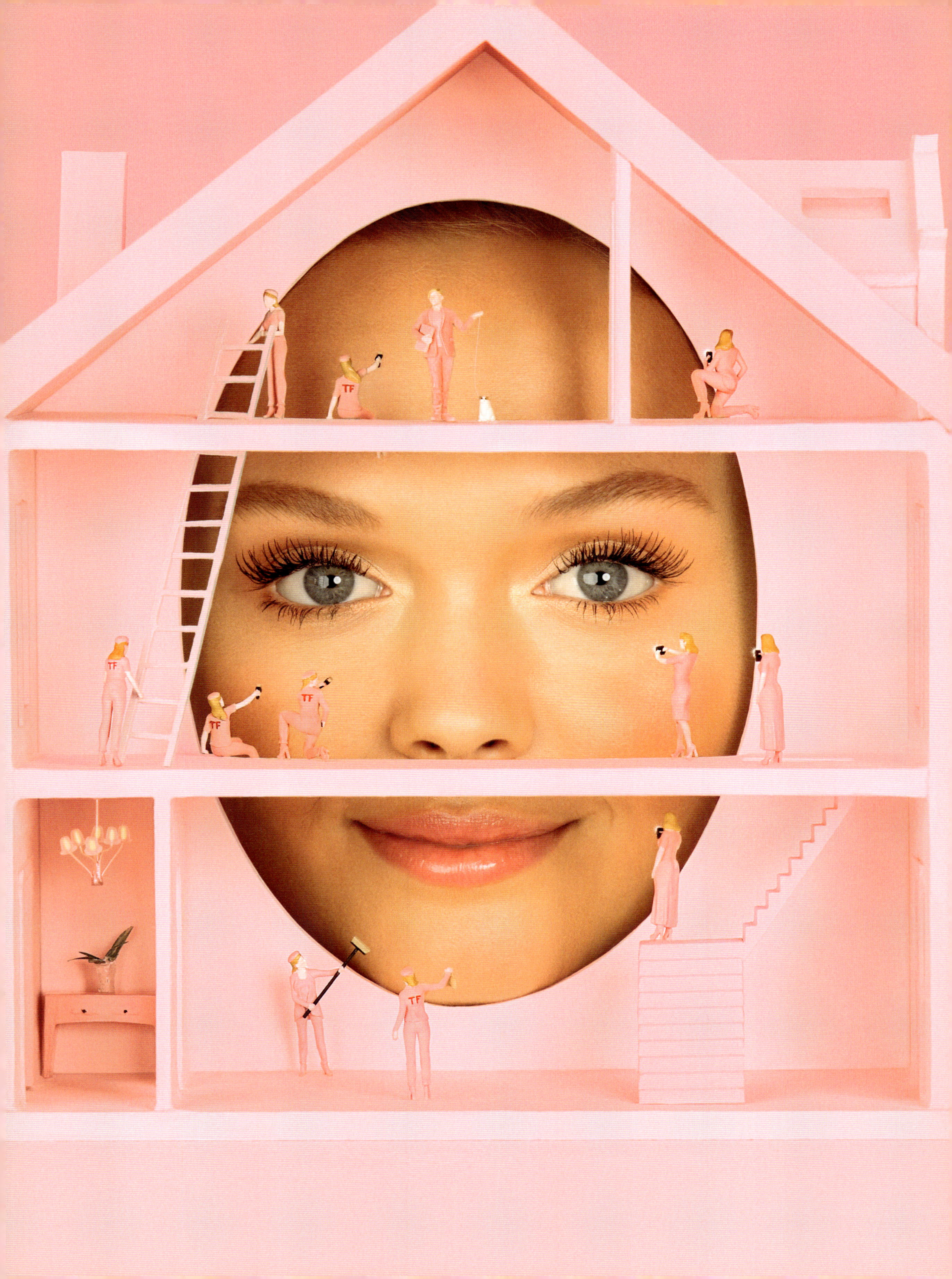

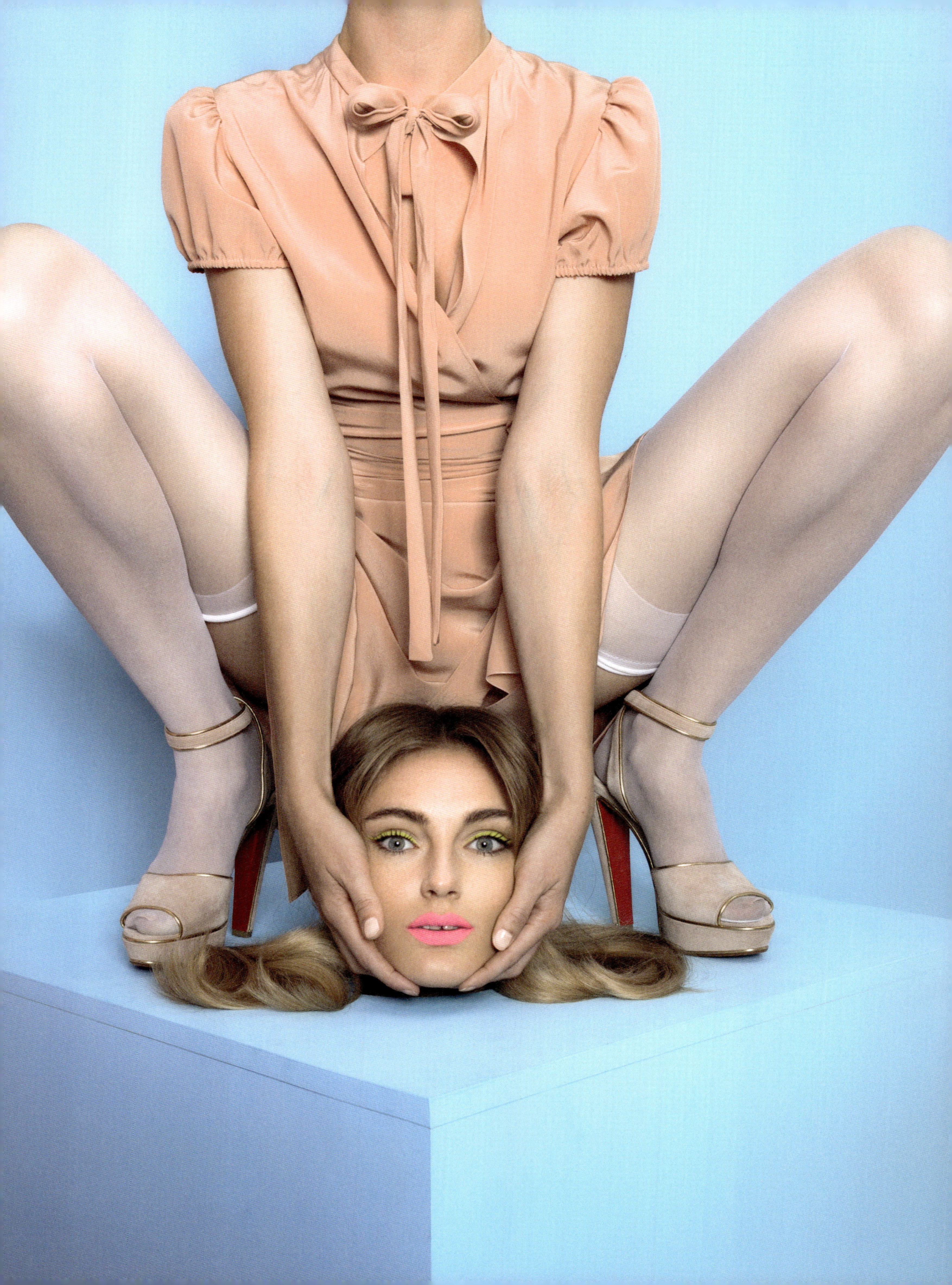

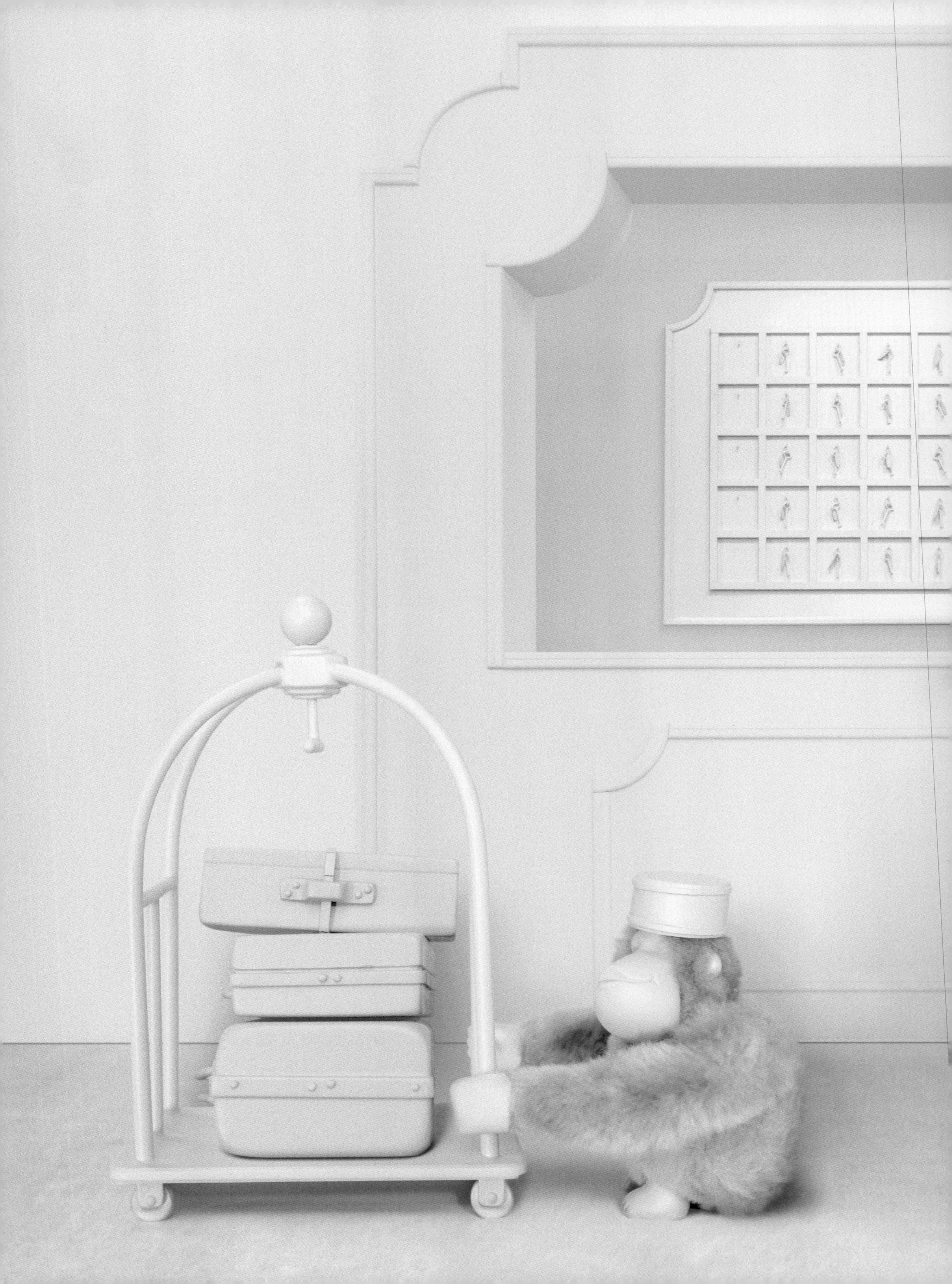

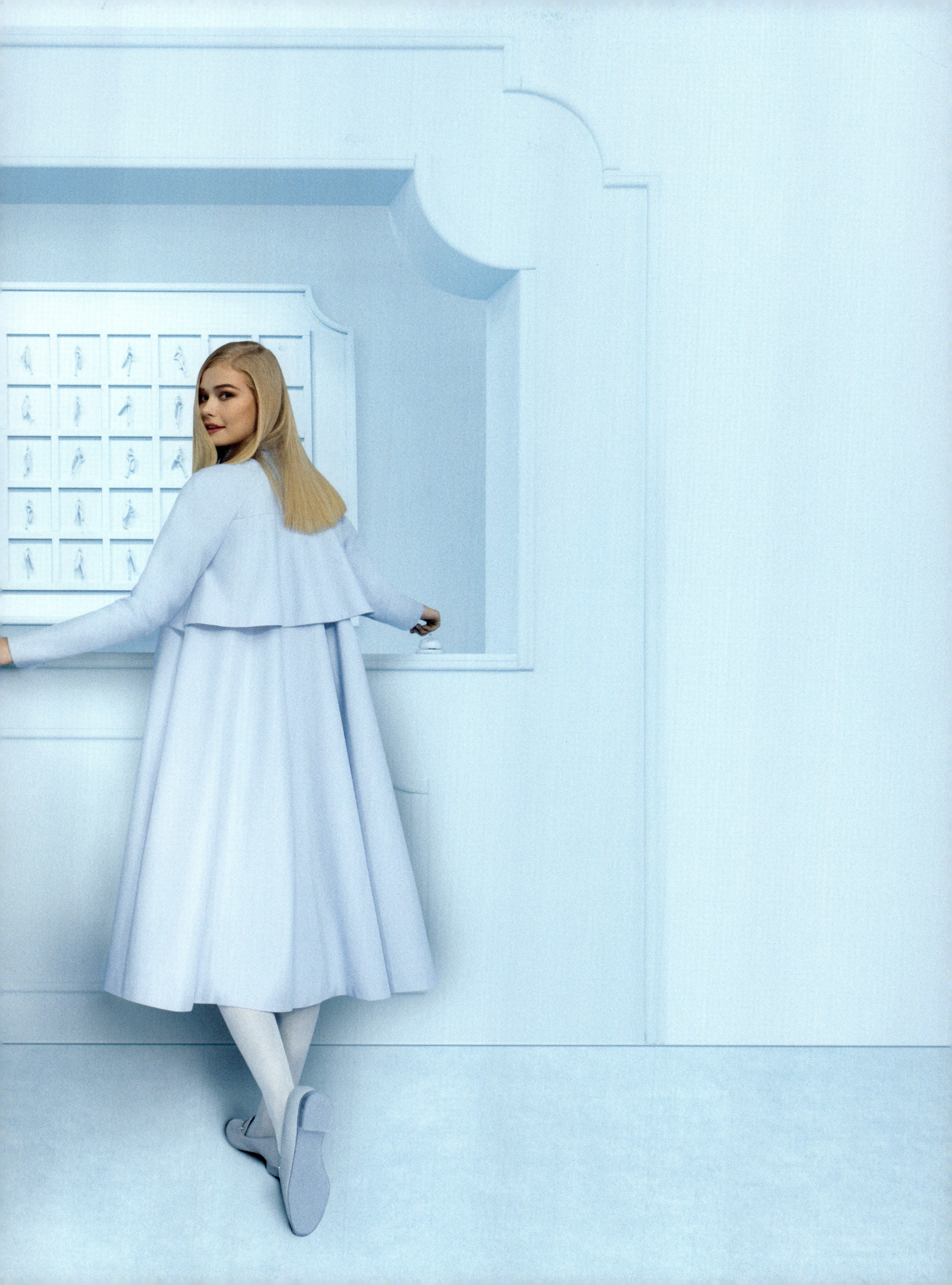

"I only became miserable when I became serious."

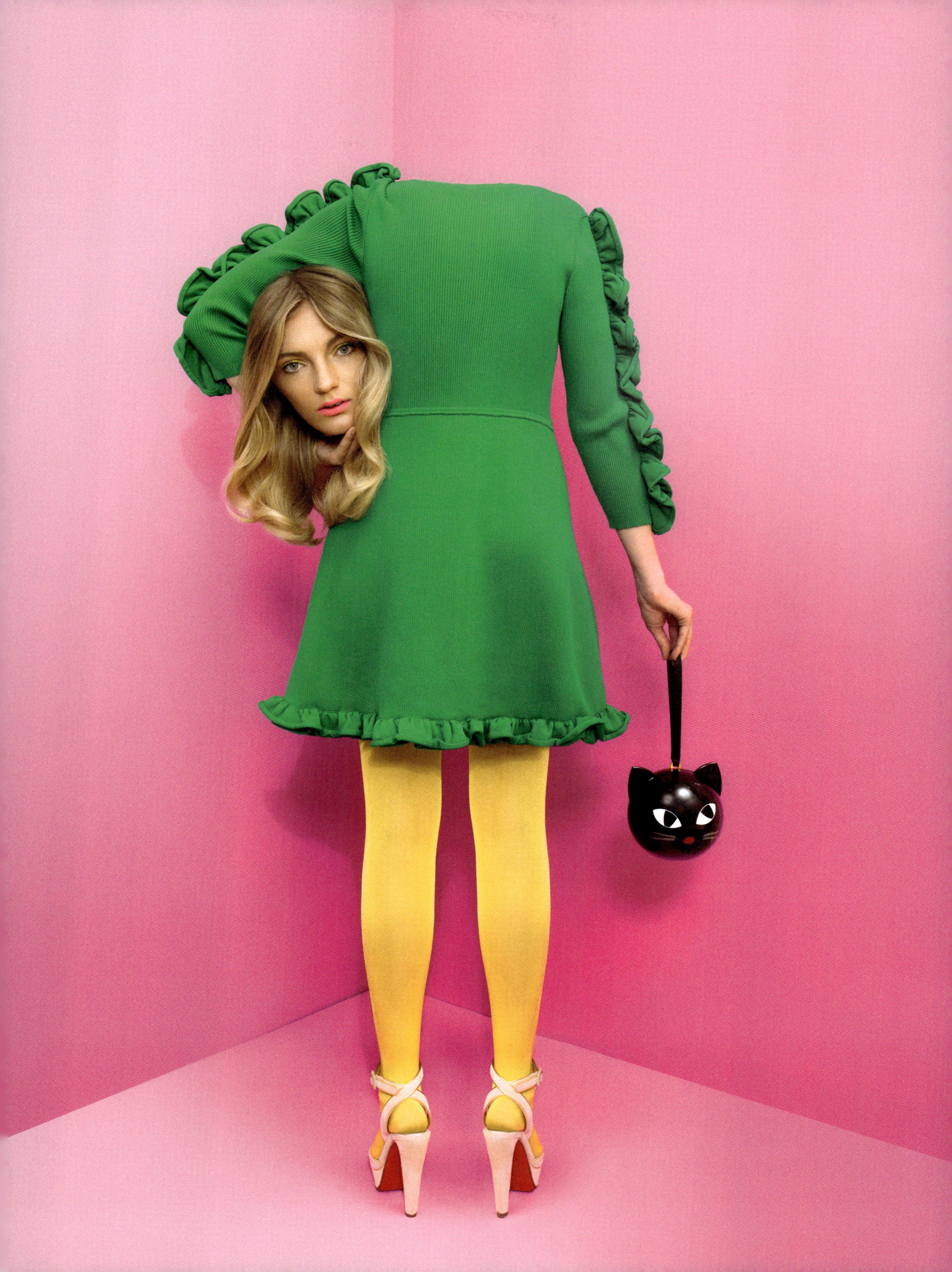

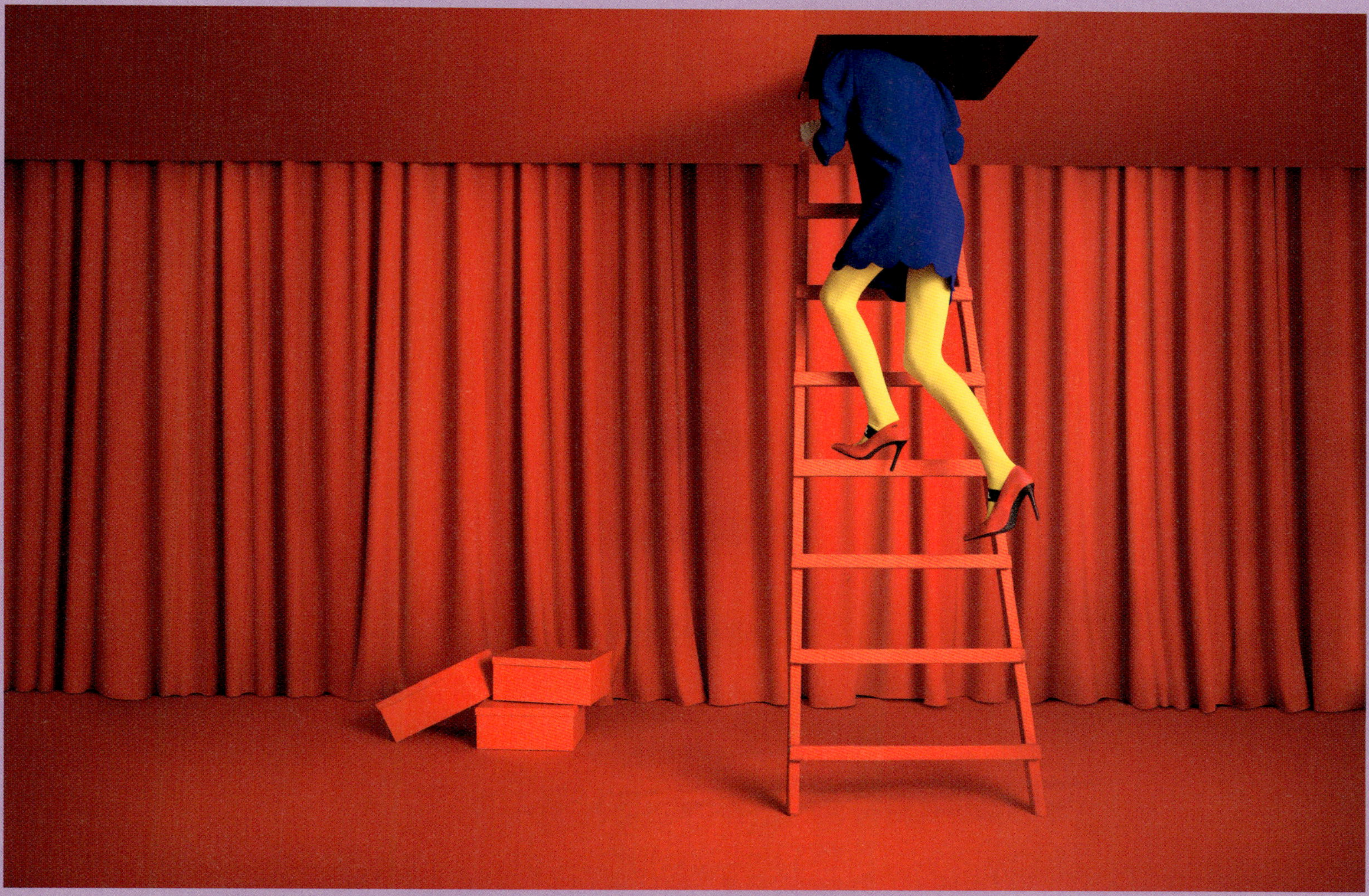

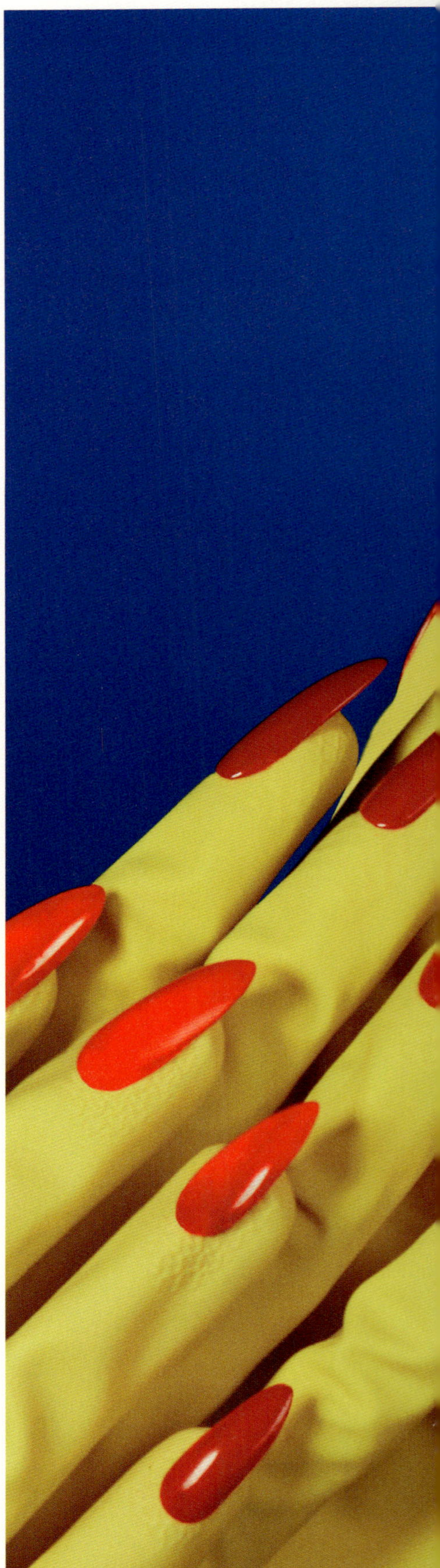

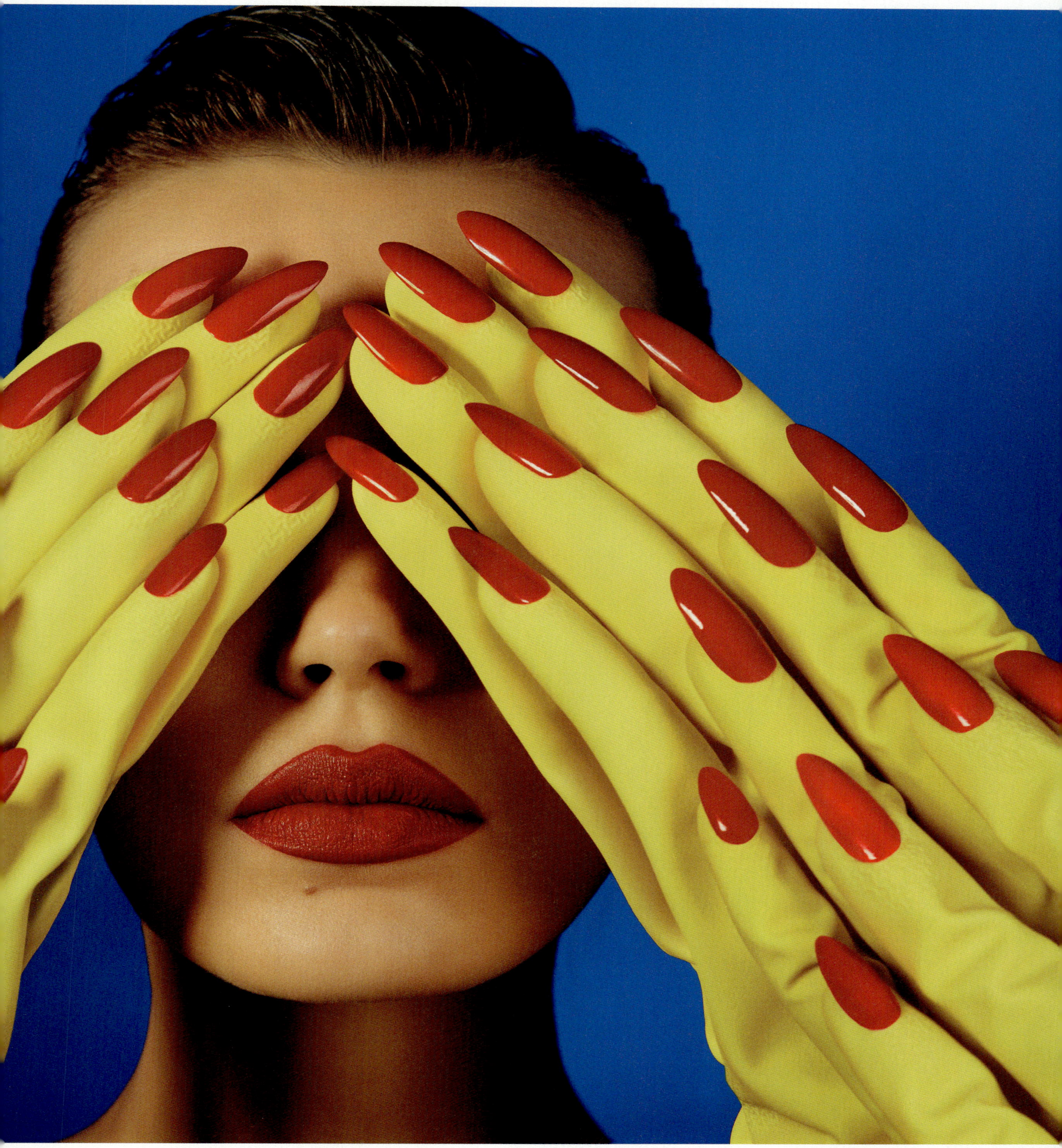

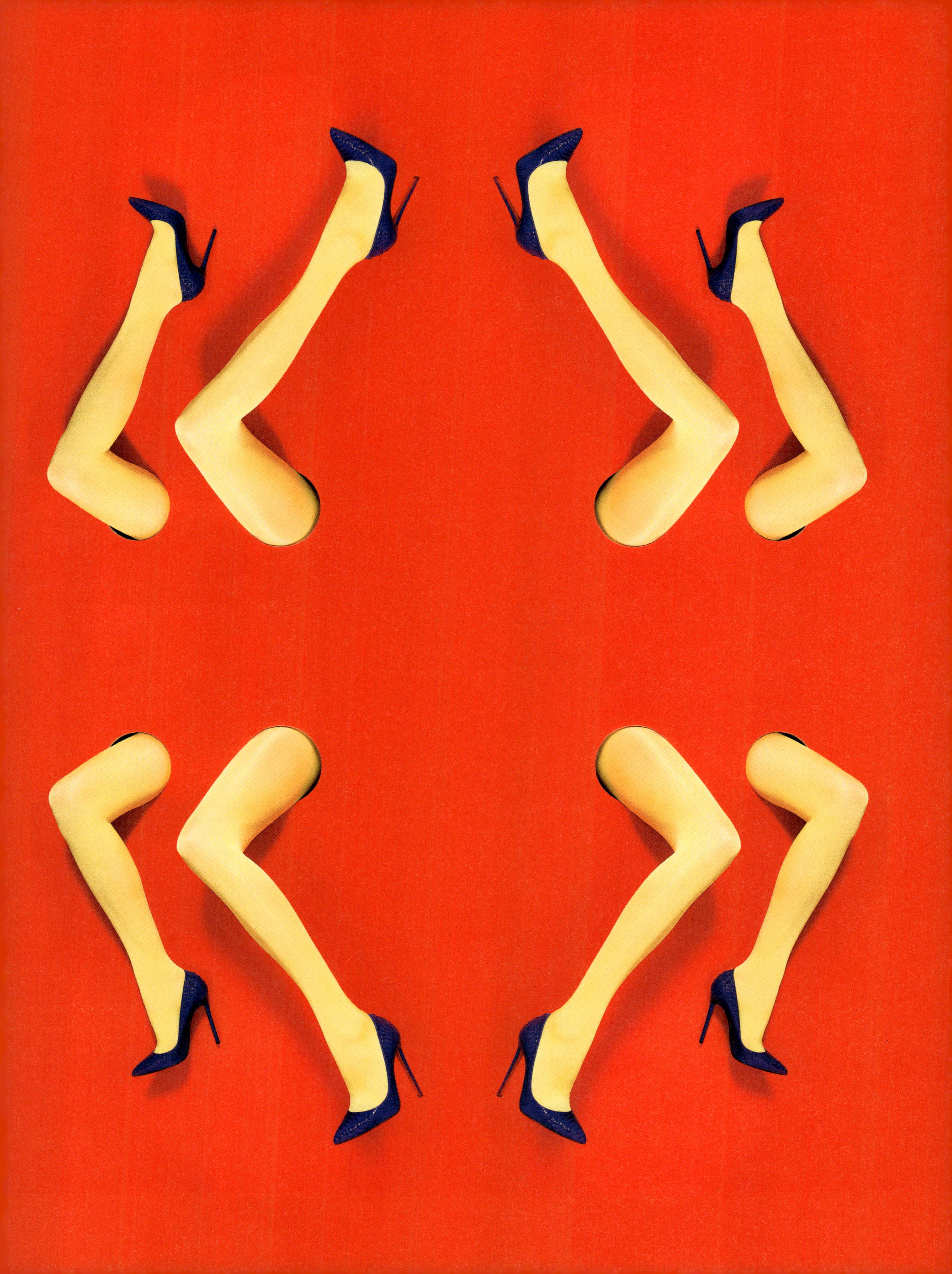

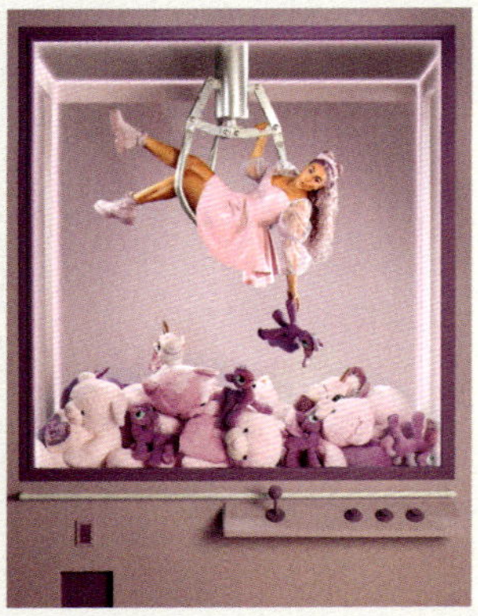

clawmachine, dubai, uae, huda beauty campaign, 2020.

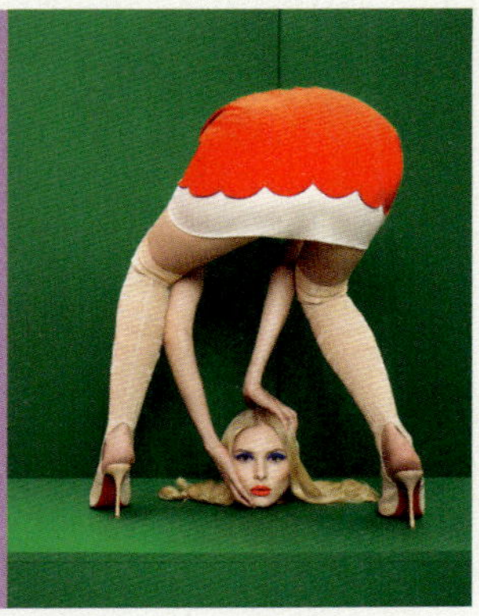

head over heels III, beirut, lebanon, *plastik* magazine, 2016.

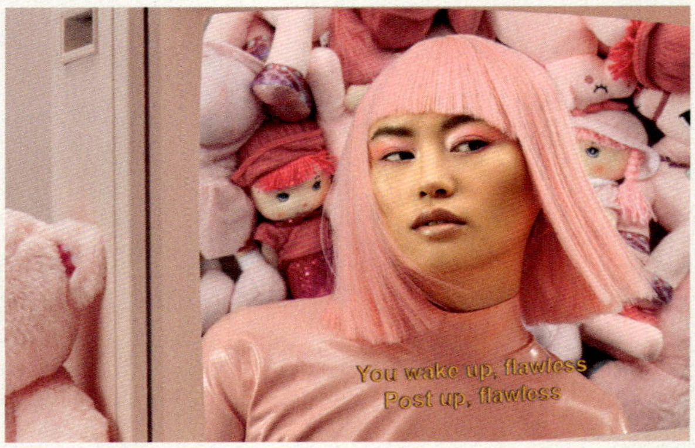

i woke up like this, dubai, uae,
huda beauty campaign, 2020.

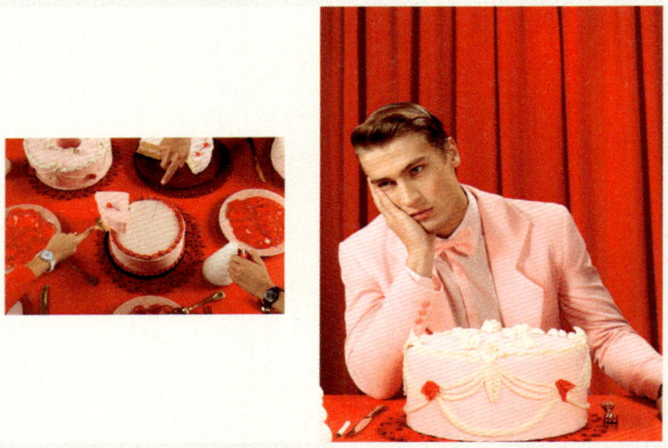

blond man with feelings, beirut, lebanon,
swatch campaign, 2019.

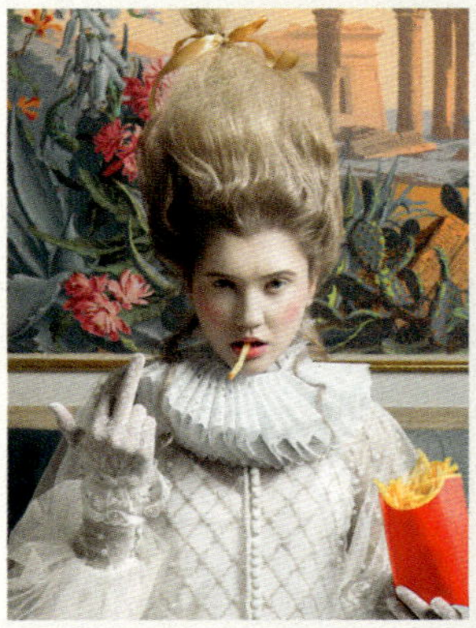

let them eat fries, beirut, lebanon, marzook campaign, 2015.

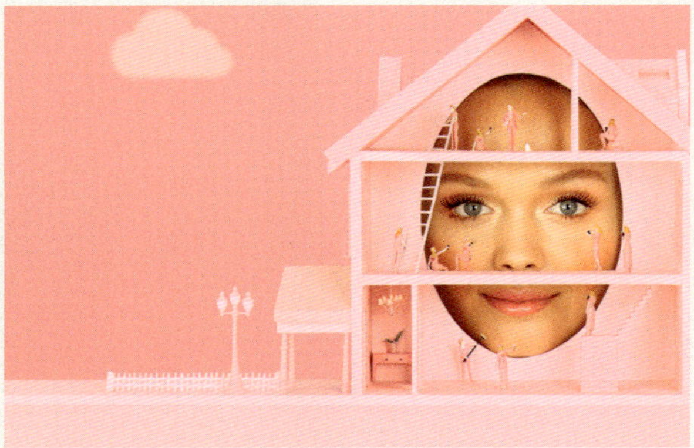

dollface, los angeles, usa, too faced campaign, 2019.

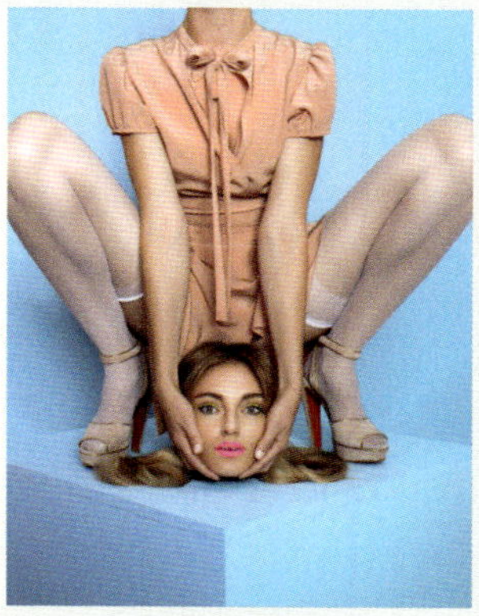

head over heels IV, beirut, lebanon, *plastik* magazine, 2016.

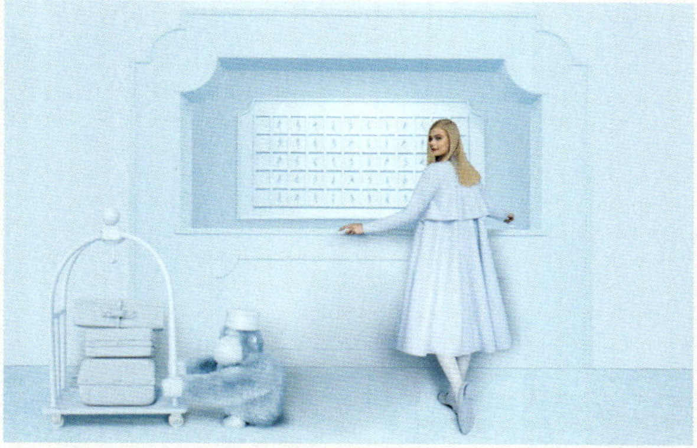

check-in, beirut, lebanon, kipling campaign, 2016.

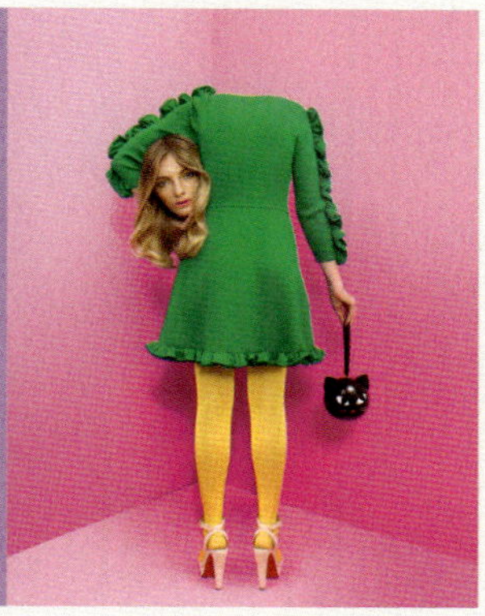

head over heels II, beirut, lebanon, *plastik* magazine, 2016.

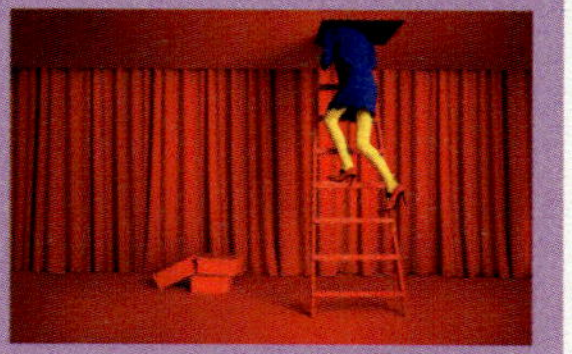

bedroom, beirut, lebanon, ABC campaign, 2018.

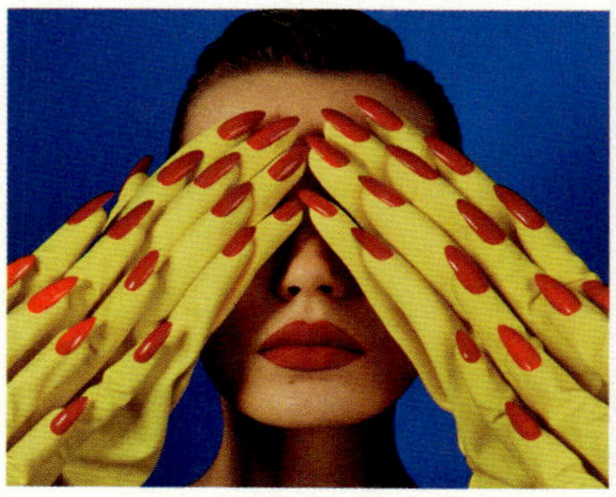

my quarantine diaries, beirut, lebanon, *plastik* magazine, 2020.

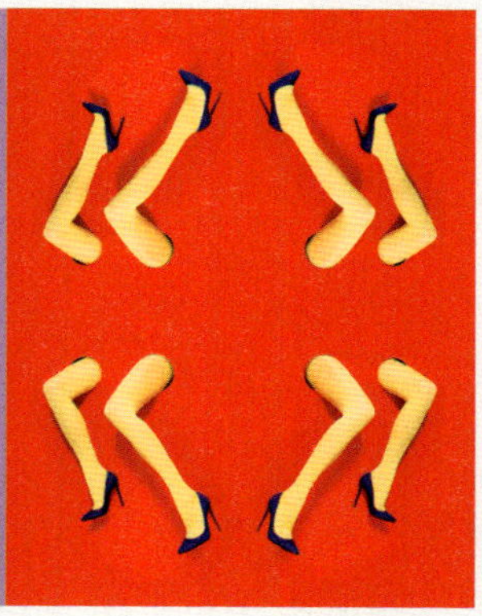

legs for days, beirut, lebanon,
christian louboutin campaign, 2014.

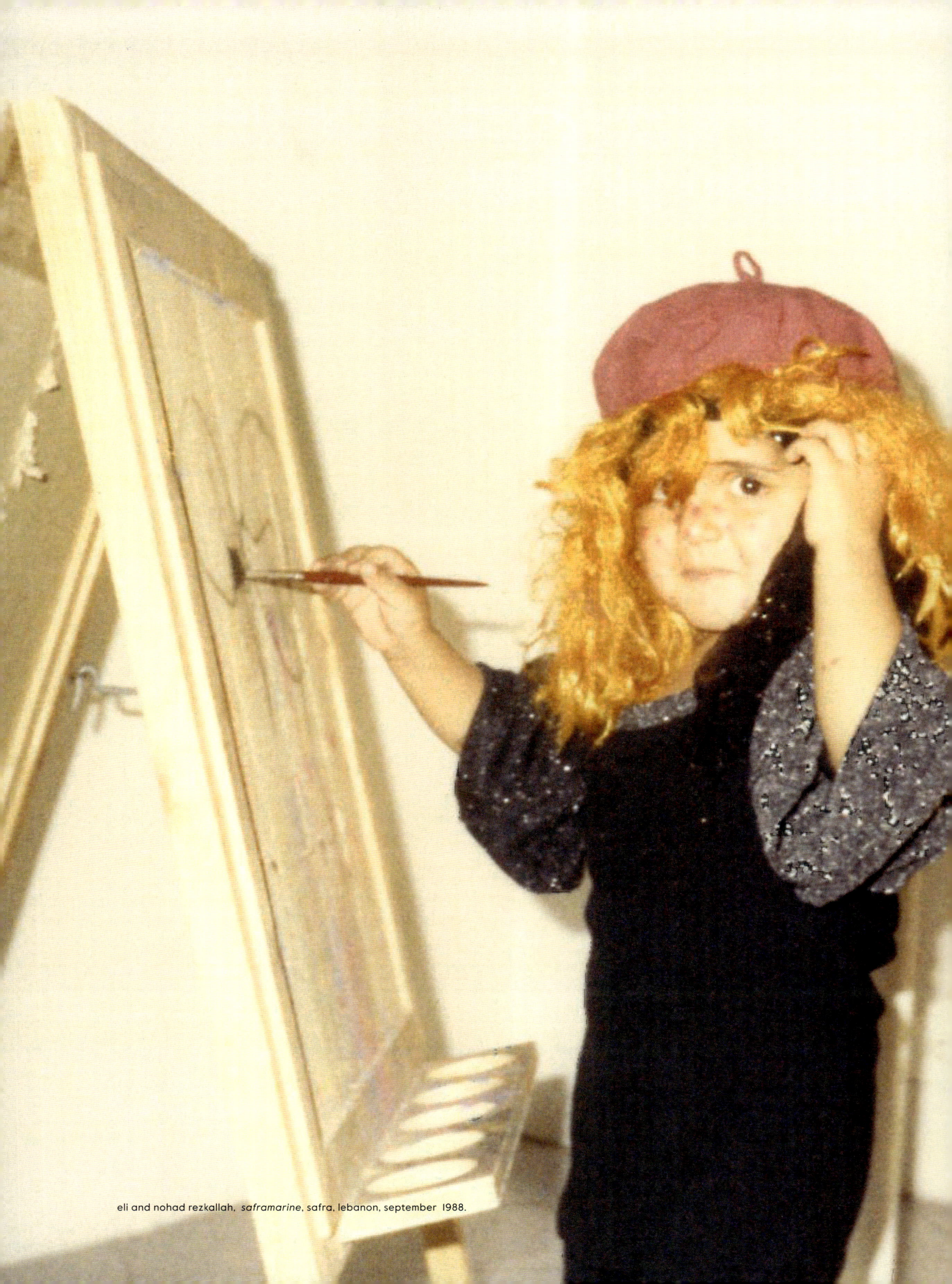

eli and nohad rezkallah, *saframarine*, safra, lebanon, september 1988.

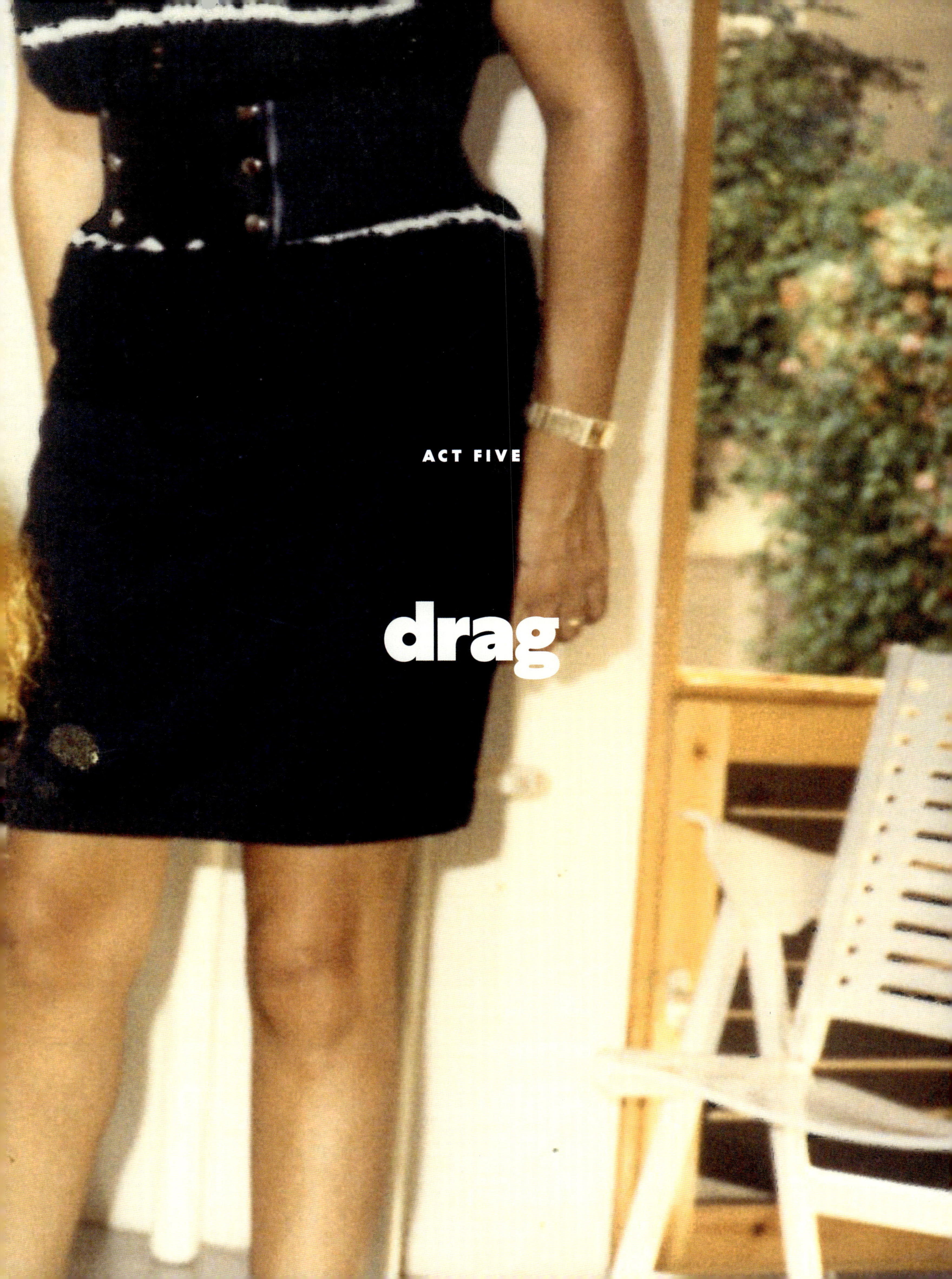

ACT FIVE

drag

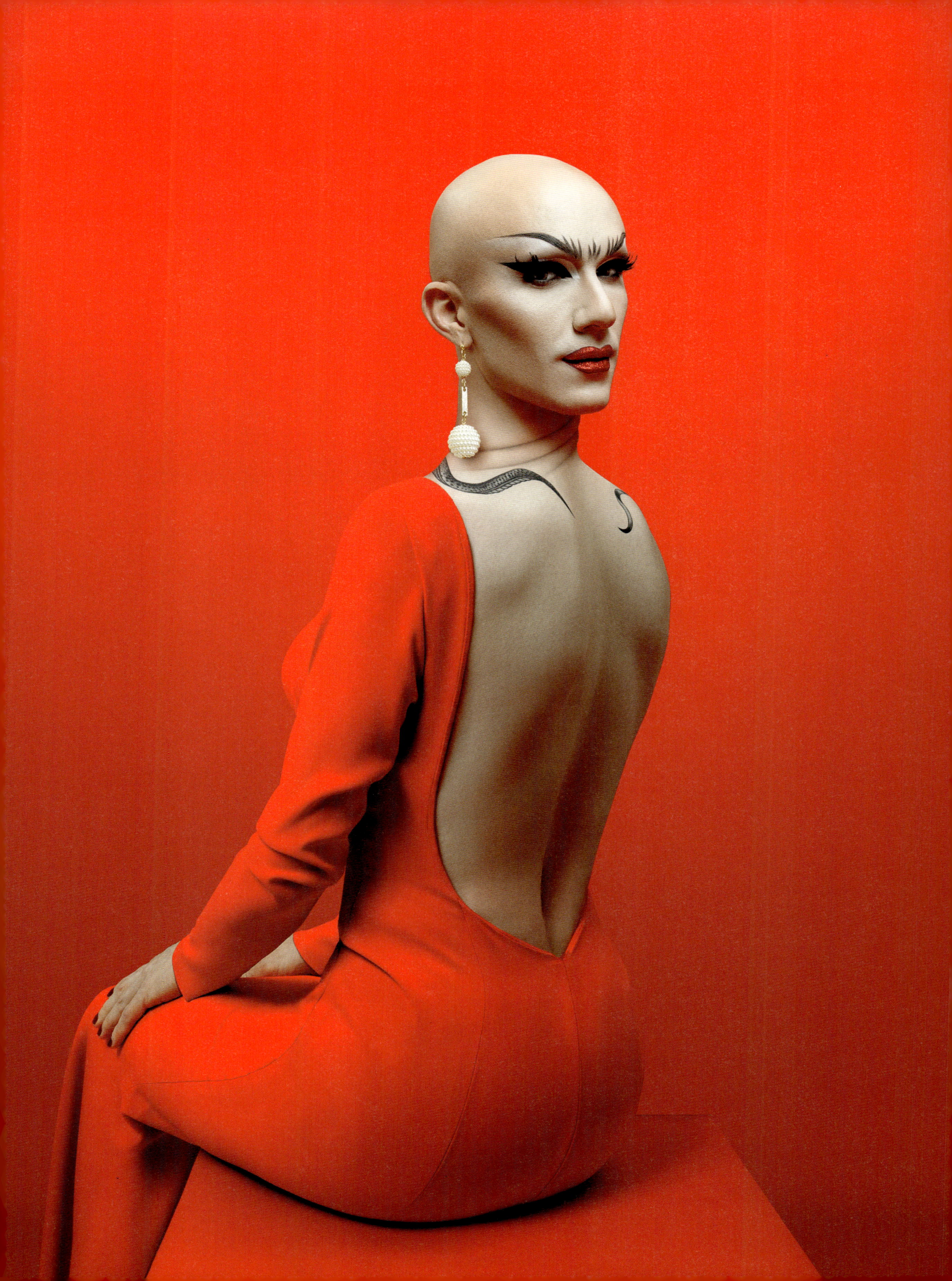

One of the most striking parallels in Rezkallah's body of work is the art of drag: colorful, extravagant, and playful illusions stemming from the heart and soul of societal renegades. To him, drag is synonymous with wonderment, living on the edge, and the opening of doors to countless possibilities by challenging social constructs and gender norms.

There's a mystical quality to his drag subjects, often depicted as untouchable deities, sometimes as disjointed/beheaded creatures. To Rezkallah, the illusion of drag goes beyond gender. Drag is a heightened means of expression, where insecurities are fodder for creativity and social archetypes are rightfully challenged; in other words, a perfect way to render broader concepts personal.

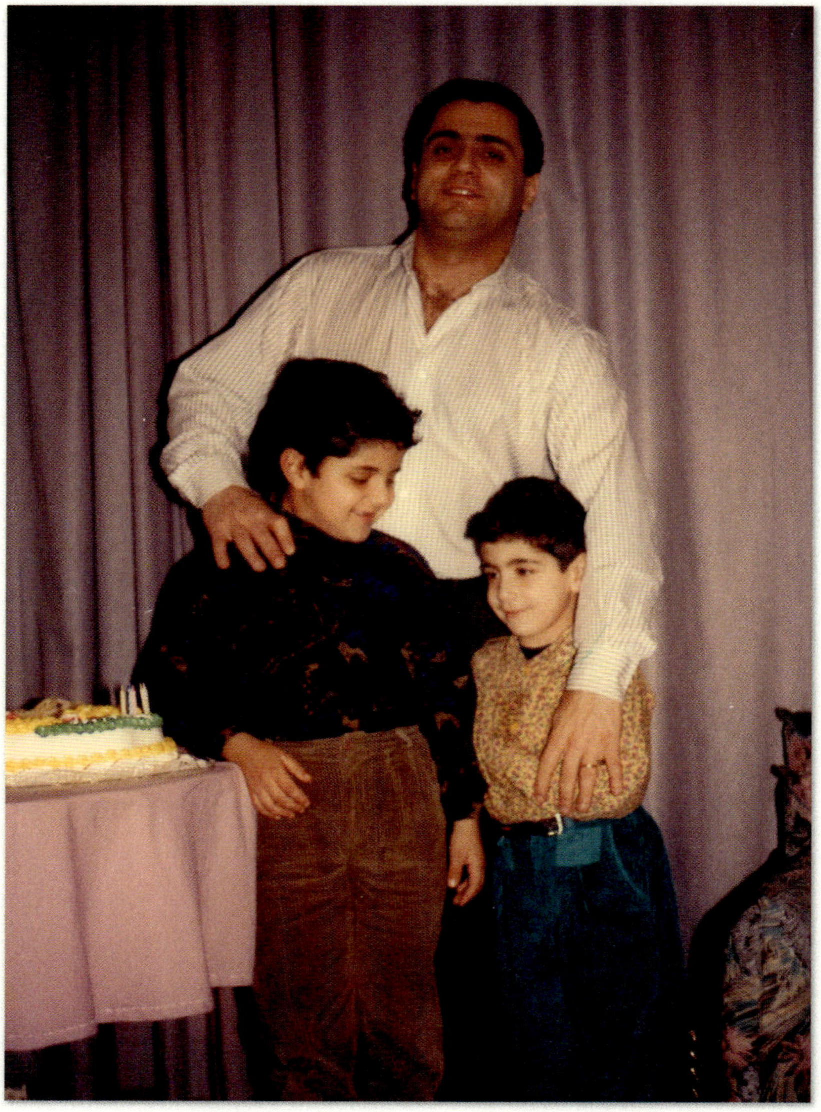

thomas, eli and rami rezkallah, santa theresa playa, okaibe, lebanon, february 1993.

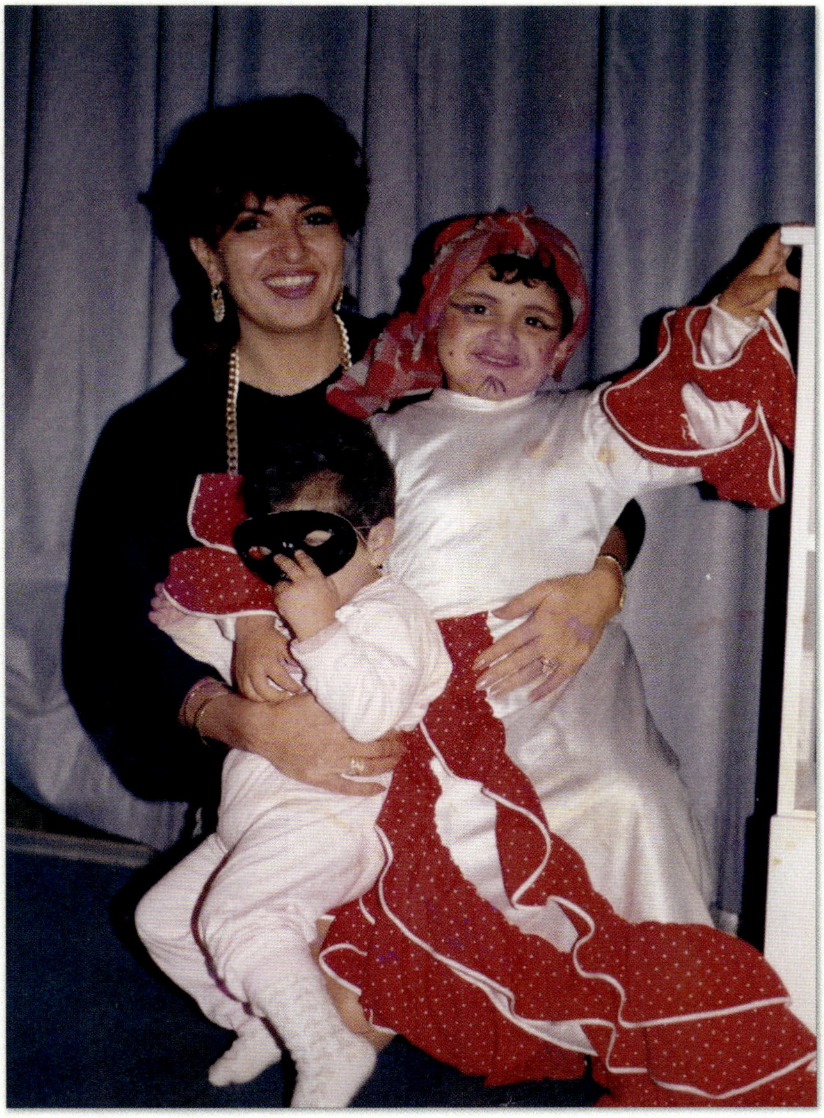

nohad, rami and eli rezkallah, santa theresa playa, okaibe, lebanon, december 1989.

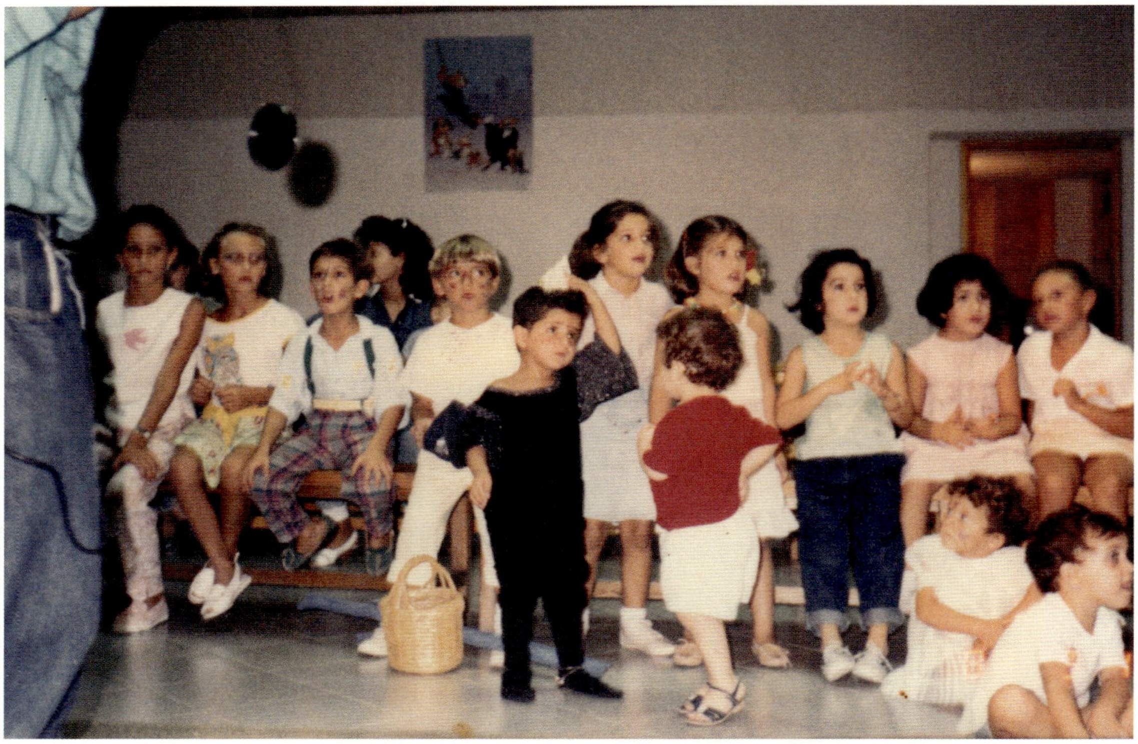

eli rezkallah, saframarine, safra, lebanon, september 1988.

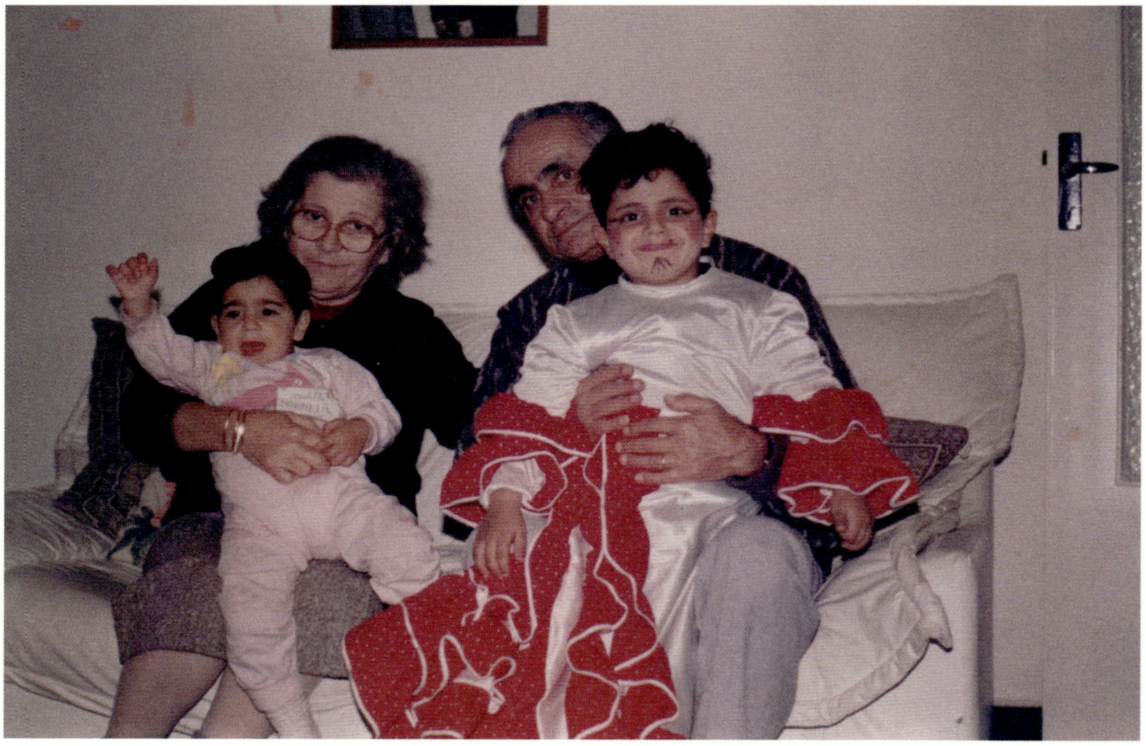

rami and eli rezkallah with their grandparents souad and elia rezkallah, santa theresa playa, okaibe, lebanon, december 1989.

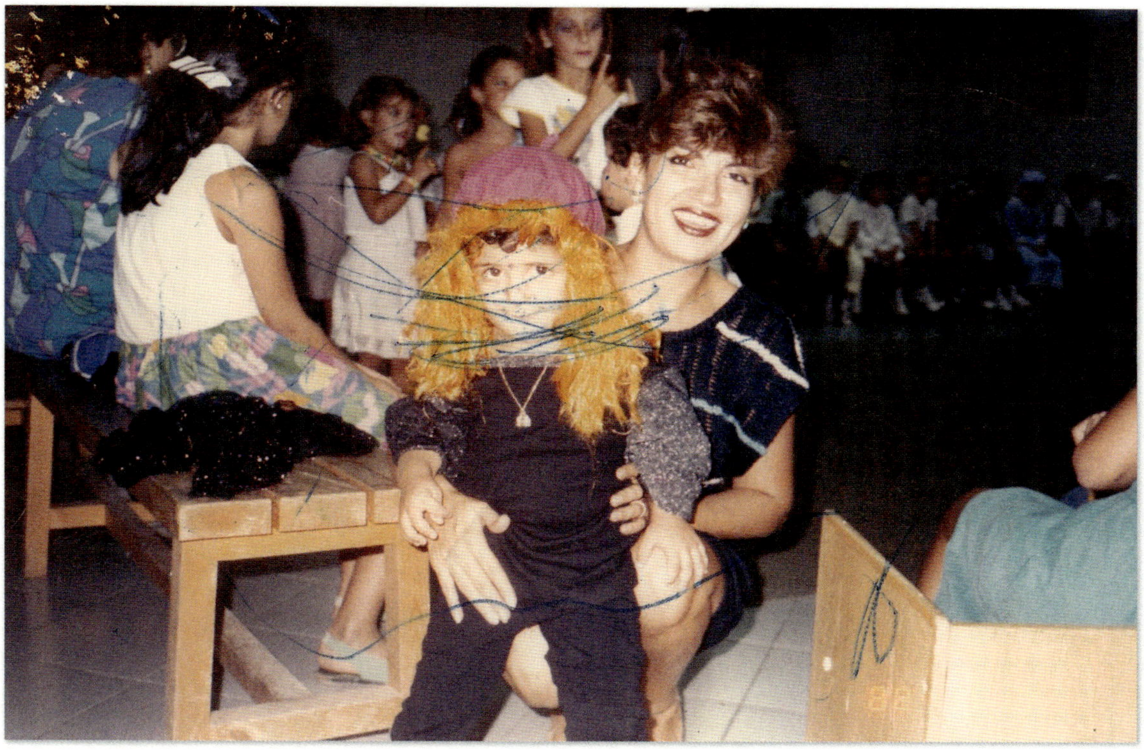

nohad and eli rezkallah, saframarine, safra, lebanon, september 1988.

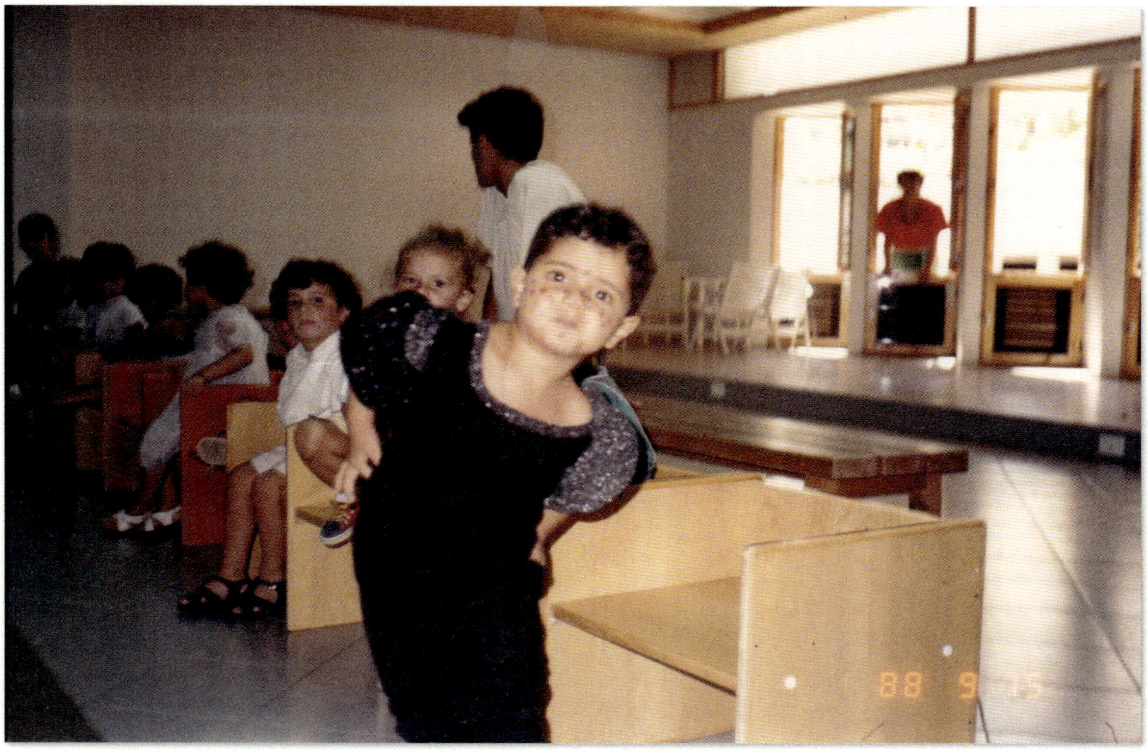

eli rezkallah, saframarine, safra, lebanon, september 1988.

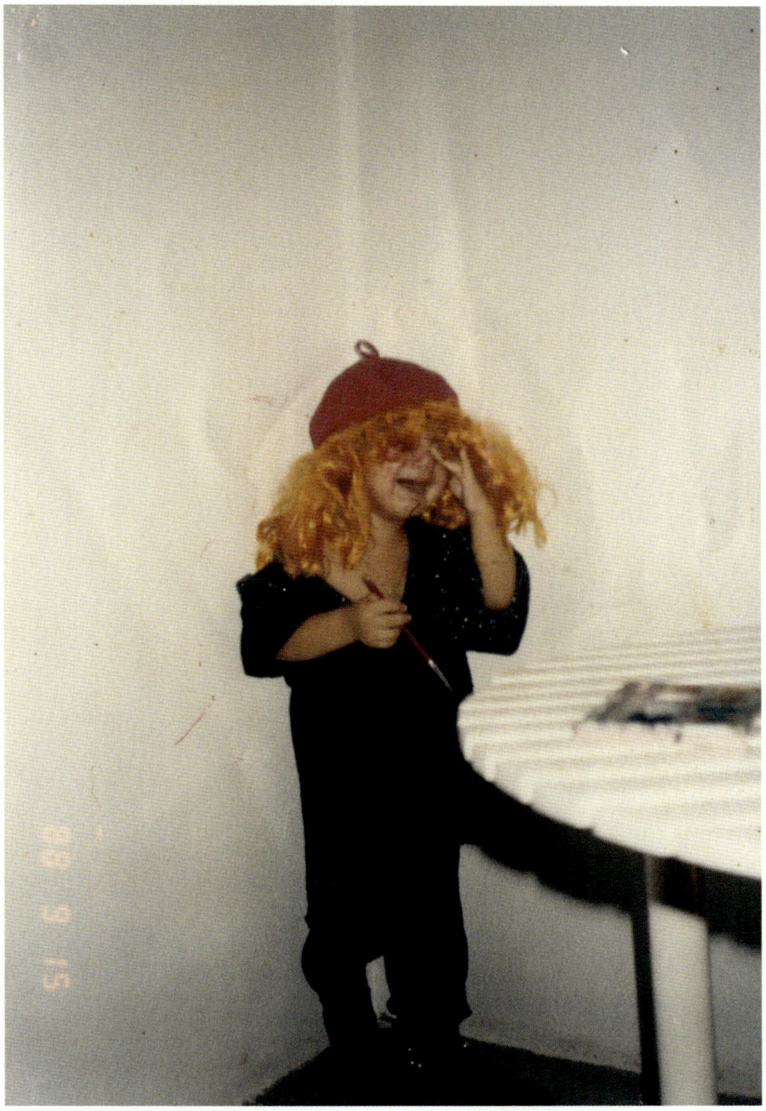

eli rezkallah, saframarine, safra, lebanon, september 1988.

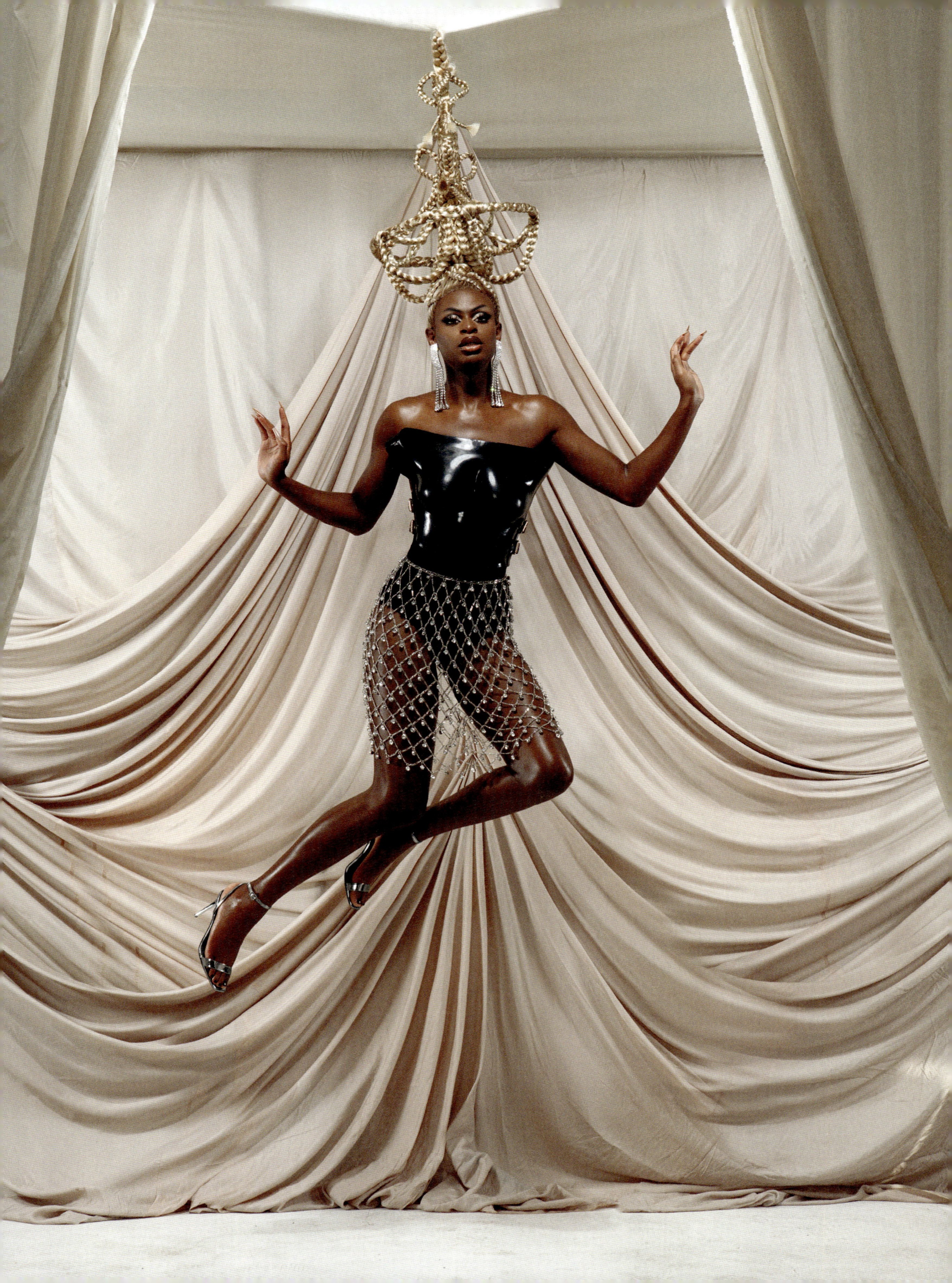

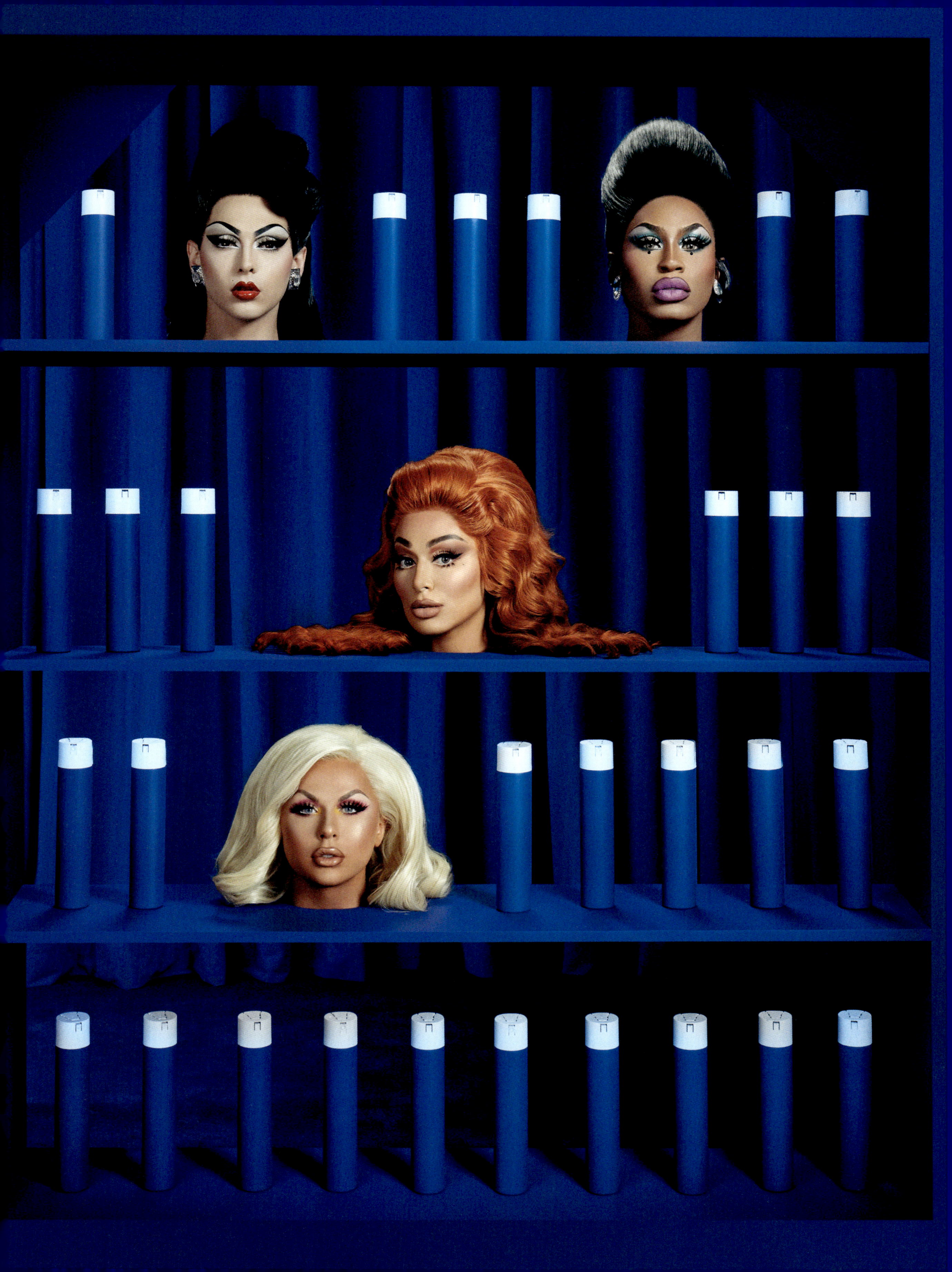

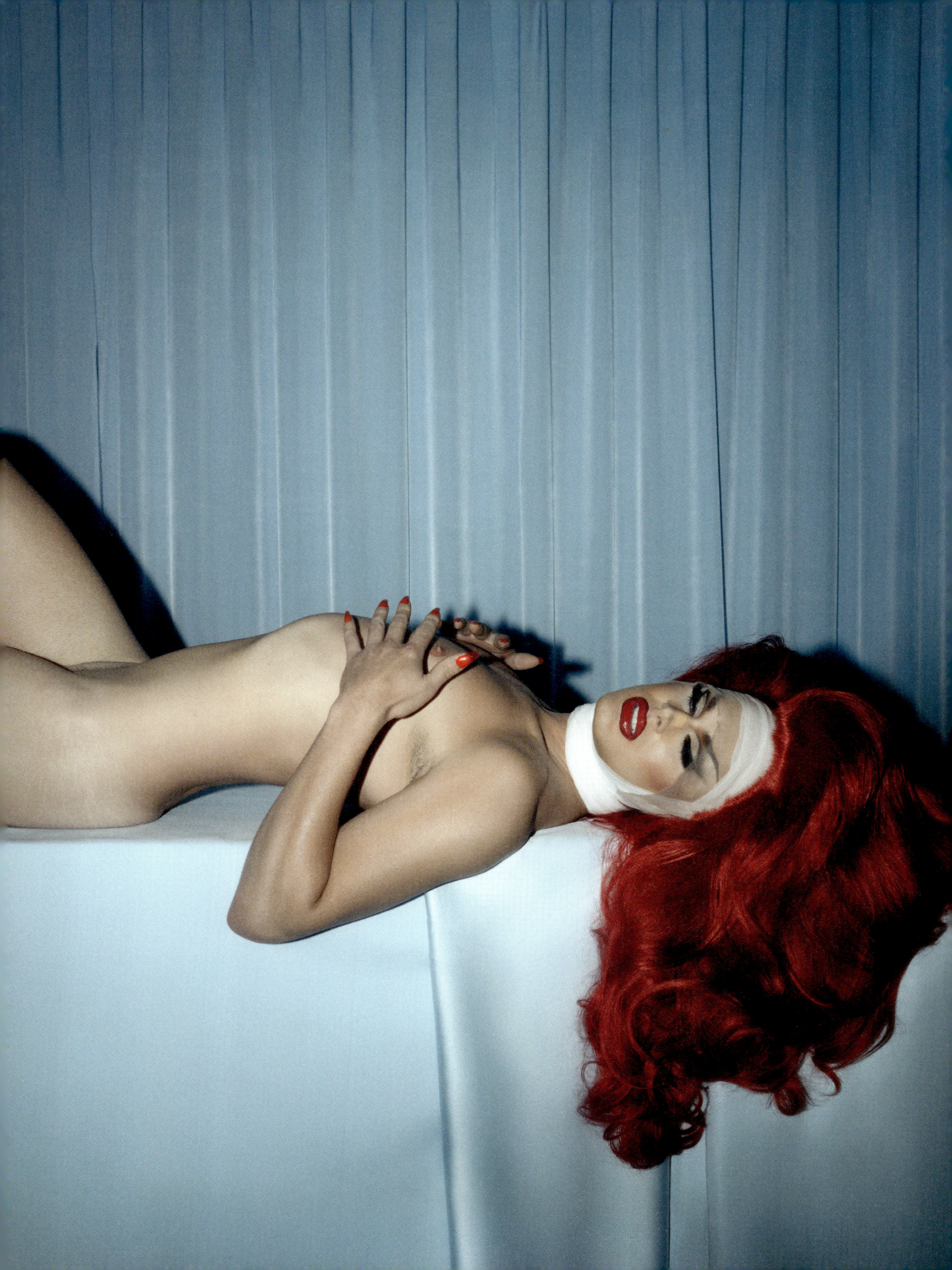

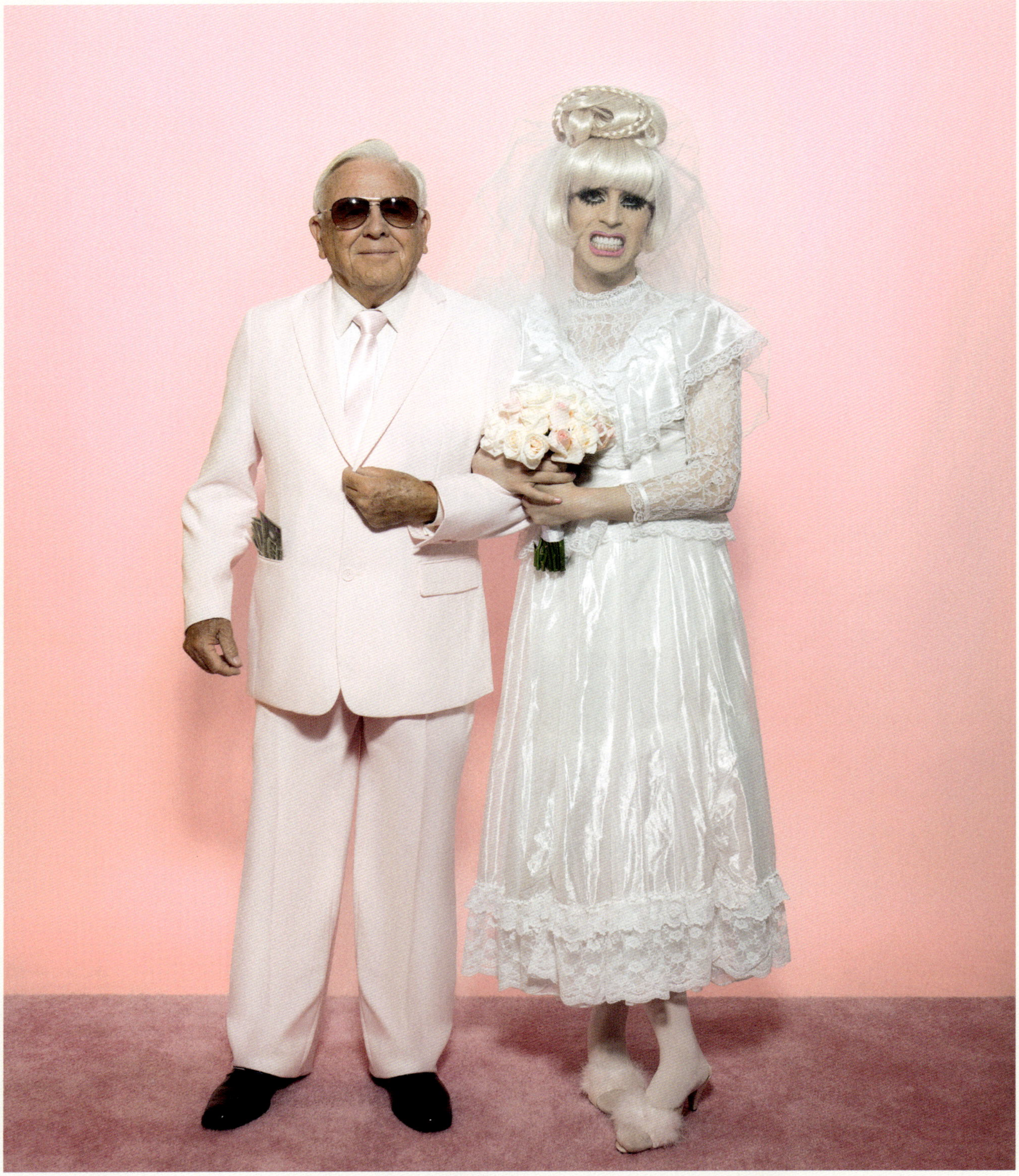

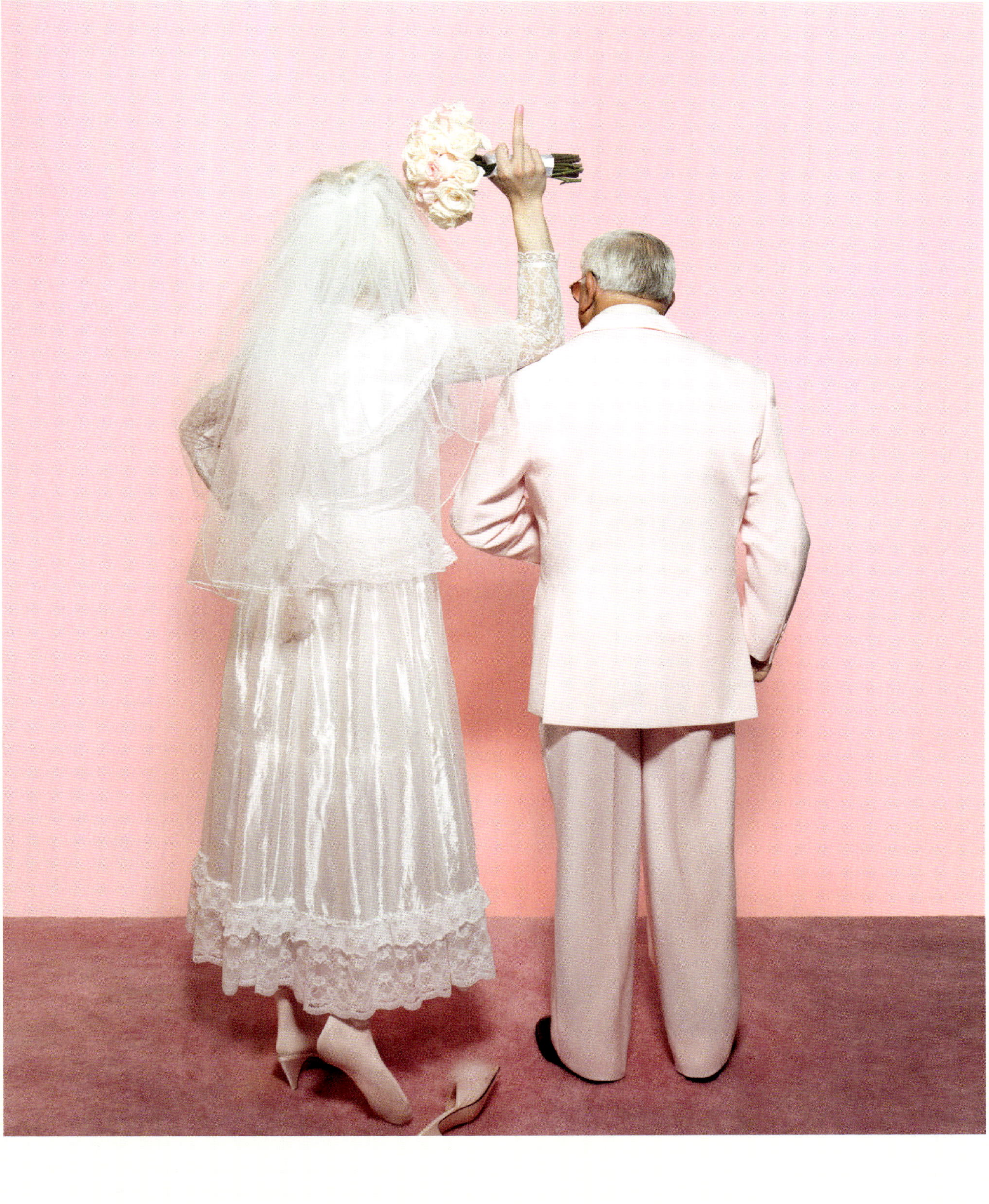

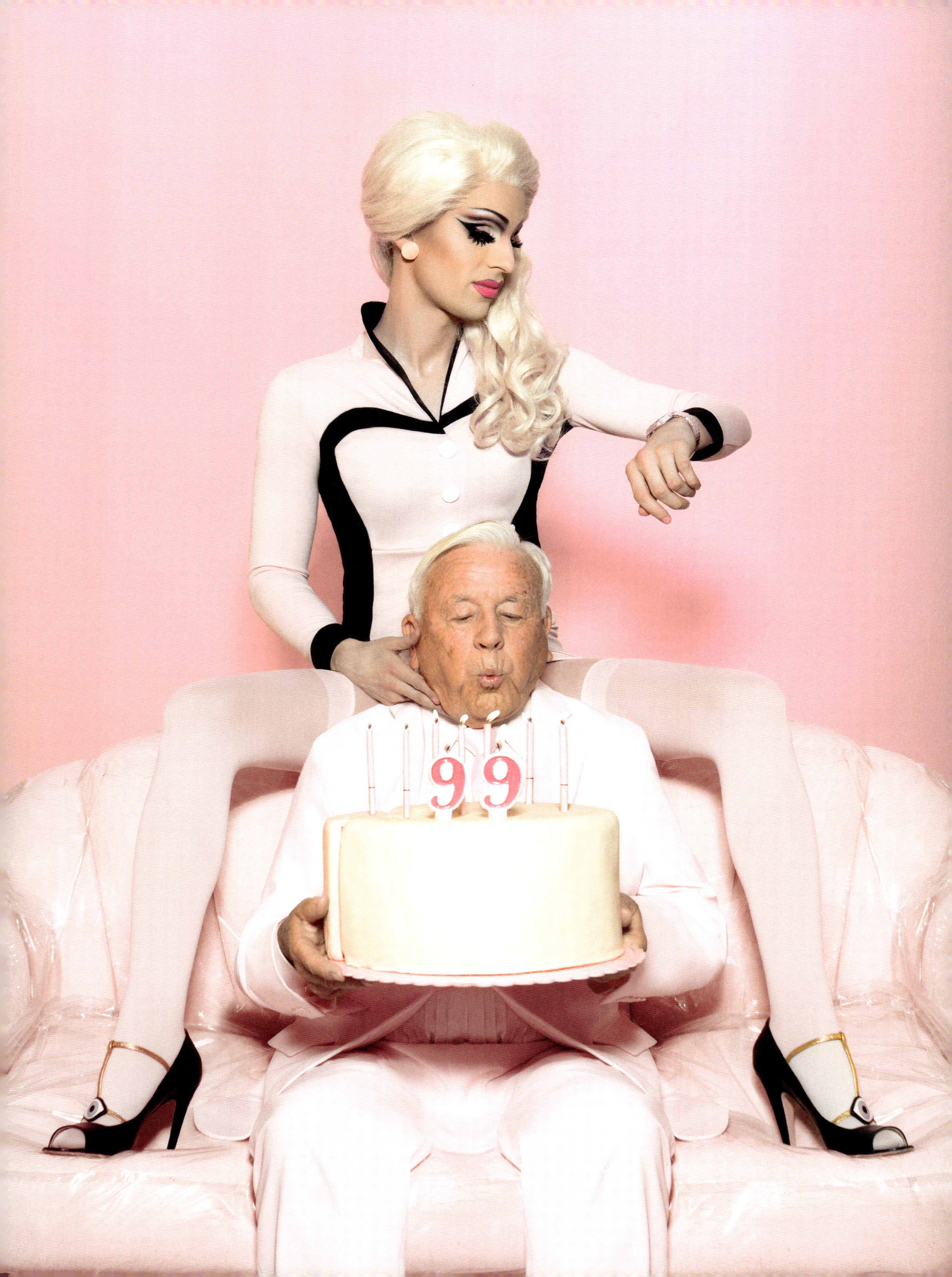
99

"When there's a drag queen in the room, everyone is on edge. There is a tension in the air mixed with a bit of excitement and magic."

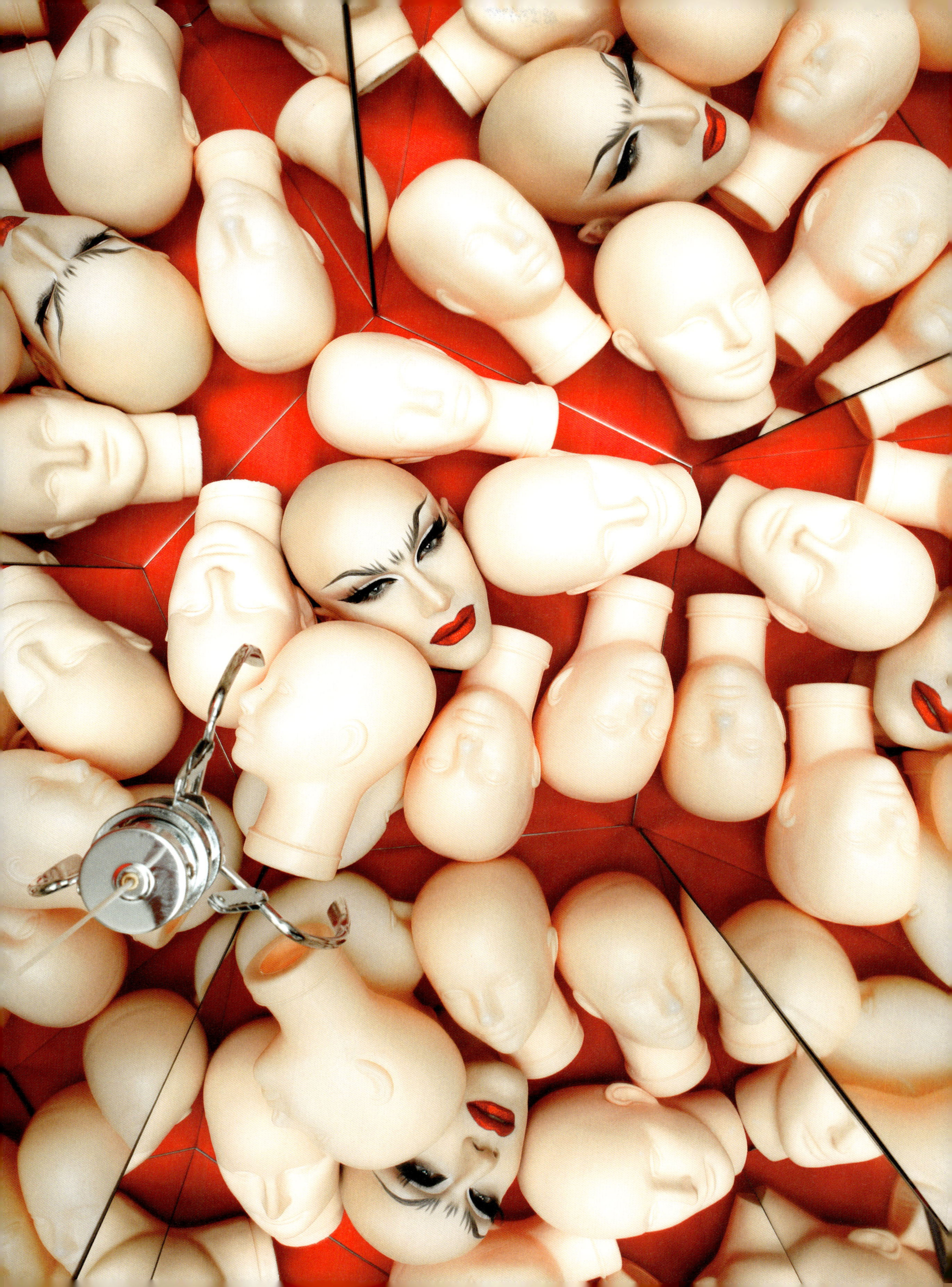

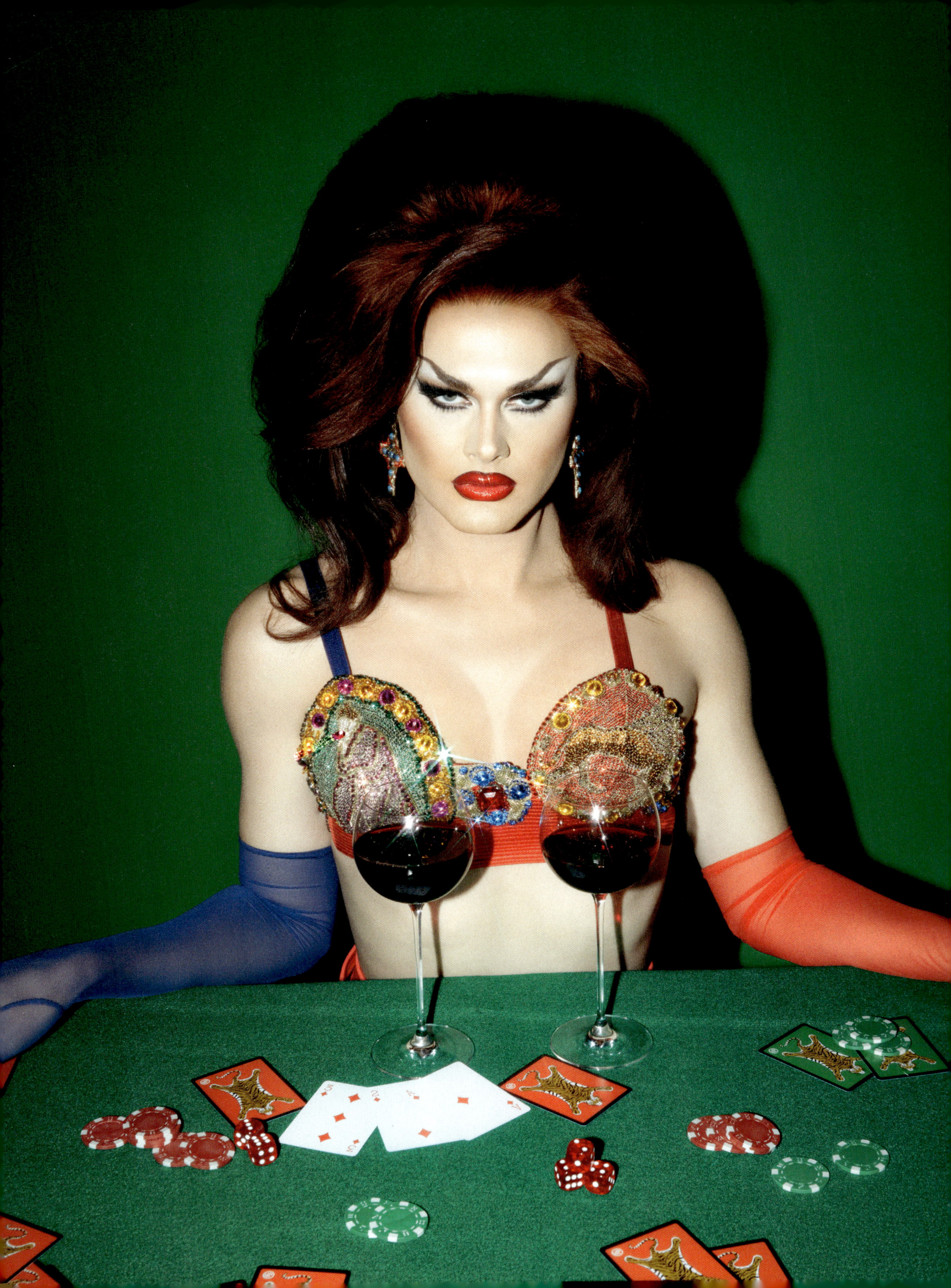

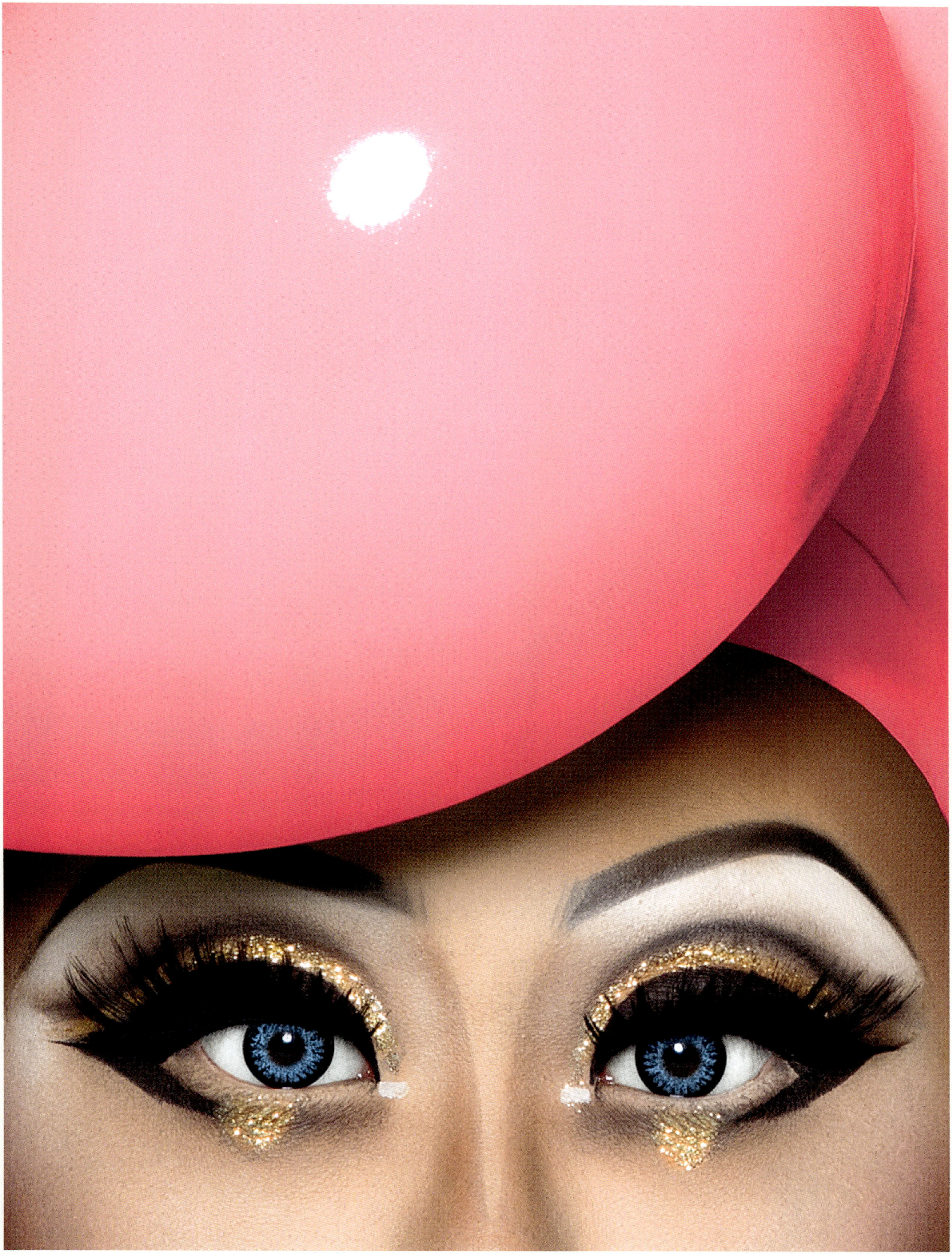

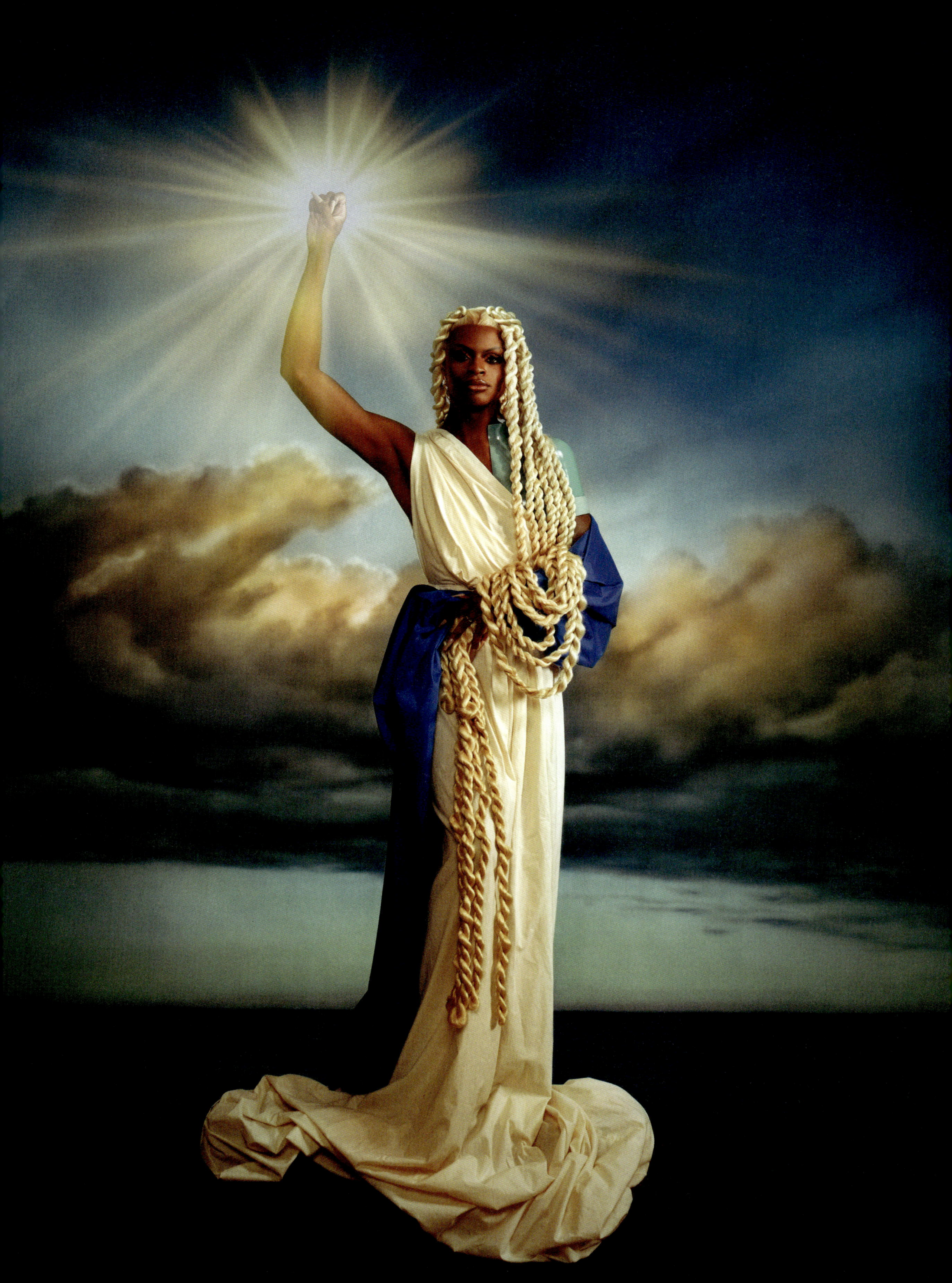

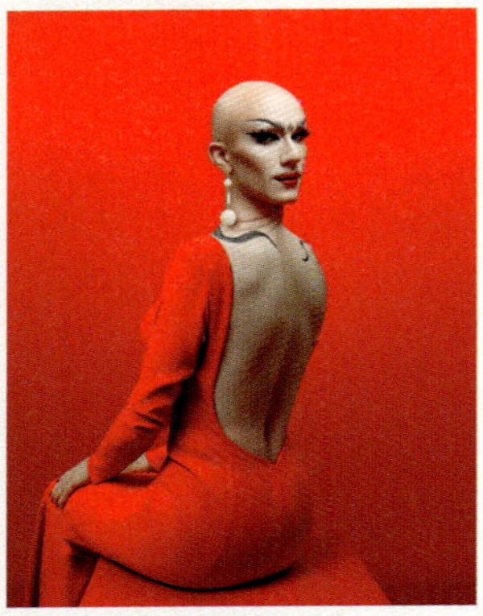

turning heads III, beirut, lebanon, *plastik* magazine, 2018.

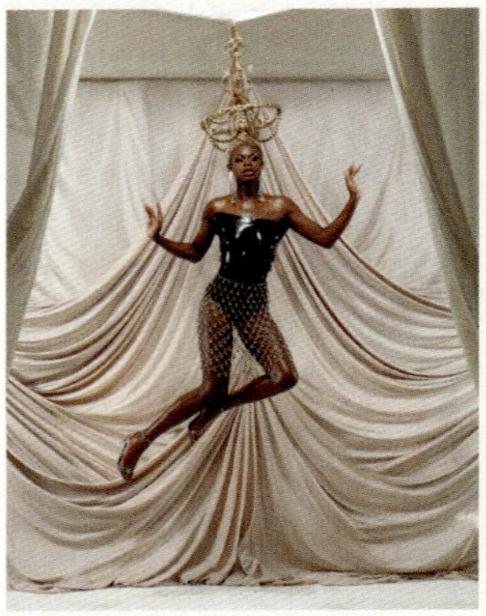

electricity, new york, usa, *plastik* magazine, 2021.

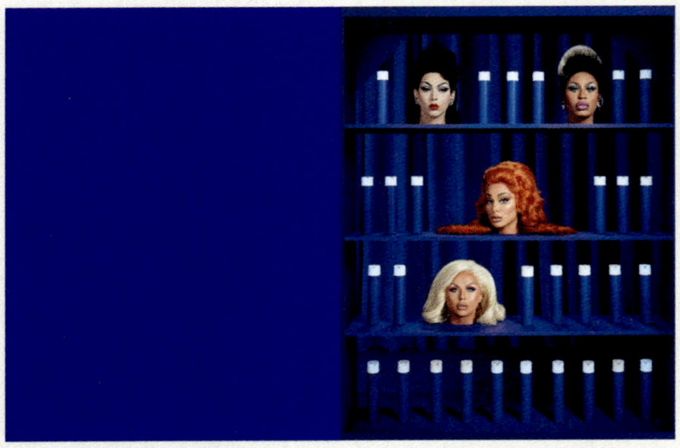

beauty parlor, los angeles, usa,
huda beauty campaign, 2019.

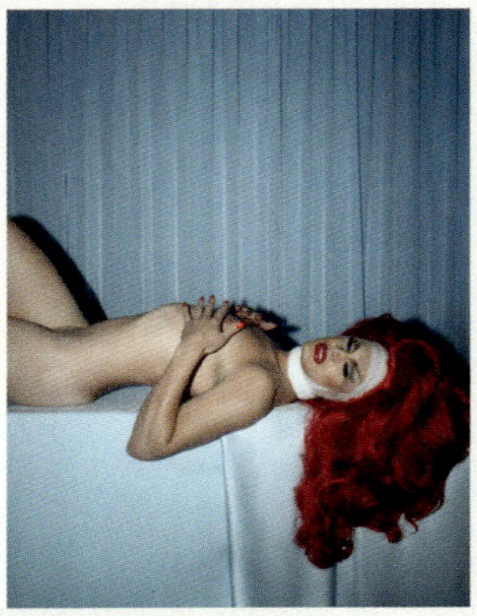

whose face is this, anyway? new york, usa,
pasqua campaign, 2021.

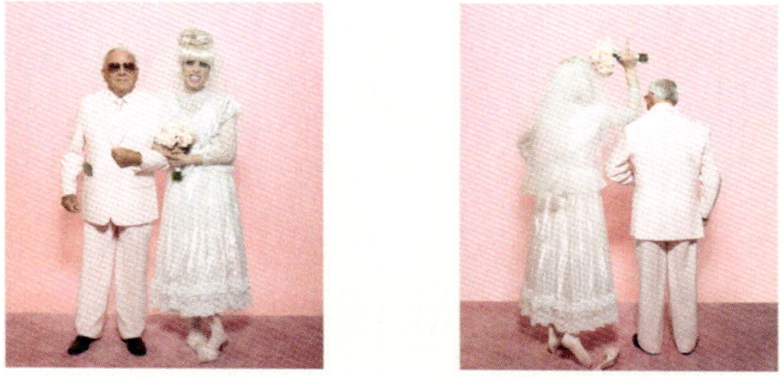

she said meh, los angeles, usa, *plastik* magazine, 2016.

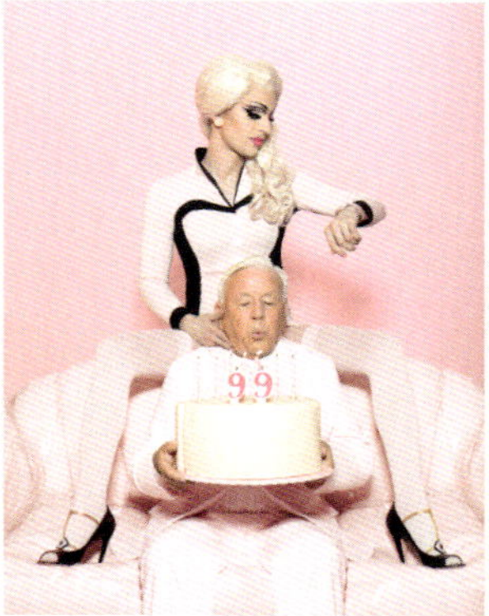

tick tock, los angeles, usa, *plastik* magazine, 2016.

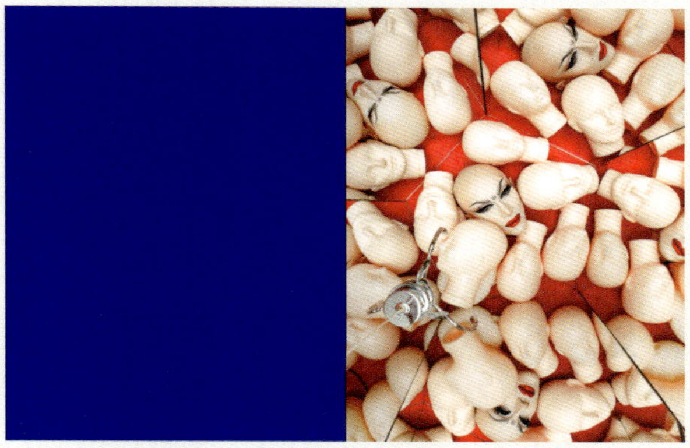

turning heads I, beirut, lebanon, *plastik* magazine, 2018.

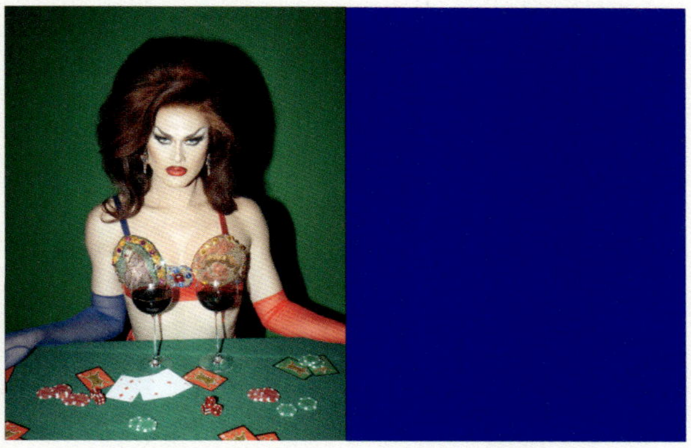

envy, new york, usa, pasqua campaign, 2021.

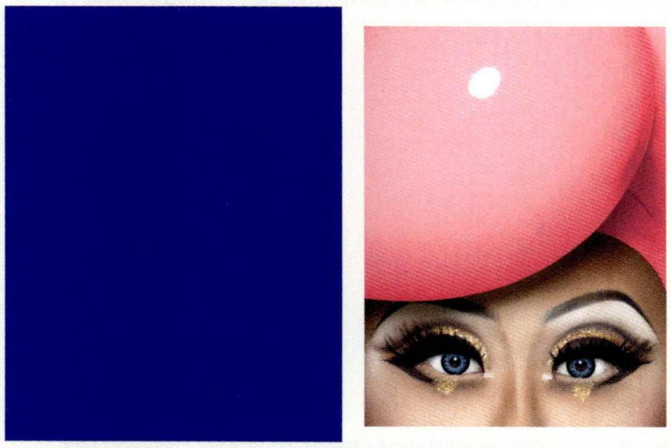

inflatable, los angeles, usa, *plastik* magazine, 2016.

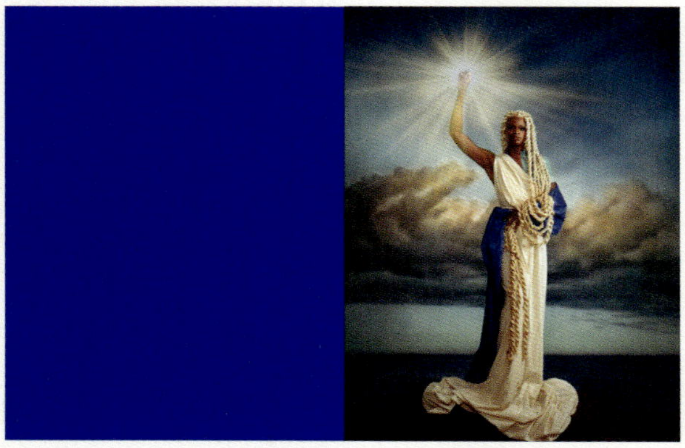

liberty, new york, usa, *plastik* magazine, 2021.

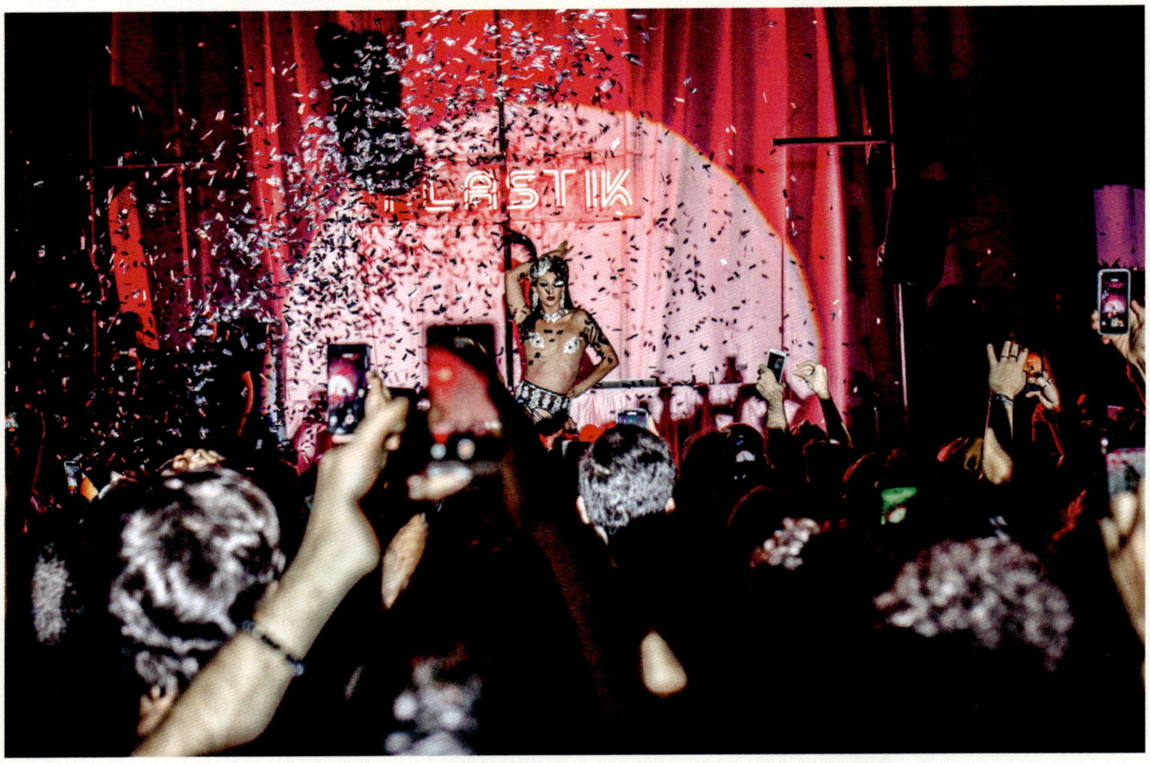

violet chachki, *plastik* magazine love night, ahm club, beirut, lebanon, 2017. photo by myriam boulos.

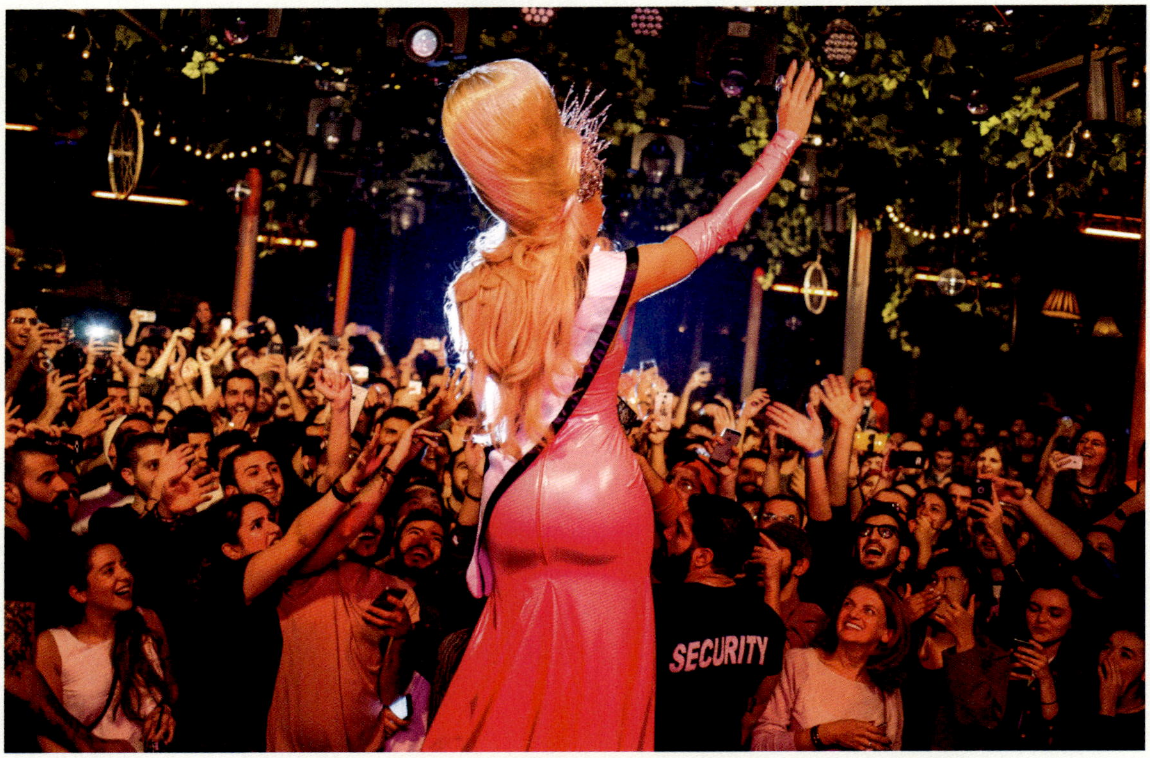

alaska thunderfuck, *plastik* magazine pop night, grand factory, karantina, lebanon, 2017. photo by carl halal.

Watching what happens when confronting the heteronormative gaze with the art of drag is a great source of exhilaration for Rezkallah. It is no wonder that the photographer took an immediate liking to the art form and drew inspiration from it, creating fantastical portraits of drag queens but also taking it further and reintroducing drag to Lebanon through high-profile performances by international queens, a first in this religiously conservative state.

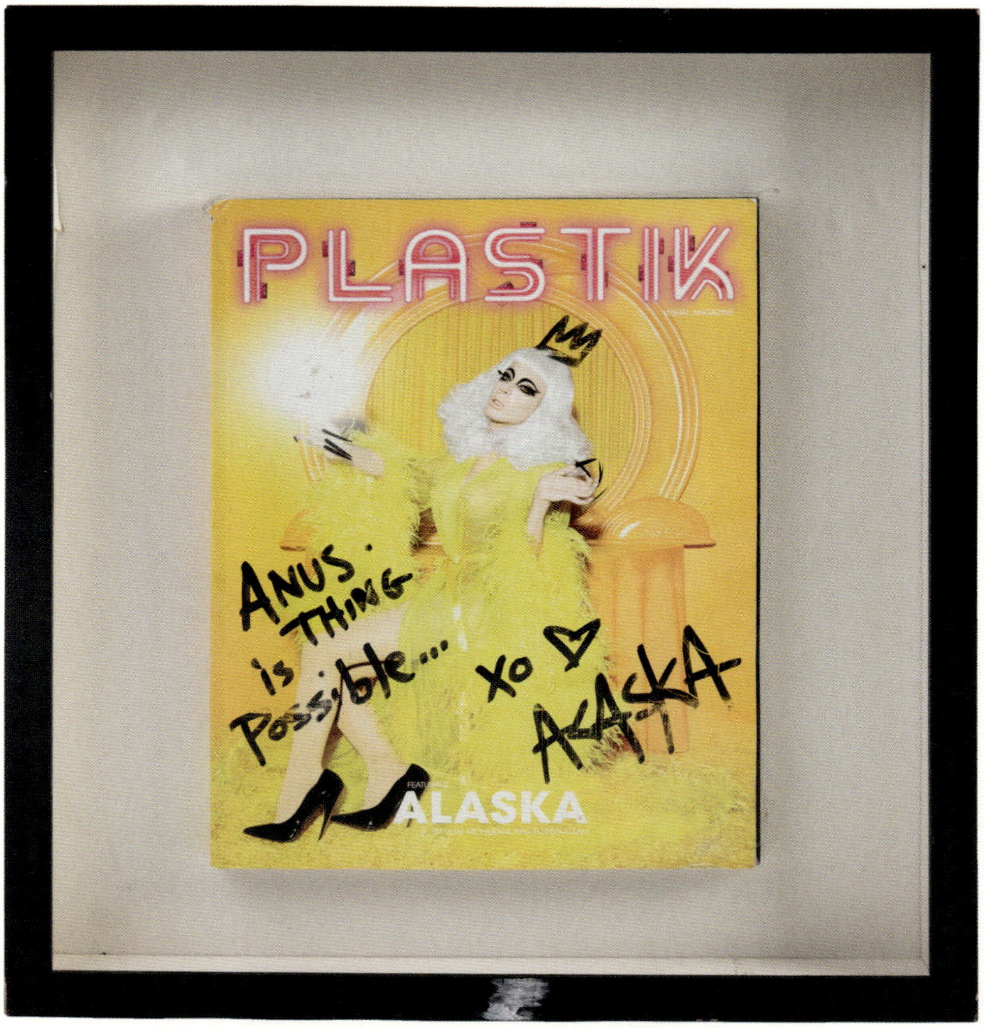
PLASTIK
ANUS THING is possible... xo ♡ ALASKA
ALASKA

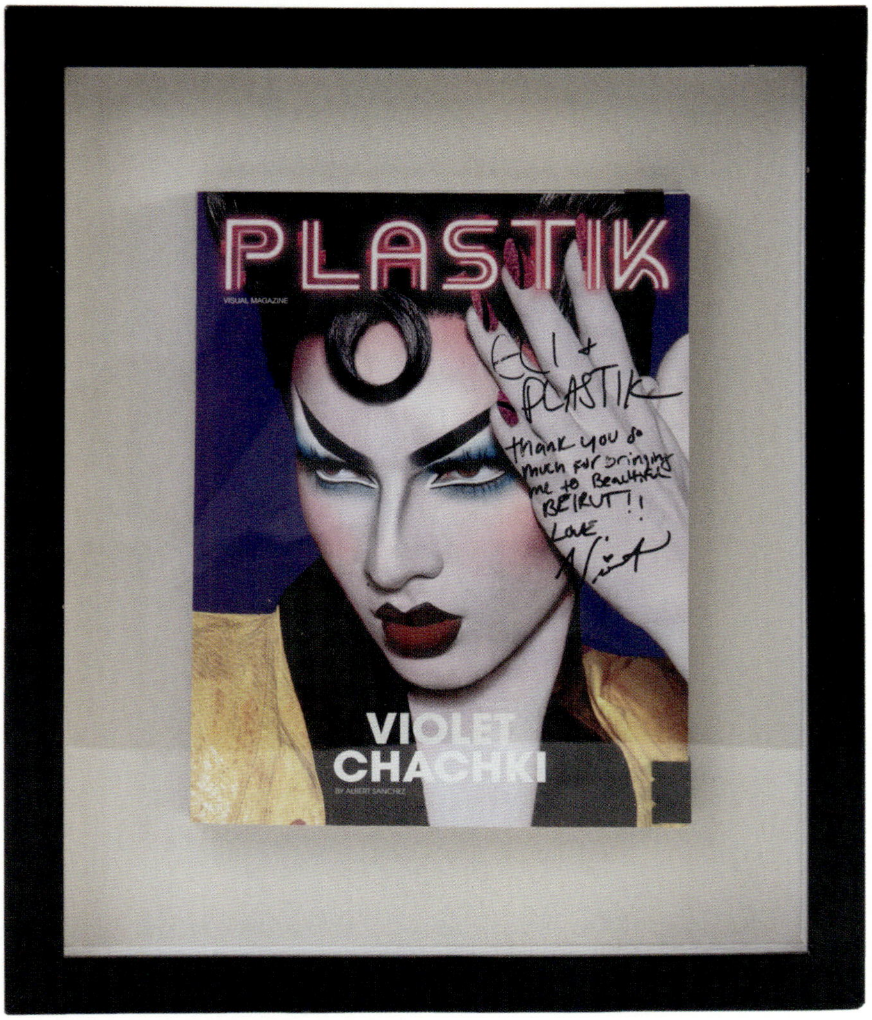
PLASTIK
VISUAL MAGAZINE
PLASTIK
thank you so
much for bringing
me to Beautiful
BEIRUT!!
Love
VIOLET
CHACHKI

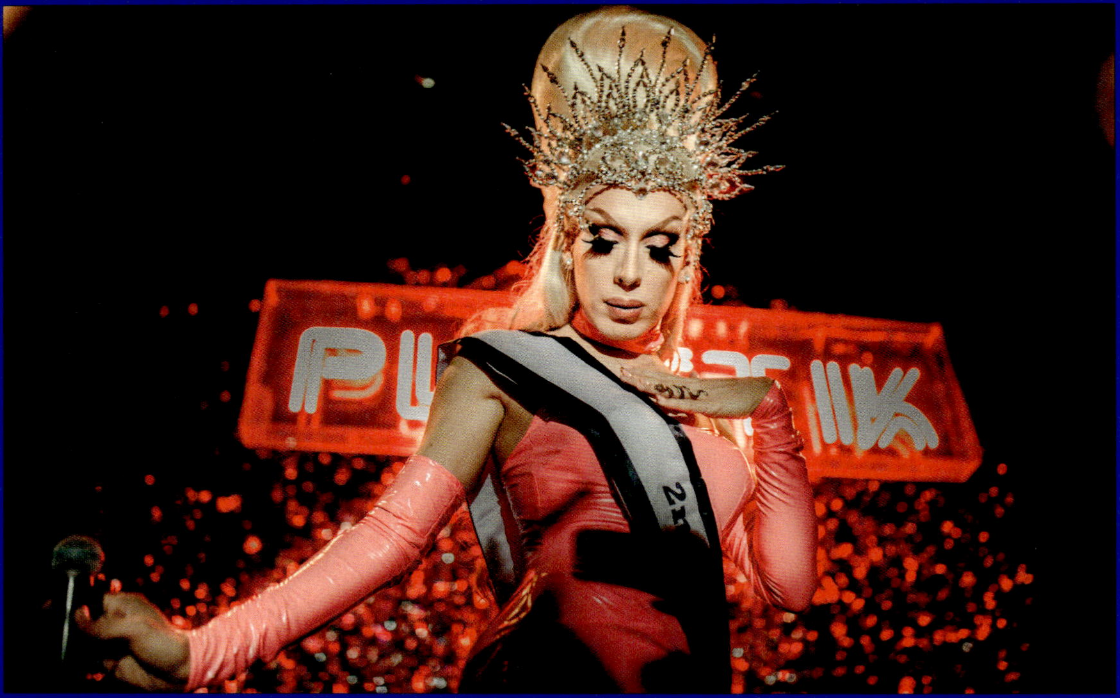

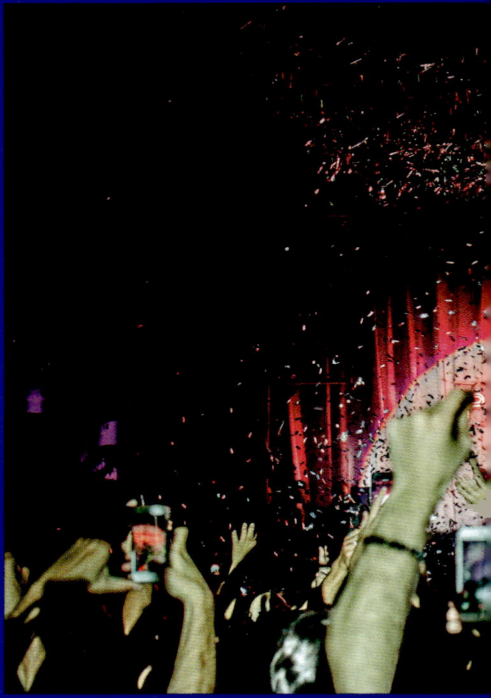

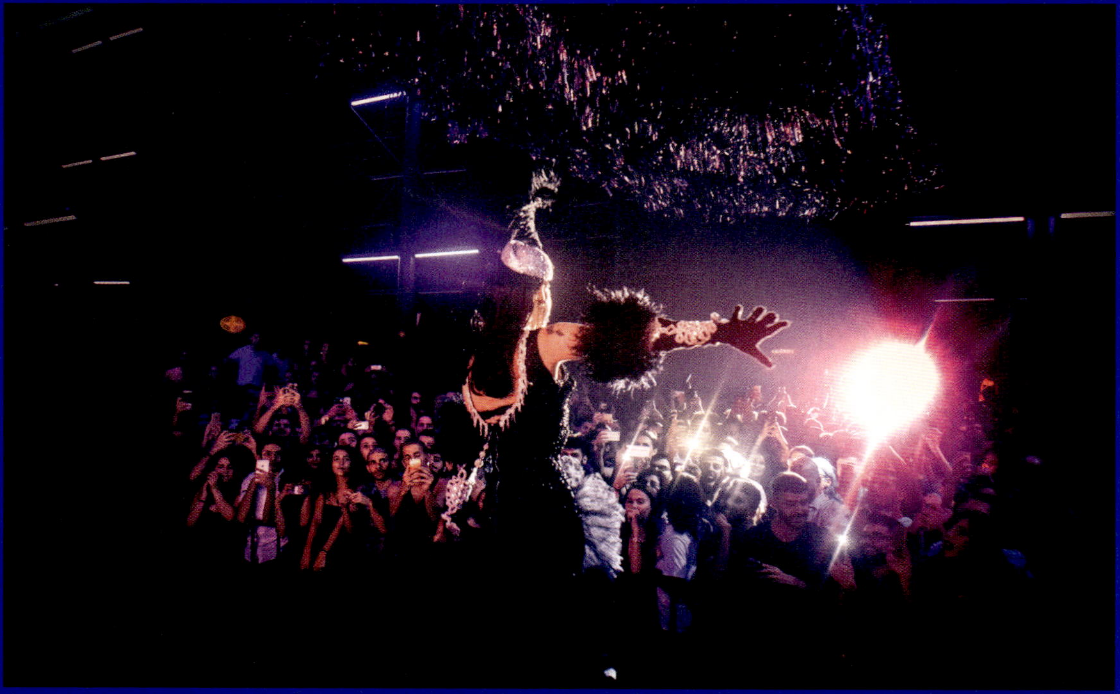

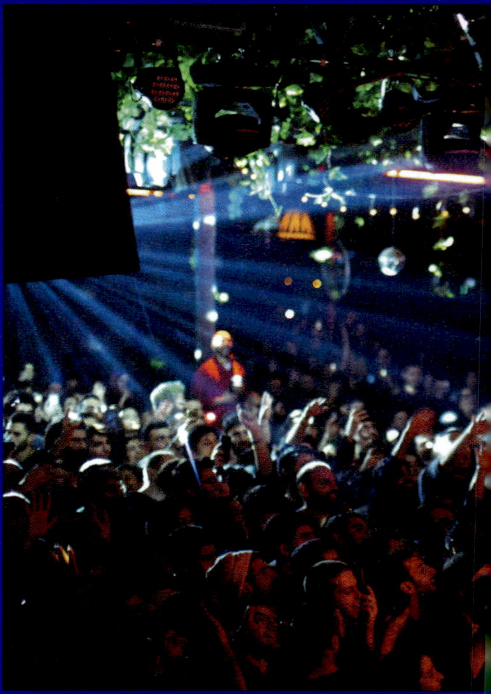

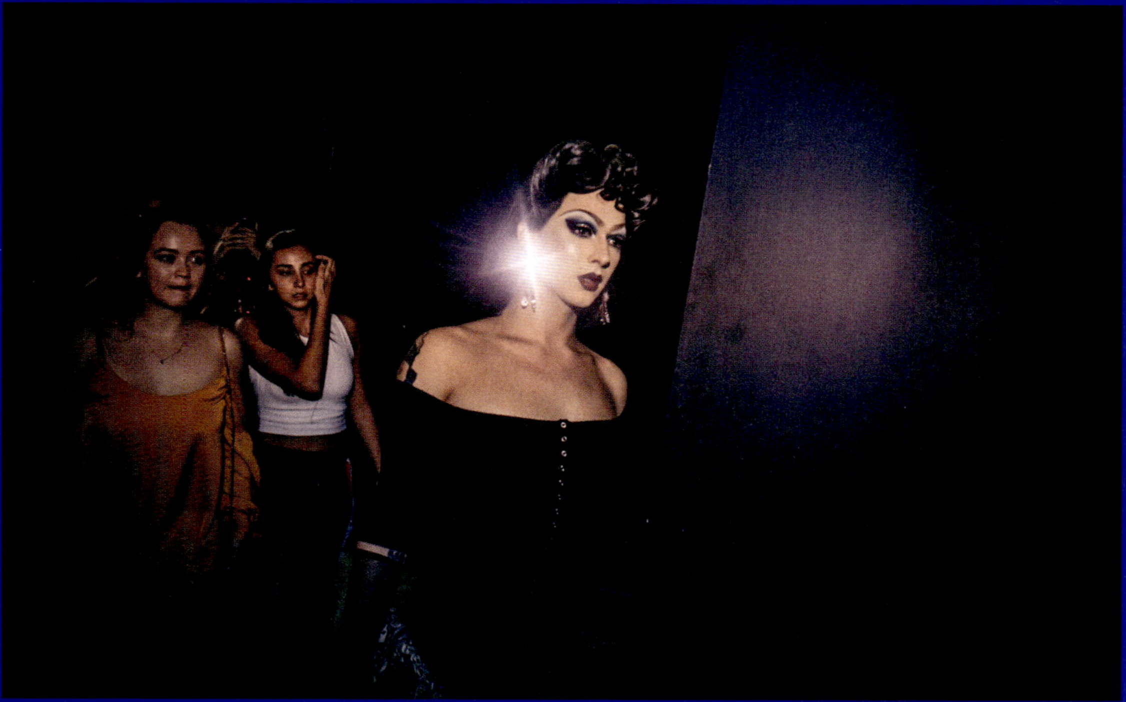

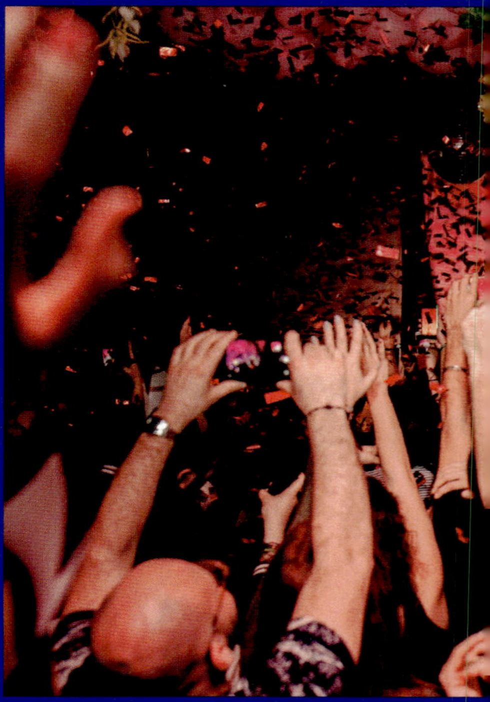

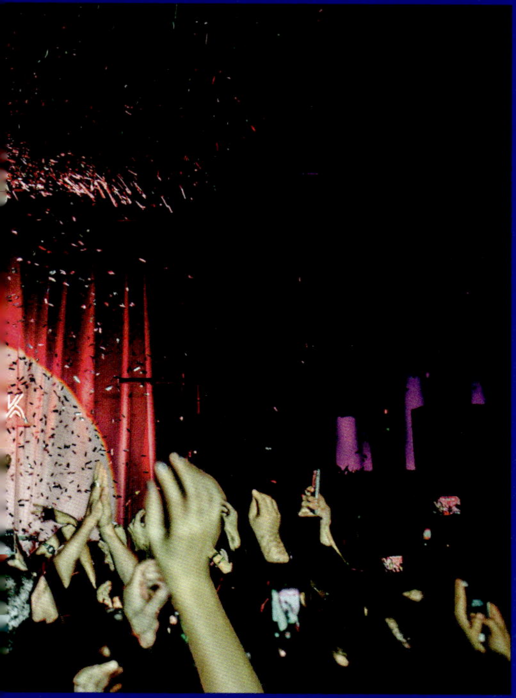
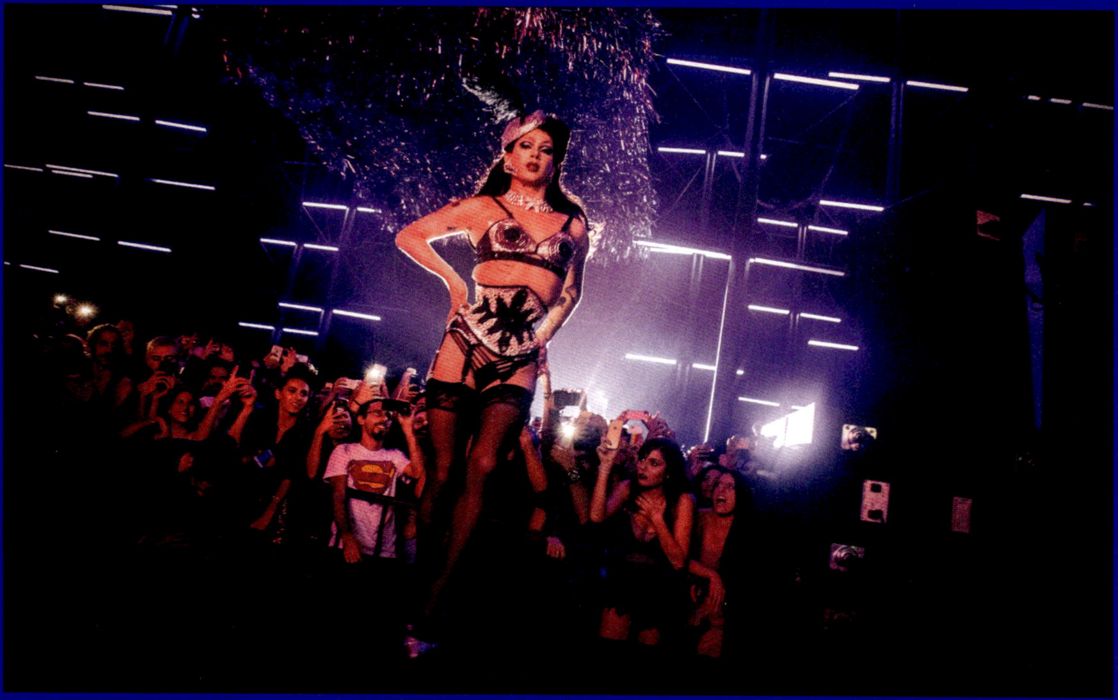
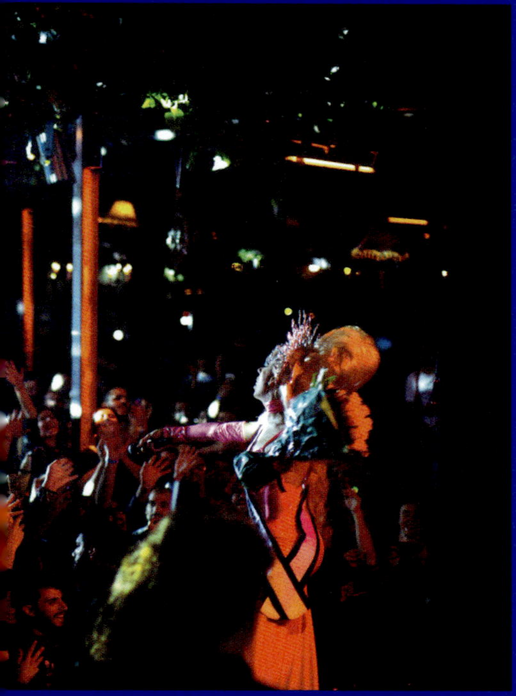
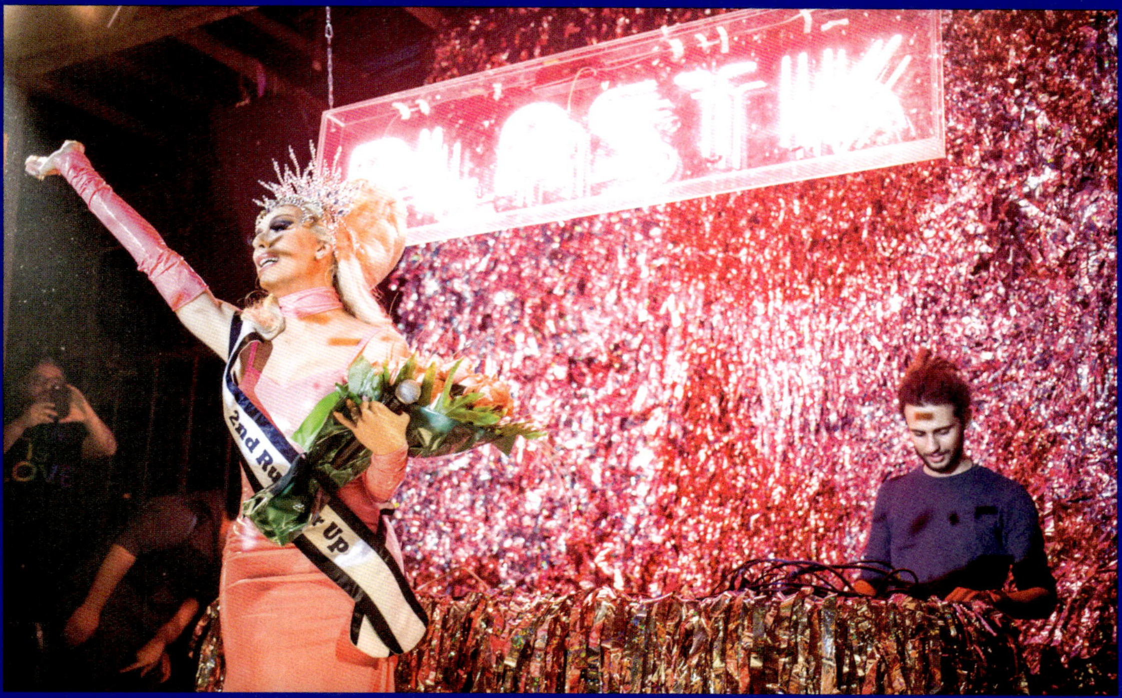
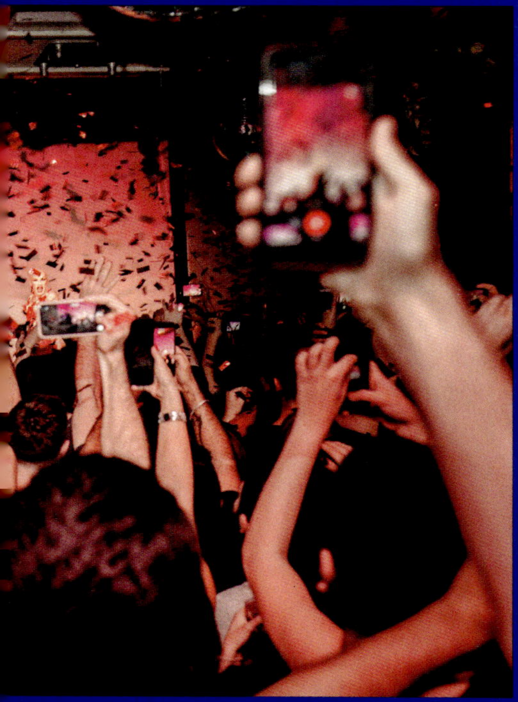
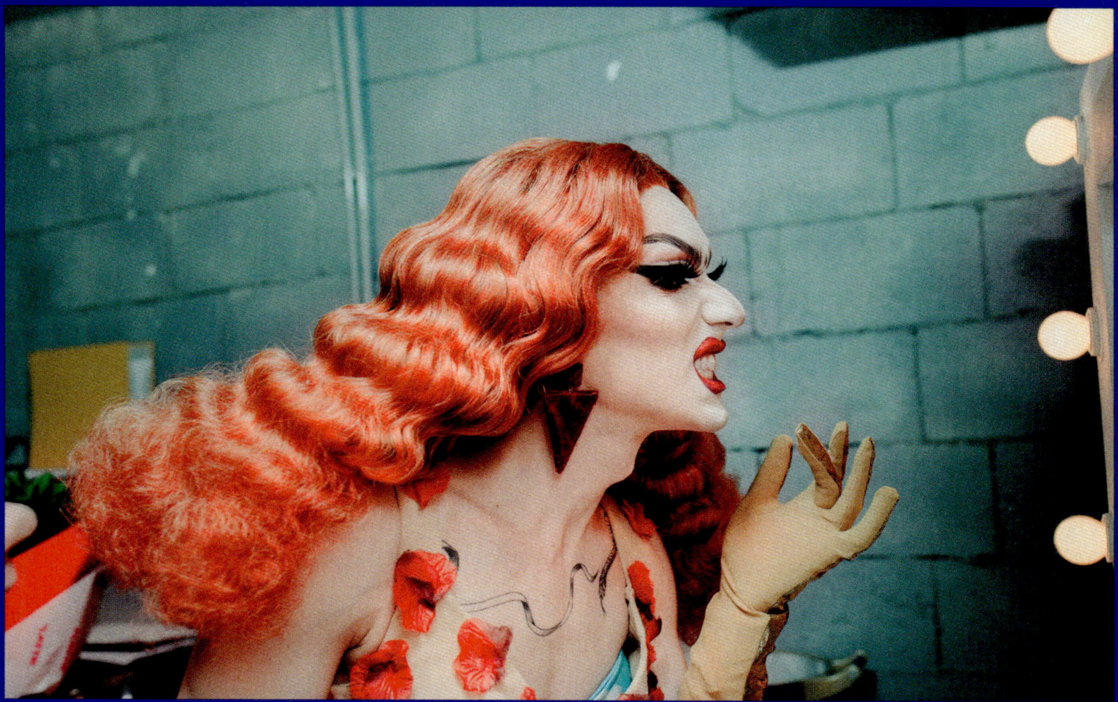

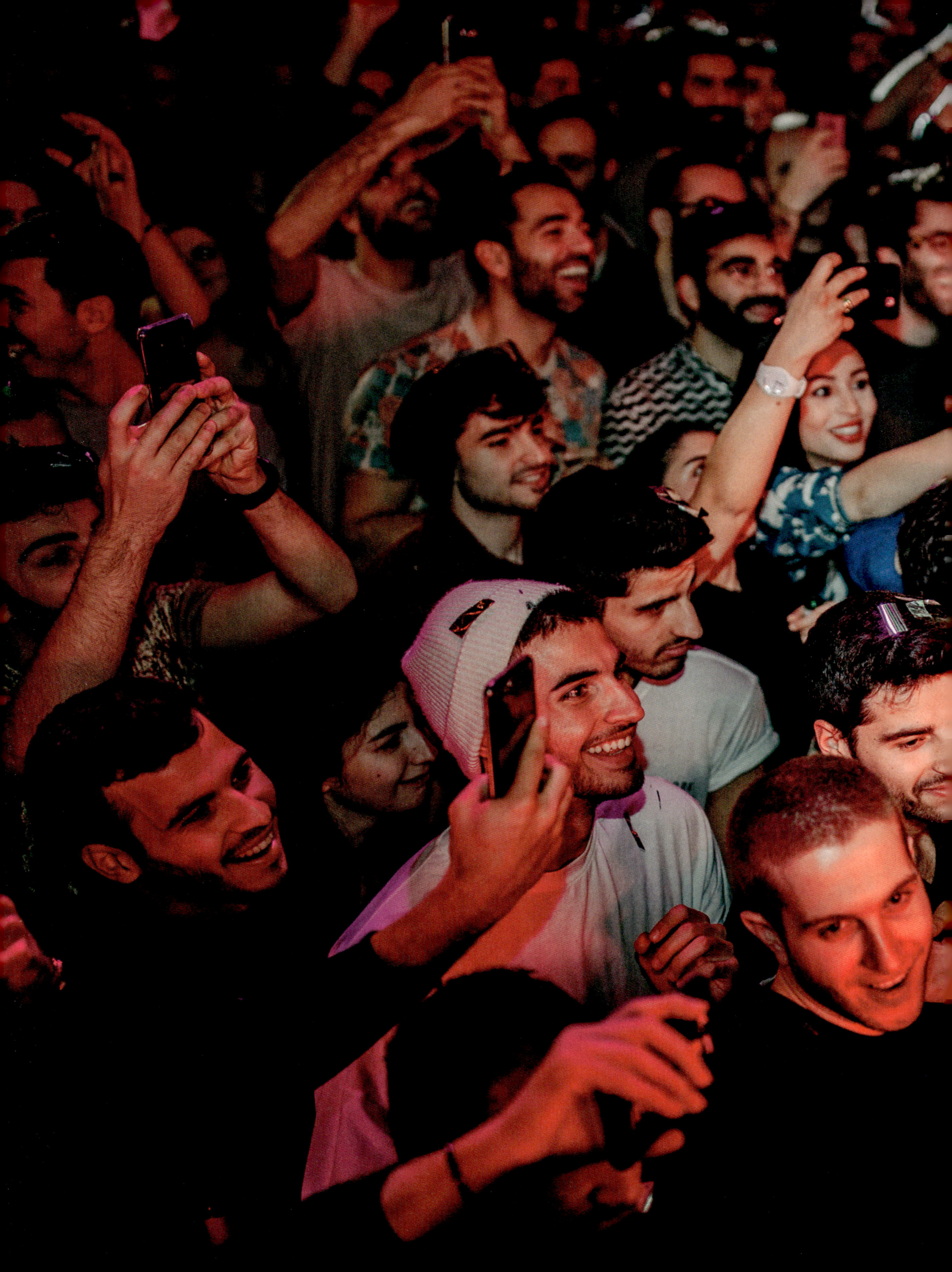

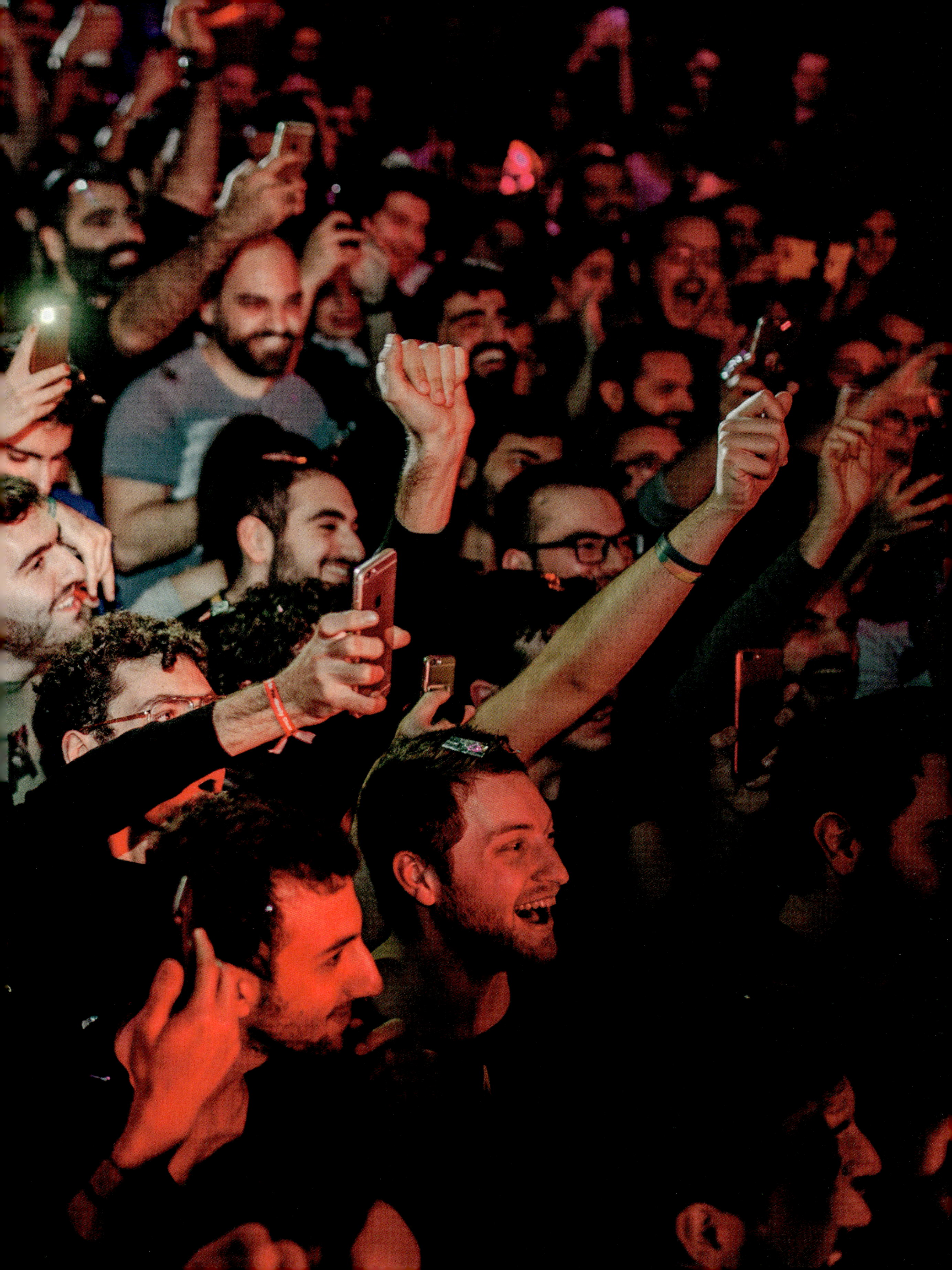

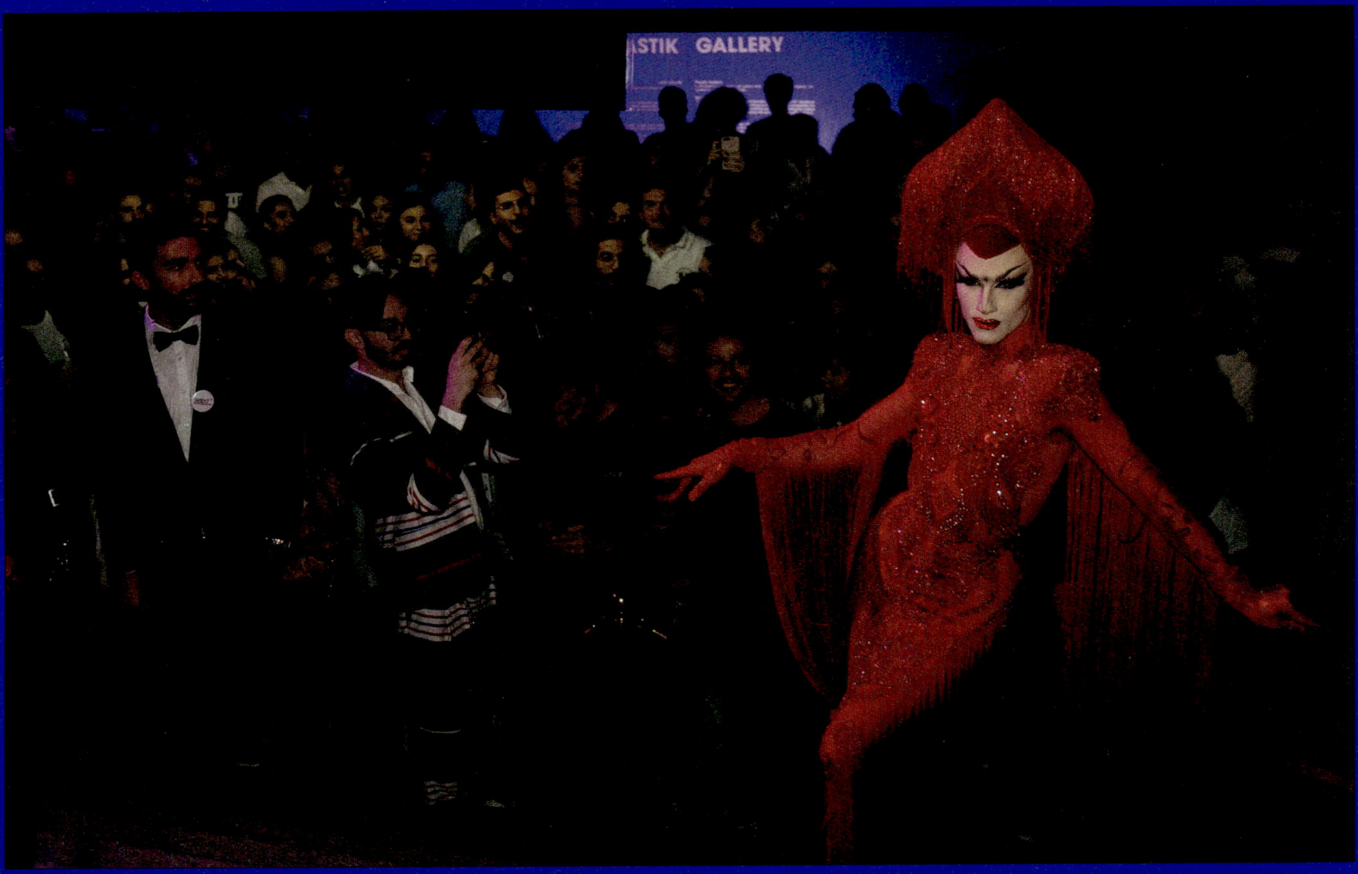
STIK GALLERY

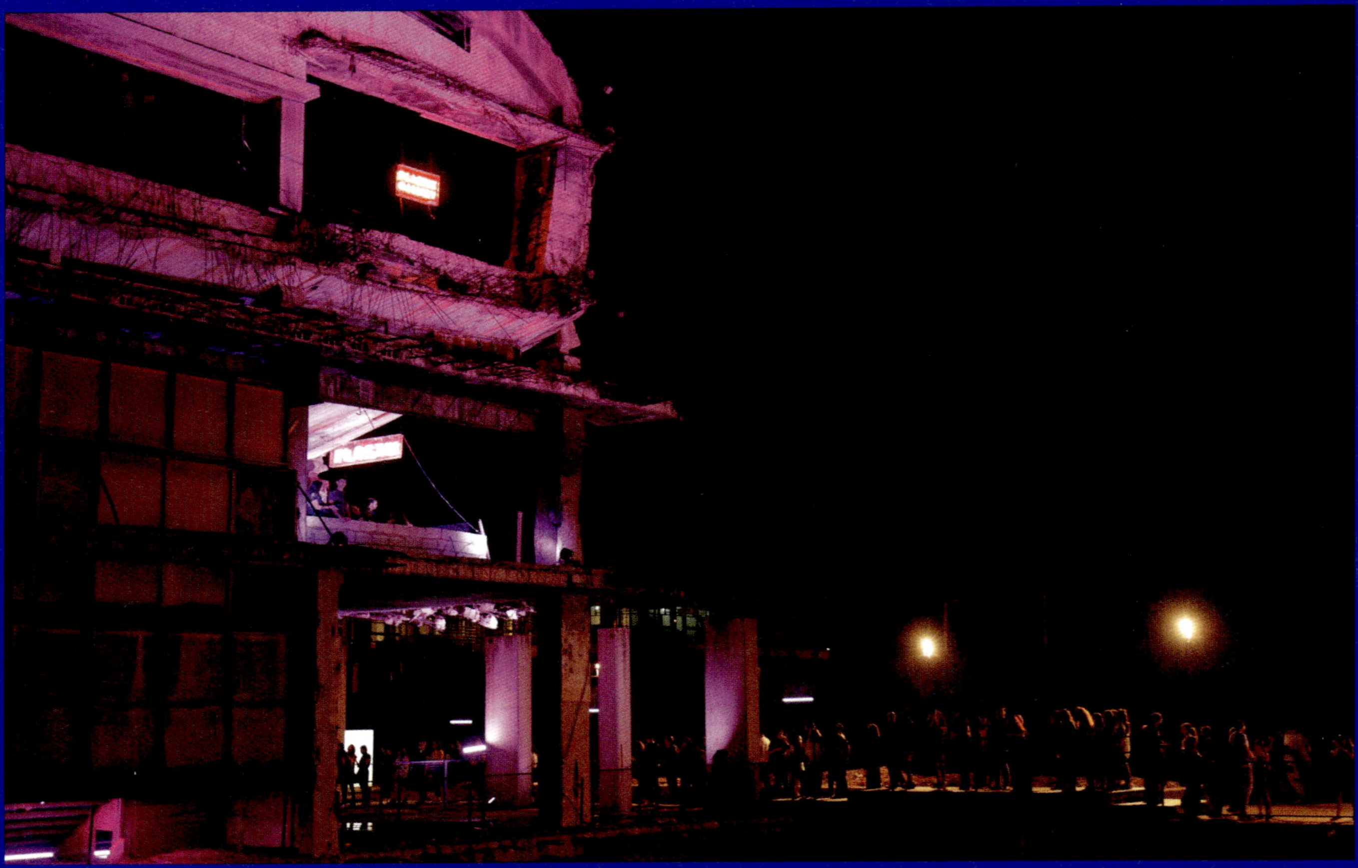

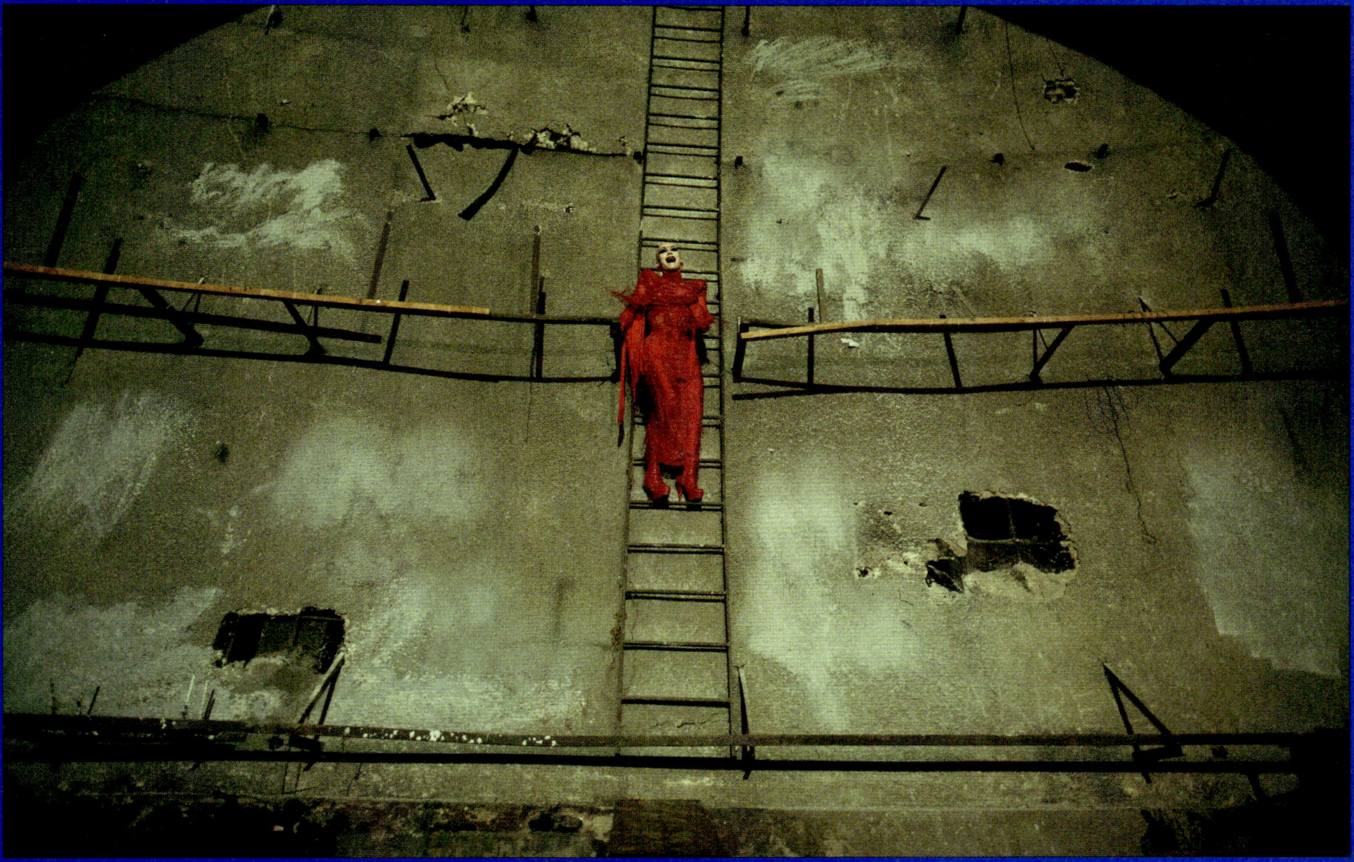

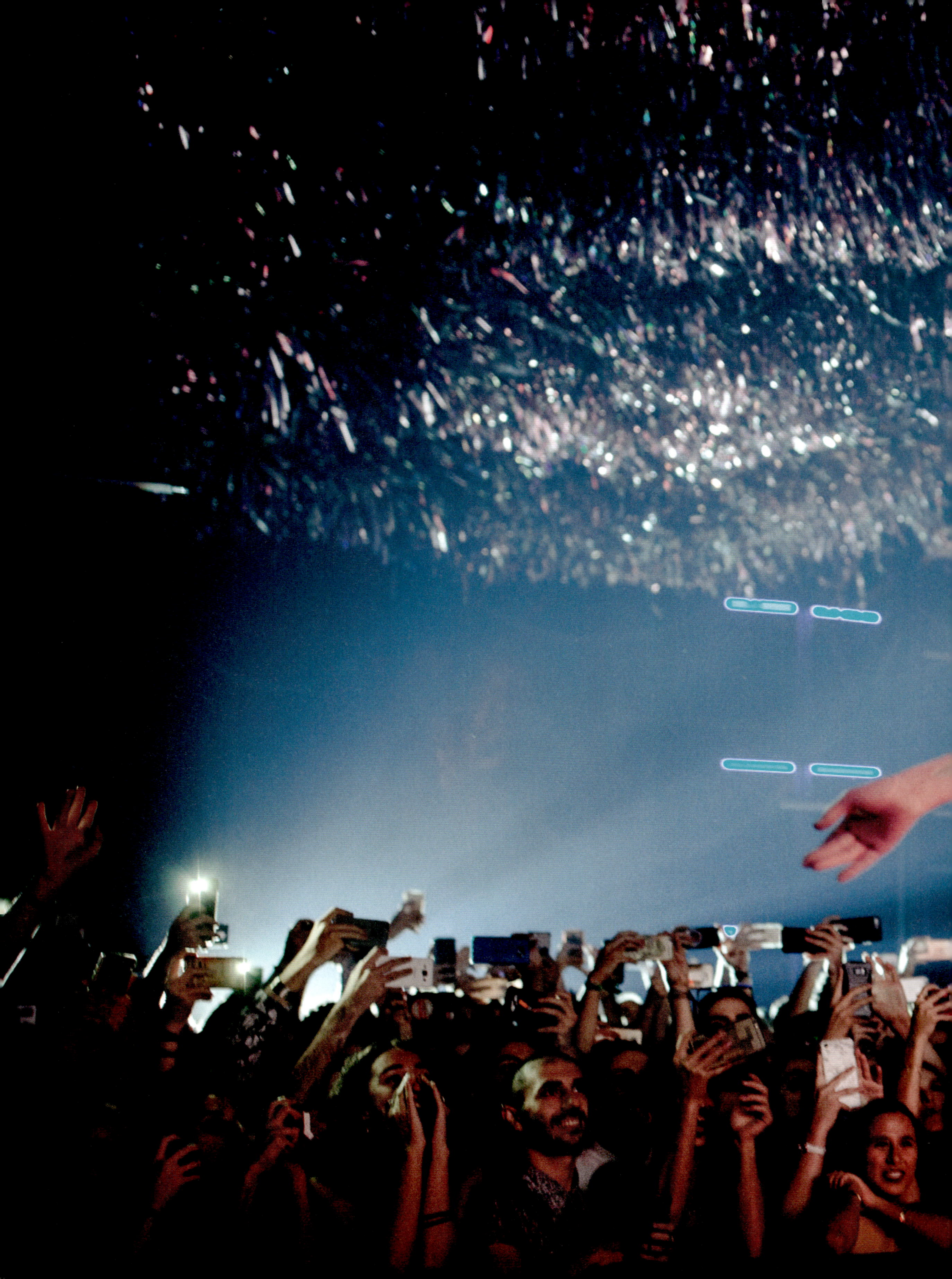

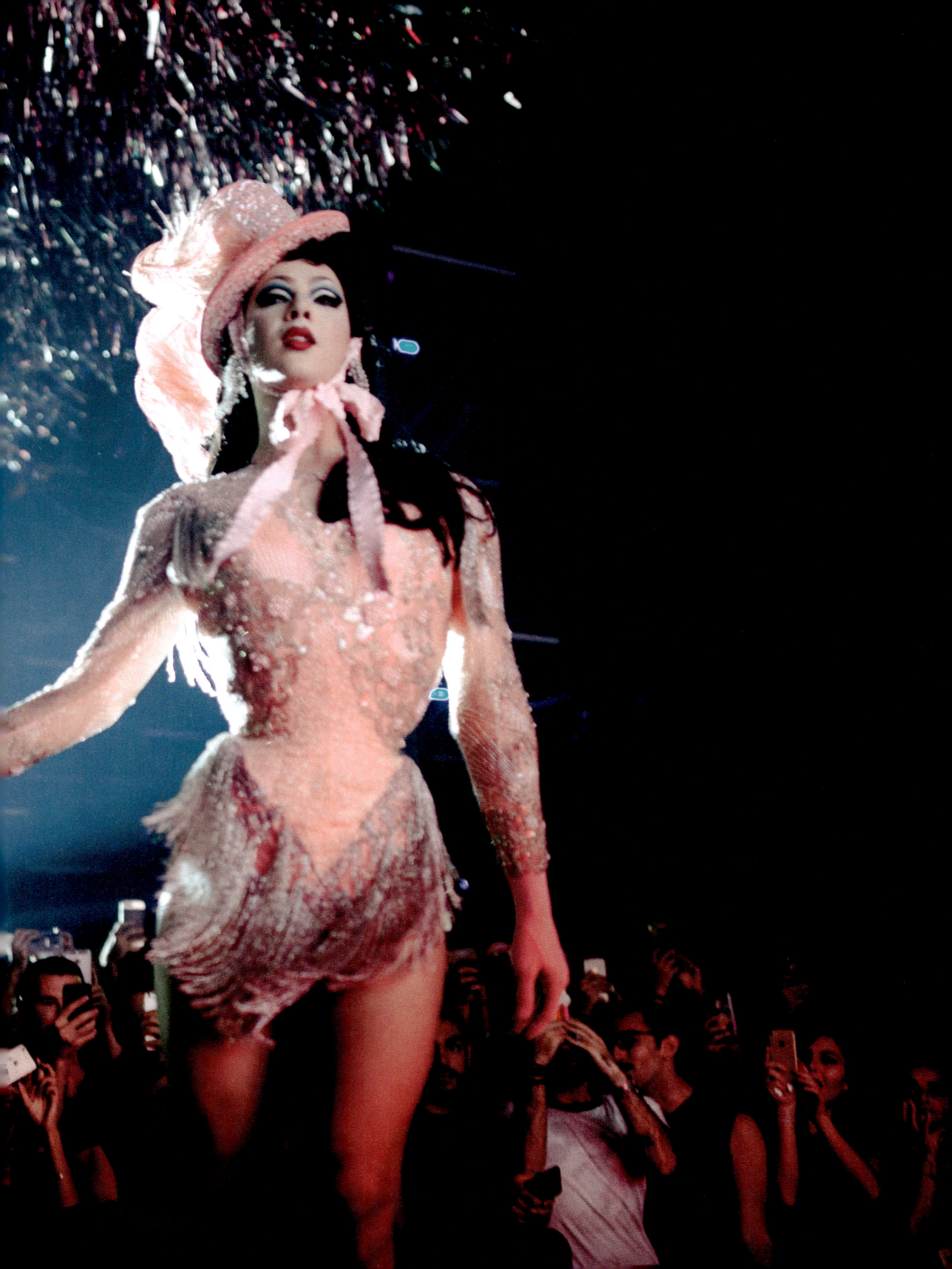

september 28, 2017

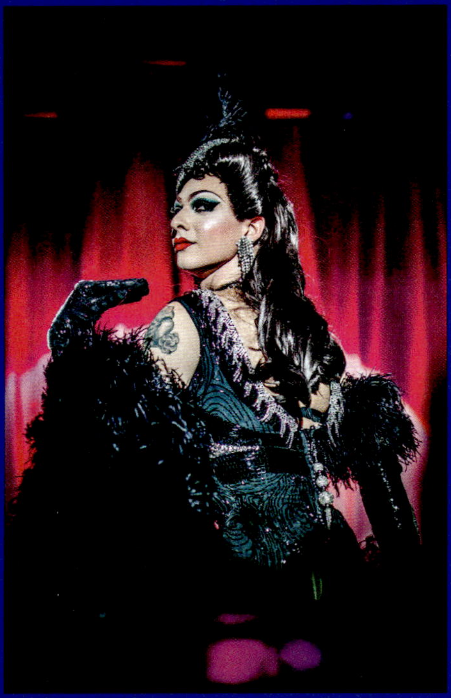

violet chachki

plastik magazine love night,
ahm club, beirut, lebanon.

photographs by carl halal and myriam boulos.

december 28, 2017

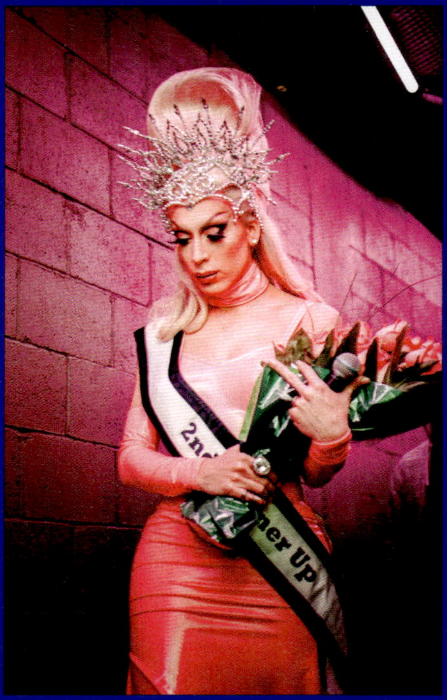

alaska thunderfuck

plastik magazine pop night,
grand factory, karantina, lebanon.

photographs by carl halal.

october 14, 2018.

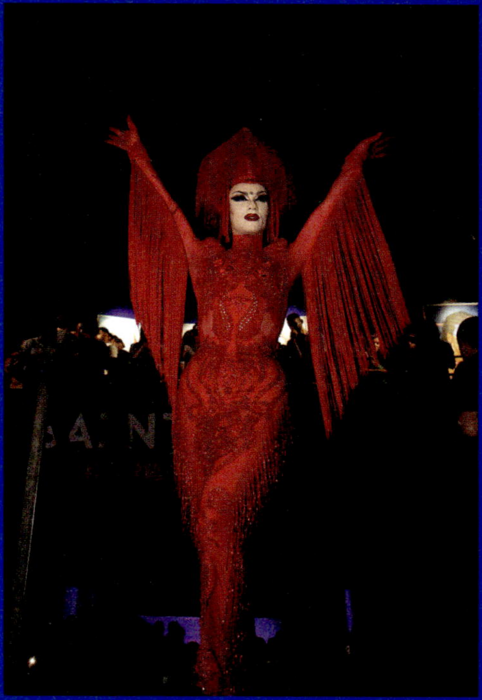

sasha velour, saint hoax

monumental exhibition by saint hoax,
the egg, beirut, lebanon.

photographs courtesy of plastik inc.

april 1, 2018

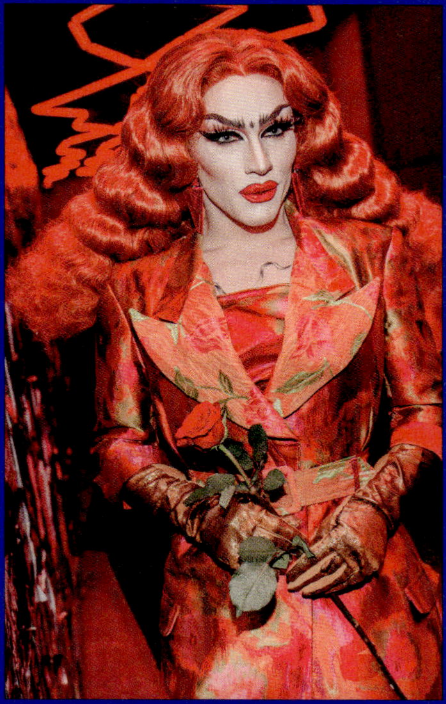

sasha velour

plastik magazine ninth anniversary,
grand factory, karantina, lebanon.

photographs by myriam boulos.

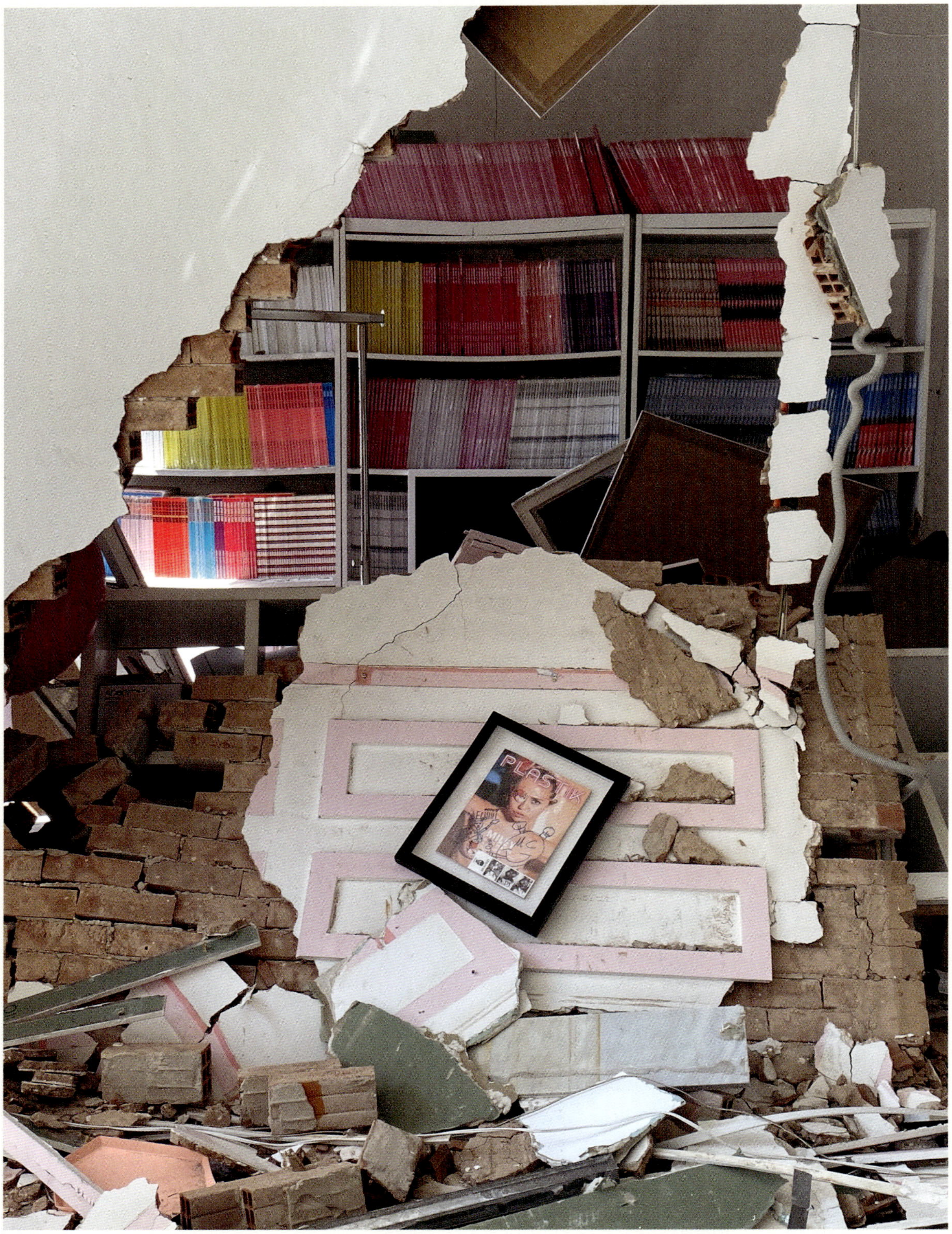

the morning after the blast, *plastik* studios, gemmayze, lebanon, august 5, 2020.

While these plastik drag show performances were a beacon of hope to the local Lebanese LGBTQIA+ community, a sign of better days to come, Lebanon soon became paralyzed by a crippling economic crisis stemming from deep-rooted government corruption. Massive civil protests, a global pandemic, and the third biggest non-nuclear explosion in human history, also known as the August 4, 2020 explosion, were all instrumental in Lebanon's tragic unraveling. All of the artist's biggest anxieties came tragically true as his country, and his personal and professional evolution, all came to a crashing halt...

As Rezkallah stepped over the remains of what he once called plastik studios, he couldn't help but notice RuPaul Charles' quote about plastik printed on one of the few walls left standing, a mission statement that rang even truer amidst the sudden devastation of the artist's world. With great tragedy comes life-changing realizations that compelled Rezkallah to confront his deep-rooted anxieties by rebuilding solid foundations for his life in New York City. These were foundations that for once, did not come with the threat of impending doom and which allowed Rezkallah and his work to bloom, this time around, with serenity and peace of mind.

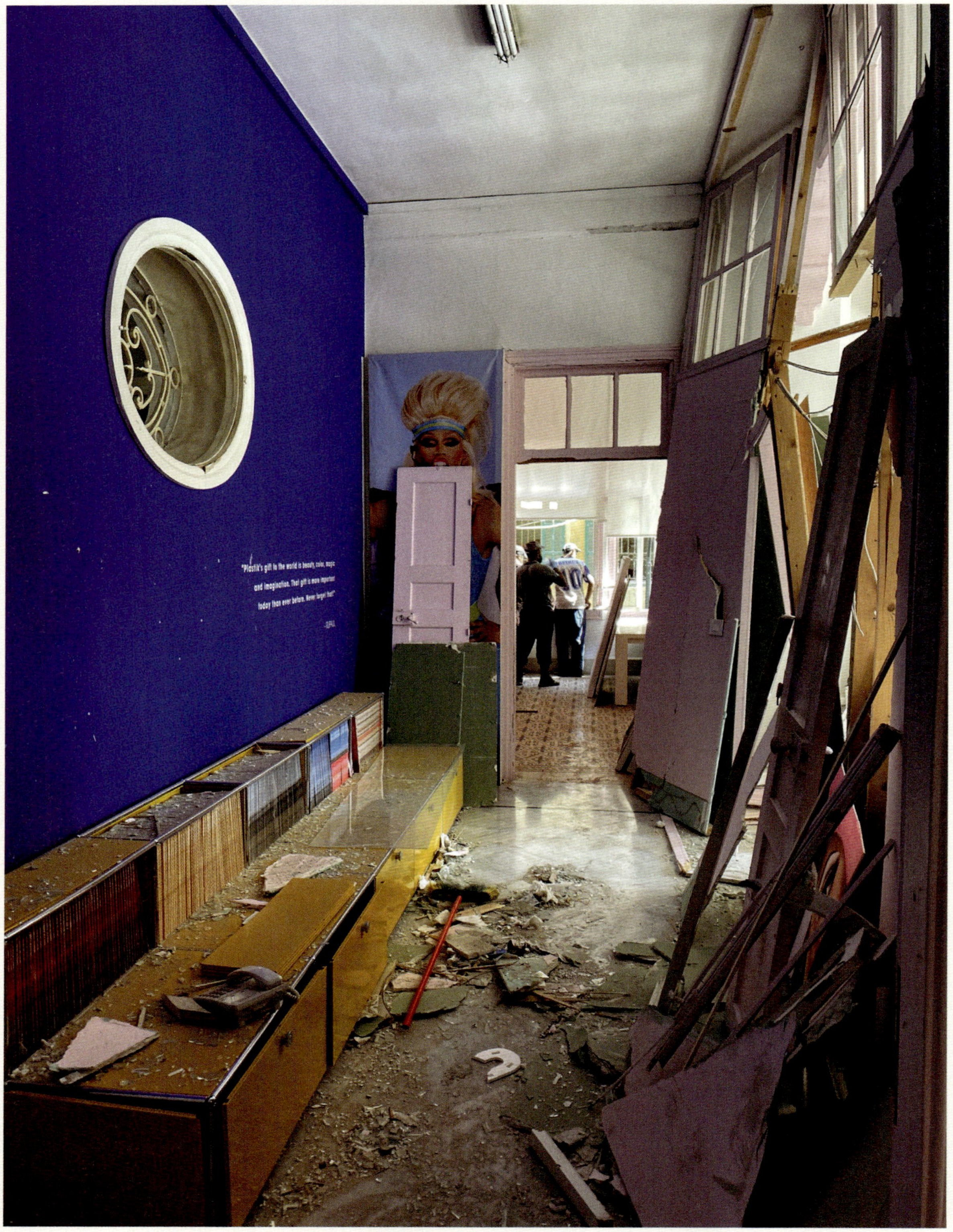

the morning after the blast, plastik studios, gemmayze lebanon, august 5, 2020.

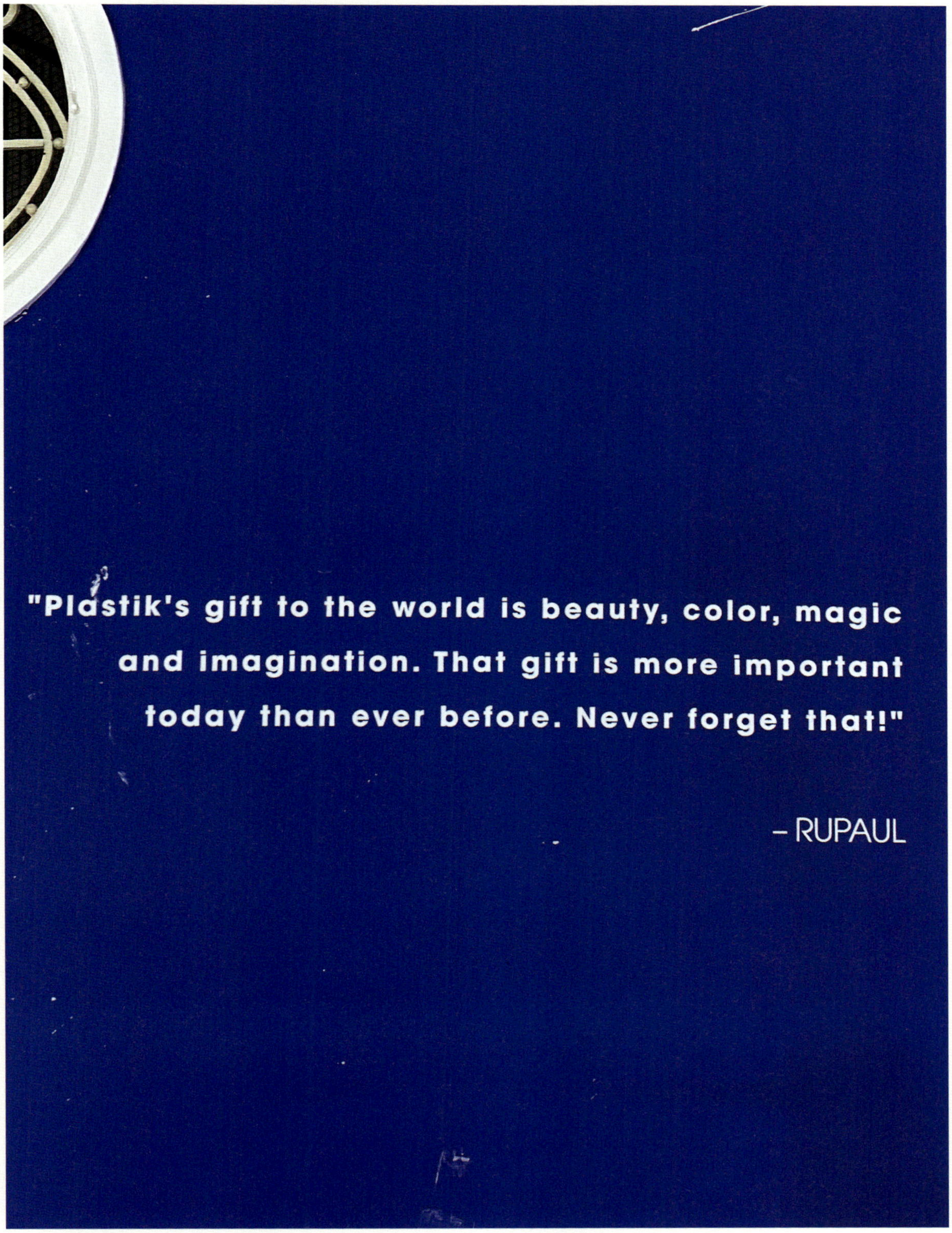

ELI REZKALLAH

the end of denial.

www.lannoo.com

Sign up to our newsletter for updates on our latest publications on art, interior design, food & travel, photography and fashion, as well as exclusive offers and events. If you have any questions or comments about the material in this book, please do not hesitate to contact our editorial team: art@lannoo.com

D/2022/45/197 – NUR 653
ISBN: 9789401483339

credits

words
ralph arida

book design
plastik studios

art direction
alex curtis

project management
camille medawar

proofreading
philippe ghabayen

publisher
lannoo

design consultancy
yummycolors

consultancy
abeer seykali
rasha shaath

production
amanda abdulhadi
bilal houssami
camille medawar
gabriella kassab
hassan kamel sabbah
lea casini
lilia laurel
stepheny kassouf

styling
amin jreissati
bashar assaf
dani michelle
jeff aoun
jihae yun
mouna harati

hair
eduardo bravo
clyde haygood
gigi goode
ivan kuz
tony sawaya
yehia shokr

makeup
bassam fattouh
christian abou haidar
ivanna osypyshyna
kade gottlieb
uzmee krakovszki
vassilis kokkinidis

photo assistants
paul terrie
pauline maroun
ram gibson
samer rawadi
thomas patton

production design
hilal abu ali
jaime terrazzino
jean paul rahal
madeleine burrow

finishing
gorgeous agency
konstantin klimin
konstantin kryukovskiy
nataly trach

special thanks
dana beydoun
lea rezkallah
randa barakat
rima mussa

to my dad who taught me how to shine even behind a camera.

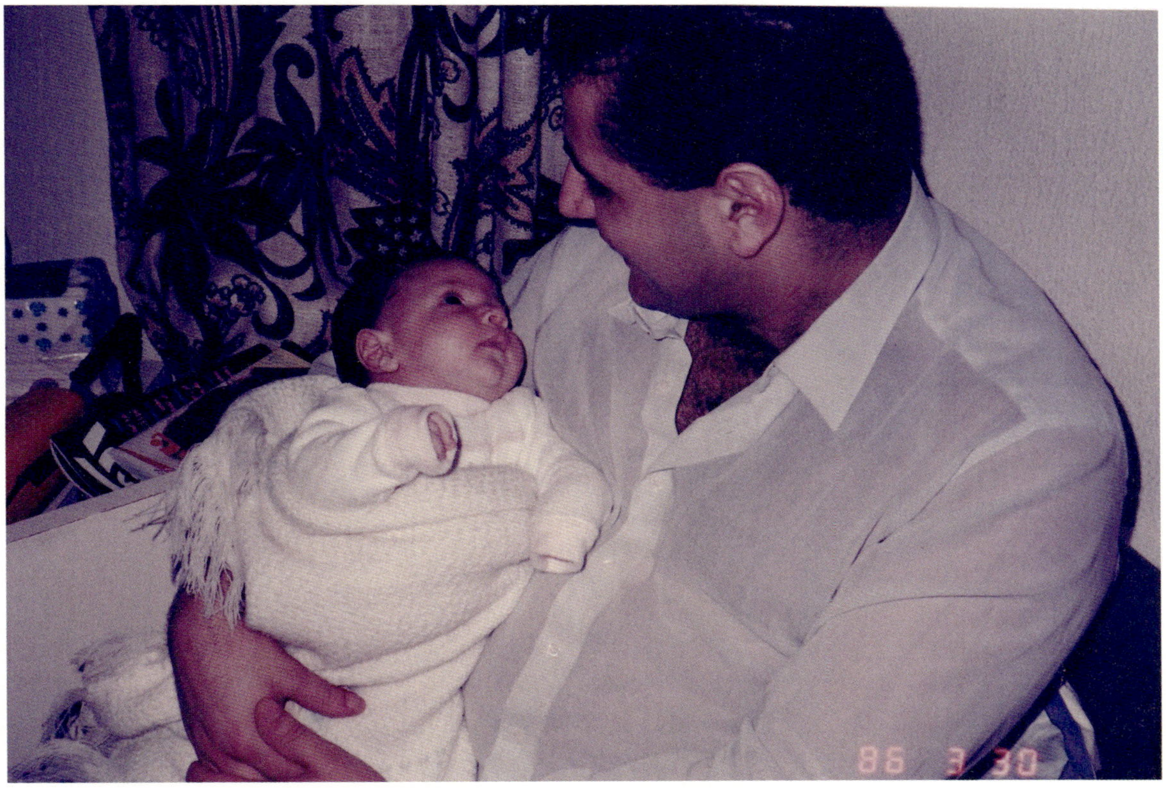
86 3 30